HARDPRESS.NET
HOME OF HARD-TO-FIND BOOKS

Memoirs and Correspondence, Illustrative of the History of the French Revolution, Collected and Arranged by A. Sayous Tr. by B.H. Paul Assisted by W.M. Rossetti and Other Members of the Rossetti Family.
by Jacques François Mallet Du Pan

Address:
HardPress
8345 NW 66TH ST #2561
MIAMI FL 33166-2626
USA
Email: info@hardpress.net

MEMOIRS AND CORRESPONDENCE

OF

MALLET DU PAN.

—

VOL. II.

MEMOIRS

AND CORRESPONDENCE

OF

MALLET DU PAN,

ILLUSTRATIVE

OF THE

HISTORY OF THE FRENCH REVOLUTION.

COLLECTED AND ARRANGED

BY A. SAYOUS,

LATE PROFESSOR AT THE ACADEMY OF GENEVA.

IN TWO VOLUMES.
VOL. II.

LONDON:
RICHARD BENTLEY, NEW BURLINGTON STREET.
Publisher in Ordinary to Her Majesty.
M.DCCC.LII.

23y. a. 105.

LONDON
Printed by Schulze and Co., 13, Poland Street.

CONTENTS

OF

THE SECOND VOLUME.

CHAPTER I.

1794.

CHAPTER II.

1794.

CHAPTER III.

1794.

CHAPTER IV.

1794.

CHAPTER V.

1794—1795.

CHAPTER VI.

1795.

CHAPTER VII.

1795.

CHAPTER VIII.

1795.

CHAPTER IX.

1795—1796.

CHAPTER X.

1796.

CHAPTER XI.

1796.

CHAPTER XII.

1797.

CHAPTER XIII.

1797—1798.

CHAPTER XIV.

1798—1799.

CHAPTER XV.

1799.

CHAPTER XVI.

1799—1800.

MEMOIRS

AND CORRESPONDENCE

OF MALLET DU PAN.

CHAPTER I.

1794.

Résumé of the financial and political state of France at the commencement of February, 1794—Moral and military condition of the army—Public spirit.

WHILE the British Parliament discussed the policy of the ministry, the latter, together with the Austrian Government, were seriously occupied with the means of giving greater consistency and energy to the efforts of the Coalition. Mallet du Pan endeavoured to furnish Lord Elgin with the correspondence which that diplomatist had requested from him; and, undoubtedly, in consequence of instructions which he had received, and which would procure for his government an exact acquaintance with

the course of affairs in Paris. He had been authorized to
spare no expense in order to obtain positive information
drawn from original sources, as far as it was possible, so that
in many respects our politician has written as a true historian
the substantial and truly curious *résumé* which follows: for
on this ground, and in consequence of their value as contemporary testimony, they are worthy of taking their place
among the documents necessary for a history of the French
Revolution.

I.

RESUMÉ OF THE POLITICAL, FINANCIAL, AND MILITARY STATE OF FRANCE AT THE COMMENCEMENT OF FEBRUARY, 1799.

BY MALLET DU PAN.

The Government of the Revolution has changed its character. It is no longer an ideal constitution, abandoned,
as in 1791 and 1792, to public disobedience; nor an
internal anarchy between two factions, contending as to the
kind of government to be given to the Republic, as in
1793; nor the confusion resulting from the triumph of a
party always threatened and ill-established, as during the
last summer.

During these three periods the Convention was still independent; each voice had more or less weight; the executive authority exercised by the ministers, continually
infringed on by the committees, and divided, so to speak,
between each member of the Assembly, each popular body,
each administration, each revolutionary agent, was destitute of vigour, harmony, secrecy, or unity.

Another régime has unexpectedly arisen out of the institution and the omnipotence of the Committee of Public Safety : the peril of the Republic and the distrust of the executive power gave birth to it ; its influence extended with the danger it established and perpetuated by success.

This committee exercises the dictatorship in all its extent : it makes plans and executes them ; the ministers are nothing better than its clerks, the Convention but a machine for issuing decrees sanctioning the decisions of this council. It exercises the sovereign disposal of armies, generals, the public funds, the revolutionary tribunals, the subordinate authorities, the innumerable agents of the public force, capital, revenue, the real and personal property and life of every citizen; it ordains inquisitions, committees of *surveillance*—the same as the clubs.

It has legalized its tyranny and rendered it systematic by the adoption of the revolutionary government, before which the rights of man, the sovereignty of the people, the preceding constitutions, and all liberty are silent. This régime has met with opposition among the anarchists ; but the credit of the Committee has silenced these murmurs, and that terrible power has been upheld by force, without a single Jacobin daring to dispute its existence. From that moment the popular power was annihilated, or at least entirely suspended. The electoral assemblies, the district administrations, the municipalities have disappeared ; the power of the directories of departments is subjected in every detail to its exercise.

The Conventional delegates, nominated in the committee, make the functions of the pro-consuls absolute in the departments ; the national agents, also nominated by the committee, second them in their districts, and execute their orders there. These commissioners discharge at will the directors, and the municipal bodies depose all the officers of the people without consulting the latter, transfer the administration to whomsoever they please, and have thus prevented the conflicts of authority of opinion or of party, and of the anarchy which was their result.

In the absence of the commissioners they are represented by the national agents, also created by the committee, and who have succeeded to the *procureurs syndics*, formerly nominated by the people, in the districts and the communes. Behind these administrations, and those of the departments, the clubs place themselves ; the smallest country town, the large villages, have each their club. From them a committee of *surveillance* is chosen, which exercises a public inquisition, not only on any particular individuals, but also on the administrative bodies, which, execrable as is their present constitution, are all and individually under the daily control of these *surveillants ;* in order to increase the precaution, the Committee of Public Safety and the clubs from which its members are selected, surround these latter with spies and informers, instructed to observe and render an account of the inquisitorial committees.

This chain of corresponding satellites, mutually informing against each other, is accountable to the Committees of Public Safety and General Security, by the necessary distrust which rules over them all. Their general instructions are to denounce and have arrested as a suspicious person whoever is suspected of secretly professing, or having professed, royalist opinions, love of religion, feuillantism, federal-

ism, or moderatism. Under the class of moderates are
included all those who are called *peaceable men:* the
decrees of the conventional commissioners in the various
departments, call the citizens *égoïstes, vampires,* and
secret agitators; almost all are proprietors; the majority
of them are imprisoned, or have been guillotined, sequestrated, or condemned to pay enormous and arbitrary contributions to defray the expenses of the war.

It is impossible to form anything like a just idea of the
submission and terror which have been produced by this
novel arrangement of tyranny. No one durst appeal to any
law or principle, or claim any right or property. The executions are as frequent in the provinces as in Paris, and in
the country as in the town. Not a word, not an act, not
an accident escapes this army of informers, who are all animated with the desire of surpassing each other in atrocity.
Last month, as some young men of the first conscription
were going to join the army in Alsace, a rich old countryman of Franche-Comté exclaimed " Poor fellows ! they are
like calves going to a slaughter-house." He was arrested
the same evening, and eight days afterwards guillotined.
A thousand such cases might be mentioned.

An organization has been formed during the last four
months, at first invisible, now openly asserting itself independent of all kind of popular power, by holding its
ground, and receiving its existence as well as its preservation from the Committee of Public Safety. All the moderate Jacobins, the undecided Republicans——indifferent men,
or those who are still capable of repentance, pity, an idea
of awe, or of the return to another order of things, have
been expelled from their situations by replacement or dis-

missal ; and now, places either in the army or the administration, are filled by fit men of decided opinions.

In Paris, as well as in the departments, the various agents
are exclusively *Sans-culottes*, in the full sense of the term
—nothing more of the old medley.   These new upstarts
tread under their wooden shoes all classes of proprietors ;
they have reduced the remainder of the inhabitants to the
most absolute nullity.   A common interest and atrocious
fanaticism, or a villany without bounds, are the guarantees
of their zeal to fulfil their functions, and to concur energetically in maintaining the present despotism.

The revolutionary power, the exercise of which is confided to them, is now carried on by fixed rules, and with an
habitual and systematic violence.   There is no longer any
fear of offending either the opinions or the principles of the
first revolution.   The commissioners of the departments
have assumed the character, equipments, and language of
pachas.   Drawn in carriages with six horses, surrounded
by guards, seated at sumptuous tables with thirty covers,
their meals enlivened by music, and with a retinue of
actors, courtezans, and officers, always threatening, and
never losing the tone of command and enthusiasm, they
have struck the people with terror.   The same spirit, the
same external forms, proportionally characterize the agents
under their orders.   In short, formerly the ministers of
the popular power affected towards the people a tone of
equality, humility, and respect, and appeared to obey while
commanding; now they speak as masters, and the slightest
disobedience is an unpardonable crime.

The treasons, conspiracies, reactions, and insurrections
which were formerly facilitated by the multiplicity of

authorities and the incoherence of their exercise are now both physically and morally impossible.

Three or four persons, unless they are the creatures of the committee, cannot assemble or converse without danger, either in public or their houses. The farmer is watched by his plough-boy, the master by his servant, the husband by his wife, the manufacturer by his workmen, the merchant by his clerks. The most impenetrable retreats are every moment betrayed. Rabaut de St. Etienne and his brother, who had been hidden for five months, at the extremity of a faubourg, in a shed covered over with a trap-door, and to whom their food was taken by their host himself, have been betrayed, arrested, and executed. Fear makes as many informers as interest or the fury of party.

It is not allowable either to speak or write. The Palais-Royal, that old rendezvous of the revolutionists, is absolutely deserted : the gardens, houses, and even the cafés, have been vacated ; every one is afraid of assembling. At night, even, one goes home ; this is called *aller coucher sa liberté*. All the shops are closed before eight in the evening. Places of assembly, trifling conversation, solitude, private affairs, correspondence, are equally dangerous. Each section in the towns has its Committee of *surveillance* ; if any one escaped it, he would be surrounded by the satellites of the commune or of the Committee of Public Safety, who rise, as it were, out of the ground.

All who might have preserved some influence by their fortune, their old credit, by services rendered, even to the revolution—every one whose name would offer a rally-ing-point, a hope to malcontents, is arrested as a fugitive,

or assassinated.   The prisons of Paris, and the houses of
detention contain eighteen thousand of these persons ; each
town in the provinces a proportionate number : a voluntary
exile has deprived, and still deprives, the guillotine of a
great number; many, too, leave every week, braving a thousand dangers.   Many of those I have spoken to have literally travelled all round France in various disguises, without
being able to find an exit : it was only after the most
romantic adventures that they at last succeeded in gaining
Switzerland, the only frontier which is still somewhat
accessible to this host of unfortunates.   They are, for the
most part, inhabitants of the towns or countries again subdued by the Convention—federalists, old constitutionalists,
and royalists of all denominations.

If the elements of an insurrection, the faculty of preparing it, that of collecting the instruments, and the will of
effecting a revolt, were not radically destroyed, there would
not be any possibility of executing one, for at this moment
the whole people are disarmed.   There is not a musket
either in the town or country.   If any can testify to the
supernatural power which the leaders of the Convention
enjoy, it is to reflect for one moment that they have, by
a mere act of their will, and without any one daring to
resist or to remonstrate, reduced the nation, from Perpig-
nan to Lille, to a state of entire privation of all defence
against oppression, with a facility still more astonishing
than that with which, in 1789, the universal armament
of the kingdom was effected.

The following is a remarkable instance of the exercise of
this power.   The haughty proclamations of the town of
Bordeaux, after the 31st of May last, the day of the down-

fall of the Girondists, will be remembered. The people
wished to march upon Paris ; they threatened and insulted
the Convention ; they separated from it, and defied it to
the contest. All the *muscadins* of Bordeaux and the
neighbouring towns were accoutred, armed, and exercised ;
they were so intoxicated with their bravery that General
Wimpfen, after his defeat in Normandy, having made proposals to them of alliance with La Vendée, they rejected
them as incompatible with their ideas as to the monarchy.
At the commencement of October, four commissioners of
the Convention set off from La Réole, with eighteen hundred peasants and brigands ; a herald was sent on their
part to summon the worthies of Bordeaux to leave the
town in battalions and to receive them at the gates. No
one was ignorant that they were followed by executioners,
gaolers, and thieves. Nevertheless, twelve thousand of the
citizens, commercial men and manufacturers, having served
as National Guards since the commencement of the revolution, obeyed their summons with great parade : they went
to the gate armed, and in uniform, headed by their leaders.
The better to celebrate the arrival of their assassins, they
had prepared wreaths of oak-leaves, for the commissioners.
Tallien, the principal of the delegates, after a violent and
outrageous harangue, ordered a detachment of his men to
go and pull the oak-wreaths, epaulettes, and cockades from
the decorated troop. This having been executed without
any resistance, Tallien broke the citizen-battalions, and
entered the town with his troop of beggars. He issued an
order to all the inhabitants, without distinction, that they
should, under pain of death, deposit their arms on the
glacis of Chateau Trompette within thirty-six hours. Be-

fore that time, thirty thousand muskets, swords, pistols, and even penknives were given up. A handful of villains conducted by four jugglers, disarmed a city in rebellion; a hundred thousand citizens obeyed the decree without daring to offer a murmur. The arrest and executions commenced the next day. They are not yet discontinued. Bordeaux is now in fetters for ever.

It is superfluous to add, that every principle of rising has been destroyed, all confidence in foreign powers—all opinions, all desire of revolt, by the ever-to-be-regretted abandonment of Lyons, Toulon, and La Vendée. Whoever may continue to believe in promises from within; in fallacious hopes, deceitful invitations, the possibility of the least success, let him turn his thoughts to the ruins of Lyons, bathed in the blood of its murdered fellow-citizens: he will be forcibly convinced that the termination of a rebellion, supported by the concurrence of foreign war, is a hundred times more horrible than tame submission to the butcher's knife and the despotism of the Convention.

Therefore, it will be prudent to renounce all chimeras on this subject, to turn a deaf ear to liars, flatterers, hawkers of false information, who wish to impress upon the cabinets that the oppressed invoke their aid, and that their assistance may be relied upon. I contradict, in the outset, these emphatic allegations, and I affirm that the allied powers have, during the last year, destroyed every power of internal insurrections in France, unless they opened a way by force into the interior of the kingdom. I strongly pointed this out to them in the month of August, in the work which I published for the purpose of disabusing them of their absurd delusions.

All plans and decrees originate from the Committee of Public Safety. It exercises the initiative in legislation; it enjoys, at the same time, the right of decision, from the subjection into which it has brought the National Assembly. This does not contain more than two hundred or two hundred and fifty members : the rest have been guillotined, arrested, or have escaped. The talk is almost exclusively reserved to thirty or forty Montagnards or more. Robespierre, Danton, Couthon, Billaud-Varennes, hold the minds, the tongues, and poniards of men in their hands; neither debate nor discussion is permitted; each representative, not belonging to that phalanx, trembles for his liberty and life, and purchases both by silent submission to the will of the leaders.

To the number of absentees must be added further, the commissioners sent with the army and into the departments. The Committee can recal them arbitrarily at any moment, and such a recal is the prelude to a sentence of death : these ambulatory deputies have but one interest, one desire, one idea: they all agree in showing themselves in their commission as inexorable and furious as those who appoint them, thus proving their unlimited devotion to the latter.

The ministry receives orders directly from the Committee, refers to it the minor details, punctually executes its commands, and, far from opposing its power, is its passive, servile and ready instrument. They are nothing more than servants. Their offices are overlooked; every clerk of any importance is at the disposal of the dictators. Bouchotte, the present minister of war, is an imbecile : he only gives his signature and bears the responsibility ; Pache, although mayor of Paris, is still the real chief of the department.

The unlimited use of the public funds is left to the decisions of the Committee of Public Safety. It is an impenetrable abuse quite : the profuse expenditure is calculated upon the richness, promptitude and nature of the resources. The finances are divided into revenue and capital : the revenue is derived from the taxes exacted from the proprietors. They alone pay taxes : the people, properly so called, pay none ; and still there is no idea of obliging them : the management and rents of the unsold national property form another branch of revenue : both are like drops of water in the ocean ; but, with the aid of the arbitrary and local contributions, which are exacted without moderation, especially from those who have any apparent fortune, they suffice for the ordinary current expenses, the amount of which has diminished, and diminishes each day. This diminution results : 1st, from the gradual and now enormous extinction of the public funds. Those which are due to subjects of the belligerent powers are no longer paid ; the capital and interest belonging to the *émigrés* has been secured ; the guillotine and confiscations have successively extinguished them ; the payment of the rents due to the corporations has been suspended ; the pensions allowed to the clergy are suppressed, as well as the salaries assigned to the constitutional clergy. Finally, the establishment of the *grand-livre,* in which the receiving persons are obliged to register the titles to their various claims under the same number, has furnished the means of profiting by negligence to make all debts disputable, to learn those which belong to suspected persons, to sink whatever is desired of the national debt. 2nd, the expenses of religious worship are null ; 3rd, those of local administration are thrown upon the departments. A multitude of other branches, such as charitable grants, public establishments, the keeping of the roads, &c., &c., are equally suppressed, or much reduced.

The *extraordinary* expenses, rendered inestimable, are liquidated from *extraordinary* resources which have been quadrupled in one year.

These resources consist in the issue of assignats, the confiscation of capital, in spoliations of all kinds, and the forced loan of a thousand millions.

As to the first particular, it is impossible to know its amount, because it depends on clandestine creations; and in various places the delegated commissioners have used, and still use, assignats. The total quantity of this paper in circulation, has diminished since the royal assignats were annulled. Moreover, it does not appear that the more or less considerable quantity of *billets* has sensibly influenced the course of the exchange, nor the price of gold and silver, during the last six months. The variations must be attributed to other causes : the state of affairs abroad ; the chances of internal war ; the manœuvres of the stock-brokers ; the more or less considerable payments for purchases and services paid abroad by government, have had a more special share in it. Thus, from the month of May to the month of October, the assignats had fallen from sixty to seventy-five per cent. discount ; they have now risen from thirty-three, to thirty-five in Paris ; from forty-eight to fifty in the countries which still keep up commercial intercourse with France. This last price was kept up for two months ; but, after the retaking of Toulon, the advantages in Alsace and the defeat in La

Vendée, the assignats have again risen in value for a moment within the kingdom. There are departments where they lose but twenty-five or thirty, and they would be still lower at Paris, without the frequent purchases of cash made by the national treasury in the month of December and the beginning of January.

Further, since the law of the *maximum*, which, by its extension to the greater part of commodities and merchandize embraces all the articles of necessary consumption, depreciation of the assignats is no longer burdensome to government, except in the purchase of foreign provisions. This law is executed with rigour; no one dares to complain of it any more : it has delivered the Republic from every expense equivalent to the overplus of price which it paid before for its consumption:—it is an enormous saving. The Convention could not compel the assignats to be taken at par; but it has attained the same end by submitting the value of commodities and merchandise to an invariable tariff.   Having succeeded in forcing the citizen, not only to sell, but also to sell at a price independent of the value which the paper-money may lose in exchange, and which, from its very nature as paper-money, must always be inferior to cash, it matters very little if the paper has more or less credit.   The Convention has, therefore, made at the same time a very economic and very popular operation ; for, to the *Sans-culottes*, consuming and not possessing, it is very agreeable to buy with paper at a price which injures those only who sell.   What is essentially to be considered is, that to-day, in spite of the enormity of the expenses, the new creation of assignats is less necessary, because a less quantity of them is wanted to provide for

the necessity of government; and, because, as I shall
show directly, it pays in money what it draws from
abroad. Besides, the Committee of Public Safety no
longer considers these new issues in any other light than
as a subsidiary resource : it manages it with caution, and
will do so in future : its efforts tend, on the contrary, to
sustain and raise the paper by diminishing its use ; to
restrict the quantity in circulation, and to raise the exchanges by payments in specie.

It is with this view that the Committee of Public
Safety has recently seized the circulation and the reserved
fund of the bank of Paris and of the kingdom, by taking
all bills drawn upon foreigners, which are found at the
bankers, and taking upon themselves to pay their creditors
abroad. The object of this operation, which is accomplished at the moment, is apparently, either to rob commerce of its credit abroad, and the foreigner of their credit
on France, or to raise the charges in favour of the latter,
by offering, as the Committee does, to liquidate the remittances in silver or assignats.

For three months the Convention has disposed of all
the property in the kingdom, capital and interest. Provisions, fabrics necessary for the public service ; linen,
cloth, metals, produce of the land, colonial commodities
—all are observed, verified, taken or put in requisition. It robs one part of its consumptions—it pays
the other at the price of the *maximum*. Whoever possesses six shirts, is obliged to give one of them for the
wants of the army. Supplies of shoes, spatter-dashes,
stockings, hats—are exacted from the proprietors of each
class ; the detachments of the revolutionary army escort

the commissioners on their rounds in the departments, make domiciliary visits even in hamlets. Besides the articles already indicated, they make the people deliver up all cast-iron, copper, and iron articles, except agricultural implements : they have taken away even the kettles of herdsmen ; they have in the same manner carried off all the jewels, table-utensils, and cash belonging to private persons, giving, however, assignats in exchange—but only to those whom they think fit not to declare *suspected persons*.

Therefore you see that, not contented with possessing the metallic and paper money—which are the signs of things—the Convention has seized the things themselves which constitute real wealth. Its immense private spoliations, added to the public spoliations, to the cash acquired by exchanging the assignats, and the faculty of regulating at pleasure the issue of this wealth of paper money (since the value of the things which are represented by this money has been determined) open to the Convention so many inexhaustible sources of accumulation and of expenditure. I repeat it, generally, all that is within the sphere of its wants and of its crimes, *is in a state of permanent requisition ;* that is to say, in its own full power ; for no one would dispose of that which belongs to him, in this provisional sequestration, without exposing himself to total confiscation or assassination.

Now, if you wish to know the actual robberies, the confiscations already executed by the Convention, you must recapitulate :

1st. All the plate, the ornaments, the monuments of metal of the churches of town and country.

2nd. The sale or the seizure of the movables of the emigrants, all that was found in their houses, in the notaries' deposits, at the bankers', in the repeated raking up of cellars, vaults, walls. Numbers of houses have been demolished, solely on the suspicion that they contained property hidden in the walls ; these attempts to discover are continued without interruption.

3rd. The forcible carrying off by the commissioners and revolutionary detachments in the departments, of all gold and silver fabricated or coined, belonging to private persons.

4th. The spoil of the insurgent towns, as Lyons, Bordeaux, Strasbourg, Marseilles: this particular is of immense value. At Lyons, almost all the substantial stock-brokers, merchants, and manufacturers, have been put into prison, put to flight, guillotined and robbed. By a trick worthy of them, the victors, on entering the town, affected moderation of language, and re-assured the inhabitants. Trade revived ; the warehouses were re-opened ; the ledgers, the portfolios, the valuable goods came forth from their hiding-places. After a few days the sword was raised again, the prisons were filled, and the confiscations renewed ; the imprudence of the stock-brokers crowned the rapacity of the commissioners, and the spoil was much more considerable than it would have been, if the massacres had commenced at the surrender of the town. The better class of stock-brokers of Marseilles and Bordeaux—the Gradis, the Tarterons—have been assassinated, and their goods have been confiscated ; all those who fled, have left a great part of their property to the confiscators.*

* I have seen the thirty-second list of emigrants of Marseilles only,

5th. Following the statements which I have procured, it appears that, without counting the great massacres, the cannonadings, such as have taken place at Lyons, the sinking by artifice of vessels laden with prisoners, who were drowned in many of the rivers, it appears, I say, that the guillotine destroys four hundred persons a-week. Besides the aristocrats, the counter-revolutionists and the federalists, we see many real republicans and rich *Sans-culottes* fall under its blade. No sooner has a revolutionist, a public officer——even a Member of the Convention ——made and displayed a newly-acquired fortune, than he is arrested, condemned and executed. Fabre d'Eglantine, although one of the twelve of the Committee of Public Safety, expiates at this moment the possession of his coach, his festivals, his mistresses, his country-seat. The sutlers of the army, the chief contractors, the generals, the staff-officers, the pursers, once grown rich, fall under this law. The Convention speculates wisely on the fortunes of these upstarts. It places no obstacle against their formation, it seizes upon them as soon as they are formed : its system consists in pillaging the rich citizens, and in afterwards successively pillaging those who become rich. The national property has reverted, four times in one year, into the hands of the nation by successive confiscations ; a great many church lands, sold since 1791, are at this moment sold by this system of robbery, which is kept up by the Convention, to the great satisfaction of the *Sans-culottes*. Thus, by guillotining the various agents who have contracted to supply the

the goods of whom have been confiscated and put up for sale ; there are twelve thousand of them, and the lists are not finished.

public wants, it recovers its assignats shortly after having spent them.

6th. The forced loan of one thousand millions is being collected, and in a great part recovered by an imperative taxation on the revenues—a taxation, the exorbitant rate of which was seen in the decree of last summer; this collection was believed impracticable, or at least susceptible of so much evasion, that the contributors might escape from it by tricks or by force. Idle conjecture! terror and informations have made the proprietors pay, even with an eagerness which they erroneously considered as a means of safety.

I shall only speak from hearsay of the extraordinary contributions exacted in a revolutionary way. They are called *taxes sèches*. At Strasbourg there have been nine millions, thirty-three thousand livres, assessed upon every one of those who possessed any fortune ; at Marseilles twelve millions. It has not yet been possible for me to obtain an approximate recapitulation of the produce of these different articles. Well-informed people have assured me, and proved by confirmatory documents the probability, that from the 1st of November, 1793 to the 1st of January, 1794, there had entered into the public treasury from three to four hundred millions specie, coined money, and manufactured gold and silver in the mints. The extraordinary expenses consume about three hundred millions a month : this state has continued since the middle of last summer. The use of the illegitimate assignats s   t understood—that is to say, of assignats struck off without decree, and of which the quantity is a mystery. Neither the Convention nor the people dare any longer ask for detailed reports of the expenditure, nor does the Committee issue any.   As the immensity of robberies and their productiveness lead to a belief in inexhaustible resources, no one troubles himself about the expenses, which will augment instead of diminish.   The Sovereign Committee has taken for the basis of its conduct effort without limit : it is to be expected that it will be as good as its word, and the certainty of its resolution in this respect must not be forgotten.   It will, for many months to come, support the burden without exhaustion.   Its method (and it is a good one) is never to regard any expense when it is necessary ; it considers first this necessity, and then the sum.   If an object costs a hundred crowns, or a hundred thousand, if the public service requires them, the difference is thought nothing of, and on they go.   I have abundance of evidence of this fact.   For instance, the Committee buys horses in Switzerland, which are not worth more than twelve louis d'or, and for which *they pay in specie* twenty, twenty-five, thirty.   At the present time it causes the forests of Savoy to be cut for the arsenals of Toulon, although that wood, delivered in Provence, must cost three times as much as the wood of Albania or of the north would cost.

For some months the Committee has applied itself with indefatigable activity to buy from the foreigner, not only what is now wanted, but also stores for preservation to meet the urgent wants of the kingdom.   Geneva and Basle are the two great arteries where its money is made to circulate, and whence it derives its merchandise and provisions.   From these two points it causes remittances to pass into Germany, Holland, England, and Italy : its emissaries are continually passing backwards and forwards; depôts are established near the frontiers in order to receive the purchases; it causes sixty thousand pair of shoes to be manufactured in the canton of Berne and two hundred thousand throughout Switzerland: it draws from Germany hides, cloth, linen, horses, arms, iron, cast-iron, copper, cattle, sulphur, which it was nearly destitute of. These articles, as well as the corn, of which we shall speak presently, are paid for liberally, so as to excite the timorous sellers to smuggling, which is done every day by means of the imbecile carelessness or the collusion of the German governments.

You may conclude from this sketch of the financial resources of the Convention—a sketch founded upon positive information—that the Republic is richer and turns out more resources than all the sovereigns of the Coalition together; for here it is the national wealth of an empire which contends with the meagre revenues of a few princes. If this truth is overlooked, it will not be astonishing to see perpetuated that miserable system of narrow economy and routine which ruined the cause of the allied powers during the last two campaigns.

II.

MORAL AND MILITARY STATE OF THE ARMY.

I now come to the army, to its command, its maintenance, its moral state; to the principles upon which it is managed, and to its numerical force.

The army has, as it were, changed its nature. Formerly it was under the control of the Minister of War, and the Military Committee of the National Assemby, the Minister and the Committee being themselves subject to that Assembly. To-day it depends, as to its composition, its government, its discipline, its chiefs, its movements, on an all-powerful council of twelve party-leaders, united by the same common danger, by the same general views, by the same passions, and invested with an almost unlimited power. The Minister can neither give nor withdraw an office, create or dispose of the funds, decide on a point of discipline, nor govern in such or such a sense the hearts as well as the arms of the soldier, without being tried by the Committee of Public Safety.

Sometimes, it is true, this Committee has shown some consideration for the nominations of the War Office; has shut its eyes to the knavish tricks, the manœuvres, the horrors of some of its *protégés*, and repulsed the denunciations which were addressed to it, in order to urge upon these wretches the exercise of their responsibility. This was the case during the war of La Vendée, when twenty-seven generals appeared successively on the stage, and when, with the exception of four, all had merited death for their folly, their robberies, their hideous debaucheries : but the Committee had its reasons for tolerating rogues who served them in other respects. Thus, as soon as they considered the time convenient, they ordered the arrest of Ronsin, Vincent, and Maillard, three arch-criminals, who figured in the reverses of last summer, at Saumur and on the Lower Loire. The Committee will deal in the same way with every cabal which it has in its power, whatever may be

its conduct, till the moment when it is able to repress it
without destroying the instruments useful to them.

There exists no longer any other title to advancement than
a ferocious zeal and an unlimited devotion to the Convention.
As for the chief-command, the promotions are determined
less by the capacity than by the fidelity of the individual.
There remains no general of the earlier times of the revolution, or of the first eighteen months of the war. Soldiers
of fortune, inferior officers, active and enterprising adventurers have replaced them. Dugommier, who took Toulon,
and who has gone to take the command in the Pyrenees,
passes for the most enlightened and capable ; he was lately
officer of artillery. It was scarcely possible that by means
of changes, there should not issue from this continual
shifting of generals, some men fit for the revolutionary
warfare in which they have been trained, and for which
they show talents analagous to the circumstances, to the
sort of troops whom they command, and also to the genius
of the generals who are opposed to them.

In placing their confidence in officers taken from the
ranks, the Committee have felt that their present elevation
was a sufficient security for their loyalty. Nevertheless,
they have surrounded them with Arguses and Mentors.
The Commissioners of the Convention who reside with the
armies are, in fact, a sort of consuls invested both with the
military and civil authority, whilst the generals represent
the lieutenants-general of cavalry of the Romans. They
preside over the councils of war, sanction or change the
plans, and give a sovereign impulse to the army. At
their beck and call are to be found a cloud of spies and informers, who give them an account of the conduct of every

chief, of his conversation, of his connexions, of his habits. This *surveillance* forms a check upon troublesome agitators, of whom the Committee have got rid in the interior by giving them employment on the frontiers.

The staff-officers, who form the council of war, are the soul of the army. They draw out and prepare the operations : most of them, officers of artillery and engineers, have been chosen with judgment. Supported by an immense array of maps, plans, observations kept in the army stores, they operate really according to the experience and the intelligence of the greatest generals of the old monarchy.

The support and the subsistence of the armies have been much improved. The Committee have given a scrupulous attention to preventing the want which entails desertion and mortality. The soldier is, generally, better clad and better accoutred. The administration of the victualling department has been perfected by punishments, by necessity : and effects more easily its supplies of provision, since all commodities are put in requisition at a fixed price ; consequently the armies are not yet affected by the scarcity which afflicts many parts of the kingdom.

They are occupied at this moment with the great measure, so long delayed, of the incorporation of the volunteers in the troops of the line, and in filling up the ranks with men of the first levy. Till now they had not dared to try this operation ; but the all-powerful Committee have surmounted the difficulties. The army will have in future more unity and solidity.

The Reign of Terror has passed from the kingdom into the camps : it has broken there all public spirit, all intimacy, all social bonds between the officers and soldiers, and between the soldiers themselves. No one dares to confide his thoughts to his comrade: every one fears to find a traitor in a confidant. This mistrust serves in lieu of discipline: effaced in the interior of the camps, and in garrisons, because the Convention wish to perpetuate the disrespect. into which the officer has fallen, it revives on the day of battle: never did a general receive from his troops more obedience in the presence of the enemy.

This effect results from the moral state of the army in general: it is no more, as formerly, arguing, talking politics, stimulated to disorder in the clubs, or excited against its chiefs and officers. The revolution of the interior, the discord of parties, the constitutions made or being made—all this has become strange and indifferent to them. No other haranguers are tolerated but those paid by the Commissioners; the use of the public papers is only permitted with moderation and discrimination, even to the officers. They are kept as far as possible in profound ignorance of the reverses which befall the Republic, of the losses it sustains, of the disputes which arise in Paris. Thus, become a stranger to its vicissitudes, the army has changed its enthusiasm: its passions are concentrated in the extreme of fanatical hatred against the enemies of the Republic, the ardent desire to defeat them, and the enthusiastic certainty of succeeding.

The foreigners and the cabinets entertain the most erroneous ideas in this respect. The flatterers, the blunderers, the ignorant, do not cease to tell them that the army is full of malcontents, and that they will be well off for boisterous meetings and agitated dissensions. Yes, without doubt, the number of malcontent soldiers and officers equals perhaps that of the zealots of the Convention. It is a positive fact that, if the latter are united by the fanaticism of equality and of license, the others are united by violence and by terror: many of them are only in the camps in order to seek safety for themselves and their families. Reduced to choose between the edge of the guillotine and the steel of the enemy, they hesitate not. Differences of opinions and of motives bring no difference into the manner of fighting: one spirit, one common sentiment, animates all the soldiers: no one will own himself beaten by the foreigners—the malcontents are first Frenchmen, then royalists. The presence of hostile armies weakens with them the interest which they take in the re-establishment of the monarchy; because the military man, without reasoning, does not wish to think, nor, above all, to act in conformity with the ideas of those with whom he is about to fight, for the sake of opinion. This observation is particularly true with regard to the French soldier, the instincts of whom are formed by vanity. Combined with the enthusiasm of the time, this passion hazards all and betrays all. Such is the true character of the French troops at this moment.

Many causes, which do not date beyond the last campaign, have produced, fortified, and may perpetuate it. The most powerful one is that art of exciting minds and feelings, of which the Convention makes a prodigious and habitual use: for that purpose it takes advantage of every event: contempt is abundantly poured upon its enemies; it represents them to its armies sometimes as cannibals, sometimes as imbecile cowards. Instructions are repeated, not now and then, but every day, and in a thousand ways.

The raving about patriotism is augmented by the opinion, universal in the army and common to all parties, that the allied powers have no other aim but to ruin France, to dismember it, and pillage the towns and country ; that their interest for the misfortunes of the royal family is nothing but hypocrisy, and that without distinction between the monarchy and the republic, it is against France herself, and not against anarchical France, that they make war. Finally, the feebleness of their operations, the desultory nature of their alliance, their eternal defensive ; the constancy with which their generals have allowed the fruits of victory to escape them and neglected to follow up any advantages—their armies all successively beaten, two campaigns lost—have carried the intoxication of the French to the highest pitch : they have indulged in festivals, hymns, orgies ; the actual exaltation passes all belief.

You will easily perceive how much energy this warlike fanaticism receives from the kind of war which is being carried on. The tactics of the Committee are not complicated ; they are to attack always, and always in great masses—that is its theme ; and we have just seen whether it is a good one : now, soldiers always acting, always moved by the hope of routing a more circumspect enemy, and being prevented by this impetuosity from seeing or calculating the danger, contract a habit of temerity and an irresistible ardour for the combat. Celerity and impetuosity are to them the two elements of war, elements perfectly conformable to their character, and to a revolutionary war. How should they fear enemies incessantly inferior, incessantly overthrown by numbers, incessantly enclosed within a circle of defensive operations, and who have never taken the trouble to show them that they are formidable? When we see an Austrian general intrenched behind a few redoubts, allowing himself to be attacked thirty-five times in five weeks without once attacking the enemy, allowing himself to be entirely defeated; compelled to make a retreat which is compared to that of Rosbach, and leaving within five days the price of the blood of the finest army; when, on the other hand, we see a sergeant of artillery (Pichegru) risen to the chief command, every day during a month, leading back his soldiers upon the Austrians, and finishing with a splendid triumph, an excess of enthusiasm may well be expected in these troops, and a most exaggerated opinion of their irresistible intrepidity.

Thus, you have to combat (what depended only on the generals and on the cabinets of the Coalition to avoid)— you have to combat what did not exist in the first campaign, and but feebly in the spirit of the second—passionate armies fighting with the passions of the sovereigns, a soldier-people made frantic, to whom are opposed soldiers indifferent to the object of the quarrel, and whose discipline has not prevented defeats.

Too much occupied last year with its intestine divisions, and living only upon assignats, the Convention has slackened the course of its foreign operations. It has taken up, extended, and fostered this kind of hostilities by pecuniary sacrifices. In the towns upon which its armies border, where the governments reside—even in the camp —it has spies, traitors, and informers. These are certain facts. The commissioners at Strasbourg knew even the minutest details of the army of Wurmser and his projects. Although Landau was blockaded, the Commissioners received a bulletin every second day. The members of the Committee of Public Safety and their creations announced the certain fall of Toulon, nearly twenty days before the attack : it was in consequence of the exact knowledge which they had of the weakness of the garrison, of the differences existing between the Spaniards and the English, and of the detachments charged with the defence of each of the forts, that the committee ordered the beleaguering army to attack it by assault. The English fleet has not made a movement or prepared an attack, of which the Jacobins have not known beforehand.

Among the infinite number of prophecies, illusions and false notions which have turned men's heads abroad and produced so many absurd combinations, the pretended dearth in France has played, and still plays, a great part. The allies have found it convenient to excuse their carelessness by the recital of extraordinary calamities, which were to have put an end to the revolution without the necessity of troubles and efforts to get rid of it.

This tale of the dearth must be considered as a fable, as well as the hope founded on anarchy, weariness, or the excess of tyranny—and other idle stories of this kind. If by dearth is to be understood a local scarcity of corn—diminution in the consumption of bread—an alteration in its quality—a want of abundance carried to the extent of leaving in the kingdom only what is absolutely necessary—they are right. But all beyond this is exaggeration.

The last harvest has been generally good in France, and excellent in some of the provinces. After having put all corn, old and new, in requisition, the committee has ordered a valuation in each department. The administration which executed it have in most instances found a deficit in the quantity necessary for the annual consumption. Informed that this deficit resulted from fraud, and that there was corn concealed, the committee ordered a second valuation by revolutionary agents; then the deficit disappeared, and a more or less considerable surplus has been discovered, except in a small number of provinces which never produced corn enough for their consumption. I have seen extracts from the two valuations made in twenty-seven departments: they show a surplus of twenty, twenty-five, thirty-five, and fifty thousand quarters of corn.

Therefore, there is no real scarcity; but the enormous necessities of the armies and the supply of provisions for the fortresses involve an accumulation of provision in the public granaries: the inevitable waste in the formation and distribution of these magazines occasions a certain dead loss. Thus, it may be presumed that there are but few departments in which there exists a superfluity at the present time, and that in ordinary times there would be a difficulty in making the corn last until the next harvest.

Many circumstances, however, modify the effect of this eaten scarcity. 1. Except in Paris, but one kind of bread is throughout the kingdom—this is called *pain de l'égalité*. It is a mixture of rye, or barley, and bran, not equal to the good ammunition bread; but the townsman and the villager are only too happy to have some of this; and if a farmer or a citizen should think of baking better bread for his own use, reserving the *pain de l'égalité* for his servants, information would be laid against him; he would be incarcerated, plundered, and probably murdered. 2. The quantity of corn necessary for each individual being fixed, no one thinks of exceeding that, for fear of being deprived of it.   3. The administrators alone are authorized to sell corn in the markets, and they deliver to each person only enough for the necessity of the moment, and that with extreme parsimony.   In the towns the consumption of every family is rigorously fixed ; no baker would dare to deliver more bread than the municipal warrants allow to each individual.   4. Chesnuts, potatoes, turnips, maize, millet—everything which can supply the place of corn—has been put in requisition.   The inhabitants of the country have to consume the provisions in order to economise the corn, and to augment in proportion the disposable quantity of the latter.   5. Finally, in spite of the precautions, weak and imperfect though they be, of the powers of war, the committee procures corn from abroad, by the powers of aid of the neutral powers, and by that of the commerce of all countries which are attracted by money. Two merchants of Havre have assured me that, during the course of the month of December alone, eighteen vessels freighted with corn had entered the harbour : they were Danish and Dutch vessels. The latter make no scruple about this traffic.   They take false bills of lading for Portugal and Spain, and discharge their cargoes in the ports of France.   Their cargoes are paid for in ready money, at a very high price, and with all sorts of encouragements.   A great many of them have already made two voyages.   Moreover, many vessels of the United States, and of all parts of the north escape unnoticed.   At the end of December, a Danish vessel, laden with thirty thousand muskets, entered the port of Havre, after having been searched by an English frigate, which allowed it to pass on a false bill of lading for Corunna.

Last year, Genoa supplied the armies of Nice, Marseilles, and Provence, with provisions. When Toulon was taken by the allies, this traffic was continued with more difficulty and less extensively, either by land or by the coasting trade at Nice and at Antibes. It has just resumed its fatal activity : the tardy blockade of Genoa, and the cruisers which the season renders insufficient, have, it is true, prevented it for some weeks ; but the evil is done, the magazines of Provence are supplied for some weeks to come. The inconsistency of the measures taken by the allies against Genoa, the haughty demands, made and withdrawn ; the declarations which have irritated men's minds ; the unexecuted threats which have become a subject of derision ; the loss of Toulon, the fermentation and preponderance of the French party, finally the inconceivable indolence of the allies with regard to this town, which has become the fireship of Italy, and which will very soon, if a decisive resolution is not taken, open the gates to the French—all this has encouraged and strengthened the boldness, the cupidity, and the emulation of the smugglers.

Since the Committee of Public Safety took the reins into its hands, the administration of the provisions has been ameliorated. Paris has principally felt the change ; it is more easily, more abundantly, supplied with provisions than it was three months ago : the bread is better, and in greater quantity : anxiety is suspended.

If you consider that the great consumers, the rich proprietors, are taken off the population, or reduced to the smallest scale of provisions ; that more than two hundred thousand of them are detained in the different towns of the kingdom, live in their gaols or prison-house only on a small ration of bread; if you observe that every day the population is diminished by executions, losses of war, emigration, you will be convinced that there is still only a relative scarcity in France, which formerly would have brought famine, and which the government of the day can sustain.

Take it for certain, that the fundamental principle of the Committee is to nourish the capital and the armies: the wants of the rest of the republic do not give them one hour of trouble. On the contrary, they speculate on suffering: they know that it has a tendency to transform into soldiers those who can no longer live as citizens: the scarcity swells the levies, the scarcity excites starved people to seek their subsistence in the camps and in invasions, which promise the pillage of the countries and magazines of the enemy. Boldly, with an utter absence of shame, the Committee, the Jacobins, the revolutionary agents, publicly propose and project massacres, in order to diminish the consumption of victuals. If need be, they will at last come to this—they will cut the throats of their prisoners, the women, the old men, as so many useless mouths.

CHAPTER II.

1794.

State of public opinion in France at the commencement of 1794
—The Committee of Public Safety, the Convention and the
Jacobins.

III.

STATE OF PUBLIC OPINION IN FRANCE AT THE COMMENCEMENT OF 1794.

February 15, 1794.

IF the French mind had been as susceptible of preserving for a long time the same sentiments, as it is of
changing them frequently, the violence of the vicissitudes
of the Revolution would have greatly modified it.   Moreover, no proposition is more difficult than that which
indicates what those alterations of opinion are; nothing
is so worthy of distrust as the reports which are heard
every day on this subject; nothing is so dangerous as the
downright hypotheses and plans of conduct constructed
on the false basis of these reports.

Last November, public opinion in France differed from
that which existed during the summer: at the present
day, sentiments are no longer the same as they were in the

month of November: subsequent events will undoubtedly develope new variations. Thus, the constructors of sketches and descriptions should carefully add the date of their representations, and, above all, guard against taking shadows for realities, and calling accidents general and permanent stabilities.

Again, people deceive themselves daily as to the causes which produce this or that disposition in the public, and thence draw erroneous inferences as to future contingencies; they argue upon conjecture the probability of such and such approaching events. This reflection has been suggested by many passages in the speeches just delivered in both Houses of your Parliament, by the principal ministerial members who have voted the address to his Majesty. They are all agreed in concluding, from the terrible *régime* of the Convention, that it has spread discontent, and that the discontent has led to the end of the tyranny. This way of viewing the question betrays a superficial acquaintance with the nature and motives of the discontent, as well as the consequences which may result from it.

Every day it is repeated that the majority of the inhabitants of France are held in subjection by the minority. This is an incontestable truth, of which, nevertheless, they mistake the limits and ill perceive the consequences. The very small minority govern with a rod of iron: another minority follows voluntarily in the track of the former, whose passions it partakes and whose designs it executes: authority, entire attachment to the Revolution, a common desire to preserve and defend it, to enjoy it by committing all sorts of crimes, are the attributes of these two dominating classes. United by interest and by common perils they tend to the same end, with an equal energy, although there sometimes exist between them differences as to the distribution of functions and profits.

The majority, on the contrary, is a scattered mass, subdivided into numerous branches without any principle of cohesion.   One part of this majority disapproves of the use now made of the anarchic and revolutionary *régime*, without disapproving of the *régime* itself.   Mitigate the atrocity of measures, contract the circle of informations, executions, confiscations, conscriptions ; lessen the scarcity of provisions and the depreciation of assignats, and this numerous class would again become almost as ardent as the former two in the service of the Revolution, and for the success of the war.   Their present disapproval, the fruit of fear and difficulties, does not and will not inspire in them a thought of revolt ; they obey without a murmur, and console themselves for their sufferings by the more or less stupid hope of a prosperous future, so soon as the war shall be ended and the Revolution consolidated.

All those also are in the majority who have differed, and still differ, in opinion from the ruling minority, either as to the formation of the republic, or as to the proscription of the monarchy.   The Monarchists, the Feuillants, the Federalists, and many of the wavering Republicans, whom misfortune has corrected, constitute this class under the influence of the knife, who are generally anathematized, and sensible that the most humble submission does not suffice to guarantee their lives and property.   Add to this catalogue the men who are strangers to political systems, who would accommodate themselves to the republic, or to the revolutionary government, as they would to the monarchy, provided they were allowed to remain in quiet; and who, in their selfishness, would receive Robespierre for King just as soon as Louis XVII., if they could eat, drink, sleep, speculate, and amuse themselves without inquietude. A description of this class is sufficient to point out that they are not the least numerous of the discontented majority.

It may be asserted, without fear of error, that a majority of the people in France abhor the Convention, the Jacobins, the rule and the rulers : this majority comprehends six-eighths of the nobility, the middle classes, and the small proprietors ; but among the latter there are still many who adhere to the present revolution from the encroachments which they are allowed to make, on very easy terms, upon the domains of the clergy and the *émigrés*. This majority contains further the greater number of money-jobbers, merchants, manufacturers, the heads of industrial establishments, men of business, lawyers, artizans who were formerly in easy circumstances, the farmers and people living by their labour, who have preserved some principles of religion and probity, or who are wanting in the activity and effervescence necessary to raise themselves from nothing, and to perceive the advantages of the condition of the *sans-culottes*.

Under another point of view, and by generalizing still further, it is a fact that the attachment to the Revolution in an absolute sense and to the present republic itself no longer exists, except among that loose and mongrel population, who, four years ago, had neither position nor existence, and whom idleness, license and impunity have greatly increased in number. The constantly increasing crowd of the oppressed and discontented, are much less divided in their political sentiments than they were six months ago : the more or less revolutionary opinions have successively subsided, so that the constitutionalists have generally abandoned the constitution of 1791, the federalists and the Brissotists, the republic, and many of the republicans Jacobinism, and the *régime* of the day,   It would, therefore, be infinitely more easy now to find a point of contact among the old parties, to rally them unanimously on common principles, or at least to prevent all resistance on the part of some among them.   The royalists yet remaining in the interior are far more reasonable thau the *émigrés :* the persecution and misfortunes, of which they have borne the whole weight, have rendered them accessible to ideas of conciliation with their former enemies, whom they see punished and in part corrected.

The progression of the ideas and desires of the majority may be defined by saying, that above all they desire to see the present domination overthrown, that afterwards they desire the monarchy, and, finally, a monarchy more or less limited.   But it would be erroneous to suppose, that in these inclinations there is sufficient energy for undertaking any salutary proceedings.   No : this numerous mass is stricken down by fear, by defeats, by the most profound discouragement : far from being in a state to venture anything, they have not even the idea of a possible resistance. Their grief is inert and passive : they are fearful of showing their suffering.   They resemble negroes, who would choke themselves with their tongues rather than complain ; and the greater number seek their safety in dissimulation, or affect the most extreme patriotism.

Such is the condition of a great number of minds.   The

idea—the image—the custom—of the monarchy is effaced, in proportion to the interval which has passed since the destruction of the throne, and in proportion to the steady hold which the republic takes. People are accustomed to regard the return of a King as a castle in the air; and from that sentiment have naturally a tendency towards the primal order of things, which promises peace and security, or even only a truce :——the distance is as nothing.

If a sense of weariness and the enormities of the Revolution have detached a great number of its adherents, many unite themselves with their enemies from the fear of falling unconditionally under the yoke of the *émigrés*, and all from a distrust and aversion for foreign force. The Jacobins abhor these latter as dangerous to their security; the discontented hate them as dangerous to the monarchy, and as incapable or ill-disposed to aid them.

The aversion for the *émigrés* diminishes day by day, but the prejudice against the foreigners is deeply rooted in the national feeling.

IV.

THE COMMITTEE OF PUBLIC SAFETY, THE CONVENTION AND THE JACOBINS.

March 8, 1794.

You have seen, my Lord, in the former part of these papers, that the Committee of Public Safety formed the key-stone of the arch. I have traced briefly the nature, the exercise, the effects of that power which has attained the phenomenon of organizing disorganization, and of uniting the powers of despotism to those of anarchy. It

now remains for me to tell you its constitution, the aim
of its leaders, the dangers which menace them, and the
divisions which shake it as well as the Convention and
the Jacobins.

Too great attention cannot be afforded to this analysis,
which rests upon precise, direct and uniform information;
for the destiny of the war, and that of the Revolution, may depend on that of the Committee of Public
Safety.

The Committee of Public Safety is composed of twelve
members, who are:

Hérault de Séchelles, Lindet, the elder Robespierre,
Billaud-Varennes, Couthon, Prieur, Carnot, Fabre d'Eglantine (accused and imprisoned) Barrère, Jean-Bon
Saint-André, Collot d'Herbois. The twelfth became vacant on the 25th of February.

Hérault de Séchelles, retained in the Committee by the
fear that he might render himself suspected by retiring,
conscious of walking on the edge of a razor, frightened by
his name, his old nobility, his late position, is desirous of
atoning for these blemishes at any cost, and consequently,
to show himself as extreme as his colleagues. Relentlessly
cold-blooded, he smilingly proposes the most atrocious
measures, endeavours to render himself popular by the
most rigorous decrees, generally gets himself named their
executioner, in order to have the merit of them; inaccessible to repentance so long as he is subdued by fear——a
flexible, sure and ferocious instrument to any one who
can inspire him with terror. Having neither the talents
nor the activity of a leader, he seems at this moment

devoted to the interest of Robespierre, whose throat he will cut if necessary, whenever the dictator shall be on the eve of his downfall.

The house of Hérault, which is very rich, and that of his relation, Pelletier, brother of Pelletier Saint-Fargeau, who was killed last year, are the rendevous where these infernal gods frequently assemble to dine, and give themselves up to the most scandalous debauchery.

Lindet, deputy of the department de l'Eure, patronised and appointed by Buzot whom he betrayed: he adheres to Robespierre, through whom he was nominated to the Committee, and to whom he would not be more faithful in the first disturbance than he was to Buzot. A second-rate chief, he will never reach the first grade.

Robespierre, up to the commencement of February, has dominated over the Committee, which dominates over all. The foreigners and the French, who judge of him by his success, attribute great talents to him. They have made him a consummate chief, a prodigy of profundity, a second Cromwell. This description is a caricature.

Robespierre never has played, and never will be capable of playing, the part which he has taken. Thought little of in the first Convention even on the left benches, where he was without repute, afterwards forgotten during the legislature, never having obtained more than a kind of half confidence on the part of the Brissotists, he has really become the actual pivot of affairs, and the principal object of attention since the death of Marat. Sombre, suspicious, distrusting his best friends, an atrocious fanatic, vindictive and implacable—his life is the image of that of

Pygmalion, King of Tyre, such as Fénélon has described him to us.

Emaciated, his eyes hollow, with visage livid, and a restless and wild look, his physiognomy bears the impress of crime and remorse. Tormented by terrors, he is always escorted by three chosen *sans-culottes*, armed to the teeth, who accompany him in his carriage. Returning to his humble abode, he shuts himself up, barricades himself, and only opens his door with extreme precaution. If he dines from home, it is never without having a brace of pistols on the table, on each side of his plate. No servant is allowed to stand behind his chair : he does not eat of any dish unless some one of the guests has eaten before him : he casts a troubled and suspicious eye on all who surround him ; fears those in whom he is obliged to confide ; sees an enemy in each of his colleagues, and drags out his existence between the terror of assassination or of poisoning.

The simplicity of his tastes, his abstinence, his small relish for pleasure, and the firmly-established opinion of his disinterestedness have made and sustained his popularity. He has not a penny : his incorruptibility contrasts with the robberies of his associates. Living on his allowance as deputy, he economises his domestic expenses enough to keep a mean carriage, which he believes necessary for his safety, and which he has had numbered as a *fiacre*, to avoid even the appearance of luxury.*

---

* In a letter from one of the correspondents who furnished Mallet du Pan with the means of tracing these portraits, is the following : " He never allows any one to approach very near to him ; even in the Committee of Public Safety, he places himself so that no one can

The Brissotists in their time, and his present enemies, accuse him of looking for the dictatorship, or protectorate, or even the monarchy. This reproach is not destitute of probability, but it is commonly too much generalized. Robespierre aspires to remain master, less from ambition than fear. Fear is the main point and feature of his character. Knowing the men with whom he shares the public fortune, a witness from the experience of his predecessors to the difficulty of maintaining the summit of power and escaping the Tarpeian rock, he dreads those whom he supposes to entertain the same terror that agitates himself—the aspirants to the highest positions, agitators, ambitious men, hypocrites. Surrounded by rivals, observers, unruly men, and not

get up to him. When he returns to his house he shuts himself up in his room, the two doors of which are of oak, and furnished with triple bolts; there he is inaccessible to every one. To hide his terror, Robespierre sometimes dines from home with some members of the Committee of Public Safety. Twice I have met him at dinner at Mademoiselle de Vir . . . . I observed him well, and saw all his fears. On seating himself at table he laid before him two double-barrelled pistols, which he always carries in his pocket. If he is offered anything of which no one else has partaken, he takes it on his plate, but does not touch it until he sees that two or three persons eat of it with him. . . . . He affects a contempt for fortune; and when some one said to him that the war would deprive the republic of all the specie, he answered : ' So much the better : the French will not be happy until there remain nothing more for them but iron for their ploughshares and their pikes ! . . .' This contempt of wealth has not a little contributed to support him in the minds of the patriots who call him—with justice, in their sense—the *Incorruptible :* it never has been, and never will be possible, to buy him. He affects the same contempt for women as for wealth ; always talking of morals and virtue, he prides himself in setting an example of chastity. He is not known to have either wife, or mistress."

having, in fact, a friend of whom he is sure, nor a partisan on whose fidelity he can rely, his project was to rid himself successively of all, and to reign alone, to deprive all of the power and the right of reigning against his will. We shall afterwards point out in what his personal power consists.

Billaud-Varennes is the fourth—a pupil of the club of the Cordeliers and of the section of Marseilles, where he fought his first battles. Insolent and audacious, cruel from insensibility, an adept in *ruses*, conspiracies and revolutionary crimes, he is remarkable for the elegance of his dress, his neatness and taste. He is the dandy of the *sans-culotterie.* Having been educated in Paris, he has acquired experience in *liaisons*, the management of intrigues, opinions, and mercenaries in the government— experience in which the provincial deputies are deficient.

Couthon, a lawyer of Auvergne, shares with Robespierre and Billaud-Varennes the supremacy of the Committee. He has intelligence, and some talents. Sanguinary, like so many others, from want of courage, disinterested from an incapability of enjoyment from loss of health, his relative capacity surpasses that of the greater part of his associates ; he is not wanting in extended views, nor of ingenuity in the conception and execution of his plans. The audacity of his genius surpasses and supports that of Robespierre.

Prieur, late deputy of the first Convention, an instrument, but an experimental instrument, of revolutionary power, a brigand in his conduct as well as in his principles, will always remain a second-rate man.

Carnot, an officer of artillery, a member of the first legislature and one of the most useful of this Committee. Intrusted with the military department, he manages it with activity, intelligence and application. He divides his time between the labours of the Committee of Public Safety, and those of the War Committee, joined to the war department. This latter office is formed of officers of the artillery and staff, the principal of whom are : Meusnier, Favart, Saint-Fief, d'Arçon, Laffitte-Clavé, and some others. D'Arçon directed the raising of the siege of Dunkirk and that of Maubeuge. He is not surpassed by any one in penetration, practical knowledge, quickness of perception and imagination : he has a fiery soul and abounds in resources.* Carnot, his colleague, assists at the sittings of the Committee of War, transmits, developes, and supports the results before the Committee of Public Safety, and, when once decided, draws up the decrees for their execution. Entirely taken up by his special functions, he mixes little in party intrigues and will serve all successively.

Fabre d'Eglantine, denounced and imprisoned in spite of the interest of Danton, his friend, and Robespierre, who had urged him on against the extreme party. The rapaciousness, venality, luxury—the fabulous extent of the prevarications of this dissembling wit—made him imprudently declare war against his rivals, who have considered it prudent to sacrifice him as well as his colleagues in iniquity, Barrère and Chabot.

Barrère, commissioned speechifier of the Committee, charged with the drawing-up of reports. Subordinate to the principal leaders, variable in his conduct, furious, as so many others, only to escape the guillotine, he will succumb with Robespierre.

* I speak of D'Arçon from ten years' intimacy with him : he is no more of a revolutionist than I am.

Jean-Bon Saint André, Calvinist preacher of Montauban, instigator of the massacre of the Catholics in that town in 1790, an indefatigable firebrand, bearing in his crimes the character of the climate in which he was born. Sent last autumn to Brest, where he established the ascendancy of the Jacobins, a good instrument of tyranny; but by his resolution and audacity, in a position to raise himself to the highest rank.

Collot d'Herbois. To define this ruffian, it is necessary to take the description of one of those imaginary tyrants depicted by poets, and whom he himself played twenty years upon the stage. All that Tacitus sang of Tiberius is applicable to him—good qualities excepted. Framed to the most profound dissimulation, no one can attain to a knowledge of the innumerable folds of his heart. Eaten up with ambition, cupidity, jealousy and revenge, he unites all the evil passions. A grim conspirator, a studied declaimer, unpopular in his tastes and habits, he has never lost the theatrical tinge. A corrupt demagogue, his true place was that of chief of the hangmen. He possesses *sang-froid*, refinement and perfidy combined—the cool barbarity of an Oriental tyrant. He orders a massacre with more indifference than one takes an ice. His conscience is never touched, nor has his sensibility ever experienced an emotion. The others are remarkable and excusable for their fanaticism, and a cruelty which is a part of violence of character : Collot d'Herbois shows no passion—he is master of himself as of his physiognomy. Proud and domineering, the Jacobinical equality was hateful to him. He was the mercenary of the Duke of Orleans, and one of the actors in the revolutionary crimes from the commencement of 1789. When he saw the Duke tending towards his decline, he carried his hopes to the most lucrative and highest posts of the anarchists.

Having succeeded by dint of intrigues in having himself nominated as principal commissioner at Lyons, he there displayed the nature of his mind, and the impassive ferocity of his character. He was for a long time on the stage in that unfortunate town : his caprices, his *hauteur*, and the mediocrity of his dramatic talents, drew many mortifications upon him : more than once he was hissed by the public. *Manet altâ mente repostum*, he did not forget this outrage, and he revenged it like Nero. A volume might have been written, as terrible as curious, on his exploits at Lyons. No pacha ever equalled the conduct, the maxims, the speeches and decisions of this triumvir. His state reception resembled that of the Grand Seigneur : no one was admitted to an audience until after three repeated requests ; his reception-room was preceded by a file of ante-chambers. No one approached him within fifteen paces ; two guards, with cocked muskets, were at his side, watching the visitors. Inaccessible at his pleasure, he never left his house without a numerous escort. All these precautions would have been necessary, and even insufficient among another people ; but the monster who had murdered four thousand citizens in five weeks, pillaged ten thousand families and thrown into dungeons seven-eighths of the proprietors of the second town in France, has not received a scratch. His barbarous *sang-froid*, his railleries towards the unfortunates whom he assassinates, the ambiguity of his replies and his orders, an ambiguity which leaves it always in his power to acquit or condemn afterwards at discretion — this incomprehensible mixture of nexhaustible cruelty and artifices combined—to give them a character of justice and legality—would form the most striking picture of the Revolution.

The following are two instances of the policy of Collot.

He had one morning sent an order to the revolutionary tribunal to arrest a young man who was suspected, to examine him and pass sentence before the evening. Toward six o'clock Collot, being at table, and at an orgy with women, dancers, butchers, eating and drinking to the sound of choice music, one of the judges of the tribunal entered. After the customary formalities, he was introduced to the triumvir; and he informed him that the young man had been arrested and examined; and the strictest scrutiny having been exercised as to his conduct, he was found to be irreproachable, and that the tribunal thought of releasing him. Collot, without noticing the judge, raised his voice, and said to him : " I have ordered you to punish that man : I desire that he may be executed before the end of the day. If the innocent are spared, too many of the guilty would escape : go." The music and merriment recommenced, and the following hour the young man was shot.

A person named Châlon presided over the Provisional Committee instituted at Lyons before the arrival of the commissioners. More honest than his colleagues, horrified at the injustice and violence of the instructions which were sent to them, he went to Collot d'Herbois to represent to him the impossibility of executing certain proceedings, and requested from him positive explanations. " The representatives of the people," replied Collot, in the serious tone of an oracle, " are here to hasten the measures of the commission if they consider them too tardy, and to repress them, if they consider them too strict. Do your duty : you will answer for your obedience." Châlon understood the meaning of the hint, and sent in his resignation the next day.

In the midst of the sanguinary destruction of Lyons, a storm was brewing against the exterminator. Robespierre, Danton, and their friends, as little touched by these scenes of carnage as Collot d'Herbois himself, conspired to make them serve for the downfall of their instigator. They arranged to recall him, to accuse and execute him, as having exceeded his powers. They would afterwards have extolled the humanity of the Convention. Collot discovered the project ; his sudden return preceded the order of recall ; he collected the cut-throats of his clique, appeared before the Jacobins, harangued them, assumed a tone of menace towards his enemies, compelled them to remain silent, and wrung from the Convention a decree approving of his conduct. From that moment he became the implacable enemy of Robespierre, and his torment in the committee. He has spread this feeling to the commune, into the sections, the Jacobins, and is made the ostensible leader of all the rivals of the dictators of the committee.

As this man will not be long in becoming important, and appearing at the head of a new ascendancy, I have considered it essential to make you acquainted with him at some length. No one is more dangerous for dividing, calumniating or embroiling a party — that is his true ability : he has none for general administration.

While describing the formations and attributes of the Committee of Public Safety, I must not omit reminding

you of the Committee of General Security. Instituted
on 2nd of October, 1792, and invested at the time with
the widest superintendance of design, discourse, thought,
action, correspondence; authorized to invite and receive
accusations, and itself to denounce and ordain the arbitrary arrest of citizens, its formidable functions secured to
it a no less formidable influence.

Even if this power is not actually fused in that of the
Committee of Public Safety, it sinks at any rate to a very
subordinate sphere: it is the satellite of the planet, the
arm which the head moves at its will, and a state inquisition directed by the Committee of Public Safety.
Hitherto it had preserved its fidelity and obedience to the
latter; Robespierre and his colleagues held it in leash;
but their enemies have succeeded in scattering among
the twofold council the seeds of discord and rivalry. I
am informed that Vadier and Vouland, members of the
Committee of General Security, have organized among
that body an active and numerous party opposed to the
Committee of Public Safety. These two men, destitute
by themselves of sufficient influence, are, in all probability, the agents of a more secret faction, governed by
more powerful chiefs.

This division will end either by leading its authors to
the scaffold, or by alienating the Committee of General
Security from that of Public Safety. The latter, losing its
sentinel, will lose one of the principal pillars of its power;
it cannot but follow that the Committee of Public Safety
must reinforce the Committee of Vigilance with its own
creatures, or else that the Committee of Vigilance must
form a new Committee of Public Safety.

This inquisitorial power which exercised its influence even over the Convention, which enjoyed the right of instituting inquiries, of accumulating suspicions, of ordering arrests, and also the right of reporting to the Representative Assembly the result of its researches, and the grounds of its accusations, prepared in fact all the judicial decrees of the Convention, and dictated them whenever its proceedings were in accordance with the Committee of Public Safety.

The latter, through the other's ministry, held then in its hands the liberty and life of all the representatives of the people, and of all the agents of the Republic. Each submissive deputy trembled to see his name inscribed on the tablets of proscription. Thus, with the exception of a few veteran members of the Mountain, the Committee of Public Safety disposed of the Assembly by suspending daily above its head the sword of Damocles.

The accusation against Bazire and Chabot, the arrest of Ronsin, Vincent and Maillard, were dictated by the Committee of Public Safety to the Committee of General Security. The same influence has led to the rejection of the accusation against Philipeaux and Bourdon de l'Oise, both of them partisans of the dictatorial committee.

The revolutionary tribunals received the same impulse ; those of the provinces, through the devoted commissaries of the Convention ; that of Paris, by the daily action of the same authority over its judgments. Innocent or guilty, every prisoner accused by the committee's inquisition has been sure to receive sentence of death. A lady of quality, whose son, an emigrant returned to France, had been condemned to the guillotine, in spite of the extenuating

E 2

circumstances of his case, was exhorted by one of the
revolutionary judges to go herself and solicit Robespierre
in his favour.   She brought to bear upon him the seduc-
tion of tears, of interest, of justice, of pity.   Robespierre,
who had listened with a face of iron, took leave of her,
saying : " Citoyenne, I have the power of punishing, but
I do not know how to pardon."

Now therefore you see, my Lord, that the terrible arm of
a judicial power the most tyrannical, the most irresponsible
to all forms, the most independent of all laws, the most
general in the exercise of its vengeance, is embodied in
the Committee of Public Safety.   It paralyses with terror
all citizens in cottages as in mansions, on the benches of
the Convention as in the beds of the aristocracy, and in
the Jacobin clubs, no less than by the obscure hearths of
the Royalist *bourgeoisie.*

In addition to the power bestowed on the Committee
by this concentration of inquisitorial, denunciatory and judicial authority, it draws another no less formidable, from
the absolute disposal of the public funds and of private
fortunes.   Free to pour forth at will a shower of gold,
sole confidant of the expenses which it directs, it can
multiply all kinds of corruption and purchase venal men,
while at the same time it causes those to tremble who
are above the necessity of selling themselves.   Independ-
antly of the public funds, it disposes of compositions, that
is, of those compromises by which an imprisoned land-
owner, placed between the guillotine and confiscation,
thinks to purchase his life by sacrificing the half or three
parts of his fortune.   It is almost always a dupe's
bargain ; for the negociators in such stipulations are too

wary to leave any alive to bear witness to their transactions. But it none the less secures daily to the Committee and its agents, the purse and papers of such of the accused as are privileged to compound, while their immovable property reverts to the nation.

By means of money, denunciations, the prison and the scaffold, Robespierre and his confederates dispose also of the revolutionary army. These are their janissaries—their pretorian guards. They are the masters of Paris and the empire, being themselves mastered by the Committee, which has appointed their chiefs, assigned their functions, allotted their divisions, and which pays each individual three times the wages of an ordinary soldier. This army, generally viewed as a new institution, has existed ever since 1789. The agents of the Duke of Orleans planted its germ : it grew, became organized, acquired commanders, rallying places, words of command—a slang of its own : I have spoken of it in a note to my *Considérations sur la durée de la révolution*, p. 64. It was successively at the disposal of every ringleader of insurrection. Each revolution was effected by its aid : where the bulk of its forces was absent, its agency stirred up popular violence : it caused the bust of Necker to be carried in triumph on the 12th July, 1789, and the theatres to be closed; Foulon and Berthier to be massacred, castles to be burned, the mob to rush to Versailles on the 5th October, the King to be arrested in the Court of the Tuileries, on the 20th April, 1791, and Avignon to reek with blood. Headed by Westermann and Fournier, augmented by the galley-slaves of Breste and Marseilles, it formed the central battalion in the attack of the 10th August, 1792 ; it carried out the massacres of September ;

it upheld the Maratists in that struggle of the 31st May, 1793, which crushed the Brissotists.

What the Committee did was openly to acknowledge this force, already secretly organized, and to constitute it legally a *public force.* Its members are worthy of its exploits and its functions, numbering the most determined wretches, the ruffians of Avignon, the scum of Marseilles, Brabant, Liège, Switzerland, and the Genoese coast. Greatly augmented since its exaltation to the military ranks, it has been recruited by barbers out of work, lackeys out of place, out of door politicians, poor wretches unfit to gain their livelihood by honest labour. The capital is kept under by ten thousand of these Mamelukes. The truth is, they are tolerated by a cowardly set of citizens. Each department maintains one detachment : they are stationed in the principal towns—Lyons, Marseilles, Bordeaux, Nantes, Amiens, &c., where they execute every species of crime at the order of the Committee. Rouen is, I believe, the only city that has resisted their introduction, and maintained its municipal independence.

The generalissimo of this army is Ronsin, an ex-attorney— by turns spy, informer, assassin, superior commissary, functionary of the War Office, and admirably adapted to this variety of employments, according to the revolutionary estimate. Pache, while regulating the War Office, took him into his confidence : he commissioned him to embroil matters, interfere with the markets, intrigue, pilfer, and calumniate in the army of Dumouriez. This general draws his portrait after nature in his printed correspondence. Devoted to the anti-Brissotists, Ronsin applied all his talents to their service ; he soon acquired consequence.

and gained credit in the war department, composed of individuals as worthy as himself.

This department, with the sanction of the committee, despatched him last summer to La Vendée, invested with a species of military dictatorship. Appointed director-in-chief of this war, under the title of minister-commandant, he shared the command with Vincent, secretary-general of the war department, and Rossignol, a stupid ruffian, always drunk, and also become a general through the vicissitudes of the times. This triumvirate, escorted by a phalanx of staff-officers, strollers, and loose women, employed themselves solely in deranging the army, degrading generals, and overwhelming the commissaries of the Convention with annoyances and mortifications. These last appealed in vain to the Committee, who had furnished Ronsin with considerable sums of money and blank *lettres de cachet*, which the general filled up at his own discretion. Had these three brutalized and thievish sharpers been paid by the royalists, they would not have conducted the campaign differently : so long as they bore sway it was one series of disasters. Meanwhile, the Committee, *judiciously blind*, but obliged to humour the triumvirs, their associates of the War Office, and the numerous cabal which protected them, turned a deaf ear to the complaints of the commissaries. Happily the revolutionary army was installed and placed under the command of Ronsin. Vincent also was located there. Ronsin, despatched to Lyons with three thousand of his satellites to inflict there the vengeance of the commissaries, fulfilled all their hopes, and showed himself worthy of his reputation.

But meanwhile the committee had become more aware

of his conduct in La Vendée.   They discovered his intimate connection with Collot d'Herbois, with the party of
the commune, with all the subordinate agitators ; they
found out certain unheard-of atrocities, committed without
orders, against orders, and for his individual advantage, by
this wretch and his army.   He was observed to affect a
threatening and independent tone.   Robespierre, without
delay, had him denounced to the Convention by Philipeaux,
Bourdon de l'Oise, and Fabre d'Eglantine.   The Committee of General Security received orders to inquire into
the conduct of Ronsin and Vincent. After some hesitation,
they ventured to arrest them along with Maillard, an orator
of the Parisian women on the 5th October, 1789, a chief
of the Septembrists, and preceptor of that popular society of
the capital where have been hatched, these last six months,
votes for massacres, incendiary petitions, and the motive
power which again and again changes the aspect of the
revolution.

You have already learned the result of this attempt on
the part of the Committee.   The outcry of the Cordeliers,
the sections, and the rabid clubs, compelled them to release
the prisoners.   Their enforced enlargement is not only a
triumph for their party, but indicates its proximate preponderance.   Robespierre, dissembling his resentment, not
only displayed complete impartiality as to the fate of these
three men, but without hesitation — lest something worse
should ensue—suffered Fabre d'Eglantine to be sacrificed,
Philipeaux to be expelled from the Jacobin club, and
rough treatment to be offered to their adherents, nicknamed
by their enemies.

These details, which may perhaps appear to you a mere

episode, by no means deserve to be considered as such, for they will give you the key to the impulse we shall now endeavour to communicate to the revolutionary army—an impulse contrary to the Committee. Whatever the factions to which the army may attach itself, it will decide their fate, at it has decided that of all their predecessors.

Having shown you that the existence of the Committee of Public Safety rests on three fundamental pillars, money, the revolutionary army, judicial tyranny and the universal terror it inspires, it would be superfluous to inquire what are the subsidiary supports of its authority. It will suffice to remark, that the multitude of public functionaries, whose salary, offices, liberty and life are at the mercy of the committee, furnish it with a host of its own creatures. The capital alone contains thirty-five thousand of these officials. Far indeed is it from a fact that all these are faithful servants, or attached partisans ; many among them serve the rulers of the day, and obey them zealously, being ignorant of the duration of a power whose slightest will would overthrow them.

" You ask me, my Lord, whither this extraordinary power of the Committee tends—what is its aim—what are its ultimate views—what limit it proposes to its labours, its sufferings and its crimes ? It would be presumptuous to return a positive answer. We must argue from probabilities, without pretending to the attainment of certainty. We cannot doubt that it is the intention of Robespierre and his colleagues to prolong the duration of their power. For what motives ? I comprehend them all under one—for the motive of fear. Whom do they now dread ? It is not a foreign war, whose influence is so far away from their

stage, whose effects have been so fruitless, against which
they all with one accord consider themselves invulnerable.
Still less is it the aristocrats, the Feuillants, the Federalists,
who drag out a wretched existence in obscure retreats.

The Revolutionists themselves are their enemies, the
object of their terror, and the concealed marks for their
tyranny.   Besieged by these terrible competitors whom
they have inured to crime, whom they know to be incapable of any feeling of friendship or gratitude, they perceive
their impatience of any sort of yoke, and their greediness
of power.   The agitators of the second rank, united to
those who appear almost of the first rank by virtue of
popularity or of important posts, are furies dogging the
steps of any one possessed of authority.   Its actual pos-
sessors, knowing themselves threatened with the chastisement they inflicted on the Brissotists, and which the Brissotists had inflicted on the Constitutionalists, have but two
chances of safety ; the one, to rival in barbarity and in the
affectation of an exterminating spirit, the demagogues,
always ready to accuse them of moderation and treason ;
the other, to repress them, and work their destruction.
To fulfil this end, they must maintain the exorbitant power
they have assumed.   Under pain of passing from the dictatorship to the scaffold, the dictator dares not retire.
Abdication itself is prohibited—Hérault and Barrère made
the experiment.   But it is not enough to keep the dagger
—it must be snatched as well from those who hold it to
your throat.   No obedience, no rest, no security is to be
hoped for, so long as rule is maintained only by the succour
of perfidious allies, and by decrees which an insurrectionary
chief will tear to fragments in an hour.

It is then in order to preserve their life, and in an auxiliary degree to preserve their power, that Robespierre and his Committee arrogate omnipotence. They work for the present rather than the future. Environed by butchers, their foresight is exhausted in the effort of self-protection. On the alternative of extinguishing these forges of interminable revolution, or of being consumed by them, the path is marked out. It is followed on compulsion; and power, which is their safeguard, can only be retained by the effort to extend it.

It seems to me, my Lord, that those projects of sovereignty, by which the public attempt to explain the hidden counsels of the Committee of Public Safety, reduce themselves to this. Numberless circumstances and peculiar facts concur in imparting to my conjectures the highest degree of probability. I think I wrote you word that last month a woman, connected with Danton and Robespierre, seeing them threatened, consulted both on the subject of a project she had conceived of quitting France. "Fly at once," they answered her, "fly: would that we were able to follow you: ere long we shall cut each other's throats, and France will be one field of carnage." The sketch I have given you of Robespiérre's habits, shows how fear predominates over all his other sentiments. Danton labours to surpass himself; and his appearances on the stage are few and far between. Their colleagues escape the intoxication of fear by the intoxication of pleasure; they maintain their courage by gluttonous banquets, in the midst of wine and the most abandoned debauchery. If you study Robespierre's speeches from the beginning of the year, you will find there a continual protest against false patriots, exaggerators and agitators.

As to the general views of the Committee, they all tend to the maintenance and consolidation of that revolutionary power, which subjugates the Republic and the troops to them. No plan of a fixed Constitution, a regular government, finds place for the present among their projects ; they are too much encumbered with the weight of the edifice to be sustained, to bestow one thought on moulding its rude mass : their attention is absorbed by the necessity of making head against imminent vicissitudes, and the factions by which they are provoked.

Up to this time the Committee of Public Safety has not belied its name—it has not even ignored its duties ; it has fulfilled them with unwearied application, indefatigable activity, talent rewarded by successes, a spirit of deduction, combination and prudent audacity. The atrocious expedients which it has made use of these five months to sustain the burden, revolt those only from whom they have nothing to fear.

The identity of its means of authority with the means of public defence, has made it adjourn peace indefinitely. Without war, no more pretexts would exist for extortion, rapine, compulsory enlistments, imposts on all the fruits of the earth and of industry—universal pillage. Without war, no more hope of maintaining in the troops that discipline, not military, but revolutionary, which anticipates conspiracies, intestine shocks, and disobedience to the Committee or its delegates. Thus, war is a necessity for the Committee. None but a Hottentot would be excusable for imagining it possible to obtain peace from the Republic. When this possibility is enlarged on, on the faith of some clandestine advances and insidious offers, the object of the Committee is confounded with its conduct, and the first is misapprehended. Assuredly, the Convention would not lose an opportunity of diminishing the number of its enemies : the Committee has made and daily repeats efforts with this aim. During last year, and even this winter, it has, for instance, made an underhand proposal to the Court of Turin to withdraw from the Coalition, unite its forces to those of the Republic, and seize on Lombardy. No less certain is it that overtures have been made to Prussia. I should not be surprised if your cabinet were to receive such as well ; but it is a mistake to perceive in this attempt to divide and enfeeble the Coalition, a desire for general peace. The Committee would treat with one of its enemies only in order to redouble, with improved means, the fierceness of its hostilities against the others.

The Committee then desires to continue the war for its own safety, through policy, through necessity, and in the constant hope that war will deliver up to its tender mercies the resources and the treasures of the provinces bordering on France. Ever since it saw the desire for peace abroad in Paris, and motions expressive of that desire brought forward, it made haste to keep it down by a new proclamation of interminable war against all governments. It will pursue this object to the last moment of its existence ; its successors will pursue the same after it, and for the same motives. No faction will attempt opposition, since all are interested in keeping the army away from the interior; and the mass of the nation is not in a condition to resist this will.

Take it for granted, then, that the war will be continued to the last extremity, the army held aloof from the scene of faction, and that a necessity exists for devastating the adjacent lands in order to support the troops.

The Committee will sacrifice everything to these three objects. Determined to conquer or die, it contemplates the expenditure of four hundred millions a month, the absorption of all private fortunes and of the able-bodied population, the seconding of its armies by these masses, the ruin of yours by constant aggression, and the laying waste the provinces into which you threaten to penetrate. —It has calculated its resources for two years. If it holds on till next harvest, it considers itself safe. The present dearth, I repeat, disquiets it only in so far as it is likely to extend to the capital and the armies. Its plan includes the abundant provisioning of the latter, of Paris moderately, and the abandonment of the rest to famine; well assured, as it is, that this will swell its legions by all the males who have no means of subsistence in the interior.

Since I commenced this *résumé*, the position of the Committee has altered: the intestine divisions which it mastered and made adroit use of, have gained strength. The forces are now equally balanced. In order to avoid the exaggeration of prognostics, I must stick to the facts, reconnoitre the combatants, weigh the respective surplus; and, with this view, discriminate exactly the nature of the divisions which set them on.

It was not till the end of last October that the symptoms of a nascent schism in the dominant faction were observable. Since the fall of the Brissotists, their adversaries, remaining united, all concurred in enthusiatic deference to the Committee of Public Safety, and especially to Robespierre. All voices lauded the latter: the public papers set the example and tone of this general veneration. None dared contradict him either in the Convention or at the Jacobins. If he appeared in a public assembly, he was applauded as the King had been. The salaried fuglemen, the mob paid to occupy the galleries and passages of the Assembly, the informers, the bravoes, all depended on him Dazzled with this eminence, and impelled forward by the violence of his character, he neglected the means of conciliation, offended the self-esteem of others, and made his designs an object of terror. He drew his faction closer round him, and the rod fell heavy on all who gave him umbrage. He sent off to the frontiers the leaders of cabals and the over-independent talkers. He gave signs of a wish to restrain the revolutionary movement, and to impose a check on those who would bear none.

The first sparks burst into a flame in La Vendée, through dissensions of which I spoke between the commissaries of the Convention, and Ronsin, Vincent, Rossignol, and their partisans. The Committee prudently abstained from either censuring or upholding the proceedings of the delegates : it appeared to fear their antagonists and the cabal of their auxiliary, the War Office. Whether this party conspired from that time to effect the ruin of the Committee by conniving at the reverses of La Vendée, or whether the mere incapacity and ruffianism of the generals occasioned it, it is certain that the denunciations made then by the commissaries, with the assent of the Committee of Public Safety, were the signal for an open rupture.

The arrest of Ronsin, Vincent and Maillard, brought forward in Robespierre's council a new faction of whose existence he already was aware, and whose power he despised. The commune, the sections, the Cordeliers, became indignant. A demand was made for the formal trial of the accused, which conveyed a tacit censure of the duration of their detention. The secretary's department of the War Office, the staff of the revolutionary army, the colleagues of the minister Bourbotte, were aroused. Secret consultations were held at Pache's house and at the War Office, hostilities from the press fomented the discord, the Jacobins were divided and stood forth in hostile parties of equal strength.

But, as yet, no one had dared offend Robespierre and the Committee ; who, maintaining a semblance of indifference as to these disputes, beheld with pleasure these dangerous cabals preying upon each other, and prepared secretly to destroy them by their own mutual agency, without ostensibly taking part in the matter. Their credit underwent no visible diminution, but their policy was divined and circumvented. Soon they became aware that a strong and practised hand manipulated these factious elements, which, when taken separately, awakened contempt rather than hatred in the Committee. The accused were set at liberty, and their accusers disgraced. Robespierre sought the means of counteracting this first check.

He consolidated the revolutionary government; he alarmed the commune by the authority of the Convention ; he seized every opportunity of depreciating and persecuting false patriots and counter-revolutionists in *bonnets rouges*; he caused Camille Desmoulins to attack them by name in a paper entitled *le Vieux Cordelier*. From the end of November, to keep ahead of the Hébertistes (the party of the commune), he united with Danton, his mortal enemy, but companion in danger who had to reproach himself with venality, sums received from the civil list, a scandalous fortune, tampering with the Temple, and opposition to the Queen's trial.

This coalition for a time secured again the supremacy to Robespierre. He ordained a purgation of the Jacobin society, that all traitors, disguised aristocrats, and faithless *Sans-culottes* might be expelled thence—that is, that he might obtain undisputed influence in the club, by ejecting the creatures of his enemies, and several of his enemies themselves.

This operation, prolonged to the end of January, added fresh fuel to the flame. A relay of opposite denunciations hatched fresh hatred, and rendered what already existed, implacable; furious debates announced war to the death—and such, in fact, it was—for exclusion from the Jacobin club, branded the excluded as a suspected person, and placed him within the shadow of the guillotine.

This scrutiny of purgation, its conduct and result, illustrate the relative power of the two factions. Victory alternated between them; but the Hébertistes were the more numerous illustrious victims. They succeeded in expelling Philipeaux, Camille Desmoulins, and Fabre d'Eglantine, in casting an indelible slur on several partisans of the Committee, and in not losing one of their influential chiefs or proselytes.

Collot d'Herbois, as I have before stated, in these conflicts, figured as the ostensible leader of the opposition. Without abusing or accusing Robespierre and the Committee, while even maintaining with his cabal an outward deference for this formidable legal authority, he studied to undermine its basis, in the following manner.

It was inevitable that, once invested with power, the Committee should choose to enjoy it; that they should require obedience after having helped to subvert the principle of all obedience : that reigning by the influence of terror, they should inculcate respect for order ; that having created the revolutionary power, they should expect also to direct it, to withdraw it from the hands of the mob and the agitators, and to arrest its motion, whenever they might seem too strong or opposed to their projects.

Such was the fatal pass which must be traversed to arrive at secure dominion—a pass in which the Brissotists perished. The Committee involved themselves in the same danger, at the hour when that scythe which mows down the royalists, seemed to menace those popular agitators who aimed at a fresh revolution. To send the anarchists to prison or the guillotine, is to raise a mutiny among one's own troops : to allow them liberty of action, is to risk their dictating to oneself.

Besides, what hopes can we indulge of securing wretches steeped in blood, and never satiated with it, by sacrificing all the victims whose death they clamour for ? To yield to the ferocity is to increase it, and to increase the opinion of their own power. Even taking the sacrifice of human life as a mere matter of cool calculation, the Committee has found out that it is not without its drawbacks. They saw that commiseration began to subdue fury in the popular mind, dread to destroy their attachment to the revolution, and the guillotine to be surrounded by nought else but a set of beggars bribed by an assignat of twenty-four sous, to roar *Vive la République* around the revolutionary tribunal and the scaffold. The Committee accordingly formed the resolution to stop the effusion of blood, to substitute incarceration for death, and to confiscate the property of such as had their lives spared.

Consequently, some of its members, such as Fabre d'Eglantine and other creatures of the Convention and the Jacobins, began to talk about clemency : indeed, Camille Desmoulins preached it openly in his pamphlets. The severity of the executions at Bordeaux, Nantes and Marseilles was abated ; some of the Lyonnese were sent to the Convention with supplications for mercy ; the ransom of life at the price of money became common ; and all the sanguinary proposals of the inferior clubs and sections were set aside.

These milder counsels afforded to Collot d'Herbois and his faction a pretext for attacking their opponents. They referred to the Clémentins, the odium which the Roland-ists cast on the Septembrists ; they represented the suspension of butchery under colour of a conspiracy of an aristocratic coalition. They made a loud outcry about the arrest of some of the patriotic party, considered in conjunction with this perfidious moderation towards rebels ; they accused their adversaries of a concerted project to sacrifice the pillars of the Republic.

Then it was that the whole company of *Sans-culottes*, Jacobins, and sections, began to manifest suspicion and cry out in chorus.   The Mountain party of the Convention re-echoed the imprecations : the Committee and Moderates were forced to draw back and dissemble their intentions : the prison doors were opened to most of the criminals confined by the Committee, who were now claimed as immaculate patriots.   These dregs of society mingling with their fellow agitators of Paris, swelled the torrent.   The despotism of Robespierre and the Committee became the order of the day: the bond was broken—mud was cast on the idol.   Robespierre, in the middle of February having, by a sudden stroke, caused to be expelled from the Jacobins two sharpers named Brichet and Saintes, who declaimed against the mild forbearance of the present measures, the next day Paris was covered with incendiary placards against Robespierre, denouncing him as a tyrant.

Never before had he suffered from such a public attack, ominous of his fall in popular opinion.   From day to day his adversaries have increased in favour : they put no limit nor moderation in their petitions.   Robespierre and Couthon having fallen ill these three weeks, through mortification, the opposition has taken advantage of their absence ; Collot d'Herbois speechifies, triumphs alone, and drinks in the applause of the Jacobins.

This party, so timid and humble till the end of last year, now audacious and unreservedly hostile, has its chief partisans in the sections and popular societies of Paris.   Though the Committee have been completely successful in suspending in the departments the anarchical influence of the deliberative democracy, it has not dared to strike a blow at its source in the capital.   Compressed for a time by the vigour of the dictatorial arm, aided in its despotic action by the peculiar features of the arena, anarchy has not failed again to raise its head.

The sections have become the refuge of disappointed aspirants, of irreclaimable rogues, of low-born rioters, of bullying *Sans-culottes*, and of many more counter-revolutionists, who, decked in red cap and brown breeches, bluster away in the gambling houses, sow discord, and attract attention by their vehement gestures. Each section comprises a committee of superintendence and a revolutionary committee, whose jurisdiction should be limited to the affairs of local police, and which in fact are so many centres of intrigue, innovation, independence, and trouble.

This elementary democracy, clashing by its very nature with the representative power, has an invincible tendency to slip out of the power of the Convention, to usurp in part its functions, and to assert dominion over it. At one time it indulges in acts of revolutionary authority, at another it vents itself in petitions : one day these acts are enforced by the Municipal Council, the next by the clubs.

The commune, emanating from these sections, the commune with its power in Paris controlled and often opposed by the Convention, the commune which, from the period of its origin, has ever regarded itself in the light of a miniature Convention, preserves its allegiance to this latter out of a mere lack of the elements of rebellion. The heads of these, entitled by their influence and situation to aspire at the highest honours, are the born enemies and ardent rivals for the Conventional power.

The Jacobins comprise in their number the most influential magistrates, the oracles of the sections, the secret agitators who beset them ; hence the popular party leavens more or less this central and primitive club.   In the Cordelier club, which has always had the Jacobins in its wake, and in the inferior societies dependent on these, it manifests itself by the concoction of repeated revolutions, and is led by its very essence invariably to rise against any authority prolonged beyond six months.

Such, my Lord, is the confederation which shakes to its foundation the Committee of Public Safety.

These, however, are but tools : the faction is set in motion by secret springs, which create and over-rule their movements.   Hébert and Chaumette have long been regarded as the principal moving powers, but yet were never sufficiently skilful, nor did they enjoy sufficient credit to play so difficult a game.   The projects are carried on by more experienced and less known hands.   A portion of the Montagnards in the Convention, the War Offices rendered influential by their number and the enormous funds at their disposal, and the chiefs of the Cordelier club, seem to be the nucleus of the faction.   We have seen how the heads of the revolutionary army pursue the same career.   Henriot, commander of the remnant of the Parisian National Guard, ex-lacquey to M. de Brohan, sides with the commune, but not openly.

In the midst of these combined forces, whose ostensible leader is Collot d'Herbois, there nevertheless exist concealed movers, whose influence has silently spread to the Convention, to the Committee of Public Safety, and to that of General Security, and counteracts unseen their measures. On the 19th February, Robespierre said to Amar, his confidant in the Committee of General Security, that for some time past he had clearly perceived that an invisible hand ever carried them beyond their own will, that every day the Committee did that which they had resolved against overnight, and that a faction existed whose aim was to abase and ruin them, while hitherto they had been unable to discover its directors. His suspicions fastened on Pache, who affected to keep clear of everything, apparently unconcerned with any party, but incapable from his natural disposition of such genuine indifference.*

Such, my Lord, is an analytical recapitulation of the elements which compose this dangerous faction, which is preparing for us a new phase of revolution.

* Amar acquainted my correspondent with this conversation on the eve of his departure.

CHAPTER III.

1794.

Opinions of Mallet du Pan on the means of repairing the errors of
the Coalition—Tardy expedients—Campaign of 1794 disastrous to
the allies—Letter from Mr. Trevor on the English policy—Letter
from the Abbé de Pradt on military events.

WHETHER Mallet had learned the doubts and hesitation
which ere long took the place of unanimity in the counsels
of the Coalition, and the coldness suddenly evinced by
Prussia, more engaged in preserving its share of Poland than
in seconding the views of Austria ; or whether he placed no
great reliance on the strategic conceptions of Mack, whose
genius, taken for granted in Vienna and London, inspired
there the utmost confidence, or on Coburg's power of
carrying out the plan of the new Major-General, he could
not refrain from great uneasiness as to the issue of the
ensuing campaign. The silence of the Coalition on the
subject of its ulterior designs, appeared to him moreover
supremely impolitic, if indeed it failed to arouse his suspicions.

It was now that he despatched fresh advices to the
London Ministry and the Imperial Cabinet, by means of

the English Commissary and Count Mercy-d'Argenteau. The opening of his despatch by its tone of discouragement, indicates that he had been asked to undertake this new labour, and that it was almost in despair of being listened to, that Mallet decided on propounding fresh views adapted to circumstances.

" March 5, 1794.

" The character of government preceptor is too ridiculous, for a sensible man to volunteer its assumption. The certainty of not gaining attention adds discouragement to absurdity. In general, both sovereigns and ministers have evinced a systematic distaste for all those who, situated in the thick of the Revolution, might be supposed best acquainted with its elements, resources, and the means of combating it.

" Their *sang-froid* has excited mistrust ; they have been generally supposed tainted with some of the passions of the time, to be more eager after personal interest than enlightened concerning that of the powers, and too good Frenchmen to be other than bad friends to Europe.

" This prejudice has caused the indiscriminate rejection of even the valuable advice of men superior to party-spirit and national rivalry, but who, having something to recover or hope for in France, in case of the re-establishment of the monarchy, have been supposed not sufficiently disinterested in the matter. From this too general presumption, it has followed that foreigners have invariably attached more importance to their own opinion than to any communicated to them from France ; that, deceived by the first erroneous reports of the emigrants, they have despised

as questionable in motive whatever information or whatever truths more tranquil spirits presented to them, and
that, straying without a compass amid the storms of the
Revolution, they pass at once from security to fear, from
terror to exaggerated confidence, instead of forming immutable plans on a thorough knowledge of the character of
the present crisis.

"The time for remedying this want of consistency, by
adopting principles based on the true nature of the evil,
has passed.   Necessity, and not foresight, calls imperatively for innumerable dykes against a torrent which
threatens to submerge all.   Now, the plans of conduct
which necessity dictates, cannot be laid down by an isolated
observer.   And how succeed in gaining the ear of several
Cabinets equally divided in views and in interest?   How
make any impression on a policy made up of heterogeneous
elements, and which, in lieu of tending uniformly towards
the attainment of the common end designated by the common danger, subordinates it to scruples about some incompatible local interests, and to considerations borrowed from
ancient jealousies between different states ?

" These reasons for the silence of every private individual,
a stranger to the administration of affairs, are enforced by
another still more peremptory.   In order to form or to
hold any opinion relative to the proper direction of plans
and efforts, it would be necessary to discern the true design
of the powers.   How indicate any course of conduct,
when the direction in which the allies mean to work, and
the end they propose to attain, are equally unknown ?

" Two hypotheses present themselves. Either the powers,
warring essentially against France, and in a subsidiary

degree against the Revolution, design to use that monarchy for their own ends, to ruin its power for ever, to appropriate such portions of it as they may find suitable for future security, or for aggrandisement under the name of indemnity, and then to abandon the despoiled throne to its deplorable fate ;

"Or else the powers propose to stifle the Revolution, and the authorities which sustain it, to end the war by the re-establishment of legitimate government, and to reserve to themselves, *a posteriori*, in a definitive treaty, such indemnity as justice, the expense of three campaigns, and gratitude, authorize them to claim.

"Ascending to the former hypothesis, that of war leading to dismemberment, no aid could be relied on but that of the strength of the foreign armies. Any project against France itself is a service to the Revolution, and the tyrants who direct its course. The Committee of Public Safety will have little difficulty in making it believed that its enemies, whoever they may be, are the allies of Pitt and Coburg. All moral means would fail, the moment the restoration of France itself ceased to be the principle avowed to the malcontents. No spring could then be touched but that of corruption ; but what treasures are to be offered to men in whose hands lie the treasures of all France?"

An exclusive system of conquests of any kind, would, by suppressing all moral and political resources, confine the chance of success to that of important victories alone ; now, in Mallet's eyes, this chance was feeble.

"As for me, my Lord," he says, "I do not hesitate to confess to you that, on the plan of warring against France, and in a subsidiary degree against the Revolution, you would be baffled both by the Revolution and by France."

Reverting to his great principle, that the Revolution must be fought with its own weapons, although without the crimes which nothing can justify, he inquires why, "while the revolutionists make a passion of war, nothing is brought against those burning passions but armies—but the old routine of warfare?"

"Seeing that this is a war of opinions, how explain this systematic and almost universal disinclination to inflame minds with a righteous indignation against the enemy?

"The Convention murders the Queen of France, a sister of the sovereign of the empire, and the event is left to the comment of some unknown scribblers. Not a single orator in your Parliament has ever deigned to allude to it: the courts seemed so little interested in the matter that the public soon forgot it. The first impression of the Queen's death was allowed to die out in a fortnight. It might have been a Cæsar's robe; but governments, although recalled to times when the magic of the ancients would be so needful to them, leave to the savages of Paris the art and the genius of electrifying men's souls by the sight of a solemn grief, which demands vengeance and popularizes resentment."

Here the memorial dilates on the necessity of assembling and organizing the armies of the Revolution, and of opposing to them the anti-revolutionary forces.

"The arming of the French emigrants, and their junction with the allied army, was a grave error in 1792: but in 1793, it was a fault of a different nature, at the instant of Dumouriez' defection, to neglect to assemble, without distinction of persons or of rank, all those French who were already expatriated, or on the point of becoming so. All who profess similar sentiments, (and the tyranny of the interior has enormously augmented their number during these fifteen months), tend to coalition and to united efforts. The evidence of a common aim, the urgency of the interests affected, the existence of a rallying-point offering peace, assistance, concert in action, encouraged the desertion. The refugees, nobles or commoners, aristocrats, royalists, *feuillants*, federalists, peasants, deserters, townsmen, driven from France by the successive crises of the Revolution, may at this moment be numbered at one hundred thousand men capable of bearing arms. Others leave France daily. Their first inquiry on passing the frontier is, where they may assemble and fight to regain their homes—such, for instance, is the question put by six thousand Lyonnese. But no one can show them any rallying point, or the smallest probability of the Powers availing themselves, in any degree whatsoever, of this immense number of deserters. I testify that soldiers, citizens, countrymen, despite the executioners and emissaries of the Committee, would flock to a French standard raised on the frontier, already surrounded by the first fugitives, and upheld by the Powers. This is the universal desire of the malcontents : a thousand concurrent facts leave me no doubt as to their inclinations. If more positive evidence is required, I appeal to the Committee of Public Safety and the Jacobins. I affirm, that they have dreaded and do dread above all, this vanguard of French assemblies, animated by passions like their own, giving the signal for insurrections, and

holding forth encouraging promises, and opening the road
to Paris for the allied armies."

Rules of conduct follow, by neglecting which the whole
project would miscarry. Thus, the emigrants should be
represented as a French auxiliary army, not subordinate to
the foreign forces ; and, above all, under pain of utter
failure, the following singular conditions should be imposed
on the Princes and emigrants :

" 1st. To abandon a too dictatorial tone, too exclusive
preferences, and the habit to which the French Princes are
but too much inured, of speaking and acting as chiefs of
the emigrant nobility, instead of speaking and acting as
chiefs of the French nation.

" 2nd. To relinquish professions of faith as the test of
reception of the refugees, to consider their sentiments
during the Revolution, instead of laying exclusive stress on
their present opinions. To humiliate no man by requiring
from him acts of repentance ; to talk of confidence, not of
clemency ; and to restrict all formularies to an engagement
to fight conscientiously for the re-establishment of the
throne, and the security of property. In like manner, clas-
sifications must be given up, and the perpetual and exclusive mention of the nobility, as if it composed the state
and could subdue the kingdom—the nation, its interests,
and misfortunes, must alone be spoken of.

" All allusion must be avoided to the old *régime*, to the
privileges of caste, to the constitutions, to all systems
whatsoever, as so many handles to disputes and disunion.

" In all future declarations to invite the concurrence of
all the enemies of the Convention, of every shade ; to treat
them with a confidence which many among them, doubt-

less, do not deserve, and only to avow the aim which unites all interests—the re-establishment of religion, of royalty, of a government, the guardian both of lives and fortunes; the annihilation of the mob's power, and its chiefs' tyranny; lastly, a promise to fulfil, faithfully, engagements for the maintenance of public liberty, entered into by the late King before the opening of the States-General."

After this exposition of the measures on which the issue of the war depends Mallet reverts to the necessity of openness, and of all operations being directed by one impulse.

" To will, command and be obeyed, are with the Committee of Public Safety the work of an instant. It acts with the speed of lightning while the Allies deliberate; all authorities are subject to it; it is able to constrain their consent, or to do without it; while ministers, separated from each other by two or three hundred leagues, and all alike distant from the scene of war, have need of discussions, explanations, endless couriers, before they can adopt unanimously any one measure. So long as the Allies have not, after the fashion of the French, their Committee of Public Safety, that is, a congress of plenipotentiaries, furnished with general and positive instructions posted in the vicinity of the troops, diligent in collecting information, and in daily ascertaining indisputable facts, authorized to set forward operations with a promptitude correspondent to circumstances, you will lose the result of your most costly efforts.

" It were useless," says Mallet, in conclusion, " to insist here on considerations which have become common-place, and for this reason are little thought of. For instance, everything has been said on the defensive system. If the experience of Cæsar, who, by prodigies of speed and the uninterrupted following up of his successes, subjugated the Gauls, who also fought in unison, and were inspired with a genuine love of freedom ; if the experience of wars in general, and of this war in particular, has failed to alter the notions of our ministers and generals, the words of an obscure individual will avail still less."

It seems that the political considerations developed in these communications obtained marked attention ; but the measures proposed received, as usual, only a tardy acquiescence. The bold and open course recommended by Mallet, had in it something vast and absolutely new, which the majority of the combined states found it as difficult to compass, as they did that great war, which neither their ministers nor their generals dared conduct with appropriately vast operations and impetuosity. Besides, statesmen only adopt those measures which they have themselves conceived. It must, too, be admitted that Mallet's proposals, with the exception of principles and maxims of ordinary conduct, were difficult of execution ; his position involved a vicious circle, which embraced all practicable means for raising France against itself : to carry it out, that spirit of union, of mutual concession, and of obedience, was essential, which was lacking in every quarter. And how much time had been lost !

Belgium, the rallying and starting-point of the nations hostile to the Convention, had been worked upon by revolutionary influence, and was, in fact, more infected than might have been supposed. Six months had elapsed between Mallet's propounding his plan of defence, and the Emperor's being inaugurated at Brussels as Duke of Brabant. During this interval the country's attachment to its sovereign had been undermined, and sacrifices could no longer be expected from it, much less enthusiasm. It is not till after the capitulation of Landrecies, at the moment when the disastrous consequences of this campaign—occasioned by the errors and inconceivable procrastination of the Prince of Cobourg—were beginning to appear, that Mallet du Pan's project is noticed.

On the 30th of April, 1794, the whole camp was gladdened by news that Cobourg had just gained a splendid victory over Pichegru, who had arrived at the head of all his forces before Landrecies. Already imagination pictures the King of Prussia marching through Longwi and Montmédi, and reaching Réthel at the same moment as the Prince reaches Guise. "This would be the moment," writes Montlosier, describing beforehand to Mallet these visionary marches, "for producing that counter-revolutionary army, which England appears disposed to organize, according to a plan with which you are said to have furnished it. I have seen here, under the title of 'Considérations,' certain extracts supplied by an Englishman to this (the Austrian) Government, and the work is attributed to you, and appears to me, on the whole, worthy of you." Montlosier volunteered his services to raise this army. But I am not aware of any fact which authorizes the supposition that the English government took any active steps towards realizing this vast project.

The disasters which followed hard on the first successes, shaking the foundations of the alliance, and deranging the army, caused other anxieties to Mr. Pitt. It was necessary to repair " the immense injury which petty considerations, those inveterate foes to great ones,"* had just inflicted on the common cause. It was necessary to conciliate the Emperor and the King of Prussia, whose views had become profoundly and bitterly estranged. In the midst of such reverses, while Europe held out to England only the insecure co-operation of weary and suspicious allies, the opposition reiterated, with increased violence to the ministry, still determined on war, the demand whether then it was a settled point never to make peace with the French Republic.

And was it so in fact ? What at this crisis were Mr. Pitt's real views ? Was his mind made up never to lay down arms until the Republic was crushed? The following letter indicates that, at least at this moment, the ministerial intentions were more moderate, and that the English government ardently desired that a government might be established in France, with which negociations might securely be carried on. This letter was addressed to Mallet du Pan by the English ambassador at Turin, Mr. Trevor, afterwards Lord Hampden, an admirer and warm friend of our author, to whom he had been introduced by their common friend, Macpherson :—

LETTER FROM MR. TREVOR TO MALLET DU PAN.

" Turin, 12th March, 1794.

" Sir,

" On my return from a little excursion into Switzerland, I found the excellent letter you have done me the honour

* Letter from l'Abbé de Pradt to Mallet du Pan.

to write me. I am deeply impressed both with the truth of the principles it embodies, and with the acuteness of their development. But for your informing me that you have already submitted them to the consideration of our cabinet, I should not have lost a moment in doing so with an eagerness equal to my sense of their value. Your remark, ' *that the armies are neither royalist nor republic, but French*,' is of the highest importance, and seems to me to supply the fittest clue for our guidance out of that fatal labyrinth in which we have lost our way, and whence we are so deeply interested to escape. But it is the diversity of this interest, too nicely calculated by a selfish and near-sighted policy, which constitutes the difficulty of a homogeneous re-union of principles and measures, and thus, *dum singuli pugnant universi vincuntur.* Shall we be wiser this campaign? I wish, as you do, that before commencing it we might heartily recognise the necessity of two things: first, that we should ourselves know what we want; secondly, that the French people should know it too. Then a large proportion of the nation, seeing what they have to expect, might rally round a fixed and central point. England and Spain have, indeed, adopted this principle in their last declaration ; but the difficulty lies in contriving that the knowledge of this fact shall penetrate into the interior of France. I believe that the congress you speak of is absolutely needful. I hope the time is come for it to be a real good ; and I shall be proud and happy to see England give a tone of magnanimity, moderation, and justice, which the other powers will find themselves under the necessity of imitating. The saddest feature of this horrible war is, in my opinion, the impossibility of concluding a peace with the

existing government; for I hope you will make the Marquis
of Lansdowne understand, that in faithfully portraying the
abnormal and colossal forces of the Convention, you never
intended, as he seems to insinuate, to reduce us to the humiliation of being induced by despair to make peace, in order
to obtain that great end for which every man and every
nation ought ardently to long.*   I think our efforts should
be directed, not so much to overthrow by force the actual
non-government, as to create a truthful and generous policy;
and, by a frank and precise declaration, to form a government with which we could treat."

Some weeks afterwards, the campaign of 1794 was
opened; and soon, notwithstanding partial victories, all
hopes vanished one after the other, destroyed by the
indecision and rivalry of the generals, by the bad feeling
of Prussia, and by the ascendancy and policy of the minister Thugut, who at Vienna was urging the Emperor and
his armies to a fatal retreat.

Mallet, again summoned to Brussels, was preparing to
depart, when he was checked by letters from his friend
de Pradt.   They informed him of the rapid succession of
reverses, of false measures, and of *idiotcies*—to use the
Abbé's expression—which were on the eve of ruining the
campaign, and perhaps all the thrones of Europe.   These
letters, composed with their author's characteristic liveli-

* Lord Lansdowne, in his speech in the House of Lords, 17th February, 1793, proposing to counsel the King that His Majesty should,
without delay, declare himself ready to make peace on disinterested
but honourable conditions, read several passages from Mallet's
"Considérations," to prove that in the opinion even of "sensible
aristocrats," mere force could never subdue the Revolution.

ness, possess an historical interest ; we cite the principal
passages.

FRAGMENTS OF LETTERS FROM THE ABBÉ DE PRADT TO MALLET DU PAN.

"April 30, 1794.

" . . . You know the course of events up to the 18th.
On that day the French army would have perished, had
not M. de Kinski amused himself with pillaging a village.
The arrival of his column was delayed four hours ; that
of the Duke of York remained uncovered, and was beaten.
From that time forward, the French have been firmly
established at Courtrai. They have worked the country
as they would a Parisian faubourg : requisitions of men,
arms, munitions, merchandise, nothing has been forgotten—
not even impiety. How to expel them now we know not.
Marshal Saxe made it his head-quarters during one
campaign, and Pichegru will do the same. On the 22nd,
another battle took place before Tournai ; but for the
Emperor it would have been lost. The French wished to
cross the Escaut : they attacked with sixty thousand men ;
happily, the Austrian on this one occasion, possessed
thrice as much artillery as the French, who were, at last,
thoroughly beaten ; and retreated, leaving above six thousand men on the field of battle. The allies lost half that
number. But such successes are not decisive. We may
obtain the victory, but our forces gradually melt away,
and we have always to begin again. The French returned
for the third time on the Sambre. On the 24th they
lost a very important battle ; eight thousand men were

disabled. But they none the less repassed the Sambre on
the 27th, and are now in the neighbourhood of Binch.
Another corps threatens Charleroi; all the country is
routed.

"All this statement opens the most alarming prospect.
On the one hand, we have armies often vanquished, but
indestructible; on the other, armies often victorious, but
harassed and wasting daily. The French tactics are
obvious: they attack the two wings to divide their forces
and crush them in detail; this done, there will be a general
attack, which the allies will not be able to stand. See
here the effect of a fatal contempt for very formidable
enemies, of selfishness, and of court-divisions. The brutal-
ization of the inhabitants has reached its height—all fly,
all tremble.

"Nine o'clock P.M.—I did not yet know all our misfortunes. Mack has retired."

"May 1.

"My last letter, my dear friend, concluded with Mack's
departure: now the Emperor himself is going. I know
not what whim, what intrigue may have suggested this
departure; the resolution dates from last Thursday morning. The alarm instantly spread on all sides: the whole
country murmurs; some tremble, others grumble; these
are packing, those decamping; it is the very image of
chaos . . . . What hope can there be for a cause deserted
by its chiefs! When those interested in the matter walk
away, the spectators may run off . . . . Most pitiful
motives are alleged: all we want to know is, whether
equally great interests can be served elsewhere as here,

and no one thinks of asking this question. Meantime, the French follow out their plan. They are huddled together in West Flanders ; they keep themselves too close for any one to dislodge them, and no one will make the attempt. I assure you, on the word of M. de Traustmansdorf himself, that at Courtrai and Menin they were not guilty of the least excess—no guillotine, no municipalities, no orgies. Certain stolen goods were restored by judicial authority : the same took place on the Sambre.

" It is hoped that the allies will now attack Maubeuge or Philippeville, and they will be considered fortunate if they take two or three hamlets in the course of the campaign. The French have not been taken in : quite sure that if they remain masters in Brabant, they will soon become so in Europe at large, and *a fortiori* in Alsace, they disregard this province, and occupy themselves wholly with the other. This calculation, as it shows they have learnt something, contributes not a little to alarm me. By comparing the energy, the activity, the inflexibility of intention and plans on the one side, with the piecemeal nature of the operations on the other, one may divine the issue of so unequal a combat."

" May 13.

" The Emperor departed this evening at three o'clock, for the army of the Rhine, thence to proceed to Vienna. It is said that he has left an edict commanding the levying within the country of a corps of forty thousand men. Going away is not calculated to accelerate the levy, but it is the new fashion.

" Rivarol carries on with spirit his great work on the

sovereignty of the people.   If the edifice corresponds with
the peristyle, it will be a masterpiece ; for, after repeated
perusals of his introduction, it appears to me a composition
full of reason, and charmingly expressed : it is truly original.
My only fear is, that the principle may escape him, as it
has many others ; and that he will lose sight of colours in
a series of tableaux and consequences, which will possess
every merit except the single one which imparts interest to
such a subject—namely, truth."

" Maëstricht, July 2.

" I did not write to you before, my dear Mallet, because
I was in the thick of a departure, hastened both for myself
and for my relations.   I will acquaint you with the details
of these remarkable events.   You know that the French,
defeated on the 16th, recrossed the Sambre on the 18th ;
they pitched boldly in the plain of Fleurus, and covered the
siege of Charleroi.   M. de Cobourg left Tournai with all
speed and encamped at Nivelle ; the heavy baggage was
posted behind Brussels.   Some days were necessary for
repose, and to prepare the troops for action.   Meanwhile,
the siege was carried on ; and Charleroi was taken after
two assaults, in default of munitions.   This is the second
city lost within the week in this manner.   Ypres underwent
the same fate, and the garrisons are taken prisoner.   Our
loss from this amounts to ten thousand men at least.
M. de Cobourg sent for M. de Mercy on the 25th : he expressed to him some anxiety as to the condition of Charleroi, which had ceased firing for the last fifteen hours ;
yet he could not make up his mind to believe it taken—the
clever men of the army thought so.   In consequence, the
attack was commenced next day at two o'clock in the

morning : forty-five thousand men against twenty-four thousand at least. MM. de Beaulieu and d'Alvinzy turned the two French wings : I know not whether this was a stratagem on their part ; but one thing is certain, the centre, posted at Gosslies, offered a fearful resistance. This post, for which nature has done nothing, became a volcano in their hands. Seven entrenchments, one within the other, an infernal artillery and musketry, had made a veritable volcano of this spot : it could never once be approached. In vain did the Archduke and M. de Cobourg place themselves at the head of their grenadiers, of the emigrants—all was useless ; the only result was the annihilation of their followers. Meanwhile, it was ascertained that Charleroi had surrendered. Then the only idea was to retreat. The French followed so close that their bullets rained down in the Austrian camp : they compelled them to shift their quarters the same evening. Since then the positions have remained unaltered, and M. de Cobourg continues invisible. In Flanders, the French had taken Bruges on the 22nd ; they attacked Ghent on the 24th, and were repulsed even from the interior of the town into which they had penetrated.

" The question now is, whether or not the Low Countries will be evacuated as far as the Rhine—whether or not the war will be prosecuted. The Count de Mercy has testified to me the greatest repugnance to everything in the shape of peace. He told me that this was a fourth campaign. He assures me he has given orders concerning the four fortresses—but all this is contingent. The French in an instant will carry the fortresses. They will not cogitate for forty-five days before Valenciennes.

" That party in the cabinet of Vienna which will have
nothing to do with the Low-Countries may get the upper
hand, and this accomplished, put an end to the war.   If
so, this cabinet will return to its favourite system of
arraying the empire in one corps behind the Rhine for its
defence.   England will protect her colonies, and an English, Dutch and Prussian army will guard the country from
Breda to the Meuse.   This is their last invention for
lulling themselves to sleep.   But, what is worse, this is the
wish of the armies.   My dear friend, you cannot imagine
what these armies are ; the soldiers are brave, but the
officers abominable.   The ill-feeling is peculiarly strong
among the Austrians : their style of conversation is truly
revolting ; they are perpetually longing to return to Germany ; they rejoice at their defeats——they like to own themselves vanquished ; they loudly proclaim the superiority of
the patriots, and their own weakness when not entrenched
behind the Rhine.   While the combat of the 26th lasted,
the French kept a balloon elevated in the air, and made
signals from it ; this put the finishing-stroke to the dismay
of the Austrians.   On the preceding day, the French made
use of the same means to reconnoitre the enemy's position ;
this reduced the poor Austrians to a situation no less
wretched than that of the Mexicans when opposed to the
Spaniards : my dear friend, I have no dependence on such
people.   As to their internal management, it has been
deplorable : they tried to bring the country under subjection at the very moment when the enemy was at the gates ;
they endeavoured to make it rise in arms, when they
themselves were setting the example of decamping.   Some
languid proclamations, some half-dozen ragamuffins rushing

about the streets shrieking 'Long live the Emperor!' a few other manœuvres as despicable as they were *asinine,* and executed in the midst of the most utter discouragement, sum up all the feats of this *idiotic government.* The Count de Mercy alone acted with resolution.

"I shall not attempt to portray all the forms assumed by grief and terror in these dreadful moments. Picture to yourself an immense country in promiscuous flight from Tournai to Breda, and from Breda to Liège; above two hundred thousand persons fleeing from their homes, carrying away their effects; the roads swarming with priests, nuns, children, old men, covered with rags, bathed in perspiration, their spirits sinking under the burden of the present and the presages of the future, defiling between two lines of wounded soldiers and military provisions in retreat. For seven days this has been going on. Try to conceive this: at Brussels there are not remaining a hundred silver covers, nor a single piece of furniture, nor one half of the shops. All the nobility of the country are fled; the bankers and merchants have done the same; the desolation mocks all description. To crown all, the French, on their entrance into Brussels, will read in every countenance and in the nakedness of every building the terror they inspire, and this very terror is but another weapon in their hands.

"I here close these sad reflections, with which I might fruitlessly fill a volume. But reflection is not enough; we and our families must live; our stomachs are not as hard as the hearts of European ministers; and these recent events, by making all Europe draw back from the struggle, place frightful prospects before us. For my part, determined to meet this sad future half-way, I have written to pass over to the colonies, and thence to America ; for the world appears me to me so near its end, that another is absolutely necessary. Yet we must think of this one still. I am bound to it by powerful ties ; my brother and his family in France, my mother, my sister-in-law, young children, my sisters and their children—we must have courage to provide for them, even in our own shipwreck— we owe ourselves to them. If the Convention expels all it may not think proper to kill, they must be of the number : they will then be ejected, and will stand in need of a man or two to protect them. My brother and I are, therefore, desirous of repairing to Switzerland, and it is on this account that I now ask you two questions : first, will our labour suffice to procure us a livelihood in Switzerland ? Secondly, shall we, in those parts where French is spoken, meet with lands we could cultivate as farmers ? In other times this would be a pleasure, in these it has become a necessity. Before I engaged in cabinets, I was addicted to country pursuits ; I am a clever manager, and possess more industry than most agriculturists. This is no romance, but a very serious reality, as I hope you will believe. Should you return me a favourable answer, I shall start with my brother at the beginning of April."

I know not what Mallet replied, but ulterior events having afforded some respite to the Abbé de Pradt's alarms, he probably thought no more of these agricultural plans.

We will now return to Berne, where Mallet determined to take up his abode.

CHAPTER IV.

1794.

Great concourse of emigrant refugees at Berne—Reign of Terror at
Geneva—Mallet du Pan sentenced to death for non-appearance
before the Court.—His employments at Berne—Negociations of
the Chevalier Lameth and some of the constitutional party with
the English government, through the requested mediation of
Mallet du Pan and Mounier—Address of Lameth—Lord Grenville
sends Mr. Wickham to Switzerland—Difficulties—Mallet's vexations.

BERNE and the neighbouring towns were at this time
full of refugees from France and Savoy, who awaited there
the decision of what their hopes still denominated the revolutionary crisis : several had had a hair-breadth escape
from the scaffold,* among others some of the defenders of

---

* Among these refugees, Mallet soon had the grief of reckoning
some of his countrymen. The plots long concocted against Geneva
by the frenzied partizans of the French Revolution at length, in
1794, succeeded in again convulsing the Republic. The heads of
the conspiracy violently inaugurated within the walls of the unhappy city the bloody rites of the revolutionary worship ; and found
themselves admirably seconded by the illusions of some, by the
feebleness of others, by recollections which they adroitly managed
to embitter, and also by the contagious madness of the times ; but
above all, by the fear which commonly cloaked itself under the

Lyons, who had succeeded in escaping from Collot d'Herbois' executions. These fugitives belonged to the various parties which the Revolution had successively absorbed ; they numbered in their ranks royalists, constitutionalists of the right, and their old adversaries of Lameth's bench ; they even included some Brissotists, expelled in their turn from the Republic by the wheel of revolutionary fortune. Mallet's accustomed society consisted of the most distinguished

specious garb of moderation ; as if ignorant that in such circumstances moderation would be no virtue in the strong, and was a mere absurdity in the weak and the oppressed. These stolid wretches had begun by imprisoning and whipping through the streets such citizens as their malice regarded with suspicion ; but to rise to the level of their Parisian models they must have blood. The established customs of the country long opposed these hankerings for assassination ; but this last obstacle overcome, fusillades, after the pattern of Collot d'Herbois, commenced at Geneva, when the reign of butchers in France was drawing to a close. Numerous victims, condemned without law, or acquitted by the revolutionary tribunal, and among the number magistrates, illustrious by their talents and their services, were massacred with cold-blooded ferocity, by a band of drunken ruffians, the new tyrants of the Republic ; who, after a century of insurrections and armaments, undertaken in the name of liberty, crushed Geneva beneath their blood-stained hands. Mallet du Pan was condemned to death in default as a *libeller* ; his brother, between whom and himself there existed a strong attachment, was arrested and imprisoned ; his eldest son contrived to escape and join his family at Berne, where from that time he devoted himself to assisting Mallet in his political labours. A pamphlet, which relates these occurrences under the title of " Malheurs de Genève," has been attributed to Mallet du Pan. This work may perhaps have been communicated to him, but it is not his. Some passages in his correspondence would seem to justify our ascribing it to another Genevese.

of these various personages; we may particularly mention Mounier, who inhabited a country house at some distance from the town. At his own house, surrounded by his family, from whom he was never willingly separated, Mallet devoted to these exiles all the time left at his disposal from the reports he drew up for the English and Austrian Ministers, and from an active correspondence with Malouet, Montlosier, de Pradt, Macpherson, and Mr. Trevor; not to speak of the difficult communications he was obliged to keep up with France, in order to obtain authentic information of the state of the interior. The *Avoyer* Steiguer also was among his most intimate friends; through this magistrate the Government sometimes requested the aid of his pen. Political consultations and confidential communications from project-mongers added weight to his burden, or rather added weight to its most onerous and most perplexing element, when he was asked not only for counsel, but for the direct support of his influence with the Governments whose confidence he enjoyed. Nothing more fully demonstrates how universal was the sense of his political independence and firm principles, than the entire trust with which the various rival factions in the Convention came to him from opposite points, when their plans, their hopes, or their alarms inclined them to conciliatory advances towards their former antagonists: to him they imparted their projects, in his hands they even occasionally deposited their pledges of reconciliation. Unhappily, in revolutions, the desire of union is rarely strong enough to produce real sacrifices; and when it came to the point of agreeing on mutual concessions, and reciprocating that heartfelt confidence which can alone guarantee a sincere reconciliation, all was broken off.

This year, 1794, saw the near approach to a happy termination of the most important of these attempts, which formed part of a great political plan.   Its authors were no less than some ex-chiefs of the constitutional party, Lameth, Narbonne, Dumas, who, as we have seen, had always been somewhat roughly handled by Mallet.

In the month of June, Mallet du Pan repaired to the little town of Morat, in Fribourg, where he found awaiting him a person calling himself Mr. Proctor, but in reality no other than the Chevalier Theodore de Lameth.   The Chevalier opened to Mallet a plan he had formed in conjunction with two friends, Messrs. Dumas and Brémond, who, however, did not appear at this first interview.[*]

It was proposed to unite all the scattered forces of the opposition—that is, all those who belonged to the more moderate shades of the constitutional and royalist parties, and to form them into one compact body, who, within the

---

[*] Brémond, a friend of M. de Monciel, had been called to the ministry for a few weeks in June and July, 1792 ; and had, in concert with Governor Morris, the Minister of the United States, conceived a plan for drawing the King away from Paris.   Brémond is frequently mentioned in the Memoirs of Mr. Morris, published by Mr. J. Sparks.   We meet with the following passage in the Journal, dated July 20, 1792.   "Brémond tells me that Mallet du Pan has been sent by Bertrand to be secretary to the Duke of Brunswick."

And again, in August, "M. de Monciel has taken as his associate in this enterprise (the liberation of the King) M. Brémond, who is honest, courageous, zealous, and faithful ; but passionate, talkative and imprudent."   (Vol. i. p. 378 and 381).

limits of France, should act in concert with the royalists beyond the frontier, and with the march of foreign armies, and so at length bring about a national rising against the Parisian butchers. " War against anarchy ! Respect for religion and property ; an hereditary monarch and national representation ;" such were to be the watchwords of the insurrection no less than of the invasion. But the Princes, on account of their extreme unpopularity, were to be wholly set aside :* there could be no thought either of forming a party in their favour, or of entrusting them with the regency. Lameth and his friends confidently expected to realize their project, as far as regarded their alliance with the moderate party, and the organization of an internal insurrection. As a commencement of operations, they were to pave the way in the Convention for the downfall of the Committee of Public Safety. The means they proposed for the attainment of this end, are precisely those which actually effected Robespierre's ruin. We

---

* Lameth, in the report he sent to Mallet, treated of this subject in the following words : " We should have had no difficulty in conferring the regency on the Queen, had that amiable and unhappy princess survived her misfortunes. No doubt she had committed some faults ; but her youth, her sex, her rank, pleaded her excuse. If one class of the people regarded her with hatred, a large number of individuals were passionately attached to her. She had lost no one's good opinion : all admired her strength of mind. Since the acceptance of the constitution she had sincerely used her utmost efforts to prevent war ; the French people had rendered her so miserable that they owed her an ample compensation ; nearly the whole nation would have eagerly offered it to her ;—in fine, she was the mother of the hope of the nation."

quote a passage on this subject from the report of the
chiefs of the Constitutionalists :

" Attention should be directed, above all, while strength-
ening and extending to the utmost the hatred inspired in
Paris by the Committee of Public Safety, to the organizing
its ruin in the Assembly, whose members must first be
shown the facility of success, and the absence even of
danger to themselves if they are prudent in the outset, and
afterwards courageous in execution.   More than two hundred individuals exist in the National Convention, who voted
against the King's death ; their opinions are not dubious,
nor, we may add, their courage.   All those whom weakness induced to adopt a contrary course, seek an opportunity to return if possible.   In what is called the *Mountain*, several are opposed to the Committee of Public
Safety.   All those who were connected with Danton,
Barrère, and the other deputies who were sacrificed,
warmly desire its destruction, foreseeing that they also will
become its victims ; hence it is evidently possible to create
a majority against it.   If only the men who head these
various sections will firmly league together ; if they will
but prepare their followers for action, be in readiness to
speak and denounce the Committee, arrange clearly in their
minds grave heads of accusation against it and its leading
members, then they may seize the opportunity offered
them by some signal reverse, to come forward energetically
and overwhelm the Committee with its own responsibility,
charging it with having exercised a most cruel and calamitous dictatorship, and with being the cause of all the
miseries of France.   The obvious conclusion would be, a

proposal for the instantaneous reconstruction of the Committees of Public Safety and General Security, whose members would be replaced by substitutes chosen beforehand. The new Committees would forthwith follow up their installation by arresting their predecessors, together with their principal adherents. This once accomplished, it is easy to conceive with what facility the revolutionary tribunal and the Committees of Sections would be abolished, and the prisons thrown open—in one word, the path would be cleared for a successful termination of the enterprise."

In return, the Constitutionalists required, and they afterwards made this demand the fundamental condition of the concurrence of their party : 1st. The liberation of M. de La Fayette, Alexandre Lameth, and the rest of the Emperor's prisoners ; 2nd. A sufficiently large sum to establish a commercial concern, the operations of which would at once cover and cement the negociations with France.

Such projects were at once delicate in their conduct and precarious in their issue ; but Mallet and Mounier, who examined the propositions together, justly concluded that it were unwise to reject these overtures, of which the chief importance lay rather in the circumstances which occasioned them, than in the character or previous connexions of the men who came forward with them. After sundry conferences, in which the grounds of these overtures were discussed and modified, Mallet undertook to forward them to the English Government. With the plan he sent an explanatory memorial, which commenced by classifying and estimating the different parties, both within and without, on whose support the enterprise was

based : then weighing the chances and interests of the
Princes as of the monarchy, he proceeded, in case of success, to a plan of restoration conformable, in the main, to
his own principles, and, as it would appear, consented to by
Lameth and his friends.

"It is," said he, "from a compromise between the legitimate heads of the monarchy, and the parties who furnished them with the means of restoration to their
thrones, that must emanate the reciprocal bond of interest
and duty.   Such a treaty is the only prop of waning
hopes ; its model may be found in nearly all revolutions
and civil wars, which, for the most part, have been terminated by similar measures.

"Henry IV. would never have ascended the throne had
he not conceded the edict of Nantes to the Calvinists, and
abjured their religion ; yet, while they required these sacrifices, neither the Catholics nor the Protestants thought of
disputing the Prince's right to the crown, nor to propose
that Biron or Duplessis Mornay should govern the state
and head the army, till the moment should arrive when the
League would succumb, and the prejudices against
Henry IV. vanish.

"General Monk neither made himself Regent of England,
nor head manager, nor supreme chief of the Restoration :
he imposed conditions on Charles the Second, and these
being accepted, he was the first to set the example of obedience and fidelity."

This document, dated 12th September, reached the
English Government through the hands of Lord Robert
Fitzgerald, English Minister at Berne, who did not con-
sider himself at liberty to respond to this overture without a

special authorization. On some occasion, which we have forgotten, Mallet thus addressed Macpherson on the subject: " I send you, Sir, the proposed basis of the treaty of union. Those who drew up these articles, and who have charged me with their transmission to you, had given them at first a much greater scope; but they were led to reduce them to the limits indicated herein, after we had discussed them together. I acknowledge beforehand all the objections that may be adduced against such a compromise, on the grounds of reason, just rights, and prudent foresight. Yet I have but one word in reply—that it is not possible for the Princes to obtain anything better, and that it would be absolutely fruitless to take a single step more in case of a refusal to comply with these points of contact."*

As the cabinets were still behindhand, unless a crisis in the convulsions of the Revolutionary Government of France

---

* These points of contact were the following : By a convention, of which the belligerent powers were to be guarantees, under the title of auxiliaries, the chiefs of the royalist parties pledged themselves to procure the restoration of the crown, in the person of Louis XVII., the just claims of Monsieur to the regency during the minority of the young King being recognized. The royal authority and the national representation, and all that the constitutional act of 1791 contained conformable, or analogous, in political principles to the legislative enactments demanded by the voice of the nation in 1789, were to be taken as the basis of the future constitution—" points," remarked Mallet, " which were in conformity with the intentions of the late King, at the moment of his departure for Varennes." The national representation was based, not on rank, but on property, and the representative body was divided into two chambers, &c.—in short, it was the charter of Louis XVIII., with the addition of the re-instatement of the nobility on their estates, on condition that they should' cede all personal feudal rights.

took place, it was to be feared that, in consequence of a
persuasion that Danton was on the eve of introducing
moderate counsels into the Revolution, when all the while
Danton's power had ceased, they might make a difficulty
about overthrowing Robespierre, who, at this very time,
was spreading the like fantastical reports in foreign states.*
In the meantime, the downfall of Robespierre took place,
and Lord Grenville, in spite of his habitual prejudices
against the constitutionalists and the *tiers partis* in general,
judged that these overtures deserved some attention, and not
deeming Lord Robert Fitzgerald adapted for a negociation
of the kind in question, he despatched to Switzerland Mr.
Wickham, who had been his schoolfellow at Eton and Ox-
ford, and whose character, talents, political sagacity, and
views he knew to be in exact conformity with his own,
and who, having married a Genevese lady of great merit,
had, on several preceding occasions, procured information
useful to the Government, by means of his family connexions.

Mr. Wickham was to have an interview with Lameth
and his friends, and obtain from them a correct report of

* The " Fête of the Supreme Being" produced an extraordinary
effect abroad : it was really believed that Robespierre was on the
point of closing the revolutionary abyss, and perhaps this ready
credulity of Europe completed the ruin of him who was its object.
Robespierre's hypocrisy provoked his friends still more against him.
At Geneva, M. de Saussure having thought proper to congratulate
the French envoy, Soulavie, on the solemn act of homage offered by
Robespierre to the Divinity . . . . " Robespierre," replied the other,
" Robespierre laughs at the good God as much as myself!"   It is
well known that this worthless Soulavie had formerly been an ecclesiastic.

the names of their associates in France, and of the means at their command. But things had greatly changed since the first overtures between Lameth and his friends. The downfall of Robespierre on the one hand, and on the other, the reverses and loss of force of the foreign powers, had considerably modified the situation and the resources of the constitutionalists : the requirements of the latter became more exacting at the same time that their efforts were relaxed, though probably they would have found it difficult to give an account of the progress they had made, if required to do so. It seemed clear that an authentic account was yet to come ; that though promised it was still to be sought for, and that, far from being in possession of adequate means, they were contented merely to demand them. Nevertheless, Mallet agreed with Mounier, that they must not yet give up the affair, and wrote accordingly to Mr. Wickham.

" Supposing," said he, " that the Revolution should continue to retrograde, or that an attempt should be made to return to the Reign of Terror, still the cause of the constitutionalists has many chances of success. Each step backwards brings the great mass of the nation nearer to them and the monarchy ; this same affinity resulting from the very nature of things, would induce a combined resistance against any novel system of oppression and the guillotine. They are placed in the position best adapted to serve as a rallying point for all who at one time or other may think proper to abjure the Republic. Any party whatever in the Convention, that should be impelled by necessity or choice to take such a step, would make the constitutionalists their agents : they, in common with the revolutionists of the day, have a dread of falling at discretion into the hands of a despotic monarchy, enforced by the princes and emigrants. It is therefore evident, either that the Republic will become more firmly established, or that the monarchy will only rise from its ruins by the united efforts of wearied republicans and the constitutional party.

"You may be assured, Sir, that the proffering at present to the Foreign Cabinets the assistance of the aristocrats of the interior, or any advantages resulting from revolt or civil war, would only prolong the illusions they are under ; and the realization of the offer would be besides morally impossible.

"Nevertheless, if the war continues, it would but entail upon the allies fresh reverses and a prolonged inability to re-establish order and royalty in France, if they were encouraged to attempt this restoration without previously securing to themselves a party in the interior. Now, this party must be sought, not amid the wrecks of the former monarchy, but in the diminished disinclination of those who, having aided to subvert it, will one day reproduce its elements."

Lord Grenville's envoy entertained strong prejudices against the constitutionalists, which their ill-timed importunities only served to foster; a second interview was even more unsuccessful than the first. These gentlemen set out with a flat refusal to treat with an English agent— a strange scruple this, after such overtures ! Mallet and Mounier succeeded in removing it ; but Mr. Wickham, an unflinching royalist in fact, failed to obtain any of those revelations which he had orders to require, and without which his Government refused to take any further steps.

Besides, the subordinate agents had been guilty of indiscretion ; suspected emissaries had taken part in the matter ; the affair, at the best but doubtful, had assumed a discouraging aspect ; the parties jarred with each other. Mr. Wickham broke off the negociation, declaring that the *moderates* were simply intriguers ; on the other hand, the authors of this project, and M. Mounier, complained with equal warmth of the English agent ; and Mallet du Pan, sensibly affected by the issue of this affair, in which, however, he had only acted as an intermediate agent, resolved to undertake no more such mediations. A letter he addressed to Lameth, explains concisely the English minister's conduct in this negociation.

LETTER FROM MALLET DU PAN TO TH. LAMETH.

" Berne, November 25, 1794.

" Since your last visit here, Sir, it appears that neither you nor your friends have acquired further information. It is no longer then reasonable to suppose that you will be listened to at Paris, or that any possible relations exist at this moment between that capital and yourselves. Consequently, Mr. Wickham regards his mission as at an end, and will depart without delay. All the blame of this false step attaches to M. Mounier and myself : we have been cruelly compromised by becoming parties to a chimerical project, according to the conversations and agreement between your two friends and us.

" Far from the moderates entertaining any thoughts of conciliation, they gull you most scandalously. This is proved by the denunciation made by one of these gentlemen, who, doubtless well aware of M. D's communication to Madame du F., availed himself of it to represent him as having an understanding with the Jacobins. Such pretended moderates are on a par with their rivals in crime; fear alone has power over men destitute of morality, honour and integrity, insensible to every consideration of duty, and whose minds and souls are not sufficiently elevated to conceive any plan of conduct but that of their predecessors, though they all fell in the pursuit, beginning with M. de Lafayette, and ending with Robespierre. We represented to you, that by making the liberation of the prisoners the condition, and not the price, of your coming forward, you provoked a suspicion that this liberation was the sole end of the negociation. By insisting on preliminaries—and on this object almost exclusively—without at the same time offering any effectual means of seconding the views of the British Government, you confirmed this suspicion. The proposal of a commercial speculation yet further aggravated the mistrust ; of which result I had warned M. Brémond. It was absurd to imagine that the resources of a party could be credited, when it needed, for receiving any information from Paris or transmitting it thither, an advance of ten or twenty thousand louis d'or, in order to commence a transaction fundamentally opposed to the interests of the power from which such aid was demanded. By mentioning the House of Bourdieu, M. Brémond put the finishing stroke to the confirmation of the prejudice, that house being notorious as the head-quarters of English smuggling with France, and having utterly lost the confidence of the government. Of this also I had warned M. Brémond ; but I could not dissuade him from naming the house to Mr. Wickham.

" In the complete failure which has undoubtedly attended at Paris the affair which we so vainly engaged in, I can only regret having been concerned in it ; for henceforward, however useful may be our suggestions, we shall not be listened to ; the liberation of the prisoners will infallibly be put off indefinitely, and the question cannot be raised again this long while.

" Receive the assurance, &c.,

" MALLET DU PAN."

In another letter Mallet said to Lameth :

TO THE SAME.

" Berne, November 27, 1794.

" Your reply to my last letter, Sir, requires an explanation from me, relative to M. de Lafayette. You misunderstand me ; none but an aristocrat misled by desperation could compare the General to Robespierre. I intended to say merely, that both fell through, and in spite of, popularity. Popularity, and popularity alone, is still the aim of the moderates : it will bring the same fate on them and on France. I have read, within these few days, twenty-four of the last numbers of Fréron and Tallien. I was not surprised to find in them all the base and grovelling atrocities of Marat against the King and the royal family, against royalty, against all those whom the sublime knowledge and experience of Messieurs Fréron and Tallien have not moulded for public liberty. Believe me, these men will never be capable of an honest sentiment or action, save through fear. Now, as neither you nor I have the means of inspiring them with fear, I cannot persuade myself that they will ever hear reason.

" I regret that my efforts should have been fruitless. I am not in luck; for, of some thirty similar negociations in which I have had the misfortune to be engaged these four years, there has not been one in which I could succeed in reconciling the different parties. The part of conciliator is a thankless one, and yet more thankless the task of supplying information to men in office. I relinquish it, and return to my usual occupations : it is better after all to have to do with the public than with negociators. I shall be none the less delighted to converse with you whenever your business calls you to Berne, and to give you fresh assurance of my esteem."

These letters show that this affair was from first to last distasteful to Mallet. The responsibility which he had declined, by refusing to take any part in it except as a mediator, had in fact devolved on him and Mounier, and his credit could not but suffer.

Soon afterwards, Lord Fitzgerald, the English minister in Switzerland, offended at having been excluded from the negociation, requested his recall, and Mr. Wickham was chosen to replace him as *chargé d'affaires* (being subsequently named minister plenipotentiary). No sooner had Mr. Wickham arrived in Switzerland, than his activity, his talents, his well-known influence with Lord Grenville, and the pecuniary resources which he was believed to command, at once gave the envoy extraordinary a character of importance and authority which gathered round him all the political speculators. The persons who had been wont to come to Mallet du Pan for advice, now went to Mr. Wickham for cash; and confidence soon attained such a pitch, as to excite in Franche-Comté, and other parts of France, movements fomented by the pure royalists, who dreamed of nothing less than the return of the old *régime*. Mallet du Pan did not share these views, and he entertained but a mediocre opinion of the means and discretion of some of the most active agents. Wickham, on his part, regarded Mallet du Pan as over favourable to the Constitutionalists, and reproached him with being, to a certain extent, the dupe of their ambitious aims. Mallet's extensive communications with so many persons imposed, however, a certain reserve on the ambassador.

In these arduous circumstances, Mallet pursued the course he had laid down for himself, and kept aloof, as far as possible, from the political intrigues of which Berne had become the centre. It is to be observed that, notwithstanding the warmth of his censure, he did not lose the esteem of the Constitutionalists; but they did not know how much he deserved it. In fact, his friendship to Mounier, and his momentary connexion with Lameth, had furnished an immediate pretext for the calumnies of party spirit, and the false reports of intriguers interested in discrediting Mallet, in order to supplant him with his correspondents.

The English Minister was vexatiously appealed to, relative to the extent and nature of Mallet du Pan's correspondence. To him was repeated all that the Prince de Condé's suite said about Mallet's connivance with the Constitutionalists, whose intrigues, said they, he actively directed. A man, who had been recommended by Mallet to Mr. Wickham, and whom the latter employed, was commissioned to speak of these rumours to the object of them. Wounded in those feelings of honour and independence, which he possessed in so sensitive and even jealous a degree, Mallet answered with this characteristic letter:—

LETTER FROM MALLET DU PAN TO MR. WICKHAM.

"Berne, June 25, 1795.

"Sir,

"M. Le Clerc communicated to me yesterday the conversation you had desired him to acquaint me with. Although I am only accountable for my conduct to honour and the laws, and though its tenor is such as to dispense me from all witness but that of my own conscience, I cannot forbear expressing to you my surprise at such a heap of fallacies. Your informers are either impostors or dupes. Whatever correspondence I may keep up in Europe, there is not one of my own seeking ; not one which I should blush to publish to-morrow under my signature; not one in which I secretly profess any sentiments differing from those publicly avowed these five years. You have been egregiously misled both as to the names of my correspondents and the object of my letters. Whatever use has been made of them, I avow and am ready to answer for them. This is enough, I think. As to the Vienna story, I admit as judges none but my correspondents themselves.

"As to the absurdities current in Condé's army and elsewhere, about my constitutional intrigues and the evil they produce, I have only one word of answer. Where is the barefaced accuser who will dare indicate one single Constitutionalist in or out of France, with whom I have conferred on public matters either by letter or by word of mouth, from the moment when, Sir, after fair warning, I broke off in your very presence the connexion which had led to your visiting Switzerland. Put this question to the Prince of Condé himself, so that he may learn to mistrust those calumnies with which he is beset by men, who are unworthy that I should so much as inquire their names. I am not ignorant that a certain woman, a vile court-intriguer, angry at having failed to extort money from M. Mounier and myself by means of abominable fictions, has reported at Manheim some such as M. Le Clerc has forwarded to you ; some emigrants, half-idle, half-furious, who console themselves under their misfortunes by injuring alternately their defenders and their enemies, both forestalled this woman and propagated her lies.

"For the rest, nothing affects me less than these gos-sipings. If anything concerning them gives pain, it is the readiness with which they are believed, and the injury they inflict on the cause of those who so thoughtlessly listen to them. No Revolutionist will change his party, who learns the unworthy treatment received by those who have defended with most constancy and courage the interests of the House of Bourbon.

"You are at liberty, Sir, to acquaint the Prince of Condé, and whomsover else you think fit, with my sentiments. So much the worse for those who will blame my views ; they do not disturb me : *stultorum magister est eventus*. These gentlemen may now make themselves perfectly easy as to the style of monarchy to be established in France, for they will not be troubled with any monarchy at all. Your later Stuarts reasoned and acted, as those without reason and act now ; their end will be the same.

"I have the honour, &c."

The influences, broils, and malevolent *surveillance*, of which Mallet du Pan was at that time the object, induced him to decline, perhaps too decidedly and with too great an indulgence of personal prejudice, an interview solicited by Madame de Staël.   The excuse he alleged was an indisposition which confined him to the house ; but this did not prevent Madame de Staël, who was well aware of the real motive of his refusal, from addressing him in a reproachful strain in a note full of impetuous irony.   She professed to have had no other aim but to obtain some information about M. Malouet, adding very politely : " M. Mallet du Pan will forgive my indiscretion in consideration of the excessive desire I felt to see him ; possibly it was this somewhat selfish feeling that had to do with my wish to talk about M.Malouet.   At any period, such superior worth as belongs to M. Mallet du Pan would undoubtedly have awakened my curiosity ; but at present I labour under an almost mad longing to hear France spoken of with reason and justice : my mind is wearied with the monotonous absurdity of extreme opinions, the resource of persons who can only compass one idea at a time ; and my heart revolts at those calumnious and violent hatreds, which, in their different proportions, govern the universe.   I forego, therefore, with unfeigned regret one hour of genuine pleasure. Such form epochs in my present course of life.   M. Mallet cannot be offended at the chagrin my sacrifice occasions me."

The correspondence which gave umbrage to Mr. Wickham and the Princes, rather deserved their gratitude, as will be seen in the following chapter.   The spirited letters which passed between the British envoy and Mallet du Pan, failed however to affect their friendly relations and mutual cordiality. On many subsequent occasions, Mr. Wickham gave Mallet du Pan proofs of esteem and confidence ; he several times promoted his interests with the English Government ; and after Mallet's death, he assisted essentially in the advancement of his son, and continued to give the family unequivocal proofs of his respect for the memory of his friend.

CHAPTER V.

1794—1795.

Correspondence of Mallet du Pan with M. de Hardenberg and with the Emperor of Austria—Situation of parties in France after the downfall of Robespierre.

TOWARDS the end of 1794, a Swiss officer, belonging to the staff of the Austrian army, was commissioned to ask Mallet du Pan whether it would suit him to furnish the Emperor of Austria with a direct political correspondence, under cover to M. de Colloredo : a precisely similar question was put to him at the beginning of 1795, by the Baron de Hardenberg, in behalf of the King of Prussia. Both inquiries had their source in the same idea. M. de Colloredo, who desiderated a vigorous struggle against the Revolution, needed reliable information from a man like Mallet du Pan, in order to counteract the influence over the Emperor exercised by the minister Thugut, who urged forward a peace on chimerical representations of the inclinations of France. M. de Hardenberg, on his part, before acquiescing in the proposal of an individual peace, as recommended to the King, was willing to make any effort to arrest him in his dangerous course. The proposition of the two ministers was accepted by Mallet du Pan, as was also soon afterwards an analogous proposition made to him by the Court of Lisbon, through its Ambassador at Turin, Don Rodrigo de Souza - Cotinho, subsequently Count of Linarès. This employment was, in fact, an opportune resource for Mallet, for the Revolution had deprived him not of tranquillity alone : for the last two years the profits of the " Mercure" had ceased ; and, to increase his dilemma, he had just been informed that, in pursuance of the decree whereby, although a native of Switzerland, he was included in the list of emigrants, his library and his manuscripts, the labour of half his life, had been confiscated beyond all hope of recovery, as well as his plate and household effects.

He therefore accepted the honourable offer made to him, and devoted himself to a conscientious discharge of the delicate task with which he was entrusted. He entered upon it with his wonted independence, and in that masculine and vigorous spirit which he adopted in addressing the public. According to what he knew of the political tendencies of his august correspondents, and according as he judged it advisable to foster or oppose these dispositions, he laid stress on the facts and considerations which favoured his principal aim, in such a way, that a cursory glance at certain periods might lead us to accuse him of assigning a contradictory importance to the same circumstances. This is merely an apparent contradiction. In addressing M. de Hardenberg, or rather the King of Prussia, who was too much inclined to conclude at any cost a separate peace, he enlarged upon the probability of enfeeblement and danger to which the Revolution would be exposed by excessive mili-

I 2

tary exertions; to the Emperor, who was urged by M. Thugut to lessen his demonstrations instead of making them suitably imposing, he showed how greatly his dominion was menaced by the ambition and immense forces of France.

As Mallet du Pan relied less on the statements of an obscure individual than on the eloquence of facts, he neglected nothing which might enable him to despatch to Vienna and Berlin, an ever faithful representation of the internal situation of France and of the parties in the Revolution. Not only had he to listen to the opinions of emigrants of every shade of colour who flocked to Berne, and from whom, in fact, he often received valuable information, but he kept up also a constant intercourse with men of note, well versed in the events of the day. But this was not enough : direct correspondents were essential, posted on the scene of action, and as near as possible to the actors—clear-sighted observers capable of themselves appreciating the importance of facts and the ability of the actors. Mallet was so happy as to be ably seconded : for some time his principal informant was one of those intelligent and valuable men of business in whom the most jealous overlook much because they cannot do without them, and who have the sense to limit themselves to their own laborious sphere of action. Although he had long shared in secret the principles of Mallet, and although he abhorred the Republic and its chiefs, he nevertheless served them, persuading himself that by so doing he averted much evil.

The Berlin correspondence had but a short and interrupted duration—we shall soon see why; that of Vienna was carried on with regularity till September, 1797 : this series of letters would have formed a sort of epistolary history of the utmost interest and value. Unhappily, Mallet only kept copies of a few of the early ones. From these fragments we must select some pages calculated to give a just idea of the historical interest of this correspondence. The Convention, and public spirit, after the fall of Robespierre, form the subject of the following extract. Mallet wrote it at the commencement of 1795.

STATE OF PARTIES AND PUBLIC FEELING IN FRANCE AFTER THE DOWNFALL OF ROBESPIERRE.

" The only existing authority in France is vested in the Convention : in it are united those powers which are more or less divided in every known government. Besides its immediate administration, confided to its committees and executive commissions, it governs the provinces and the army by pretors taken from its own body. These ministers of its will, absolute under the reign of Robespierre, now exercise only a subordinate and evanescent power, of which the action is necessarily weakened.

" The committees of the Assembly have their share, also, in this change of rule. Every month a fourth part of the members go out : their legislative authority has been restricted ; the awful abuse which the Committee of Public Safety made of its power, wholly subordinate to that of Robespierre and his accomplice, has rendered its directors objects of suspicion to the Convention, who watch them jealously, and who, fearful of their becoming dangerous, have deprived them of a portion of their strength.

"Executive Commissions have replaced the Ministry; they compose its departments. Each of them is subordinate to the respective Committees of the Convention by which they are all appointed, and form in a manner its secretary's office; their functions are confined to receiving and despatching orders. Hitherto they have been composed of coarse, ignorant, inexperienced men, whose sole merit was serving as instruments to the chiefs of factions as they successively obtained the preponderance. To purge them, it has been found necessary to substitute for the dregs of Jacobinism which filled them, persons less zealous for the Revolution, and consequently less incapable. The Convention feels so strongly the need of servants fit to sustain the burden of its difficulties, that it now seeks them out even among decided royalists. For instance, it has just offered the direction of the treasury to M. Dufresne, ex-chief of a department in the late King's reign, and pensioned off since 1790. In the same spirit, and by a choice yet more extraordinary, it thinks of confiding the commission of foreign affairs to M. Gérard de Rayneval, head of the corresponding department from the Ministry of the Duke de Choiseul to that of the Comte de Montmorin inclusively. He is a man equally rigid in opinions and in character; and I remember that, in 1790, he left the department through aversion from the maxims which had been forcibly introduced with the Revolution.

"This monstrous Convention of deputies of the people, concentrating in their own hands all the legislative power, offered nothing but an assemblage of unconnected parties. At this moment, perhaps, not ten individuals could be found professing the same opinions, bound by a common sentiment, and carrying out one uniform plan. Such a state of isolation is the result of that mistrust to which men, agitated by the contemplation of their own perverse passions, are a prey, fully cognisant, as they are, of the excesses each is capable of, and seeing an enemy in every colleague and accomplice. The enormity and precarious tenure of the power they have usurped, incessantly urges them to mutual spoliation, to prevent the prosecution of purposes to which it might be applied by the most popular among them, after the example of former actions.

" This dissension, repressed by the iron hand of Robespierre and his committee, burst forth as soon as they had disappeared. The members of the Convention, however, instead of finding a rallying point in their emancipation from a comprehensive and unexampled despotism, hastened to separate, terror giving place to discord and a spirit of revenge. Though tolerably unanimous in a desire to prevent the return of danger, each set to work under the dominion of his own particular passions and resentments; and, with such contrary views, that falling again into a state of anarchy, the Assembly is once more without a head.

" All the actors who, at various periods, played the first parts on the revolutionary stage, having either perished tragically or taken flight, the Convention and its partisans are left destitute of men of talent and principle, and even of such as possess but a moderate degree of administrative capacity. They resemble valets, who step into their master's shoes, after having assassinated them.

" Not one of them enjoys popular esteem or credit, nor any weight in public opinion. Not one of them possesses either the powers or the character of a party-chief, and infinitely few of them even advance the slightest pretensions of the kind. All have learned to beware of so perilous an elevation. Even were they tempted to aspire to it, they would not attain their object; for the roots of all individual authority are dead. Neither the Assembly, warned by the example of Robespierre, nor the people, disgusted with its demagogues, would tolerate it. The existence of the popular idols and arch-quacks may, therefore, be considered irrevocably passed.

" Various cabals divide the Assembly; and all mask their secret intentions under appearances, and seem to be playing a game opposed to that on which they are really intent.

" The only one of these cabals which, four or five months ago, deserved the name of a faction, is that of the Mountain, or Jacobins. It had partially inherited the genius and the measures of Robespierre, and proposed to continue after him the revolutionary and exterminating system. There were the head-quarters of sans-cullotism, of universal pillage, and of indiscriminate sentences of death against all owners of property. The Jacobins were in favour of an agrarian law, the community of goods and powers, and the institution of an agricultural, military, and aggressive democracy. They had declared war against commerce, arts, industry, and would have changed France into a nation of military labourers.

" This faction fell by what appeared its very means of life—the refugees, that is—whom the members of the abolished committees of public safety and general security, the depositaries and executioners of Robespierre's barbarities, sought in its bosom. The great majority of the Convention, rancorous against them for this complicity, and for having excited for their destruction public horror and hatred—these dragged down in their discredit the Jacobins, who had seemed likely to sustain them.

" His Imperial and Royal Majesty is aware how this infernal society was suppressed, without, however, being formally proscribed. The execration of all France responded to the signal given by the Convention, in the departments as well as at Paris. The Jacobins, expelled from their clubs, from administrative posts, from public offices, have become afraid of even meeting together—public hatred pursues them everywhere.

" Their party does not number fifty members in the Convention,—a minority condemned to the humiliation and silence it was wont to impose on its adversaries by force of arms. But it would be a mistake to imagine that the faction is crushed.

" This dangerous faction, although abhorred by the public, and in a minority in the Convention, might yet regain its ascendancy by a stroke of policy similar to those which decided the several epochs of the Revolution, and for which the duration of the Republican form of government will, sooner or later, supply them with an opportunity.

" The party in opposition to the Jacobins has received the name of Moderates. It deserves this appellation only in a relative sense ; for, but for the conduct of the Jacobins, properly so called, that of the Moderates throughout the Revolution would deserve to bring them to the scaffold. The chief members of this party have figured in all the crimes of the period : they were accomplices in the massacres of the 2nd and 3rd September, 1792 : for the most part they voted the execution of the King, and shared in the debates preliminary to it. Up to the middle of the present year, they belonged to the Jacobin club, of which they were then the orators and props. But, being reduced to a secondary position by the supremacy of Robespierre and his coadjutors, they ranged themselves under the banners of Danton : they shared his fears, his projects, and all but shared his fate. Like that leader, and intimidated by the Revolutionary Tribunal, in the institution of which they took part, they let the Queen of France and Madame Elizabeth die, although anxious to save them. Beginning to suspect Robespierre, and excluded from the Committees which covered France with blood and ruin, the decree of their proscription was already signed when, on the 29th July last, they anticipated their executioners by dragging them to the scaffold.

" This act of necessity invested the Moderates with the character of liberators of the Convention and the oppressed, and gained them the public applause, but without either esteem or confidence. They rightly perceived that they would never become popular, unless they made the Revolution retrace its course, and declared war against its partisans. Thereupon the prisons were opened, the permanent guillotine disappeared, the revolutionary tribunals were closed, and the measures of the Reign of Terror were represented as crimes. Liberty of speech and of the press was restored : security within was promised, and the hope of peace without propagated. The public movement excited by this unexpected change imposed the necessity of its extension and prolongation. This maintained the milder system adopted by the Moderates, far more than did any efforts of the Moderates themselves : this aided them in obtaining in the Convention a sufficient majority against the partisans of terror. As yet, therefore, this party has derived all its strength from the popular feeling, which it obeys, after having merely revived, not created, it.

"No member of this party has faith in the future existence of France as a Republic. Every day, while feigning to proclaim its immortality, they labour to shake its foundations; but these men, narrow in mind and yet more despicable in character, are blown about successively by the mere force of circumstances, from ambition to fear, and from fear to ambition.

"But for the fears excited in them by the fate of their predecessors, they would wish to preserve the Republic in order that they might continue its dictators; but there is reason to think that their views and their plans tend at present towards the re-establishment of royalty. A host of accurate and uniform details of their clandestine measures, and an attentive examination of the direction in which the Moderates are gradually leading the Assembly and public opinion, leave me little doubt in this respect.

"Soon after the fall of Robespierre, I was consulted by some leaders of the Constitutional party, exiled from France, as to a plan of conduct and conciliation suggested by them to the Moderates. The latter, without returning any direct answer to the communication, have so exactly followed the course marked out for them, that scarcely anything remained to be accomplished but the final act of proclaiming the young King. Had the army of his imperial and royal Majesty maintained its position on the Meuse, and the English theirs in the Pays de Généralité; had not the Spaniards lost two provinces in six weeks;

had not the King of Prussia failed before Warsaw, and threatened to withdraw half his army from the Rhine, these preliminary steps towards monarchy would have rapidly gained strength in the Convention.   But the hope of detaching from the coalition the King of Prussia and the southern powers, that of seizing Holland and holding it to ransom, and the cry for peace artfully propagated from the Diet at Ratisbonne throughout the empire, have persuaded the Assembly at Paris that, having the option of finishing the war on its own terms, it was equally able to fix the fate of France and itself in the most independent manner.

"The re-establishment of a King being, through this combination of circumstances, no longer a matter of necessity to them, will the Moderates, through an enlightened policy, or a sagacious perception of their own interest, do what fear does not now oblige them to do ?   It is impossible to answer this question in the affirmative, since its solution depends on men governed solely by their passions.   But I may assure his imperial and royal Majesty, that the Moderates, disgusted individually with the Republic, have not lost sight of the project of restoring monarchy.

"What kind of royalty do they propose to restore, and when, and how ?   These are questions which time and circumstances alone can decide.   The Moderates and their adherents, whether ambitious of government or weary of it, will not relinquish their transitory power unless they can strengthen their security for the future.   It can only be on positive guarantees for their lives, the illegitimate fortunes they have gained to the scandal of France, and the certainty of not being called to account, that they will ever consent to resign the sceptre into the hands of the sovereign : they will reserve to themselves the form of government, as a bulwark against the administrators of the regency.

" The difficulties of this problem attach to the Republic, in spite of themselves, those revolutionists who would be willing to abolish it. If their insensate and criminal hands had spared the Queen and Madame Elizabeth, one of these two princesses, when the Convention should have capitulated with them, would have served to solve the dilemma of a regency ; but they shrink from conferring it on the princes, brothers of Louis XVI., yet know not whom to substitute for them. The same principle of fear and hatred against the emigrant princes divides those republicans, also, who split on the choice of a king. Some direct their thoughts to the young orphan who languishes in the tower of the Temple ; others to the Duke of Orleans, retired to Switzerland—a prince who, without sharing the vices and the crimes of his father, served the popular party until the King's death, and who, having made a profession of his attachment to the Constitution of 1791, is much less dreaded by the republicans, who, on the contrary, flatter themselves on having all to hope from him. The third party thinks of changing the dynasty, and bestowing the throne on a new line.

" Whatever the ultimate decision of the Convention, it may be considered certain that that body would take care to reduce the royal authority to a merely representative function, and would reserve to itself the sub-

stance of its power.   The period of such a revolution is,
therefore, necessarily uncertain.

"The means by which they would effect this undertaking would consist, in general terms, in successive pro-
scriptions of the Jacobin party, indirect efforts to disgust
the people with republican government, the mitigation of
the revolutionary *régime*, and the discountenancing of its
maxims ; a reconciliation with the constitutionalists, authors,
or partisans of the law of 1791, and the formation of a
majority in the Convention and in Paris so preponderating, that the decree ordaining the restoration of monarchy
might be proclaimed without danger.

"The party here described numbers from one hundred
to one hundred and fifty members in the Convention : its
ascendancy is owing solely to the hatred of the Jacobins
entertained by the great majority of the Assembly.   But
not one of these Moderates deserves to be called the leader
of the party, or is capable of sustaining such a part.   The
people have no affection for them individually : it would
be impossible for them to interest it in their personal cause
so soon as it ceased to be that of the public.

"The third party in the Convention is composed of
about one hundred and fifty-four members, who refused
to vote the death of Louis XVI., and of seventy-four
deputies almost all in the same case, and imprisoned ever
since the revolution of the 31st of May, which decided the
superiority of the Jacobins, and led to that of Robespierre.
These one hundred and fifty-four representatives escaped
confinement only because of their want of influence, and
of the profound silence which they imposed on themselves

in the Convention. They belonged to it for eleven months without daring to utter an opinion, paralysed by terror, and expecting every week the moment of their execution.

"The preservation of their seventy-four imprisoned colleagues, demanded every day by the Jacobins, is due, in all probability, only to the number of more important victims whom the Committee of Public Safety had to sacrifice before them. In pursuance of a recommendation from Switzerland to the Moderates, the latter have set at large these seventy-four deputies, and, in spite of the opposition of a portion of the Convention, have succeeded in replacing them in the Assembly.

"United in 1792 and 1793 to the faction of the Brissotists—so called from the name of Brissot, one of its chiefs—or of the Federalists, because to them was attributed a project of converting France into a confederation of republics, presided over by a king, this section of national deputies includes some honest men, a proportion of hot-headed and impracticable persons, and yet more of the weak-minded, accustomed to yield to the force of circumstances. Most of them, in 1792, voted for the Republic without desiring it, and even without considering it possible. The terrible experience they have had of it has sufficiently opened their eyes; it has even restored to them a degree of courage of which they feel the necessity. The present sentiments of many among them are known; and the greater number may be regarded as secret partisans of monarchy, and as determined to second its reestablishment whenever the state of affairs may permit them to avow such an intention.

"The Moderates have reinforced themselves with this

party, which, however, not being chargeable with the same crimes, nor being so damaged in character as the majority of the Moderates, sides with them only as supporters. Until the latter adopt a more decided course, the Federalists will mistrust them ; and the more so, inasmuch as the leaders of the present Moderates persecuted them, when time was, fiercely, and concurred in the guillotining of the twenty-two chiefs of the Federalist faction, in the month of October, 1793.

"The last party remaining to be described consists of the class of deputies intermediate between the Jacobins and the Moderates. It is more easy to define their characters, than their intentions. Most have signalized themselves by atrocious opinions, and their practice was on a par with their precepts. Were it not for the Jacobins of the day, the revolution would have had no more perverse fomenters or instruments.

" If this league of the mitigated republicans were to acquire consistency, and some amount of ascendancy, it would supplant the Jacobins, with the sole modification of their daring, their ferocity, and their final aim.

" In their own despite, the system of moderation has prevailed : although they did not dare display open opposition, they have aimed, and aim still, to prevent the weakening of the revolutionary system.

" The Moderates oppose the Royalists tamely, the Jacobins furiously. The mitigated republicans would pardon the Jacobins if they did not fear their chiefs, and would seal their reconciliation with the blood of the Royalists.

" In their party is recognized the fundamental principle of the revolution——that of sacrificing all to expediency, and of never hesitating for any motive of morality, justice, right, or duty. Among them, as among the Jacobins, prevails the system of confiscation, but by methods less sanguinary.

" This rapid sketch of the several parties into which the Convention is divided, will assist his Majesty in appreciating the general character of that anarchic congress.

" The means of working upon it consist in the general opinion, which is common to the great majority of the individuals who compose it, that the existence of the Convention is compulsory, dangerous to the members themselves, and that it is destined to perpetual crises. Consequently, it is generally admitted that a form of government must be attained, less terrible than that of an assembly, in which the faction which usurps absolute power may, at any moment, send the minority to the scaffold.

" But, while agreed on this point, they are not in the least so as to the means of compassing their object, nor on the nature of the government to be substituted for that of the present day.

" Hyprocrisy and fury lord it by turns over the scene. Every sitting is a lie several hours long, by the aid of which their own intentions are disguised. The fear of being suspected of ideas contrary to those they profess exaggerates dissimulation still further. The public papers which report the debates of the Convention represent, therefore, nothing but the history of a masquerade. This habit of falsehood in all matters of opinion yields to brutal passions, hatred, jealousy, revenge, as soon as it becomes a personal question.

" Individually, the Convention is composed of pigmies ;

but these pigmies, as often as they act altogether, possess
the strength of Hercules—that of delirium ;   for they are
urged by passions, and by the momentous object of escaping
the fate with which five years of crime menace them.

" Although only a minority of these deputies seriously
think, of founding a Republic, the physical majority of the
Convention is still republican ; in other words, the dangers
attendant on the re-establishment of monarchy dismay
them   more than the storms of anarchy and the vicissitudes of the power which they have seized.

" Having described to his imperial and royal Majesty
the cabals and the spirit of the Convention, it remains for
me to speak of the parties which exist beyond its limits.

" The sword of Robespierre, by striking for a whole
year revolutionists as well as royalists, has considerably
diminished the numbers of the republicans.   The number
of stubborn republicans is therefore reduced at present
to : Firstly, the adherents of the Jacobin party and of
the mitigated republicans in the Convention ; Secondly,
the enthusiasts, for whom the dogma of equality is far
dearer than liberty itself ; Thirdly, the limited intellects,
who, seeing no medium between the Republic and the old
régime, cling to the former to avoid the latter ; Fourthly
and lastly, young political romancers, crazed by reading
Rousseau and the history of the ancient republics, to
whom the palace of the Tuileries is the Capitol, the
Convention the Roman Senate, an expedition against
one or two provinces bordering on France, the conquest
of the world, and who persuade themselves that the
French Republic is destined to display the morals of
Sparta, the legislation of Plato, and the grandeur of

ancient Rome. These are almost all bad authors, college-ushers, men of letters, *café* orators. So long as Jacobin clubs existed in Paris and the provinces, they served as a rallying point for the crack-brained and speculative republicans. Since the suppression of those societies, the party floats, scattered, obscurely and without compass. It has lost in power, and loses daily in adherents.

"The number of men, of whatever kind, who invariably aim at maintaining the Republic, cannot without exaggeration be estimated at more than a fourth part of the inhabitants of France.

"The royalists bear a larger proportion, if we include under this name all citizens, without distinction, who desire the re-establishment of royalty and of religion. One may average them at a third of the inhabitants; but nothing can be more dissimilar than the various sections of these partisans of monarchy : they differ essentially in force and opinion.

"That class, originally distinguished by the appellation of aristocrats, comprising the clergy, nobility, great capitalists and principal landed proprietors, has lost by emigration or executions the greater number of those whom illustrious birth, government offices, situations in the magistracy or the army, or their fortunes, had placed at the head of the state. Confiscations and sequestrations have destroyed their opulence. Among those who yet remain in France, only a small number retain the wreck of their patrimony, and even this on a precarious tenure : there are scarcely any whom the nation's voice would at a favourable moment call to take the reins of government and found a Restoration. The last remnant of the genuine aristocrats now comprises only old men, women, children, and a few ecclesiastics and gentry concealed in their native provinces.

"We may add to these the brave population of La Vendée and of a portion of Bretagne. Fewer of these perished in the war of 1793 than of the patriots; these latter own to a loss of two hundred and fifty thousand individuals of both sexes, killed in the war, or murdered. La Vendée lost about two thousand of its inhabitants, either on the battle-field, by executions, destitution or transportation.

" In the same section of the royalists rank a number of persons of the *tiers-état*, whether lawyers, commercial men, or any other class of citizens, who, having at first adopted some of the ideas of the Revolution, now bitterly regret that it ever commenced, and would joyfully acquiesce in its termination, though purchased even by a return to the former government.

"His Imperial and Royal Majesty will observe that among these three classes of genuine royalists, one only, that of La Vendée, can be regarded as active and important. The other two have not yet recovered from the terror which stunned the entire kingdom ; for the most part they are utterly incapable of action, and even of will. There is no one to rally or lead them. They could only become useful by uniting with the Constitutional party, which founded the Constitution of 1791, which professes the fundamental principles of monarchy, and since 1792, has been more oppressed than even the genuine royalists.

"Although terror, ambition, interest and the guillotine,

have thinned it ever since the birth of the Republic, the Constitutional party still includes a considerable proportion of the middle classes and landed proprietors. Undoubtedly, in 1791 and 1792 it numbered among its members the majority of the French nation; King Louis XVI. elicited this truth. Eighteen thousand military officers of every grade, appointed by the Constitutionalists, seventy-one out of eighty-two administrators of departments, the greater part of the tribunals, the merchants, the manufacturers, the bulk of the Parisian National Guard and all its chiefs, belonged at that time to this party. Several of its chiefs have perished; more still have left France; its adherents have been, and continue to be, condemned to dissimulation and obscurity; but its roots, spread far and wide, will shoot forth in all quarters at the first moment that the republican tyranny declines.

" To numerical strength, the Constitutionalists unite the advantage of the closest vicinity to the Revolution, of the most intimate knowledge of its resources and tactics, and of the ability to make common cause with the deserters of the Republican party. Their ancient theory, rather democratic than monarchical, is thus more acceptable to the crowd of ignorant men or enthusiasts who are infected with the doctrine of equality and the people's sovereignty. Placed midway between the aristocrats and the republicans, their faction not only serves as a refuge for all converts, but holds up to the nation a system already known, consecrated, and elevated into law, and whose destruction was mourned over by the majority of the people.

" Yet this party is now as scattered and almost as insignificant as that of the aristocrats. Deprived of chiefs and of the power to reunite and assemble itself, it would scarcely suffice, by its own unassisted strength, to shake the monstrous edifice of the Republic, and to overturn it. But there is an affinity between these members and the old federalists of the Convention, who may now be re-garded as covert Constitutionalists : even the Moderates, who would re-establish royalty only on constitutiona principles, tend, in the nature of things, to the same junction.

" The actual opinions of this party and its chiefs have been bettered by the mournful experience of their first attempts. All men of note among them, whether rendered prominent by talents or credit, agree in condemn-ing the bases of that constitution which they fabricated, and which ruined them : convinced that it requires to be reformed, they would now institute a limited monarchy— but not like that of 1791, crushed by the power of the people or their delegates : they would concentrate the energy of the royal government, while circumscribing its authority in questions of legislation and taxes by a national representation, which would be divided, as in England, and limited to proprietors only.

" Though the Constitutionalists agree as to fundamental principles, their personal views are widely different : numerous are the individual rivalries which exist in this party, fruitful in intriguers, ambitious men, and men who long to play some part. M. de La Fayette has his cabal, MM. Lameth have theirs, Dumouriez has his partisans ; other Committees have also their heroes and their personal aims. The common misfortune has done but little towards uniting these opposite interests. As to the nation, it extends neither esteem nor attachment to any of the factions actually existing in the Convention, much less to their prominent members—it will see them reign or cut throats with equal indifference."

CHAPTER VI.

1795.

Letters on the peace of Basle to the Abbé de Pradt, M. de Hardenberg, General Heyman and Marshal de Castries.

Of all possible contingencies, none caused Mallet greater
uneasiness than the peace concluded with the Convention
by various states of the Coalition.   The Coalition would
be relaxed and the Convention saved, at the very moment
that, already shaken and almost overbalanced on the
shifting surface of opinion, clamorous for peace, it tottered
to its fall.   As far back as November, 1794, Mallet had
imparted his apprehensions to the Abbé de Pradt.

LETTER FROM MALLET DU PAN TO THE ABBÉ DE PRADT.

"Berne, November 1, 1794.

" Would you believe it——Coblentz and the states of the
Church hooked without a bait ! The Prussians have
recrossed the Rhine and abandoned Mayence to the
Austrians.   Mollendorf has promised his army good winter
quarters, on which he is about to enter, and a peace to be
shortly concluded between his master and the enemy.

These disasters and scandals have their rise from one source. It is clear that people will defend themselves. Less than you propose would suffice to terminate within six months the Republic and the Revolution. Whether the allies were on the left or the right side of the Rhine, they would equally triumph, and almost without striking a blow. So irresistible is the torrent of popular feeling in France, that the Convention is lost unless it can point to a peace concluded before next spring. There exists now but one passion; a thirst for peace. I repeat it, if only the powers stood firm and presented to the nation this alternative : ‘ war and the republic, peace and the monarchy,’ the issue could not be doubtful, so long as all was avoided which might tend to rouse men’s passions or their fears. But everything leads me to apprehend that peace will be hurried on and concluded, just as war was made, without due examination or appreciation of the enemy. Then the Convention will take breath, and olive branch in hand, will impose—be sure of it—a sample of republican government in conformity with its own views. Remember, peace is universally desired, whether with or without a monarchy. The latter has as yet only timid partisans ; the bulk of the nation begin to forget that they ever had a King, and when once peace is established without, and a mild government within, it will no longer be the people’s interest to desire a different order of things. Those who now aspire to one, having once escaped incarceration and the guillotine, will content themselves with a sorry inn, rather than take one additional step which might carry them to all the comforts of a mansion.”

Meanwhile, M. de Hardenberg having requested to have him for a correspondent, Mallet failed not, while depicting the state of France and its altered position, to lay stress on the continuance of the revolutionary doctrine, a real and formidable danger, ever overhanging Europe.

" That which changes not, he forcibly observes, is the essence of the revolutionary doctrine. All who in France choose the Republic, are infected with it ; it bears sway in administrations, sections, clubs ; the popular societies of every city, town and village—those mighty resorts of the lower orders—harbour and foster it. This anti-social theory serves as a creed to the partisans of Revolution. This is what is ignored by that throng of futile writers and ignorant reasoners who labour in Germany to mislead both sovereigns and people, by invariably representing the French Revolution as merely local, the result of causes peculiar to France, and prolonged only by the necessity of resisting foreign warfare. Nothing can be more false than these assertions. The revolutionary system is applicable to all nations ; it is based on philosophical maxims which suit all climates and oppose every government. Its authors show no more favour to that of England, than to an Eastern government ; their doctrines corrupt republics and monarchies alike. We both have seen, and do see, their emissaries tutor the inhabitants of the neutral states, of Genoa, Switzerland and Sweden, precisely as they would the subjects of the belligerent powers. The three Assemblies which have subverted France, and particularly that one which now exists, have regarded this system with blind enthusiasm. The fanaticism of irreligion, equality and propagandism, is to the full as inflamed with zeal as any religious fanaticism, and employs means a thousand times more atrocious.

"This formidable sect has affinity with the English Presbyterians, the German *illuminati*, and all the disciples of modern philosophy throughout Europe. These all regard France as the metropolis of their doctrine, and the centre of union. Hitherto, all religions have tended to subdue the passions : this creed excites them all, and sets them free from restraint. In the north and south alike, in every region, rank, and country, it enlists the unsuccessfully ambitious, men ruined or discredited, men of letters, each of whom conceives himself alone capable of governing malcontents, visionaries, enthusiasts, and the lower classes of people. It developes and propagates itself like Islamism, by arms, and by opinion ; in one hand it holds the sabre, in the other the rights of man. One of the principal motives which induced its founders to commence a war with the powers, was the hope of accelerating the spread of revolutionary principles, by the conquest and corruption of nations and soldiers. The Convention and the Jacobin club have organized their missions of proselytism at home and abroad, as systematically as the Jesuits have organized theirs in America and China."

Ere long Mallet du Pan's suspicions were confirmed : there arrived at Basle deputies from the Convention, appointed for secret service, a Prussian chamberlain, some diplomatists, the Swedish ambassador, M. de Staël, and finally Barthélemy, in person. All denoted that this town was the place of meeting of negotiators, assembled to confer.

At this sight Mallet's imagination, opening to him a vista of baseness and disaster, for a moment rendered him unjust. Already he beheld Austria withdraw discouraged, or resolved to turn its arms against Prussia; a general defection follow in consequence, and the English, paying dearly for their policy, remain alone and powerless at their post. He considered that his correspondence with M. de Hardenberg became useless under these circumstances, and suspended it. His surprise was great when he received from General Heyman, on the part of the Prussian Minister, urgent solicitations to continue the correspondence.

He replied immediately.

LETTER FROM MALLET DU PAN TO GENERAL HEYMAN.

" . . . . I will not conceal from you my astonishment at this unexpected application. I was the last person that could have anticipated it; and I see with more regret than surprise, that this new engagement will be as perfectly useless as the preceding. I accepted it out of regard to you, and deference to an honourable minister, but without the hope of producing any effect. The experience of the last three years has cured me of the mania of volunteering my advice. Those who choose to poison themselves can only be left to perish. Europe is going to wrack and ruin. It will fall into the revolutionary vortex at the moment when we shall see France issue thence. That is what would have been the result of a war which the late King Louis XVI. had so much reason to dread, and the effects of which he foretold to me. It will have served to prove one thing—that there is nothing in the world so feeble, so disorganized, so impotent, as a coalition.

"A correspondence like that in which we have been engaged, is so much waste paper. . . . . I had reached my fifth number, which is despatched to-day, when I learned, by letters from Frankfort, that you were resuming with more determination than ever your negotiations with the ruffians of the Tuileries, and that Baron de Hardenberg was about to repair to Basle with this object. That is a very significant commentary on my labours; had I foreseen it, I could not have entered upon them. I regret extremely that I should have undertaken a task, merely to abandon it at the end of a month, from so humiliating a motive. It appears to me that, since the negotiation was resolved upon, in despite of the most sacred circumstances and interests, it was perfectly superfluous to have recourse to information from me. Experience will pass judgment on the motives of your cabinet, the consequences of its proceedings, and the extraordinary conduct which his Prussian Majesty is induced to pursue.

" Baron de Hardenberg, I presume, will have no further occasion for my services, being, as he is, on the same spot as myself, and in a position to procure whatever information he may need. The very nature of his mission overrules my correspondence, which is a perpetual pleading against the fatal negotiations which I foresee.

" It is quite possible that the Convention has ceased to exist at the moment when your court contemplates signing a peace with it. Ever since the origin of the war, the allies have had the art of putting themselves in opposition to facts, and of letting slip, or annulling by their own act, such as were favourable to them.   What a world it is, my dear General !   I repeat to you, &c.,

" MALLET DU PAN."

The answer did much to reassure Mallet.   His objections were removed by the General's warm representations of the minister's principles and character, of the loyalty of his sentiments, the integrity of his personal views, and, above all, his express desire that Mallet should not avoid even unpalatable truths, while increasing the force of his arguments.   Our author could not but seek some other aim than that of a partial peace in these conferences at Basle : for a moment he believed it a preconcerted plan, whereby a few palatinates might be pared from the Court of Vienna. He then addressed M. de Castries :

LETTER FROM MALLET DU PAN TO MARSHAL DE CASTRIES.

" April 4, 1795.

" I have private reasons for believing that Baron de Hardenberg is equally removed, by his opinions, by the intelligence of his mind, and the nobility of his character, from so disgraceful and delusive a transaction.   Three months ago this minister sent to request me to explain to him fully my opinion on the questions of the day.   My reply was supported by such convincing proofs, facts, and inductions, that I learned without surprise that M. de Hardenberg concurred entirely in my views.   He started for Berlin, assuring me that he would forward them to the utmost of his ability ; but the only result was a renewal of negociations.

The minister came to Basle in person: soon after his arrival, he requested an interview with me and the continuance of my correspondence; I refused both the one and the other, declaring that, devoted as I am to the cause of the French monarchy and of Europe, I would take no part in transactions to forward the private interests of Prussia with the Convention.

"You will conclude from these last requests, that the designs are far from being fixed, or the arrangement from being concluded; but I imagine you will approve of my reserve on this topic."

He had scarcely closed this letter when he heard of the treaty of *peace and amity* signed on the 3rd April, at Basle, between the King of Prussia and the French Republic. M. de Hardenberg had arrived from Berlin to renew the negotiations, which had undergone a momentary interruption through the death of Baron de Goltz. The consequences foreseen by Mallet ere long began to be developed: Austria alone, which had just lost the Netherlands and its Dutch dependencies to Pichegru—Austria, elevated by its misfortunes, its menaced isolation and just wrath, instead of succumbing, boldly carried on the campaign, backed by the single alliance, rather than the successful concurrence, of England.

A confidential letter, in which Mallet gave vent to his first impression, came to the knowledge of Baron de Hardenberg, who, in his turn, complained of it in terms of the liveliest dissatisfaction. Mallet, while protesting against the indiscretion which had placed him in so insidious a position, frankly defended himself.

LETTER FROM MALLET DU PAN TO BARON DE HARDENBERG.

" Berne, May 17, 1795.

" Monsieur le Baron,

" It was only last week that I was made aware of your Excellency's letter to General Heyman, dated the 15th April last, wherein you desire him to express to me your dissatisfaction with the opinion I had communicated to M. de Tolosan, and which the latter had thought fit, without authority and without informing me, to make known to a friend. Such a communication was injurious to your Excellency and myself: I flatter myself that you did not suspect me of having been concerned in it.

" I should find it very difficult to justify myself in regard to a letter written by M. de Tolosan, in which he translated rather than transcribed my expressions: but I can affirm that what I said did not contain a syllable offensive to your Excellency. I never for a moment questioned the honour of your sentiments, or the rectitude of your personal views. In several private letters, more important than those addressed to M. de Tolosan, I expressed this opinion decisively; and I have repeated it in public, uniformly, ever since the signing of the peace. The Chevalier de Gallatin, my countryman and friend, who recently had the honour of an interview with your Excellency, could attest that, in his presence, and under all other circumstances, I never adopted a different tone.

" In accepting the proposal for this brief correspondence, I reminded General Heyman that my opinions were incompatible with the apparent tendency of his Prussian Majesty's cabinet. He overruled this difficulty by giving me a very faithful account of your Excellency's principles and character. After this precaution, and upon the repeated solicitations of the General, I did not hesitate to lay before you what he asked for—that is, *even disagreeable truths*. On your departure for Berlin, M. le Baron, he expressed to me your thanks for my *sincerity*, requesting me to give my arguments with *even greater unreserve*.

" I may perhaps be excused for my surprise at your departure for Basle—an event which I learned through the papers at a time when I was continuing to address to you, at Berlin, a correspondence nugatory in this new state of matters, and without having received from your Excellency, directly or indirectly, either an intimation to persevere, or even a circuitous assurance that your Excellency's mission was still compatible with the opinions and the cause to which I have publicly devoted myself these six years.

" This silence, and your Excellency's sojourn on the French frontier, sufficed to convince me that my correspondence was without an object, that peace would shortly be concluded, and that, under these circumstances, any letter from me would be an act of importunity, indecorum, and absurdity. As to an interview ;—your Excellency had, like myself, perceived the objections to it : it could scarcely by possibility have been unknown. Eight days later, the "Moniteur" and the tribunes of the Convention would have been certain to add to their unremitting inventions, that I was an emissary and an intriguer : the emigrants, whose want of employment foments their gossiping and idle exaggeration, would have spread the great news from

one end of Europe to the other, with the embellishments
familiar to them.   Your Excellency will do me the justice
to think that the opinion of this set affects me little : but
more respectable connexions—my duty towards the memory
of Louis XVI., who honoured me with his confidence,
but never with his bounty—bound me to guard against even
the suspicion of sharing, in whatever manner, in any
accommodation with the National Convention.

"None of these motives, M. le Baron, were personal to
you.   It is precisely because I am not called upon to
discuss the interests of your Court that it became my duty
to cease writing to you.   Surely, you cannot blame me for
having been hurt at seeing peace signed at the very moment
when the Convention was abdicating its functions in dismay.   I regret the fact, without judging the motives of his
Prussian Majesty ; and I am too well aware of your
magnanimity, M. le Baron, to doubt that your reasons
were as well-grounded as imperative, &c."

The bitter disappointment of Mallet may easily be understood.   The peace of Basle threw fresh uncertainty over the
hopes and projects which he had indulged, on seeing the
turn matters were taking in the interior of France.   He
had fancied that the signs of a return towards monarchy
were manifest in the general tendency,—although not to
the old régime ; for he said candidly to the Abbé de Pradt:
"It is as impossible to restore the old régime as to build
St. Peter's at Rome with the roadside dust."

"Would you believe," he writes again to the Abbé, "that
I am urged every day to return to Paris ? and would you
believe that it hangs on a thread whether I do not return ?

You were thinking over this resolution fifteen months ago. The moment is at hand for thinking of it seriously. You, a banished ecclesiastic, will return without peril, and, probably, by legislative authority. Your fellows are preceding you in crowds. Opinions are in an inconceivable chaos. The Abbé Morellet has resumed his pen : he is the author of the 'Cri des Familles.' His pamphlet, which has been astonishingly successful, has compelled the Convention to give in, and withdraw the sequestrations. The ' Accusateur Public', which comes out in numbers, has taken up the tone which I had maintained in the ' Mercure' : it has crushed the Abbé Sieyès. 'It is with your *declaration of rights* in their hand,' says this paper to him, ' that they have butchered your colleagues, your benefactors, your relatives—a whole generation. Look, eager metaphysician, you stand knee deep in blood.' Numberless papers say again and again : ' We will have no democracy which does not ensure to the people security, justice and liberty. Equality is in the kennel.' Again I say to you, prepare to return."

However, the peace of Basle did not deprive Mallet of these hopes. He considered that their fulfilment was only postponed. On the 19th April, he wrote to the Abbé de Pradt :

" Rumour which, like the plague, spreads poison, will have informed you of the treaty of ' Peace and Amity,' signed at Basle on the 8th. You will see the articles of it in the papers. I could not muster courage to tell you at the moment of this event, so precipitate, so incomprehensible in the circumstances under which it has been

L 2

carried out, and so fatal through the delay it occasions
the conclusion of our misfortunes."

"I have been long convinced of the necessity of peace,
since war is no longer possible, either by befitting means, or
by concert, or by the indispensable instruments. But to break
up the coalition, to reduce its members to isolation by partial
treaties——to sink so low in humiliation——to admit their own
feebleness so imprudently, to sacrifice the hope of a general,
certain and glorious peace, which three months of manly
perseverance would have brought on without the burning
of a match ; to sacrifice this to the design of destroying the
empire by a war with the house of Austria this will be
severely judged by posterity.

"Six weeks more patience, and the Convention would
have crumbled to pieces. The King of Prussia gives it a
helping hand, sets it afloat once more, reanimates its partizans, fosters its exhausted quackeries. He inspires patience
in the nation, when the burden of its sufferings was about
to make it rise up in all quarters. But this peace is only
a momentary respite ; it cannot stop the effect of motives
for reaction so powerful, so active, so manifest. The
Convention is used up, despised, hated more than ever ;
and the primary assemblies are universally demanded. I
subjoin an extract from a letter I very recently received
from a steadfast and sagacious friend at Paris, just returned
from a tour in the South :

"The Convention," he says, "is generally despised.
Those who cry, 'Long live the Convention!' do not fail
to add : 'But we have no bread.' Nowhere, not even in
the most dangerous quarters, is the 'ça ira' to be heard.

The *tutoiement* is beginning to disappear. In Lyonnais churches are built. On the whole line from Antibes to Geneva, Sunday is kept, and the *decadi* laughed at. A decided preference is everywhere given to the non-juring priests. As to the others, those only are tolerated who, having taken the oath under the compulsion of violent threats, have since conducted themselves well. It is hoped that religion will soon be again in vigour. The restitution of the goods of the church is considered inevitable, except, perhaps, in the case of the monks, and some of the higher clergy. But little of the property of emigrants is sold : almost every one says that their property should be restored to those who have not borne arms against France. No one will hear of re-establishing the nobility in its hereditary privileges, or the parliaments in the exercise of their functions. All classes of society, to the very lowest, display in divers ways a desire for monarchical government, particularly by the frequent repetition of these words : ' Eight and nine make seventeen.' In addition to this desire of restoring the Dauphin to the throne, it is considered fair to confer the Regency on Monsieur. As for the Comte d'Artois, there is a very decided ill-will against him. The majority of the people are inclined to the Constitution of 1791, with an augmentation of the royal power."

CHAPTER VII.

1795.

First Prairial—Death of Louis XVII.—Mallet is again applied to,
and the Count d'Artois sends M. de Sainte-Aldegonde to him—
Letter from Count d'Artois—Questions put to Mallet—His answer
in two notes addressed to Louis XVIII.—July, 1795—Letter to
Marshal de Castries—Count François de Sainte-Aldegonde.

THE desperate attempt of the Jacobins on the 20th of
May (1st prairial) was not deemed by Mallet to be of a
nature to arrest the impending crisis : the victory of the
Convention especially was a victory gained over terrorism ;
the feculent dregs of Robespierre's tail had disappeared—the
reign of pikes was at an end.*   The Convention could not
hold out much longer against the overwhelming hatred of
the people themselves.   But another disappointment—or
rather a terrible misfortune—once more changed the face

---

* One of Mallet's correspondents writes him word : " The 6th
Prairial, order to give up the pikes to the section—that is to say, to
disarm three-fourths of the inhabitants, under pain of imprisonment—
all is done without a murmur; people wait patiently at the doors for
their turn, I, myself, have waited three-quarters of an hour to deliver
up my pike. All France might thus be disarmed without the striking
of a blow."

of the question, by depriving the royalists of their prop and stay. The young King, the captive in the Temple, Louis XVII. died.

The following letter, addressed to Marshal de Castries, proves that Mallet du Pan instantly perceived all the consequences of his death, and clearly foresaw what in fact occurred; that the event would tend to the establishment not of monarchy, but of an executive council which would be installed with the approbation of the people.

LETTER FROM MALLET DU PAN TO MARSHAL DE CASTRIES.

"June 17, 1795.

"Monsieur le Maréchal,

"The death of the young King has put an end to all questions about the regency. You must already have heard, Monsieur le Maréchal, that the unfortunate prince expired on the 8th, after being during three months in a gradually declining state; and Desaulx, the surgeon who attended him, only survived him two days. Paris is persuaded that there was poisoning in the case . . . .

"Paris and the royalists are in a state of consternation. All that I hear and my own reflections suggest the apprehension that this unlooked for loss will serve to consolidate the Republic. It takes place at the precise moment when the Convention is on the eve of publishing its plan of constitution. The monarchists, not feeling themselves, and indeed not being, strong enough to set up a king, nor even to return to the Constitution of 1791, had found themselves compelled to compound with the Girondists, and to rest satisfied with the hopeful anticipa-

tion that the monarchical edifice might yet rise from its
ruins.   The Girondists having adopted the damaged foundation of the Constitution of the United States, the
Monarchists demanded that they should carry out the
imitation to the fullest extent; that holders of property
alone should be represented, and representative ; that the
legislative body should be divided into two chambers
instead of forming two sections of one and the same
chamber ; finally, that a chief should be elected, and not
an executive council.   During the minority, they proposed
to put a vice-president at the head of the council of
regency, and this *mezzo-termine* rallied many of the
republicans round the royalists.   Now, the death of the
King sweeps away this plan, and forwards the project of
an executive council.   I fully expect that the Convention
will definitively fix on this form of domination ; the public
will grieve, the people will applaud, all will obey.

" Such, M. le Maréchal, are our prospects at present,
and such are the prevalent tendencies.   His Majesty's
council must profoundly meditate on the course of conduct prescribed by such difficult circumstances : my own
consternation is too great, and the intelligence is too
recent for me to venture even to give an opinion on the
subject.   I shall, therefore, limit myself to the reminding
you of what vital importance it is to acquire correct ideas
of the actual condition of affairs, and the true state of
men's   minds, of the necessity of repressing illusion,
romance, exaggeration, and party statements.

" The famine is as severe as ever ; people get used to it,
and cease to grumble.   At Paris, on the 13th, the louis
d'or was worth five hundred and sixty francs ; it is ex-

pected to rise to a thousand francs next week. The provinces take advantage of this distress, demand an exorbitant price for all sorts of provisions, and are highly delighted with the present state of things. The towns are in the depths of despair — despair which suggests no remedy; credulous people look to the new constitution for that, as well as for a general peace.

"Receive, &c."

According to hereditary right, on the death of Louis XVII. Monsieur claimed the title of King, and the Count d'Artois found himself a step nearer the crown. A serious embarrassment, this, to the foreign powers, suggestive of fresh difficulties in the situation not only of the emigrants, but of the princes themselves. If the regency question had proved difficult enough of solution, how would they solve that of the recognition of the rightful claims of the new legitimate king? Whoever he might be, the heir to the throne of France was truly a pretender as the state of things ordained it, and all of the foreign courts were not inclined to uphold the title of king by their recognition of him, a step which would have placed them in a most difficult situation. The effect of these peculiar circumstances should have been to turn the attention of the party attached to the princes and emigrants to the tone of public opinion, the public being most interested in ascertaining what chance they had of success, and most versed in the necessary conditions of that success. As usual, application was again made to Mallet, at the same time that Ferrand and d'Entraigues were authorized to prepare their lying manifestos, and their silly manœuvres. Count François de Sainte-Aldegonde, in whom the Count d'Artois had great confidence, and who, through the medium of his mother-in-law, Madame de Tourzel, governess of the royal children, had been brought into a friendly connexion with Mallet, was commissioned to seek an interview, and to put a series of questions· to him.   Count d'Artois, writing to Count Sainte-Aldegonde on this occasion, said : " I am aware of the talents and good sense of M. Mallet du Pan, as well as of the purity of his sentiments and the strength of his principles, and I know the high esteem entertained for him by my virtuous brother.   I shall not now enter upon the subject of the minor differences in the views we take of the actual situation of our unhappy country.   I am sure that it cannot be difficult to come to an understanding with an upright, sensible man like M. Mallet."

The meeting between the Count and Mallet took place at Schaffhausen, in June, 1795.   Mallet, first in a paper intended for the eye of Louis XVIII., and then in various other summary documents, replied to most of the questions put him, concerning the state of France, of politics, of the principles to be maintained, and the ulterior steps to be taken ; to some, touching the re-establishment of the clergy, he declared himself incompetent to reply, on the ground of want of information.

The paper previously despatched to Louis XVIII., set out by explaining the real state of things and persons at Paris, and in the interior : with this sketch we are already acquainted.   This foundation firmly fixed, the politician entered on the all important question——how far successful could Louis XVIII. hope to be in the re-establishment of the monarchy; and above all what measures was he to take to develope and attain his object. We can imagine his answer; but the consultations in question form too important a feature in these Memoirs, and, indeed, in the historical record of this critical period of the Revolution, for us to pass over the subject in silence. We, therefore, extract the most interesting portions:

MEMORANDUM BY MALLET DU PAN FOR LOUIS XVIII.

"July 3, 1795.

"We have no ground to expect that any spontaneous insurrection in favour of royalty will take place in Paris or elsewhere. The Convention rules the people, and all the rest of the population dreads the very idea of a fresh convulsion.

"This disinclination for any general insurrection in the monarchical sense, would render partial insurrections disastrous. The Convention would wield against such an attempt the weight of its power, its armies, and the *vis inertiæ* in the public, which would take its part as being the safer.

"Civil war is a delusion of the same kind. The elements of civil war do not exist without princes, without nobles, without eminent generals, to bring over to their party provinces, armies, and the chiefs of the hierarchy; they do not exist where there is no rival faction, on which its credit, its opulence, and the personal resources of its leaders, confer firmness and strength. Under popular anarchy nothing is seen but ephemeral demagogic cabals, ruffianism, murders, of the 2nd of September, 31st of May, and 9th of Thermidor.

"The resource of foreign war is no less worn out now: in fact, and in opinion, nothing equals the contempt felt in France for the armies and the policy of the allies, unless it be the not less universal detestation they inspire. These feelings are equally decided in the monarchists and in the republicans. Lyons, the most royalist city in France, is not less incensed against the English than is a club of Jacobins. The whole realm, without distinction of party, will everlastingly unite against the foreigners, considered as enemies of France, and not as enemies of the Revolution. No modification of this animosity can be expected, unless the powers, abandoning their systems, their vacillations, their embassies, their negotiations, secret or public, should display at once imposing, united and victorious forces, and should, on the other hand, declare in an authentic and solemn manner, that they make no pretensions to attacking the integrity or the legislative independence of France, or to establishing its government ; but, that they are ready to offer peace, and re-open the doors of commerce and exchange so soon as monarchy of any kind shall be restored. So long as they keep silence without laying down their arms, they foster mistrust and fanaticism ; so long as they remain inactive, disunited, professing war, and taking steps for peace, they are neither feared nor respected.

"There is at present no perceptible means of force which does not counteract the slow but certain return of the revolution towards monarchy. All efforts should be directed to the seconding of this tendency : this alone can create the power which would be sought for in vain in internal insurrection, or the force of foreign arms. To discover this tendency, and make use of it without falling into blunders, we must become thoroughly conversant with the true state of the realm, and consider the point from which our efforts must start, instead of abstractly considering the point to which we would bring it."

Here Mallet gives an abridged version of the picture his correspondence has already offered to us, and he derives from it this primary fact, that the Constitutionalists, who are at the present moment of no account, are none the less foremost on the road towards monarchy, and that the tendency is towards the Constitution of 1791, imperfect as it is confessed to be.

" It is the general conviction, that it will be requisite first of all, to repass through the forge of 1781 in order to arrive at a good monarchy. Any other transition offers too many difficulties and dangers to men intimidated by two years of ferocious tyranny, which has made the people lose the very feeling of its power, absorbing it in that of the power of its oppressors.

" Generally speaking, it is but too true that the great majority of the French nation, having taken part in the Revolution through errors of conduct or of opinion, it will never surrender at discretion to the old authority and its representatives : we need only enter into the human heart to be convinced of this fact. The national vanity, maddened for three consecutive years ; wounded but not stifled by the system of terror, revolts equally at the idea of a pardon, especially when offered by the legitimate heads of the monarchy, who have not the power to re-establish it, and to a mass of men who consider themselves alone in a position to become its restorers. I may add, it is impossible to conceal that a portion of the principles of the day has survived the horrors of the Revolution, and that the present generation, infected with this leaven, can only deliver itself from it in course of time, and with a firm and enlightened government.

"The constitutionalists who abandon the act of 1791, consider from a hundred different points of view the method of remoulding it ; but the fundamental points, in general opinion, are the diminution of popular privileges, the relinquishment of the farrago of the rights of man, a considerable augmentation of the royal power, and a reservation of the national representation to men of property alone.

"Such is the spirit, the inclination, the desire of the towns in general, of the townspeople of all classes.

"In many respects, but from different motives, the country districts share these inclinations more or less. Crushed under Robespierre, they breathe again to-day, fatten on the misery of the towns, and make fabulous profits : a sack of corn pays the farmer's lease. The peasants in easy circumstances have become speculators, stock-jobbers, buy costly furniture, contest the sales of emigrants' property, pay no taxes, congratulate themselves daily on the abolition of tithes and feudal rights, and will continue— until this prosperity alters, until a new form of oppression arises—contented enough with their lot to receive the Republic without grumbling. They will receive it without putting faith in it; for, while liking the present system, they all think the country will one day return to a king of some kind.

"The new constitution will be received without opposition. Whether approved or blamed, it will be recognised, the oath of fidelity to it taken—even the absurdities of 1791 will be repeated. They will lie down on this volcano as on a bed of rest, and expect on awaking a general peace, an increased value and a diminished number of assignats, the return of plenty, and one half of the golden age.

" It will be asked what course of conduct, according to this rapid sketch, ought the King and the august Princes of the house of Bourbon to follow ?

" The reply to this question would be as complicated as the difficulties which surrounded its solution. Not one method—nor two—nor three, but a concurrence of resources would, perhaps, be demanded by such unprecedented circumstances.

" Two broad plans present themselves—either to incite civil war in the interior, for the re-establishment of monarchy; or to profit by the existing elements for its restoration, do no more than second their action, and combine with them to endow their development with the strength of union.

" The time is gone by when the banner of honour and duty, when the blood of Henri IV., inspired bold and warlike enthusiasm. The character of the age, the ravages of the revolution, the weakening of all energy, have suppressed in France (as in all Europe) those heroic and deep sentiments of fidelity, attachment, exalted loyalty, which determine men to great sacrifices, electrify them rapidly, and rally them without reflection. There is not at the present day a Frenchman in the interior who does not calculate his duties by his danger.

" I venture to affirm, therefore, that the most eminent, the most honourable chief entering France without means,

or without having created beforehand such as might be
seized and employed at the moment of his appearance, will
find himself either deserted, or incapable of making head
and contending against the resources of the Convention.

" It would then be necessary, I repeat, before taking the
field openly, to create these means, and render them of
sufficient importance to become means of war and sustained
resistance.   Nothing is easier than to foment and produce
some local insurrections.   Such sudden strokes, which have
been far too much relied upon these five years, are pernicious, unless their morrow has been provided for.   Experience has proved, and will prove everlastingly, the ease
with which such movements can be crushed.   I am not
sufficiently familiar with the condition of La Vendée
to know whether that district offers those preliminary advantages, without which any invasion, conducted
by one of the august Princes of the house of Bourbon,
would end in disaster.   In Paris, and throughout all France,
esteem and good-will are entertained for La Vendée : the
Convention fears it, and will always treat it with caution ;
but if it should resume arms without being justified in the
eyes of the nation for its hostilities by renewed oppression,
it will be abandoned to its own resources, will gain but few
proselytes, and will be attacked by all the disposable troops
left to the Convention by a peace more or less general.

" Such a renewal of oppression appears to me the only
case, whether in La Vendée, at Lyons, or elsewhere,
which can furnish the hope of forming a nucleus of
resistance.

" So long as the Convention abstains from peopling
either the prisons or the tomb, so long as it does not

make its yoke felt intolerably, a revolt of any importance is not to be expected. A nation reduced for the past five months to living on from two to four ounces of bread a day, to paying sixty francs for a pair of shoes, and to a conflict with hourly destitution, will remain quiet under usurpers, whenever it has not before its eyes prisons, or revolutionary committees, or guillotines, and so long as it does not despair of a turn of fortune.

"No royalist party exists; now, without a royalist party, there is no war. To form such a party, no elements exist except interest and sentiments of the most general kind, common to the partisans of monarchical government. The first study should therefore be devoted to this interest and these sentiments, and the plan of conduct, whatever it be, based on these data.

" I take the liberty of respectfully soliciting a distrust of visionaries and men carried away by party-spirit. The former represent France as opening its arms to receive the old *régime ;* the others take fright at any constitutional or limited system as at an irreparable evil. These two methods of viewing matters are equally false in fact and in hypothesis. The vast majority of the French repudiate the old *régime ;* but, whatever may be its desire for another system ; that is—will be—and can be, nothing but a transition from the Republic to a monarchy."

In a seemed note written some days after the first, Mallet du Pan indicates the measures which circumstances appear to him to demand.

"July 10, 1795.

" Any military means whatever are too inadequate to the difficulties, to leave any hope of ever restoring the monarchy by force of arms, if such means do not proceed *pari passu* with a reliance on policy and opinion.

"I do not except even the attempts in La Vendée. Were that department to resume arms, were it to receive one of the Princes of the blood or His Majesty himself, and were the disembarcation of the forces destined to pass into Brittany effected—these projects, this success, would not harm the Republic; unless, at the same time and above all, men's minds and interests are gained over by an appeal to those principles on which aspirations and efforts may be hoped to meet. So long as La Vendée presents itself in arms to re-establish the old *régime*, all France will fight against it voluntarily or on compulsion, and will end by crushing it.

"These reassuring tendencies for gaining proselytes and fixing the wavering purposes of the well-intentioned will become all the more necessary in that alarm, which will seize on all if the English uniform should appear in Brittany or Normandy, especially with an aspect of command: hatred, suspicion, fear, will bestow incalculable advantages on the Convention.

"I again beseech, and with equal fervency and respect, that, above all, the importance of levies and military enterprises may be rated at its right amount of value, and that hopes may not be founded upon them.

"The conquest will be completed and preserved by military means; it must not commence with them. They, in their extreme imperfection, must be considered as subsidiary, and as adapted solely to seconding operations of another kind.

1stly. "The first operation, that which the monarchists in

Paris and the provinces expect, is the moral resuscitation of royalty. It is desired, demanded—it is imperative, that His Majesty should speak and act without delay in this capacity.

2ndly. "That he should speak, not only by a public declaration of his accession, but by a solemn appeal to the nation. The rational royalists, the only ones who enjoy at this moment any credit or take any part in the public movement, are working for the convocation of the primary assemblies, in order to make them recognize the legitimate head of the nation. The general hope of honest men unites there, and there limits itself, because they know that an absolute counter-revolution is the absurdest of chimeras. The appeal of His Majesty to the nation presents them with a fixed basis—a puissant motive—a germ of fruitful resources—if it be managed wisely.

"The nature of this appeal will determine its efficiency. It is not enough that it should be drawn up on honourable principles, conformable to the fundamental laws, to an enlightened view of the public interest; its whole force will consist exclusively in the relation of such a manifestation to the feeling and desires of the majority. It is chiefly important that its principles and the conduct it shall announce, should be compatible with what may be hoped for, and practicable in the interior by moral and political means, to induce the recognition of the King by the assembled nation.

"It is considered that this appeal might contain 'a short, rapid, and energetic view of the crimes committed against the house of Bourbon and of its bounties, especially those of King Louis XVI; that it should show the nation

its calamities as having been consentaneous with the misfortunes of the royal family, of tyranny with the Republic,
all its plagues with the anti-monarchical revolution :

" Cite the unanimous desire expressed in the official acts
of 1789 ; the universal consecration of the monarchical
government by the Constituent Assembly, notwithstanding
the errors it committed, and by the all but unanimous voice
of the nation in 1791 ; and the memorable execration to
which Paris and seventy-three departments devoted the
Republic in the month of July 1792.

" Recall the fact, that subsequently France, delivered
over to the Convention, tortured by its successive factions,
decimated by its executioners, crushed down by a system
of savage and bloody oppression, knew no moment of civil
liberty and free opinion.

" Finish by proclaiming the permanent and indestructible rights of His Majesty ; invite the nation to rally
round him ; promise it succour ; announce hopes and
measures with dignity ; and appeal to it to co-operate
with His Majesty in re-establishing monarchy, religious
liberty, property, and public order, on bases of which
experience has more than proved the necessity.

" Promise a amnesty to the culpable who shall return
to their duty ; protection, impartiality, distribution of offices
without distinction of persons or past opinions, on consideration of talents, probity and services, even in the
case of such as were led astray for a time by the Revolution, without having imbued their hands in blood,
given France up to brigandage, and shared in the ferocious
insanity into which the minority of the nation was hurried
by a minority yet more ferocious.

" 3rdly. That His Majesty should act, and in conformity with his declarations, by testifying in his deeds the purity and sincerity of his bountiful and merciful intentions.

" That he should *act*——for feebleness is the reward of misfortune ; that his existence be felt, his resources perceived, or movements be seen, to create resources analogous to those which engage attention in the kingdom.

" 4thly. That negotiations, conferences, relations with the interior, should be commenced.

" 5thly. That no agents should be selected or employed but those who may be fully confided in, who have not been distinguished by too conspicuous marks of favour, and whose name, reputation and character may be sufficiently well known to facilitate advances.

6thly. If such a plan were adopted (and, indeed, under any plan possible) it is of sovereign importance to vest its superintendence in a central power ; of sovereign importance that His Majesty should be pleased to use his authority to prescribe imperatively to every agent his line of conduct, and abolish that shoal of emissaries, peripatetic ministers, crackbrains, legates, who swarm in all quarters, and especially in Switzerland——some with brevets from His Majesty ; others with the patents of the Prince de Condé ; a third set with British commissaries, crossing each other in all directions, perpetually in activity to do nothing but harm, recounting their missions at tavern-tables, and entailing on the royal cause, a disfavour, a confusion, a contempt, which absolutely keep aloof all rational men, whose zeal and efforts would be rendered equally fatal and nugatory by such coadjutors."

Several of the twenty-eight questions which M. de

Sainte-Aldegonde brought to Mallet from the court of
Verona had been answered by anticipation in the two
notes ; to the others a succinct reply was given.

To show the tendency of the ideas which now occupied
the councils of the Princes, we give the most important
of these questions, with the answers.

" Q. What do you consider to be the general desire
with regard to the future government, distinguishing
the views of the provinces from those of the metropolis ?
What are the wishes of proprietors, artisans and capitalists, divided, as they doubtless are, between a republic
and a monarchy ?   We should also be glad to know what
kind of monarchy is meant, and how far sacrifices would
be made to obtain a strong government, such as the
present state of France requires ?

" A. In my note of Schaffhausen I have replied to this
question.   I will add, that in the provinces, public opinion
consists in a vague and indefinite monarchism, totally
devoid of energy, and slavishly copying all the fashions
of Paris.   The desire most generally felt is for a constitution analogous to that of 1791, but purified in its
democratic portion, and invigorated by means of a strong
government.   Such is especially the wish of proprietors
and capitalists.   Artisans who work for absurd wages,
farmers who sell at exorbitant prices, well-to-do peasants
who purchase the property of emigrants without paying
any duty, are less desirous of change than of a settled
order, whatever it may be.   As to the lowest class,
particularly at Paris, workmen, bricklayers, blacksmiths,
water-carriers, carters, small shopkeepers—all these are
still Septembrists by taste and from custom, and always at

the service of any one who may be disposed to mischief and disorder.

" *Q.* Have the sufferings attending the republican government brought the multitude to their senses, and, if there is a general wish for a monarchy, will that wish be so decided as to constitute a fixed determination ?

" *A.* The multitude have not, and never will have, more sense than they had before. Their sole lot will ever be to abuse their strength when it is called into action, and to tremble when authority is strong. Chastisement and experience have, as yet, been powerless to correct the mass of the nation.

" *Q.* We should wish to know how far the royalists are likely to carry their perseverance in maintaining the two principles (God and the King), which they asserted when they took up arms ?

" *A.* My knowledge of La Vendée is not sufficient to enable me to answer this question."

The following question is put in a form worthy of attention.

" *Q.* We ought to know with what intention the royalist chiefs (of La Vendée) called in foreign aid ; and whether they can do without it ?

" *A.* I am not acquainted with the views of the royalist chiefs in summoning foreigners to their assistance : they cannot carry on the war without such succour ; but they ought to dispense with it, if, appreciating the full strength of their moral and political position, they were to advocate principles rather than fight battles, and seek to win hearts by influence, rather than crush them by physical force.

" *Q.* How far may we expect the clergy, who have

sworn to the constitution, to be of service, supposing them to remain ?

" *A.* This portion of the clergy are, like the Constitutionalists, convinced that they would be expelled and punished after a counter-revolution, and are therefore interested in preventing it. A large number of the most despicable members of this class having, under Robespierre, abjured the priesthood and denied all religion, those who remain consider themselves as of the faithful, profess the greatest zeal for the Catholic faith, and are ruled by their bishops, who put forth mandates and pastoral instructions, and direct the publication of an ecclesiastical periodical, written for the purpose of proving that the jurors are in no sense schismatics, that there exists but one Church, and that they are its perfectly lawful ministers. Most of the jurors would again submit to the monarchy and the ancient Church, if their conduct were buried in oblivion and their benefices preserved to them : they have influence in many provinces, and might do much harm by exerting themselves to hinder, as far as possible, the full and complete restoration of the orthodox Church.

" *Q.* If the non-juring clergy were to be recalled and to return, would it not be possible to introduce into France a system which might content scrupulous consciences, and be administered (for a time at least) without the aid of a hierarchy, excepting a few bishops for the purpose of ordaining priests ?

" *A.* I cannot answer this question, which is not in my line. I will only observe that, a hierarchy exists in the constitutional Church ; and the people will probably, in default of any other, content themselves with that.

" *Q*. Is there any unfavorable disposition towards the Princes ? And, in the affirmative case, what should be done to win back opinion ?

" *A*. The prevailing opinion represents the Princes and the emigrants as implacable and irreconcileable enemies, from whom no more liberty, treaty, security, or mercy, is to be expected than from Robespierre. The writings, daily published abroad, have made this prejudice as strong as it can be. I have pointed out in the notes the only means of diminishing it ; such as, declarations in which the predominating sentiment should be treated with forbearance ; public proceedings to prove the sincerity of professions, and the most signal disavowal of all those incendiary pamphleteers, all those frantic slaughterers, who, in the army of Condé, in pot-houses, in society, talk as Genghis-Khan did not talk at the head of 200,000 Tartars.

" *Q*. What is the accusation against the Princes ? What is feared ?

" *A*. They are accused of an utter abomination of all liberty, of exclusive attachment to the first two orders of the state, of inexorable resentment against all who shared in the errors of the revolution ; of having stirred up the war, of allying themselves with the foreign powers, contemplating the re-establishment of despotic power, and bestowing their confidence on persons who can inspire in France nothing but fear of their principles and designs.

" *Q*. Up to what point does the rural population lay stress on its emancipation from tithes and seignorial rights ?

" *A*. The rural population will never surrender the

emancipation from tithes, and it could only be by great dexterity, and after repeated efforts, that it could be induced to give compensation for the feudal dues.   They are pretty nearly unanimous as to these two advantages, which the revolution procured them.

" *Q*. What means might be proposed for encouraging the well-affected, and arming them against the evil-minded ?

" *A*. The notes furnish an answer to that question ; but it cannot be solved till a definition shall have been given of those whom it is intended to comprise among the well-affected, and those who are considered evil-minded.   In the sense of emigrant pamphlets and talk, the well-affected are reduced to the Vendeans, the Chouans, and a handful of individuals in each town, individuals absolutely destitute of means, credit and energy.

" *Q*. What is the temper of the army ?   What means can be employed to win it over—distinguishing the feelings of the officer from the soldiers ?   Does the general possess the influence attributed, and fairly belonging to him, over the subaltern officers, and these over their soldiers ?   In Dumouriez's time, experience showed that the representatives in the Convention had more influence over the spirit of the army than the generals.   There is reason to believe that this disposition is altered.   Now, a knowledge of all these particulars is necessary, in order to carry on the work it is expedient to commence.

" *A*. The reports relative to the temper of the army are so contradictory, that it would be rash in me to define the sentiments of the officers and the soldiers.   Fanatical against the foreign enemy, passive instruments of the

Convention in the interior, they exhibit, unmistakeably, these two symptons alone, and these are as certain as their sorry condition and discontent.

" The general does not possess more personal influence at present, than did La Fayette and Dumouriez. It is twenty to one that, in a conflict between the authority of the military chief, and that of the deputy from the Convention, the latter would gain. The fall in assignats, the immoderate increase in the price of provisions, and the misery to which these two causes must reduce the soldiers, will beyond a doubt abate their submission more and more, unless new victories should further keep up their excitement."

The final question in a postscript was the most delicate ; and the reply was frank to a degree that would have been cruel, had it not been imperatively necessary.

" Q. What effect did the death of the young King produce ? Favorable or unfavorable to the monarchy ? What are its consequences in relation to the actual King ?

" A. The death of the young King strongly affected honest men, disconcerted the monarchists, astonished the public. It was forgotten at Paris as quickly as the taking of Luxembourg : it only served to quicken the pity felt for the Princess Royal. Under the circumstances, his loss is a calamity : it has deferred the restoration of monarchy, and serves as a basis for the coalition aimed at between the Republicans and the Constitutionalists. As regent, his Majesty was comparatively unthought of ; as king, he is dreaded."

These questions were doubtless sincere. To address them to the intractable Mallet du Pan, was to ask

seriously for truth without circumlocution; but it soon
became evident that this desire had arisen with the persuasion that the recent change would render that truth more
palatable.   The language held by the majority of the emigrants and counsellors, favourably listened to at Verona, in
the little court of the new King of France, must have
rendered unpleasing the candour of Mallet, and especially,
perhaps, the silence to which he condemned, as among the
King's chances, certain qualities of mind on which the
latter piqued himself, and which were accounted high by
his suite.   Baron d'Erlach, on returning from Constance,
where he had met a great number of Frenchmen, wrote to
Mallet :——" They make much ado just now, and are greatly
taken up with the subtle, delicate, amiable, recondite, and
indeed rather affected turns of thought and expression contained in the numerous letters of their new King—who,
for a king, appears to me to aspire a good deal after distinction in such matters."

Scarcely had Mallet quitted Schaffhausen, when he had
occasion to perceive that his information would be fruitless.
He wrote the following letter to Marshal de Castries :

LETTER FROM MALLET DU PAN TO MARSHAL DE CASTRIES.

" M. le Maréchal,

" I hear from Constance that you have not left, and that
it is uncertain whether you will leave, for Verona, to which
place I had the honour to address you two successive mis-
sives.   In the second, to comply with the desire of M. de
Sainte-Aldegonde, I informed you that my travelling expenses to his house had amounted to sixteen louis d'or,

leaving to your convenience the time and the means of defraying the sum.

" I have, at the present moment, nothing to add to the extract enclosed from a letter I wrote yesterday to Berne. The state of affairs deteriorates more and more. His Majesty had honoured M. Mounier, two months ago, with a letter no less decisively written than judiciously conceived, and which expressed a plan of conduct extremely wise in conjunctures less disastrous ; but the objections to making it public struck M. Mounier and myself sufficiently to make him resolve to keep it private : he had the honour of informing Baron de Flachslanden. And now, this letter, sent from Verona to Paris, is printed and circulates there, and has produced the effects we saw reason to fear. I find with deep regret that self deception as to the state of men's minds and the affairs and resources of the interior is preserved in, and that false informations are relied upon. I can be of no further service in the system which is pursued, and which will soon occasion unavailing regret.

"Receive the assurance, &c., &c.

" P.S. I have received letters from Paris to the 22nd. On the 18th, there was a very serious uproar at the Opera, where the young men—that is, the remnant of the old National Guard, compelled the playing of the *Réveil du peuple*. The Convention was overwhelmed with imprecations. The cavalry made its appearance, and was repulsed. Three actors who were arrested, were demanded on the following day by the young men, sixty of whom are imprisoned, as well as several journalists. The excitement, desperation, and alarm are very great."

But these efforts of thought and labour, which were profitlessly undermining Mallet's health, were at least recompensed on this occasion by the intimate friendship which arose between himself and the worthy nobleman who had been despatched to him at Schaffhausen.   Count François de Sainte-Aldegonde, of a highly distinguished Flemish family, was the model of a nobleman ; of elevated heart, delicate mind, and most amiable in intercourse : openhearted, devotedly loyal without being a courtier, extremely moderate, and of very sound judgment.   The austerity of Mallet, whom he had known at Brussels, did not repel him: he could appreciate the generous soul which animated the somewhat misanthropical thinker, the often severe judge of men and their errors.   A brisk correspondence was afterwards kept up between the intimate of Charles X. and the Genevese republican, and the reciprocal sentiments of esteem and affection were never altered.   We will gather from this political correspondence some confidential communications, suppressing as far as possible the repetitions unavoidable in such an intercourse.   Indeed, Mallet's correspondence comprises the whole interest of his biography for this year and for that which followed, and here we shall meet him ; choosing from among the letters written or received by him, such fragments as relate to public events, or to the personages who acted in them.

CHAPTER VIII.

1795.

Letters from Mallet du Pan to Count de Sainte-Aldegonde and Marshal de Castries (July to September, 1795), on the state of the interior, the plans and expeditions of the emigrants—*Sortie* from Quiberon—Mounier—The Constitutionalists.

LETTER FROM MALLET DU PAN TO COUNT DE SAINTE-ALDEGONDE.

" Berne, July 9, 1795.

" WHEN I arrived here last Tuesday evening, I found bundles of letters from Paris. I at once took my pen and completed the note by the accompanying supplement, which I recommend to your care and persuasive powers: it indeed deserves the most serious consideration. The resources are extensive ; we must make use of these, and not pursue a mere chimera ; the first steps will be decisive ones. The necessity for a central point on which the Marshal insists, is urgent—is imperative. Switzerland is thronged with hare-brained individuals, and emissaries of every kind, all the envoys plenipotentiary, agents for five or six powers. Some come from Verona, some start from Condé's army ; the English employ a host. All these deputies babble, intrigue, heap folly upon folly, compromise the Princes, ruin the cause, and repel all sensible men. A stop must be put to this disorder ; immense sums are wasted on these follies. If they continue, I shall withdraw altogether ; for it is impossible to arrange or do anything amid such a labyrinth of views, envoys and authorities. In Paris the sensible monarchists are uniting in one aim ; those in the interior must be listened to, if anything tangible is to be undertaken. I hope that ideas are more altered in your vicinity (Count d'Artois) than is the case at Verona and Mulheim. Montgaillard has just shown me a declaration of royalism and fidelity sent him by Count d'Entraigues, who writes him word that if the King has not spoken to him of his last work,* he thinks it is on account of the eulogium which he (Montgaillard) has made of me ; that the King hopes he will not swear in verba magistri ; that he (d'Entraigues) acknowledges as royalists those only who have never departed from our holy laws ; but that he favours me so far as to doubt my entire devotion to the Jacobins. I send you the very expressions of the original letter. This singular compound of audacity, insolence and bad faith is certainly laughable ; but what deserves our tears is, that the writer speaks and acts in the King's name, and appears undoubtedly high in his confidence. It should be understood that confidence cannot be shared between M. d'Entraigues and myself ; and that if his directions are to be followed, mine should be thrown unread into the fire. I will do everything, except ever resort to means which I conscientiously believe calculated to ruin the royal cause beyond recovery.

* " L'an 1795," by Count de Montgaillard.   Hamburg, 1795.

" The new constitution is about to be discussed. The public view it in a thousand opposite lights : all sensible men deride it ; the people laugh at it ; the boobies hold forth. ' It is not the thing yet,' was remarked the other day by a leading republican of my acquiantance in a circle of the capital. The majority of the National Guard is of the eighty-nine school. Raffet, their commander, is a constitutionalist. The Jacobins are on the alert, watching and spying : the Sablon camp, arrrived at Marly, amounts to thirteen thousand men. The wishes and endeavours of all worthy men aim at an appeal to the primary assemblies, and at inducing them to acknowledge the chief of the nation. The Chouans kill and pillage indiscriminately : as yet the war is not renewed, nor indeed is there any perceptible movement in La Vendée : Tallien is proposed as Pro-consul of the Western army.. It is reported that General Canclaux has been dismissed—what a pity ! Lyons has verified your predictions and submitted without a word. All its cannons and ten thousand guns have been taken away. The Jesuits have emigrated."

TO THE SAME.

"July 16, 1795.

" A coalition between the republicans and the constitutionalists is under discussion at Paris. To the latter is promised total oblivion, a share in employments and profits, the recall of La Fayette by the Convention, which would give in exchange the German hostages ; finally, the return of the constitutional emigrants and the restitution of their property. I have not kept the causes of these overtures

from Verona, nor will will I disguise them to you : their
first effect will be the indefinite adjournment of the
monarchy, if the majority of the constitutionalists acquiesce in these proposals. The exasperation of the old
emigrants against the later refugees, the propositions of
members of Condé's soldiers, who, at the table d'hôte at
Basle, devote to the wheel all who have not shared their
sentiments ; this profession of faith published in a host
of daily pamphlets ; finally, the young King's death, which
would consign the constitutionalists to the mercy of the
emigrants, were the new King acknowledged, are the principal causes of these negociations between the republicans
and the constitutionalists.

" D'Entraigues has had reprinted and circulated in Paris
his ' Observations sur la conduite des Puissances Co-
alisées,' in which he pronounces all those who took the
oath of the *Jeu de Paume* to be first class regicides ;
declares that man's justice cannot pardon them ; and in
his scale of punishments and ignominy, gives the monarchical revolutionists precedence of the Jacobins. Himself
and friends have accompanied this incendiary document
by some atrocious pamphlets, which serve as its comment.
In one of them, entitled ' Révélations Importantes,' a
boastful avowal is made of their party's having provoked
all the excesses of the Jacobins, in order to outwit the constitutionalists and the monarchists, to urge the revolution to
extremes, and to arm the powers. I leave you to imagine
the impression these horrors make in Paris : every one has
read in them his doom, and said : ' Between such implacable enemies, and the republicans who invite us with open
arms, we cannot hesitate.'

"The moment the news came of the disembarcation on the coast of La Vendée, Doulcet announced, in the name of the Committee of Public Safety, on the 1st of this month : ' Hitherto the republicans have fought for glory ; to-day every Frenchman must fight for his life. Anglo-maniac republicans of 1789, constitutionalists of 1791, one doom awaits you ; march then all of you, march together to exterminate these executioners who thirst for vengeance only, and are as unwilling to pardon those who, after talking of liberty, desired an impossible monarchy, as they are to forgive the founders of the Republic.'

"Such is the feeling prevalent throughout three-fourths of Paris : a royalist, extravagant in theory, but judicious in practice, and an acute observer, wrote me word on the 5th of this month; 'You must expect, on account of this invasion, to see all parties rush in a spirit of emulation to fire on the enemy. All constitutional royalists, and all who took the slightest part in the Revolution of 1789, have been repelled.'

"They speak of clemency and pardon ! Henry IV., the conqueror of Paris, in pardoning his disarmed subjects, really showed mercy, because it was in his power to punish ; but is that indeed our case ? Is it believed that the amnesty signed at Verona in favour of the first revolution-ists, affects one of them ? If beneath the sword of the all-powerful republicans, they laboured, at their own proper peril, to cause the King to be recognized, would they not look rather for gratitude than for pardon ? Such acts derive all their force from the position of the doer : and besides, they ought not to be belied daily by a multitude of speeches and writings. Never will this immense majority

of monarchists of all shades, and repentant revolutionists
surrender at discretion : if this evident fact be disregarded,
an abyss of calamities gapes before us.   All will demand
guarantees, conditions, and will seek them in the form of
government.   But the subject is exhausted : I will not
return to it.   I perceive an obstinate intention of persisting
in the course adopted ever since 1789.

" The constitution is generally hooted at; but it will not
be the less freely accepted, on pain of death.   The
monarchists are labouring to get it submitted to the
primary assemblies ; but, disunited as they now are, their
efforts will be incomplete."

TO THE SAME.

" August, 1, 1795.

" You may take this as tolerably certain relative to the
state of Brittany on the 15th July.   The royalists encamped at Carnac compose, together with the Chouans,
from eighteen to twenty thousand men, masters of the
peninsula of Quiberon, maintaining themselves there, and
unable to extend beyond two leagues.   They have not even
kept Auray, nor dared to advance to Vannes, evacuated as
it is.   Their first steps had sown terror.   But confidence
revived : the Convention commands thirty thousand men
in Brittany : fifteen thousand men of the Army of the
North were crossing Normandy to reach it.   Musters are
marched forward from all quarters, and they are but feebly
resisted, as I expected.   Had the emigrants been in
strength, more active, more enterprising, they would have
arrived at Rennes unopposed.   Now, the army is between
the province and them.   So long as this position lasts,

do not look for the adhesion of those in the rear of the army. The road from Vannes to Lorient is intercepted : bread sells at fifty francs in the latter town, for which some fears are entertained, as well as for Belle-Isle. In general, Paris is not in the least alarmed at this expedition, and very few persons expect the slightest success from it.

" The Spanish peace, signed at Basle on the 23rd July, will restore two armies to the Convention : of these, one will march towards Italy ; the other to La Vendée, which, on the 15th, had not again taken up arms. It is strange and admirable to behold a grandson of Louis XIV., swear fraternity and concord to successors of Ravaillac, reeking with the blood of a king of France, of his son, his wife, his sister. This treaty consists of fifteen articles. Spain cedes its share of St. Domingo to France, and regains the conquered territory.

" This treaty is said to be directed wholly against England : it is the result of the jealousy inspired by the colonial and encroaching system of that power, whose fatal policy has lost the Antilles and now arms a counter-coalition.

" You wish me to labour at dimishing the hatred borne by the French against the English. My dear Count, how can you expect the words of an individual like me to destroy a prejudice, the work of six centuries, which is become a mania, and is justified by the conduct of the English ministry these three years ? It only is able to diminish this fatal and profound impression, not by un-meaning declarations, but by positive acts ; by recognizing the King, promising the restitution of its own conquests,

and formally engaging not to interfere with the independence or integrity of the kingdom.

"One of my friends wrote me word from Paris on the
26th : Mme. de Tourzel is always the same, attached to her
masters and regretting them.   She has failed to obtain
the favour of remaining with Madame.   But every day
she goes to a terrace near the Temple, whence she can see
the Princess walking : she cannot speak with her.   Mme
de Chantereine, one of the late Queen's ladies in waiting,
is with Madame."

TO THE SAME.

" August 2, 1795.

"I wrote to you yesterday, my dear Count, and I take
up my pen again on opening my letter from Paris of the
28th.   It is with great grief that I announce to you the
melancholy result of this landing, which has always
inspired me with more fear than hope.

"On the 20th of July, Hoche attacked the emigrants
and the Chouans, who had joined, or rather had allowed
themselves to be surrounded in the neighbouring island,
to the number of ten thousand men.   The fort Penthièvre
was taken by storm ; there was a hot fight there ; but the
whole of the royalists, prevented from embarking, apparently from contrary winds, were at last cut to pieces or
taken prisoners.   Rohan, Béon, Dumas, d'Hervilles,
Périgord, have laid down their arms : Sombreuil is a
prisoner ; the magazines of muskets, ammunition, and uni-
forms all are in the hands of the enemy.

" Tallien, arriving from Lorient, announced this victory on the 9th Thermidor (July 27th) to the Convention in great detail. Imagine what a sensation the approach of the anniversary has made ! Let us renounce for ever all those chivalrous expeditions, which are destitute of common sense and shackle the resources of the country. We are now thrown back—perhaps, for several years—at the moment when with prudence, management, and conduct, a port of safety might have been attained. The prisons and scaffolds again receive their victims, and the royalists in the interior are reduced to the most deplorable situation."

TO THE SAME.

" August 16, 1795.

" Ah ! without doubt, my dear friend, all is vicissitude and change in this disordered world : it was only the imbeciles who did not think so, in desiring obstinately to carry their principles into practice. Good God ! I fancy I hear Brissot or Robespierre.

" I told you that affairs suddenly became worse since the landing ; to-day they take their necessary and imperative course. During the landing, the Committees have been in the ascendant. Sieyès, escorted by Louvet, Sevestre, Rewbel Guyomard and others, seized upon this moment to re-establish the terror ; no one could or durst speak of royalty, while the *émigrés*, allied with the English, talk of it in Brittany with arms in their hands.

" This incident over, and the peace of Spain, like the general peace, being looked upon as very near, people's minds have recovered their elasticity, the Convention its disorder, the sections their resistance, the press its liberty, and honest men their courage. Those who think with Sieyès have been checked in all their measures; they have sounded the tocsin in a multitude of pamphlets. I cannot tell you all that has been written daily during the last three weeks against the Convention generally and especially. The leaders became conscious that the liberty of the press, after having created the revolution, was about to destroy its own offspring; they issued *lettres de cachet*, and sealed up the presses. Futile efforts! a general outcry was raised. The section of the Arsenal has just demanded in a body from the Convention, the liberation of the editor of the 'Gazette Universelle,' a paper advocating liberty without bounds. Those who voted against the death of the King, have again begun to speak out: they have effected the abolition of certificates of citizenship, and the withdrawal of the decree which protected the Montagnards by submitting them to a committee of the Convention, and not to the ordinary tribunals. No denunciation of royalism is any longer received by the sections. The eighty-nines dominate more and more, and have three-fourths of the public papers on their side. Besides, the hatred for the horrors of the revolution becomes more pronounced each day, and in it are included avowedly the 10th of August, 1792, and the 21st of January, 1793.

"But if they wish to lose all, they will repeat the foolish attempts of Quiberon, the extravagances of Coblentz, the romances of chivalry, the Dunois, the Gastons de Foix—the kings who talk of conquering their kingdom when they have not a batallion, and who speak of Verona as Henri IV. spoke, and could speak, upon the plains of

Ivry. · In the name of Heaven, my dear friend, once for all, let this flood of absurdities have an end; silence your impudent pamphleteers, shave your moustaches, tell the emigrants to desist at length from cutting their own throats, if they desire to re-enter France and recover their possessions. If they wish their country not to remain a Republic, let them be quiet, and not mix up their unfortunate interference with the progress of internal events, which they counteract incessantly. It is not our part to regulate the interior ; that, on the contrary, must regulate us. The monarchists deprecate nothing so much as our grand measures, our grand armies, our grand projects, from which we have obtained such grand results.

" I desire general peace, and look for it. The powers have certainly no better alternative. The empire will come round : you may expect the Kings of Sweden and of Naples to imitate without delay the example of Spain, grown weary of waging war in favour of the English. All these European broils no longer concern us. Whether or not they acknowledge the King, does not signify a straw ; it is France which must recognize him, and not a posse of strangers, beaten, spit upon, and hated. If he is of another opinion, he will end, like the King of Sidon, by turning gardener."

LETTER FROM MALLET DU PAN TO MARSHAL DE CASTRIES.

"August 28, 1795.

" Monsieur le Maréchal,

" I have received the letter you did me the honour of addressing me on the 13th of this month, and the order for sixteen louis, which has been paid. Your very obliging enquiry on this subject, Monsieur le Maréchal, would heighten, were it possible, the gratitude and attachment I feel towards you. I have lived and can subsist for some months to come, on such fragments as were saved from the ruins of France and Geneva ; hitherto I have not experienced physical wants, and this is much. The uncertainty of events, hope not yet lost, my connexion with France, have hitherto prevented my settling ; I know the limit of my resources ; this will determine the duration of my present mode of life, and of my irresolution. Whoever can barely live, must not abuse the benevolence of those victims whose misfortunes he shares, and must feel honoured by your generosity, whilst postponing its exercise to a less calamitous period.*

" In the work which has undergone your inspection, and of which your approbation is the recompense, I have depicted with courageous sincerity that which concurrent facts, reports, letters and consultations convince me is the true state of France. My warmest wish would be to

---

* We cannot forbear doing justice to the spirit of order and simplicity of manners which furthered this honourable independence. Mallet habitually kept an exact account of his expenses, and of his moderate resources, which he never exceeded. The Bernese aristocracy was not very hospitable, and Mallet's life essentially domestic. His daily recreation was a stroll, usually a solitary one—giving opportunity for meditation—in the lovely environs of Berne, where, as in England, the woods and meadows are intersected with paths ; and even at a period when his family had their meal from a tavern, at the rate of ten-pence per head, he did not neglect the education of his children, and even afforded them masters of Italian and music.

furnish another picture ; but the painter is not answerable for nature, nor must his intentions be impugned because he does not steep his palette in rose-water, &c."

LETTER FROM MALLET DU PAN TO COUNT DE SAINTE-ALDEGONDE.

"September 16, 1795.

" I have received no answer, nor any kind of notice from Verona, except two lines from the Marshal, informing me of the reimbursement of the expenses of my little journey. He adds concisely, that his views tally with mine, but that opposite counsels counteract my views and opinions. Mounier has been treated even worse than myself : having complained of their printing his Majesty's reply to him without giving him any previous notice, which might expose his family, in France, to incovenience, M. de Flachslanden answered him with contemptuous harshness. It is a settled plan, my dear Count ; you see how speedily they have carried out the principles of the declaration by disgracing the Prince de Poix and depriving him of his office. He has written the King a noble letter, full of spirit and energy : he concludes by protesting against the assurance given him by the King, that ' this act of his will would remain secret.'——' My honour demands,' answers the Prince, ' that this act of your will should be public, in order that my offers and your refusal, your commands and my submission, may be known. On this same day, the 10th of August, three years ago,' he adds, ' I covered his Majesty, Louis XVI, with my own body, to protect him from the shots fired

at him in the Tuileries; for six weeks I heard the price
of my head cried about ; I have lost my father and mother
on the scaffold in the cause of his Majesty.   After all·
this, I had expected some consideration from the successor *and brother* of Louis XVI.'

"The royalists within France are in despair at this
conduct of the King and the emigrants.   I have received
from persons of the most distinguished name and most
deserving of respect, bitter reproaches on the subject.
They complain, that the emigrants set the heads of their
relatives and friends on the throw of the dice ; that they have
no idea of what France has become, and that their language
and projects are an order for the martyrdom of all connected with them in the interior.

"The monarchists are defending themselves at this
moment against the Convention, to escape from tyranny
far rather than to restore royalty.   It is wished for, but
without any feeling of devotedness ; and out of the kingdom everything has been done calculated to destroy the
germs of its reproduction.   The Duke of Orleans and his
young brother gain partisans ; but the King loses his
every day, as well as men who would have become his
adherents, had this unhappy prince been guided in a course
conformable with his own situation and that of France.

" Paris (that is to say, the sections) almost unanimously
has deprived the Convention of its powers point blank,
and annulled its decree of re-eligibility ; they pronounce
with rare vigour.   This is the fruit of the dispositions I
have more than once stated to you.   Meaux, Versailles,
Chartres, Montargis, the greater number of the environs
of the capital, Strasburg unanimously, have imitated the

sections; but Rouen, Lyons, Grenoble, Besançon have already accepted under the influence of the terrorists. I fear lest Paris should succumb, and have the majority against it."

TO THE SAME.

"September 23.

"My dear Count,

"I have received your letter of the 10th. My constant desire gains strength that they should renounce these privateering expeditions once and for ever, and deign to be persuaded that the best service they can do the cause is, to do nothing at all. Be quite sure, that, as often as, and whenever you show yourselves in arms, you become the allies of the Republic, and that you produce no effect but that of perpetuating the power of the Convention, paralyzing the royalists, driving them to despair, raising up a thousand dangers against them, and reviving the detestation of the emigrant system.

"I am so convinced of this truth that, if the courageous and unanimous resistance of Paris should triumph, I am quite for disbanding Condé's army forthwith, recalling M. d'Artois to the continent, dismounting your white and black cockades, and laying aside your hostile attitude altogether. Without this, and without a council around the King, composed of men in whom the nation may repose confidence, the new monarchy will not be your work. You will be repulsed by its restorers as well as by its destroyers, and his Majesty will yet linger out long years of exile with you. Once more, lay down your impotent thunderbolt—sit is a game at chess you have to play, not drums to beat.

" On the 18th, the sections maintained their attitude ; the nine departments nearest the capital had adhered to its example almost unanimously.   The influence of Paris and its environs is immense.   The hatred of republicanism has manifested itself there most signally : the papers describe the spirit which animates the sections.   It is the patriots of 1789, the friends of the constitutionalists united with the royalists, who have the good sense to cling to them, and the republicans are in disgust, who have produced and regulated this impulse. Dumas is named Elector as well as Gorgerau, Quatremère de Quincy, Lacretelle, Chéron, Peuchet, my successor on the ' Mercure ' up to the 10th of August, and many others belonging either to the right side of the Legislative Assembly of 1791 and 1792, or to the first municipality of Paris.   If the re-election of two-thirds of the Convention be rejected, this party will compose almost the whole of the new legislative body, at least for all the places refusing the re-election.

" Remember what I told you at Schaffhausen of the influence the constitutionalists would infallibly recover. Yet war, to the uttermost against them, is more the less persisted in from without indiscriminately.   With a million crowns, a million livres, the victory of the sections would have been gained decisively.   Reiterated and urgent applications have been made to me from Paris on this point. But what can I do ?   I have solicited, remonstrated with the ministers, the nobles — not a doit.   They will spend thousands of millions on fighting, but not a crown on self-preservation.   I could tell you abominable things on this subject : my blood boils when I think of it."

CHAPTER IX.

1795—1796.

Military events of the autumn of 1795—Letter of Mallet du Pan—Vendémiaire—Letter of M. de Hardenberg—Mallet maintains three great political correspondences—Letters of the Chevalier de Panat, and de Lally-Tollendal.

The correspondence of Mallet and his friend was interrupted by the military events of the autumn of 1795. In the midst of its victorious career, the French army of the Rhine was suddenly repulsed, but rallied with an unexpected vigour and rapidity. Taking advantage of the indignation and the desperation of the Austrians, forsaken by the Prussians, and reduced to their own resources, General Clerfayt, animated by the critical position of his army, executed with impetuosity and firmness a series of dexterous manœuvres which changed the destiny of the campaign.

In the interval, Paris has been the theatre of other events, far more important to the destiny of France. The strife between the Convention and the sections, that is to say—between those who wished for the Republic, and those who did not—had prematurely broken out in Vendémiaire. But this new 10th of August had to encounter, in the place of a

King amiable and weak, a power determined to defend
itself.   The letters of Mallet upon the occurrences of this
day, fatal to his cause, deserve to belong to his history :
moreover, they present a useful lesson to parties who prefer
their passions to their principles, and even to their interests.

LETTER OF MALLET DU PAN TO COUNT DE SAINTE-ALDEGONDE.

"October 28, 1795.

" The victories of M. de Clerfayt having set free the
means of communication, my dear Count, I take up
my pen.   Your last letter is dated the 2nd of October :
how many events have occurred since—and of what a
nature !   We have now fallen back again into a bottomless pit : it is those only who know by what efforts,
patience, writings, influences and faults on the part of
the Convention, Paris has been roused from its lethargy,
that can form an opinion of the difficulty there would
be in bringing back such conjunctures.   This affair of
the sections is, like all others, regarded in a false light
abroad.   The object of the enterprise was mistaken, and
the limits which prudence should have prescribed to them.
Our emigrants are generally well satisfied with the catastrophe, because a number of constitutionalists were mixed
up in the movements, because they did not at once don
the livery of the old *régime*, and because the loyalty
of its prime movers could not generally show its sixteen
quarterings.   On the triumph of the sections, the first act
of the legislative body would have been the restoration
of monarchy, the restitution of conquests, that of their property to the emigrants, their recall, and a general peace.

" The electoral body has nominated all those members of the Convention who acted in concert with the sections, and in favour of the new third——Messieurs d'Ambray, late Advocate-General in the parliament, a man of first-rate merit ; Lafont-Ladebat and Muraire, royalists of the Legislative Assembly ; Gibert des Molières, a notary of the old school ; Portalis, senior, a distinguished advocate at the Aix parliament, and a decided royalist, and Le Couteulx de Canteleu. The legislative body will be a regular Horace's monster ; there we shall see the aristocrat sitting beside the Jacobin, the Constitutionalist by the heroes of the 10th of August. Conceive the scenes of such a chaos! it must have opened to-day. The Thermidorists, terrified at owing their safety to the Jacobins, already dread their rising again. They are quite willing for terrorism, but not for its ancient chiefs, whom they have persecuted, and who would soon pay them in kind.

" I will not hazard any conjecture : none but a madman would venture to do so. Had the King followed the plan we suggested, he would have become the head and director of the sectional movement. The declaration served only to divide, irritate, incense, and chill. The Doulcets, Bourdons, Legendres and Talliens said to the people : " That's what the King promises you," and the King replies : " Quite true ; I will sign it." How guilty are those who dictated this manifesto, and who regulate affairs at Verona ! You know that Marshal de Castries has returned to Eisenach ; he has not written me one line : the silence maintained by him at Verona is a formal reprobation ; for this I can console myself, but not for these mad measures.

" The Chevalier de Guer has been despatched to Lyons to manufacture a Vendée in that town and the adjacent provinces. The Prince of Condé has sent with him a logger-headed Jacobin of the aristocracy, named Teyssonnet, aide-de-camp to his Highness. This Teyssonnet was despatched to Franche-Comté three months ago, to get up a Vendée. On reaching the inn there, he declared before ten persons his mission, his project, and that he brought five hundred louis-d'ors for its execution. Fifty emissaries of this stamp are employed : two have just been sent to Paris, to carry off the Princess Royal on her issuing from the Temple, and conduct her to La Vendée, in order to liberate her from the Emperor.

" All this is no fiction ; not one word of it is false. You will hear of La Vendée, Haute-Loire, great hopes, great doings in those quarters : well, let me tell you that the whole matter reduces itself to five or six thousand armed or unarmed peasants in the environs of Issengeaux; considerable forces have been marched against them, and they will vanish within a month. I have already named the machinators, and leave you to deduce the rest. We owe this vast plan to D'Entraigues."

The following letter reverts to this topic :

TO THE SAME.

" November 4, 1795.

" Once more we are fallen. into an abyss, of which I can measure neither the width nor the depth. I fancy you have been ill-informed on the subject of the sections : whoever may have doubted their enthusiastic royalism, has only to glance at the new third returned by the electors of Paris a week after Barras's cannonading, the incarcerations, the shootings, the decrees of terrorism. Do you think that men who chose as representatives M. d'Ambray, M. de Bonnières, the Abbé Morellet, Gibert des Molières, Portalis, are Republicans, or even Constitutionalists of 1791 ? Out of eighty-five thousand voters, seventy thousand desired a king ; and, once victors, would have attacked the revolution, its principles and actors, and the Republic, with a weapon a hundred times more formidable than all the armies of Europe. He who denies this is an ignoramus, such as the Abbé de Calonne, who in his prosy ' Courrier,' is pleased to doubt which party deserves our good wishes, and adds that the sections are too republican for us to feel any interest in this quarrel.

" The sections have succumbed, because their onset was premature ; fire-brands were cast among them from this country, from London and from Mulheim : they were induced to join battle without cannon, munitions, plan, or general. They were playing a game at chess, and carrying off a piece daily : with or without the two thirds, their force would have remained entire after the formation of the legislative body ; to strike terror was enough without giving a taste of their quality by musket shot. But national impetuosity waits for no opportunity—presumption makes sure of the most precarious success, and resentment allows no time for events to ripen. Believe me, the original plan was laid down by men of weight, better royalists than the babblers who bear that name, and than the round table of Mulheim. These should have been allowed to act, instead of the sections being prematurely incited to an insurrection, which was desired by the conventionalists. People might have been certain that the Committees would not imitate Louis XVI. by shutting themselves up in the Tuileries.

"The Convention had dug its own grave; we have filled it up again. The new Assembly was composed on the 4th. It is divided into two distinct classes, two fundamental factions, that of the regicides, and that of the non-regicides, headed by Lanjuinais, La Rivière, Boissy-d'Anglas, Fermont, or supported by the new third of whom three fourths are royalists. The general peace, and even that of the empire, are adjourned. This would not be an indifferent occurrence, in another age and with other men; but . . . Twenty-seven thousand millions of assignats are current, not counting forgeries; I have this *first hand*."

TO THE SAME.

"November 12, 1795.

"Since the 5th October, my dear Count, I have received no news of you—my man is not come, and has not written: fear has put a stop to everything; besides, this infernal correspondence of one of the agents of Verona with the master, has rendered Switzerland suspected. It is not prudent to send any letter there containing suspicious matter; with great difficulty I have some crumbs of news from my correspondents.

"This memorable month of October ushers in most important results: the aim of partial acts of pacification is missed, and the Emperor is once more become the arbiter of peace and war in Germany. Victory will probably put an end to manœuvring at Basle, to the abortive congress, to separate peaces :——it will not be the fault of the Baron de Hardenberg, I can assure you, if all this is not soon brought about. He hopes (between ourselves) to return in a month to Anspach : I have passed three days with him here. In his character of minister, he was not much elated by the extent of the success of the Imperialists ; but as a loyal, honourable and most sensible man (as he is), he highly approves of it. He is disgusted at the tone, the discourses, the insolence of all the French agents and representatives ; he is quite convinced of the impossibility of treating safely and honourably with such a sort of men. The choice of the Directory——of which he has been informed here——has been the finishing stroke ; for the five viziers who have been elected are the suggestors of the passage of the Rhine, and the reunion of Belgium, the promoters of conquest, and of the disorganization of Europe."

TO THE SAME.

" December 12, 1795.

" The whole diplomatic body has decamped (from Basle). The Baron of Hardenberg must have set off yesterday ; the ambassadors from the Palatinate, Hesse and Wurtemburg are now on their road back to Germany. M. de Clerfayt has given this congress its deathblow : the negociations are completely broken off ; the recall of M. Barthélemy was the finishing stroke. Though this minister still remains provisionally, his disgrace may be regarded as complete and irrevocable.

" Before you receive this letter, you will have heard of

the shameful defeat of Baron de Vins on the 23rd November, and the consequent imminent peril of Piedmont and Lombardy. This disaster once more alters the face of affairs, and will destroy much of the effect of the successes on the Rhine. The Directory will now right itself, adverse courts will sink back into their terrors, the French army will regain its reputation, and requisitions will be as easy as ever.

" I see, on the other hand, that M. de Clerfayt finds plenty of occupation in the Hundsrück, where Jourdan has assembled sixty thousand men. Kreutznach has been ceded to him perforce. I should not be surprised to see the Austrians compelled to recross the Rhine.

As we see by one of the preceding letters, M. de Hardenberg had returned to Mallet du Pan and had seen him at Berne. Some days afterwards, on leaving Switzerland, he asked him to resume the political correspondence, interrupted by the peace of Basle, in the spring of the first year, as we have mentioned.

LETTER FROM BARON DE HARDENBERG TO MALLET DU PAN.

"Zurich, December 13, 1795.

" Sir,

" Your letter of the 6th could only be handed me by M. Broë just at the moment of my departure from Basle, and I have much regretted my inability to cultivate his acquaintance, and prove to you, by the reception I should have been eager to give him, the value I attach to your recommendations. The intelligence which has reached me confirms all you say on the affairs of France. You must have heard of the extraordinary step which has been hazarded against Count Carletti. I am very anxious to ascertain the motive, which is yet unknown. One cannot too deeply bewail the fate which awaits France. May the most serious efforts be made to prevent the conflagration extending to the rest of Europe! Perhaps it is too late; but the means which still remain must not be neglected. If it were possible to compel the French Government to a satisfactory peace, the horrors which will not fail to disgrace France after that event would probably be the best remedy for the evil. You would exceedingly oblige me, Sir, by resuming—at least for some months—the course of that interesting correspondence, which was interrupted on my arrival at Basle. It is of great importance to me to watch the affairs of France as well as I possibly can, and your enlightened judgment, the views which you could give me, would be of infinite value. If you will grant me the favour I request, Sir, not only will you be by no means compromised, but, should you desire it, no one shall know that you write to me. Make your own terms, Sir, and direct your letters to Anspach, I pray you, until I inform you I am going to Berlin. My presence was absolutely useless, and perhaps even injurious at Basle. The plenipotentiaries of the Princes of the Empire who were there, have also quitted that spot. My wife begs you to accept her compliments, Sir, and I have the honour, &c. &c."

Mallet assented to M. de Hardenberg's desire, so that, at the end of 1795, he was keeping up three extensive correspondences. For some months he had that of the

Court of Lisbon, addressed to M. de Souza-Cotinho, who, on his part, wrote to him regularly, and on a footing of almost familiar intimacy.   On the other hand, all connexion had ceased with the English cabinet, which, harassed by the constant proceedings, and yielding, rather than assenting, to the policy of the emigrants, was bent on favouring the plan of descent.   Without sharing the suspicion which this conduct excited in some observing minds, Mallet du Pan had no indulgence for ministers who managed so ill the affairs of France, and but too well those of her tyrants.   Refraining from political conversations with Mr. Wickham, he received direct information from England only through his friends in London, some of whose interesting letters will find a place here.

There is much mention in these letters of the Count d'Artois.   This Prince, whom at that time many persons judged superior to his brother, and who had his secret party among the emigrants, is here represented under a not very favourable aspect.   The moderation for which Mallet gives him credit, is set to the account of his present adverse fortune ; and his views are not considered more intelligent than those of Louis XVIII., however he may make them appear to be so.   At all events it is curious to notice, that, with regard to the two brothers of Louis XVI., in the first years, opinion was absolutely opposed to the judgment which the two reigns of Louis XVIII. and Charles X. have enabled us to form definitely on their wisdom and political talents.   Further on, in the course of these Memoirs, we shall meet with other proofs of the art with which the Count d'Artois contrived to conceal the obstinacy of his views under an amiable exterior of flattering deference, and of a confidence which, in reality, he only felt for counsels dictated by himself.

LETTER FROM THE CHEVALIER DE PANAT TO MALLET DU PAN.

"London, January, 1796.

" I find at last, my dear friend, a safe opportunity of writing to you; it is the first that has offered since my arrival in London.   Montlosier and Malouet gave me news of you when they received them.   They have communicated to me your letters, which are always full of interest.   I have also noticed in them that you have not forgotten a man who is tenderly attached to you. . . . I left Brussels with Cardinal de la Rochefoucauld.   We stayed there till the last moment.   Business called me to London : I separated from my uncle.   I have done nothing in London, and I have had the misfortune to lose my brother here.   It is impossible to be more deeply wounded in my affections and interests at once.

" I have not sought to be placed in any French corps, because a naval officer of thirty-two years of age is but ill-fitted to be a lieutenant of infantry; my health was another obstacle.   And besides, my disfavour with the aristocratical party is such, that I should assuredly have obtained no employ if I had solicited it.   There remained that multitude of occupations, embraced by those noble French chevaliers, who wished to re-elevate the throne and the altar, and who shuddered at the very name of an accommodation. This resource was of no avail for me.   Such, my dear friend, is my sad situation : I wait for peace that my

lot may be fixed.   Then, whatever government may rule
in France, whether the present constitution be maintained,
or overthrown by the terrorists, I will go and offer myself to
the poniards of Rewbell or of Duheim, rather than perish of
opprobrium and hunger in a foreign land.   You will receive,
my dear friend, a little work which has appeared under the
name of one of my comrades, but which I have edited.
You will find in it some interesting details on the affair of
Quiberon, and you will be satisfied, I hope, with the spirit
in which it is written.   I have gathered this spirit of reason
and wisdom from your works and your conversations.

" You often tell us of the follies at Verona.   Alas ! my
dear friend, this folly is general and incurable.   How you
are deceived in thinking that there is any reason at the
brother's court !   We see all that near at hand, and we
sigh : no one has improved—no one has known how to
forget, how to learn anything.   All the chiefs of the aristocracy, all the men of influence, go far beyond the ideas
of Coblentz.   No hope therefore can be indulged.   The
nature of things will indeed bring back the monarchy; but
never Louis XVIII.   The senseless proceedings of this
Prince have hastened the destruction of his ancient house :
he has ruined himself, and drawn with him all those men, so
constantly blinded, and who were victims and examples at
the same time.

" I often see Montlosier, Malouet, and Lally ; we bewail
so many faults committed, so many misfortunes which have
resulted from them.   We look for a remedy without dis-
covering one.   But still this intimacy, this community of
ideas and sentiments, has many charms.   How much we
find you wanting !

"Adieu, my dear friend : when shall I see you again ? Our destinies are too uncertain for me to form even a hope ; I am sure at least that you will never forsake your interest in me, and this thought is sweet to my heart."

LETTER FROM LALLY-TOLLENDAL TO MALLET DU PAN.

"London, January 10, 1796.

"Montlosier, Sir, has afforded me a great proof of friendship by informing me that a traveller was on the point of setting out, who might be safely intrusted with anything one wished to address to you. I am only sorry that the opportunity is so sudden, for I felt a great need of chattering to you rather lengthily. First, I wanted to thank you for remembering me when writing to Malouet ; and then you cannot imagine what rapture I experienced from your last two letters. You would have conceived it, I am certain, if Mounier had been with you, if he had read with you the packet which I begged him to communicate to you, and which I very much wished you had opened. *Pæne gemelli*, Sir, and when we understand each other so completely, so miraculously, without any inter-communication, we must speak to each other afterwards, in order always to keep up the understanding.

"Mounier's idleness is a thousand times worse than mine, it is the greatest excess known. He writes to me that he will write to me ; he tells me cursorily that he employs every means of promulgating useful truths at Verona, but that they are rejected. And there he leaves me, adding only that he believes the King has the best intentions in the world. I send him a literal copy of my despatches to

Verona, of the declaration I have proposed, of twenty pages of reasonings and positive facts with which I have caused the project of manifesto to be followed up. I give him an account of the first answer I had from the Marshal. I tell him I am better instructed than he in the intentions of the King, and that there is too much imposture, too much nonsense even in speaking of the good intentions of a reign (since there is a reign) which commences thus. I ask him if he has received two copies of a book of mine, in two volumes, which I sent him a year ago, one for him and one for you. He does not answer me.

" If you know, Sir, where this incorrigible Mounier actually is, whom I do not the less love with all my heart, though I scold him heartily too, tell him, I pray you, that I request him to communicate to you the two pieces of which I have just spoken.

" M. de Castries, to avoid discussing with me the proclamation adopted, wrote to me the first day of his arrival at Verona: ' I have not yet seen the proclamation which His Majesty has published.'

" I do not know what the Duke of Bourbon is in his father's army ; but here it is impossible to be more modest, more interesting, more engaging, than the Duke of Bourbon is. When he arrived in this city for the first time, before the foolish expedition of l'île Dieu, he went to lodge at an hotel kept by a Frenchman, named ' La Sablonnière.' On the second day ' La Sablonnière ' offered to send out of the house some republican officers and soldiers who were going to leave England to be exchanged. ' Why so ?' asked the Duke of Bourbon ingenuously. ' I have met some of them, and they have offered me no offence ; they

are of one party, and I am of another : I do my duty.
They are perhaps very honourable people : let them alone.'
These fierce republicans were affected by it ; they never
met him without showing their respect. 'If they were all
like him !' they said.

"There has been much anxiety about the Count d'Artois,
who was supposed to have been cast away on the coast of
Norway. At length it was known last evening that he
had arrived at Edinburgh, at the mansion which the King
assigns him as a residence, which he will only be able to
leave on Sunday, or run the risk of being arrested for his
debts, and where the King will defray all his expenses
during the winter. The ardent portion of our ministry
are always thinking of a new campaign and new descents.
Peace is most certainly the first desire of Mr. Pitt ; and
Fox himself whispers to his friends that he now thinks
his rival sincere in the project of terminating the war. I
can give you that for certain.

"The cause of the sections has appeared to me as sacred
as that of Louis XVI. I have offered from afar all my
vows, all my admiration ; and I have sighed at not being
able to consecrate all my efforts for those who directed this
movement, so pure, so moral, so just, so noble, which was
only miscalculated by a day, and which unfortunately was
lost by the miscalculation. Since you have had the consolation and the glory to be one of its first inspirers,
accept, I beg you, in this deeply sincere homage, all the
share which belongs to you. Whilst this great struggle
was in agitation, you cannot have heard more prayers than
I for the triumph of the Convention, and you have not
heard them with more horror.

"You think the King's brother more reasonable : yes, just now—since the failure on the coasts. The proclamation of Verona is now disapproved. His moderation is asserted, and is made the common topic of conversation by all his adherents. But at the moment of hope, they have rejected as absurd and insolent some ideas of a more moderate manifesto communicated by M. de Calonne himself. They have refused to see M. de Calonne, who has sacrified in their cause a revenue of a hundred thousand crowns, who has now nothing to get a dinner with, and changes his lodging—that is to say his room—every week, to escape the pursuit of creditors who, after having set up all he had, to sale, are not yet paid.

"A fortnight since these gentlemen were quite delighted on hearing that this wretched pretender had a tumour in the neck, and I don't know what in the legs. They killed the poor man in less than three months, with dropsy, apoplexy, and all the diseases with which a miserable creature can be oppressed—and then one would see what a difference between his brother and him! That was the man who would be another Henry IV! He would not give way very easily! and all such nonsense. If you only knew how all moderate intentions disappeared!

"I have gone on writing to you as if we were chatting. Must I ask pardon for having arrived at the eighth page? Be considerate enough to see in it at least a pledge of esteem, of confidence, and of the friendship whose ties I wish may bind us ever closely."

CHAPTER X.

1796.

Correspondence of Mallet du Pan with M. de Sainte-Aldegonde—
Letter of the Count Souza-Cotinho on the new dispositions of the
Court of Verona—Questions of the Count d'Artois about the
Duke of Orleans (Louis-Philippe)—Mallet's reply—Fragments of
correspondence on behalf of the Emperor—Letters of Mallet du
Pan, Louis de Narbonne, Sainte-Aldegonde and Malouet.

THE year 1796, the fourth of the French Republic, offers
in the interior the curious spectacle of the revolution,
tired of itself continuing its march towards the precipice
of a despotic monarchy, and of the new society eager to
resume the pleasures and manners of the old ; whilst,
without, General Bonaparte gains victories at full speed,
revolutionises Italy, and startles the Directory by speaking
to them of his army, as the chiefs of the revolution spoke
but little of the people, when they were preparing to
overturn the throne. Never also, notwithstanding the
retreat of the French armies on the Rhine, and the talents
of the Archduke Charles, who begins to take his place
among the great names of history, had the other powers of
Europe experienced more lively alarm. The character of
the struggle had thoroughly changed, and a new and

formidable phase was opening for them in the development of the revolution, at the very moment when the latter, exhausted and transformed, was about to see the ultimate objects carried off, the Republic its conquest. The correspondence of Mallet du Pan, the information he receives, the reflections with which it inspires him, his letters and those of his friends, reflect quite vividly the flexible physiognomy of this singular epoch. We will, therefore, continue to offer extracts of this correspondence. First, among these circumstances, however, will be the only personal incident which the biography of our Journalist offers us during this year, 1796—that is, the publication of his treatise on French republicanism.

LETTER OF MALLET DU PAN TO COUNT DE SAINTE-ALDEGONDE.

"January 10, 1796.

". . . . I now answer the important questions in your letter. As soon as I was informed of the project regarding the Duke d'Angoulême and his marriage with ' Madame Royale,' I laboured to oppose it. I sent to Paris a very strong memorial on the subject, and I do not cease discussing it by letters in a discouraging point of view. To break the line of succession arbitrarily, to dispose of the crown revolutionally, to regard the monarchy as on the day of its creation, are pernicious ideas in every sense, and fraught with incalculable consequences. Neither Monsieur nor his son would ever lend themselves to such a violation of fundamental laws. I have thought it my duty, and the fulfilment of Monsieur's intentions, to represent all these considerations. I beg you, my dear Count, not to allow the Prince to remain in ignorance of it; for, although an historian of the project formed at Paris, I am not its apologist, still less its promoter. It must not be expected that this crowd of people returning to monarchy will voluntarily adopt a king without preliminary guarantees: all that can be hoped, is, that they will address their capitulation to the King, and treat with him as recognizing in him the legimate heir to the crown. No doubt, if this Prince, consulting the ' d'Entraigues,' rejected all conditions, and took his ground on the terms of his declaration, the throne would be offered to others, or perhaps a republic be organized. The fate of the King and the monarchy would then be definitively connected with the resolution of Verona. If, therefore, it is desirable to invalidate or weaken these projects of displacing the throne, and at the same time, to give to the monarchical resources all the value they can preserve, it is necessary for the King to make himself accessible and conciliating, that his disposition may be evident in his steps, in his choice of counsels, and in all the ways indicated by me in the month of June. I learn then, with a lively satisfaction, my dear Count, that Monsieur is exerting himself to bring back Verona to this system of reconciliation. The arrival of MM. de la Vauguyon and Saint-Priest is a good augury."

M. de Saint-Priest had, in fact, been called to Verona *, and he quitted Sweden to attend to the King's desires, but

* See " Lettres et Instructions de Louis XVIII. au Comte de Saint-Priest," preceded by a notice of M. de Barante's. Paris, 1845.

he received a countermand on the road, and proceeded successively to St. Petersburg and Vienna, to prosecute the interests of Louis XVIII. with Catherine and the imperial cabinet. This veteran minister, this faithful friend of Louis XVI. was assuredly the best counsellor that the new King could call on. Such was Mallet's opinion, who replied to the questions of M. de Sainte-Aldegonde, on the wisdom of this choice : " I esteem and love M. de Saint-Priest much : he has experience, firmness, a good range of opinions, capacity, and everything necessary to be a good minister, without being a first-rate man. I watched him in 1791, in very delicate and difficult circumstances, and he conducted himself with dignity, dexterity, and success. He and the Archbishop of Bordeaux were in the council what they ought to be, whatever may be said of them, and the King did them justice."

LETTER OF MALLET DU PAN TO COUNT DE SAINTE-ALDEGONDE.

" January 28, 1796.

" I have no faith in the peace, or I am greatly mistaken, because the Directory will keep everything, and always hopes still to isolate one power after the other, as it did last year. Besides, its tyranny requires armies removed from the interior, and its wants require invasions ; it will try them in the spring with all its remaining resources. You will see it, as in 1794, cast a second time France entire and destitute in the face of foreign countries, and crush them with her *débris*, if they are not on their guard.

" The requisitions are worse than under Robespierre, and,

thanks to the quality of the executive agents, are every-where submitted to. One delivers up his corn, another his horses, a third his fodder, and a fourth his children. It is a blight on the youth, who are carried off in Paris from the streets: citizen Thureau, ex-Montagnard member of the Convention, charged with this work, goes from house to house, inspects the inhabitants, and carries off whomever he thinks fit. Numbers of young people, after having obtained their final *congé*, had married; Thureau has marched them to the frontiers without any other form of process, after having robbed them of their certificate. The forced loan is worked with as good a grace. Whole sections are taxed at six hundred thousand livres a head. Thus, the levy is stopped quite short, not from a spirit of rebellion but from inability to pay. Paris will not furnish ten millions in ready money; and this loan, compared to which that of Cambon was a paternal impost, will not give an effective return of a hundred and fifty millions, in cash and assignats together. Paper money returning to the treasury is cancelled, and a much greater proportion is issued; this issue reaches from four to five millions daily. That is the reason, when the government was receiving them at a hundredth (centième) that they constantly remained lower: the unanimous opinion of the Bourse is, that in six weeks they will be at ten thousand francs the louis d'or.

"Notwithstanding this horrible state of exhaustion, their returns, whatever they are, from the loan, the money which they get against assignats, the sale of gold and silver stolen articles and diamonds which is being effected, the requisitions in kind, the contributions they have pumped

out of Holland and Belgium, the trifling assistance which
Hamburg and other commercial towns have the criminal
folly to advance them ; lastly, the engagements and deli-
veries to which they will force the contractors—all this
will suffice to support them.   If they are beaten, they will
shut up shop, if they triumph, they will sack the
stranger.

"The Jacobins daily acquire a more marked ascendancy.
Tallien occupies the same relative situation among them
as Robespierre held, after he had passed from the commune
of the 10th of August to the National Convention.
Neither Tallien, nor Carnot, nor Louvet like the Jacobins,
who are ungovernable ; but they make use of them
to crush the royalists, with the reservation afterwards, *si
fata sinant,* of reducing the Jacobins.

"Neither time nor misery has changed the common
people : they still nourish a hatred of the tyrant and a love
of equality.   Do not listen to those who tell you that the
people are reactionary.   At the first sound of the tocsin
they would have another 10th of August and 2nd of
September ; the demagogues are always sure of them,
whenever the question is to make war against the proprietors.*   A great number of *bourgeois,* annuitants, and men
of letters, have become good royalists again, but the whole
of them are not worth fifty *sans-culottes.*   The latter

---

* Mallet's correspondent adds : "The people cry out misery, they
swear against the Republic ; but talk reason to them, tell them they
were formerly happy, &c., they reply that they no longer want a
master, and that the aristocrats wish to make them demand a king
through hunger and pain, but they will rather eat the paving-stones.
They are still quite enraged."

relies on his arm; the royalist on his neighbour. He of Paris places his hope in the departments; he of the departments, in Paris. Public spirit, to speak properly, is a spirit of resignation and obedience; every one seeks to withdraw himself, at any cost—that is, by a thousand infamous meannesses, from the general distress.* Since the 13th Vendémiaire (5th October), the discouragement has been general. This does not hinder the *beau monde* from going to the theatre, taking their way over pavements yet stained with the blood of their relatives or neighbours, killed by the grape-shot of Barras. No one can speak of the King at Paris, without getting well snubbed. The sovereign powers have hardly as much consideration there. No doubt is entertained of soon bundling them into the Rhine.

"The Directory is under the auspices of the leaders of the regicide faction. It upsets the constitution every minute; decrees, annuls, commands, vexes, without attracting the slightest observation. By its imperious initiative, it is the legislator. Its messages become decrees *d'urgence*; the two councils are two boards of reference, where they register the laws at the will of the ' Five.' The legislative corps is used up, deserted; it is a declining spectacle: it is the French comedy ' Les Jours de Molière.'

---

* It is a recent observation of M. Barante : " It was no longer a period of terror and scaffolds ; but the disorder in the administration, the changeableness of the legislation, the want of faith in engagements, the absence of security, were still the manifest signs of a revolutionary epoch."—*Notice sur le Comte Mollien*, par M. de Barante, p. 10.

More than a third no longer attend ; the remnant of the
opposition is silent and approves every thing.

"The Chevalier de Guer has escaped from Lyons, and
prates away at Lausanne with a swarm of adventurers,
loungers, and undertakers of counter-revolutions, at two
hundred francs a-month, paid by the English minister.
All these swindlers do an infinite injury, and make this
frontier more and more uneasy, because the attention of the
Directory is fixed on it."

TO THE SAME.

"January 31, 1796.

"What is written to you about the 'Chouannerie'
makes one shudder, and the Marquis d'Autichamp seems
to me little fit to bring the dissensions of these brawlers to
an end.   This revolution has gangrened all.   Though
those countries might have given me some hope, what you
communicate to me would take it away.   What the Abbé
Dillon relates to you about the King is accurate : the personal conduct of this Prince is worthy of respect ; but he
is surrounded only by courtiers and mediocre and ambitious
men ; there is no getting out of the deluge with those
oars.   The spirit of intrigue was the poison of the court
and the monarchy ; it survives both, and will not revive
them.

"I shall resume the pen, because circumstances are so
desperate that they quite restore my independence. Strong
considerations have withheld me for six months : they have
ceased ; but, instead of a bulky work, I shall publish his-

torical and political letters which will appear successively : they will be printed quite near you at Hamburg, and you will be the first served."

"February 7, 1796.

"My brother was forced, in the month of December, to make a journey to Paris ; he brings me some information on various things, and some very grievous for me : of all that I had left in deposit at Paris, plate, jewels, bills, he has only been able to recover my muff, confided to my furrier. Be it faithlessness, be it fear, all other depositaries have excused themselves on the most shameful pretexts. Paris is a cut-throat place in every respect : no more duties, decency, honour, or probity of any kind. I have made the same remark as you on the benevolence of the Scotch towards the emigrants ; the remembrance of the old relations between France and Scotland, and the resemblance of the fate of the Jacobites with ours, have a great influence on those sentiments. I am charmed at the respect paid to Monsieur, which may assuage the pain of his situation.

"The council of the Ancients has had the courage to put its *veto* on the atrocious law which plunders the fathers and mothers of emigrants. This success is due to the Abbé Morellet, who, in four successive pamphlets, has defended this cause with a force of reason, a courage, a logic worthy of the greatest praise. He has even dared to treat of the cause of emigration, and to point out the principle of it in the anarchy and fury which since 1789 have taken hold of France. This rebellion of the Ancients may cost them dear.

" Expect a terrible display at the opening of the campaign.   If the Austrians do not take care, we shall see again the spring of 1794.   There are the same means, terror, and requisitions : they have, it is true, neither money, nor paper worth money ; but they take the things themselves, all that is necessary—men, horses, cattle, shirts, stockings, shoes, corn, hay, &c.   They will have wherewith to open the campaign energetically, and support it three months.   I cannot avoid anxiety : professional men all agree in saying that the present position of the Austrians is excessively bad.

" They have just stopped the issue of assignats for the 30 pluviose (19th February).   The reasons for this are simple : 1. The assignat is no longer worth the cost of manufacture. 2. Government circulates in its stead ' rescriptions,' or bills of anticipation at three months on the produce of the loan, with which it pays its contractors.

" The Duke of La Vauguyon has arrived at Verona, and the Bishop of Arras has been recalled thither.   He has just charged a foreign minister at Turin, with whom I have intimate relations, to inform me that he has received a letter from Monsieur, who desires him to persuade his brother that he should consider France as divided into two parties, the royalist and the republican, and should rally to his standard all those who hold with the first, whatever may be their differences of opinion.*   They write to me also that

* These are the very terms in which Don Rodrigo de Souza transmits to Mallet du Pan the curious communication of the Bishop of Arras.

" Turin, January 30, 1795.

" The Bishop of Arras, who had quitted Verona with disgust, has

intentions change visibly at Verona, in spite of the efforts
of the intriguers and the Parlamentarians. The latter have
just published, without the consent of the King, a bulky
book in which, by the side of the sure principles of the old
constitution of France, they reproduce their whole system
of remonstrances, of the *veto*, of the states-general upon a
small scale: the Chancellor Maupeou would have had this
work burned. These pretensions are a lesser evil; but
what really is one, are the virulent notes in which they
declare monarchists, anglo-maniacs, constitutionalists and
Jacobins equally culpable, and in which the design of
punishing indiscriminately all who have swerved from the
opinion of the Princes, is openly announced."

just been recalled, and having received a letter from Monsieur (the
Count d'Artois) who charges him to persuade his brother that he
should consider France as divided into two parties, the first royalist,
the second Jacobin, and regard the second only as an enemy, whilst
he should ally himself firmly with all those who hold with the first,
whatever may be their particular opinions about the monarchical
form which suits France; offering loyalty to the royalist party to
adopt the constitution which may be judged convenient, and to propose the reunion of the whole party by reciprocal and mutual services,
which every one will do for the general good at the moment when
the common enemy is overthrown. He not only communicates this
letter to me, but he entreats me to inform you of it, only begging of
you to keep the secret as to your being informed of it through him.
I have undertaken to write to you, because all this is conformable to
what you had written me four months ago; and besides, there is at
present some appearance that views and policy may be changed at
Verona."

TO THE SAME.

"February 20.

The Duke of Orleans * quitted Switzerland a short time before you arrived last year ! He is gone to the north : he was to embark for America. You are by far nearer to his residence than I am ; you must direct to Hamburg. He has partisans and no party : these two things are confounded every day. The chiefs of his pretended party are some constitutionalists, such as Montesquiou, who is obliged to hide himself in the mill of Maupertuis ; the Duke has no one either in the legislative corps, or in the government. Sieyès whom our emigrants do not know what to make of, belongs, I repeat it to you, to no one but himself ; he is the partizan of nothing but of his genius, of his pride, his universal republic, and his atrabilious temper. These are unquestionable facts : I sigh on seeing that our Princes and the emigrants are so ridiculously informed, and that they continually fight with the air.

" If, by a conduct compatible with the persons, with the prejudices and the interests of the time, with the imperative force of circumstances, the King does not change, and does not attract towards himself or his family that multitude of revolutionists, old and new, half royalized, or on their way

* Here Mallet replies to a question which had been put to him by M. de Sainte-Aldegonde, evidently on the part of the Count d'Artois ; " I should like to know where the Duke of Orleans (Louis-Philippe), usually resides, and where he may be at this moment ; who are the chiefs of his party, and the principal agents whom he employs ; you could not tell me too much on this point : it is of the highest interest to Monsieur, and above all to his son."

to be royalized, you will see them taking the first king who will arrange with them. I protest to you, that if there were a foreign prince rich enough, skilful enough, audacious enough, you would see in France a revolution like that of 1688 in England. This change of dynasty is, more or less, what all those who reckon and act at this moment are aiming at.

" Here is a proof of it which will surprise you greatly.

" Tallien is by no means embroiled with his wife, as our news-writers of the emigration spread about. She has procured him first-rate connexions in Spain ; he has been the mediator of peace ; he has just caused his father-in-law, Cabarrus, to be re-established in all his honors, employments, and property, even with enormous indemnities. He keeps up a regular and intimate correspondence with the Duke of Alcudia. This latter announced to him, in the middle of last month, the reinstatement of his father-in-law in a letter full of fulsome flatteries and protestations of friendship. Tallien has read it to two hundred persons ; one of my correspondents has seen the original. Well, my dear Count, Tallien has imagined and proposed to give the crown to an infant. In order to prosecute this enterprise, he wanted to appoint one of his agents to the consulate of Cadiz : Rewbell, who detests and fears him, has refused it, aud has named a certain Roxantes whom Tallien has circumvented in every sense, in order to induce him to resign. Not having succeeded with him, he has demanded this place for himself—a second refusal : *inde iræ*, and misunderstandings in the Directory, where Barras and Letourneur are the trusty friends of Tallien.

" Here is what a confidential person writes to me from

Paris, on the 12th, who is very active, very intelligent, at the fountain-head of information, and as royalist as you. Your court at Verona, to speak plainly, has no great things to expect from its agents here.   They are all men strange to revolutionary arts, men of straw, who see steeples in the moon, and who think they have done all for the peace of Europe, and the re-establishment of monarchy, when they have chanted *l'é...républicain*, or read an aristocratic journal—which they alone read.   Their insignificance is so well known, that the revolutionists take hardly any account of their proceedings ; it is not the same when suspicion falls on a converted revolutionist, or a monarchized patriot. *Diable !* The latter is to be feared, and that is true.   For this reason I repeat still, that the royalists have been fools not to attach to themselves Tallien and seven or eight others, who would have been more useful than the Clerfayt and La Vendée.

" This moment brews new troubles. Intestine agitation, animosity, divisions, rivalries, ambition, will give us a new taste of *vendémiaire*.   But always no chiefs, no men worth thousands, no nucleus of an army, no centre of opinions and doctrine to which one can adhere."

LETTER OF COUNT DE SAINTE-ALDEGONDE TO MALLET DU PAN.

" February 28, 1796.

" You afford me the greatest pleasure by informing me that intentions change visibly at Verona.   Count F. d'Escars had announced it to me at the time of his journey this way.   These intentions will require to be maintained; you have the means on your part in the Bishop of Arras, who is truly full of esteem for you, and who renders you all the justice which you deserve; and for my part, I undertake to continue showing its indispensable necessity. Monsieur is all we can desire, and I would, with all my heart, give all the money that I still have left, in order that he might be well known in the interior : I enjoin you to labour for it on your own part. This Prince really deserves that interest should be taken in him, and no one would be more grateful for it than himself. The Count, who writes to me also by the last courier, makes use of these very words : 'Monsieur is perfectly content with M. Mallet du Pan, and you cannot repeat it too often to him on his part.'

"I thank you once more, too, for the Duke of Croy. The advice which you give him is the best he can follow. My mother-in-law agrees still with you upon that. I shall write to him immediately. He is residing at Prague with his interesting family. The father is a very learned man, very intelligent, and perfectly acquainted with business. I am extremely attached to him."

Here we must again insert the fragments of the correspondence of Mallet for the Emperor.

CORRESPONDENCE OF MALLET DU PAN FOR THE EMPEROR.

"February 20, 1796.

" .... The project of penetrating at any risk into Piedmont and the Milanese territory occupies the Directory more than anything else. They have consequently disposed, and still dispose of, considerable forces in order to join the army of Italy. These troops pass daily through Lyons in numerous detachments ; they repair also to Nice from Languedoc, as well as large trains of artillery and convoys of ammunition. They propose to anticipate the allies, to open the campaign very early, and by acting vigorously on the offensive. It is a positive fact, of which I am informed from the fountain-head.

" Jourdan is the favourite of the Directory, as he was of the Committee of Public Safety. It is he who has given the plan and the finest hopes for the next campaign. Pichegru, on the contrary, has spoken of the exhaustion and discontent of the armies : he displays doubts about fresh advantages, consequently Jourdan has been overwhelmed with presents, festivals and confidence, and they have shown Pichegru nothing but ill-humour.

" Besides the motives formerly announced to his Majesty, which urged the Directory to a new campaign, there is still one very manifest it is that, even allowing for some reverses, they would only bring the allies to the gates of the French fortresses. The Directory thinks that then it would still be time to consent to the conditions which it refuses to-day ; a fresh attempt may preserve the actual conquests, whilst defeat leaves nothing to fear for the interior of France. Such is the reasoning which the principal leading men have opposed to the advocates of peace. But his Majesty the Emperor will pardon the sincerity with which I have the honour of assuring him, that the Directory places far less confidence in this alternative than in the irresolution, the want of steadiness and audacity, the fear and changeableness which they impute to their enemies. They do not disguise to themselves the extent of their exhaustion, but they are convinced that the foreigner will not know how to wait for the period of their extremity, and its infallible consequences, nor to profit by it by bold operations and formidable means. They know the hatred which all France bears them, the disgust of war which has seized the people and the armies, the terrible consequences which some serious reverses at the frontiers would have in the interior, before the military machine is completely reorganized; but they rely on the examples of the past, and the little confidence which the nature of the foreign war inspires in the malcontents of the interior. Never was their presumption more excessive, or their effrontery more open. The members of the government speak quite aloud of the corruptions which they hope to practise among the hostile generals, and of the terror which they have infused into all the cabinets.

" Their insolence and audacity have increased to such a point, that they treat the foreign envoys who are at Paris precisely as they would treat those of their tributaries. There are no insults and marks of scorn which they do not make them endure. The meaner they are in their proceedings, which are mere apologies, the more the Directory treats them with outrage; it is the tone of Roman Consuls with the Kings of Cappadocia.

" I have had the honour to describe to his Majesty the Thermidorians—of whom Tallien is the chief—as lost men, indifferent to every system of government, republican or monarchical, making a traffic of the revolution, and seeking at any price their security, their domination, and their fortune. Seeing in the republican government only alter-

nations of massacres, by factions now victorious, now vanquished, they would get France out of it, if they could find
a monarch devoted to them, one of their choice, and grateful
for this benefit ; an usurper of the crown from its legitimate
possessor, and consequently dependent on them—interested
like themselves in maintaining the new order of things
which they would establish."

[Here follows the history of the intrigue of Tallien with
the Duke of Alcudia.]

" I had the honour, six weeks ago, of informing his
Majesty of the division which was approaching in the
Directory, and which is now public. Barras and Letourneur
side with the allied Thermidorians and Jacobins ; Rewbell,
who is no better, but who hates them, and whose coarse
insolence does not harmonize with that of his colleagues, is
their principal opponent. Carnot, cunning and acute, never
forgave the Thermidorians for having wished to destroy
him after the death of Robespierre, whose colleague and
co-operator he was in the Committee of Public Safety, and
has joined Rewbell ; finally, La Réveillère-Lepaux, insignificant as he is, has given his voice against the Thermidorians, and completes the triumvirate which forms *for the
moment* the majority in the Directory.

" In order to find an excuse for expelling Barras from
the Directory, they have attacked him on the subject of
his age, by publishing a public deposition upon oath, which
he made in 1790, from which it appears that he is not yet
forty, the age which is requisite for entering into the Directory ; but this stratagem of which Rewbell is the instigator,
has not reached the pages of the public journals. Barras has set

this accusation at defiance as false. No one has dared to support it in the Legislative Corps, whatever evidence there might be for it.

"This Barras, a genuine buccaneer, has the direction of the safety of Paris, and holds in his hand all the assassins, the Septembrists, the cut-throats of the Republic; he and Letourneur hold secret cabals with Tallien, in a country-house at Montrouge, near Paris.

"The contempt and hatred for the Directory are manifested in every way in the towns and in the country. The peasantry designate them only by the ironical name of *Kings of France and Navarre*. In a coffee-house of Paris, they were speaking about the difficulty of victualling the army: 'Yes,' cried a wag, 'for we have only five cartouches left.' All those who were present, applauded, and this witticism has been repeated in all public places.*

"The administration was never more complicated, its difficulties were never more openly acknowledged. It would be a strange mistake to imagine that the money in circulation in the coffers of the Republic is in proportion to the millions in metal, which the legislative corps grants on paper to the ministers and the Directory. I have certain information, that on the 10th of this month, the funds of the treasury, with the little quantity of bullion which is at the Mint, were limited to nine millions and four hundred thousand livres. Besides this, 'rescriptions,' bills of anticipation on the forced loan, have come in to

* A traveller wrote to me that in a post-house near Dijon, he heard the master of the house bid an hostler go in search of the *representatives:* those legislators were the turkeys of the farm.

the amount of five millions, by the sale of the movables of some royal houses, and by the payment of the forced loan ; for, as those bills lose forty per cent., every one is eager to send them in, in payment of public money, where they are received at metallic value."

Whilst Mallet, writing to the friends of the Princes, expressed himself severely on the mistakes of Verona, he endeavoured to diminish the effects of it by seizing upon every appearance of conversion to a better policy, in order to reconcile to the brothers of Louis XVI. such of the constitutionalists as he could influence.   Thus, he had communicated to Louis de Narbonne, then retired to Gleresse, in Switzerland, the recommendations addressed by the Count d'Artois to the Bishop of Arras, whom the Prince requested to persuade the King, his brother, to reunite into a single party the Monarchists of every shade (see the letter of Mallet of the 14th of February).   M. de Narbonne replied to Mallet.

LETTER OF LOUIS DE NARBONNE TO MALLET DU PAN.

"Gleresse, March 1, 1796.

" M. Brémond, Monsieur, has communicated to me a letter of M. le Comte d'Artois, which you have requested him to show me ; I am exceedingly thankful to you for it, and feel much flattered to think you felt how much pleasure it would cause me.

" A royalist on principle, and attached to the royal house by bonds which nothing can   sever, I should with true happiness see it follow up the line indicated by M. le

Comte d'Artois. Although I believe this measure excessively tardy, I shall not the less look upon it as a sacred duty for every man in my position to do all that is in his power for the success of a cause which, maintained with ingenuousness and loyalty, would at length discharge that which an honest man owes to his country and himself. What is now the stand which can be taken by the man who desires to obey reason and his conscience? You, Monsieur, who are so well adapted to enlighten both, have you not been condemned to displease all parties, by telling them stern and useful truths? If they would have heard you, this letter of M. le Comte d'Artois would, doubtless, long since have appeared instead of a proclamation; but I fear very much that, even at present, it is not adopted by the King. The phrase of: *I charge you to persuade my brother*, is solely with the intention of frightening. Is there any indiscretion, Sir, in asking you for some explanation about it? Is this quite authentic? to whom is it written? what may have been the occasion of this form of instruction? If it is possible for you to satisfy my extreme desire to know the truth on a subject so calculated to interest all Frenchmen, I shall be truly obliged to you, and my conduct, of which you have sometimes misunderstood the motives, will prove to you, perhaps, that I am worthy of this confidence, and of the advice which I shall always deem it an honour to follow.

" I have the honour, &c.

"LOUIS DE NARBONNE."

M. de Sainte-Aldegonde having sent to his friend a

letter of Monsieur* which filled him with delight, for it must, thought he, shut the mouths of his calumniators, Mallet du Pan—for whom, in fact, this communication was designed, because they desired to obtain for him information and advice—answered these advances in the following letter :

LETTER FROM MALLET DU PAN TO COUNT DE SAINTE-ALDEGONDE.

"March 27, 1796.

" I send you back, my dear Count, the letter of Monsieur, begging you to express to the Prince, on my part, my appreciation of his kindness and acknowledgments, as well as the extreme desire I should have of responding to his intentions.   Unhappily, in the present state of things, I can do nothing at all.   Correspondence with Paris has, for six weeks, become impracticable : all foreign letters are opened, and are only delivered when the receiver proves his regular and commercial relations with his correspondent. Besides, even if the road were free, what influence could I expect ?   It would be in vain for me to do a hundred times a-day what I have already done, namely, reassure men's minds as to the sentiments of the Princes : who do you think would believe me, on seeing them constantly on the path which they have trodden for five years, without the least fact to support my remonstrances, and to give me credit with the French ?   My brother has furnished me with a report of great extent, and conformable almost in all points to what you know already, and what my correspond-

* This letter has not been found.

ents write me every week. Here is the summary of the information it contains :

" The royalists side exclusively, neither with one nor the other of the Princes. Some desire the King, some Monsieur, some the son of the latter ; finally, the Duke of Orleans has many partisans. If care is not taken, he will easily reunite the great mass of the people who have been something in the revolution, those who have made a fortune in it—the whole class of four hundred thousand individuals, who have bought, sold again, or who are still proprietors of national domains.

" All opinions are infinitely ramified ; but the first who is able to make himself King, and to promise early tranquillity, will absorb them all.

" The habit of misfortune and privations, the frightful state in which the Parisians lived under Robespierre, causes them to find their present situation supportable. The peace that would ensue would fill the nation with joy. Lassitude is at its height ; every one thinks only of passing in tranquillity the rest of his days. If Carnot or the Duke of Orleans ; if Louis XVIII. or an Infant of Spain were to become King, provided he would govern tolerably well, the public would be contented. They think only of themselves, firstly, secondly, and always. The lower classes have not recovered from their hydrophobia ; they are still mad animals, in spite of their profound misery. Reason does not reach them ; they suffer, and attribute all their evils to the royalists and the war which they keep up.

" It is losing time to wish to counteract this feeling, and it is perfectly suicidal to endeavour to get up local insurrections. It is Paris—it is the authority itself—which must be attacked; not with the army of Condé, but with the bayonet of interest, hope, security. It would be necessary to make one's self a party in the councils, to treat with the new third, with the honest members of the old Convention, such as Boissy d'Anglas—even with some Thermidorists—conduct one's self afterwards according to the instructions of this party, and let them do the rest. I see no other resource; but, once again, its indispensable basis is the union of all monarchists to common elements and a common interest. We are near the last gasp: royalty will surely disappear; but, from day to day, it becomes more than doubtful whether its reappearance will be in favour of the direct line. The Princes have ruined, and are still ruining, themselves. The monarchy will be recovered only on heaps of ashes and corpses, and after having seen an usurper seize, and hold the reins for, perhaps, a very long time."

TO THE SAME.

"April 2, 1796.

"I have gradually drawn you a picture of the chances at Paris; it was to that of the re-establishment of royalty by the Legislative Corps, and the Primary Assemblies, that it was necessary to apply one's-self exclusively. It is the only means which does not frighten the nation, and in which the body of the people will be eager to concur. The most formidable obstacle to the monarchy is the universal terror which is inspired by the thought of once more going through a sanguinary revolution in order to attain it. All will abandon you if you display your swords, your English, your Austrians, your projects of conquest.

" Judge if there is matter for despair. The follies of the Directory, its insolence, its predilection for giving employment to all the criminals of 1792 and 1793, have reanimated a faction which was only asleep. A strong, systematic, and positive coalition has just been formed in the two councils against this Directory and its faction. It is composed of the *new third*, led by Portalis, Dumas, Marbois, Doumerc, Lemérer, a man of great talents, Jourdan (of the Bouches-du-Rhône), who emigrated in 1792, 1793, &c.; besides, from a hundred and thirty to a hundred and fifty members of the old Convention, Vendemiarists, or men who become such, Boissy-d'Anglas, &c.

" This coalition has upset the project of Sieyès, Louvet, Chénier, and the regicides to muzzle the press; it has obtained the presidency and the secretaryship of the Five Hundred; it has recalled and brought to account Fréron and other proconsuls; it will hamper the Directory—the days of subservience have passed. This association will demand the report of the law of the 3rd Brumaire, which excludes from public offices the relations of emigrants and Vendemiarists.

" The definitive end is the convocation of the primary Assemblies and of the Sections, namely, to renovate entirely the legislative corps and nominate deputies, who will discuss and put to the vote the re-establishment of the monarchy. That is the scheme; it will be executed sooner or later, and with more or less rapidity, according to circumstances. The Directory will try to do so on the 31st of May; but the fear of terrorism has taken a greater hold than terrorism itself, and the Directory is far from being able to promise themselves a certain success.

" Be this as it may, it is to this coalition, its objects and
its means, that one should attach one's-self as to a plank of
safety.   What frightens me above all, is, that by prolong-
ing the duration of the Republic, the alienations of confiscated property are multiplied ; the mass of the new
proprietors is swelled ; and when all is sold, who will be able
to strip two millions of invaders ?   Adieu, &c."

LETTER OF COUNT DE SAINTE-ALDEGONDE
TO MALLET DU PAN.

" April 17, 1796.

" I thank you, my dear Mallet, for your kind and very
interesting letter of the 2nd of April. I hastened to send extracts to Edinburgh.   We must not hesitate about the plan
which you propose to me. It is the only one, in my opinion,
which can save the King, and perhaps the monarchy.   I
have written in this strain to Scotland, and profited by
the confidence which is shown to me, in order to demonstrate the necessity of prosecuting the scheme which you
propose.   It is Verona that must be converted—but how
are we to hope for it ?   I shall see, I hope, the Bishop of
Arras on his journey this way, and I shall learn from him
many details, of which I will inform you immediately.
He is a convert who will not leave us in the lurch, I
warrant it. If the Count d'Avary has shaken off his
prejudices, he will bring us back the King, because this
Prince regards him with the tenderest friendship and most
entire confidence. As for the Duke de La Vauguyon, he has
too much sense, and surely too much ambition, not to see
that Louis XVIII. is absolutely in the same position as
James II., and that no time is to be lost in extricating him

from it. You render them, my dear Mallet, the most important of all services, by enlightening them on their unhappy position, and by making them acquainted with the projects which are meditated.

" The last news from England (of the 5th) is less pacific. It appears, that the government has thrown difficulties in the way of the Directory, and that it wishes to gain time in the hope of obtaining better conditions. Besides, there is the same going to and fro, and surely the same underhand dealing between London and Paris, as that which you tell me exists between Vienna and Paris. I tremble, and I am not the only one, lest they try a second *quiberonnade* within six weeks.

LETTER OF MALLET DU PAN TO THE ABBÉ DE PRADT.

"April 22, 1796.

" . . . . We know now in what have consisted the pacific transactions ; they have just printed the documents here : you will find them in the English papers. On the 8th of March, Mr. Wickham, the British minister in Switzerland, sent a note to Barthelemy, to propose a congress, or any other method of negotiation, in the name of his King and his allies. On the 28th, the Directory replied in a most insolent and haughty answer : it ridicules the proposition, rejects any congress, and declares plainly that it will never hear of treating about the restitution of *the annexed countries.* The British Government, on receiving this rescript, has published a very quiet and feeble note, which has no other advantage than that of proving to the peace party in France, that the fault of the war is on the side of the Directory, and to the peace party in Europe that, in spite of their thirst for it, peace can only be obtained at the sword's point. It is this answer of the 28th of March, which has determined Vienna, and the departure of the Archduke. The Directory, in the course of the winter, had sent to Vienna an intriguer to offer exchanges and secularisations as an indemnification for Belgium; they made a similar proposition to the King of Sardinia, and only with the view of dividing and cooling, but without any sincere intention of bringing matters to an end. Their answer to Mr. Wickham contains their true principle."

LETTER OF MALLET DU PAN TO COUNT DE SAINTE-ALDEGONDE.

"April 24, 1796.

" I received your letter of the 10th, my dear Count, on Thursday last. My pamphlet must certainly be in your hands at the moment I write. I am finishing the second division, which will appear at the end of May. All this comes the day after the fair, and is perfectly useless to the foreigner : I write for France. I do not wish to persuade you; you know as much of it as I do. I address those whom it is necessary to bring over to us, not those who side already with us. That is all my answer to the clamours of the Guers, d'Entraigues, and the mob whom I hear beforehand.

" Danican, of whom you speak to me, has been four months in this country. We have had time to form a judgment of him. He has a good heart, and a detestable head : if I am not mistaken, he will do nothing in La Vendée, although he knows that country well.

" That Alexander de Lameth has been in England at the request of the Government, outrages all probability. The British minister in Switzerland has raised up a very serious broil with Theodore Lameth ; he abhors the constitutionalists ; he persecutes them on all occasions ; this is not done without instructions from his Court. I rather suppose that Alexander Lameth has proposed some scheme to the Government, which will not listen to him any more than it has done to us.

" The ministerial papers announce the capture, near Saint Malo, of poor Count de Serrent, and twenty-two other emigrants disembarked with him : all have been taken and shot. They have carried off the ammunition and the arms which they had brought. I had a presentiment of this misfortune when writing to you on the subject. These absurd expeditions—these parcels of emigrants, which are thrown, one after another, on coasts covered with enemies—this squandering of resources — these puerilities are inexplicable. At this rate they will have buried the very last nobleman before regaining an inch of ground. I have had a letter of the 21st of March, from Nantes, written by an eye-witness, of the death of Charrette, for whom the people showed so much interest. The writer looks upon the affair of La Vendée as concluded. Commissaries organize it at this moment on a republican footing. Hoche has transferred his headquarters to Rennes, and will handle the Chouans very roughly.

I tremble for this campaign. There is the Austrian

army of the Rhine, commanded on one side by a deaf and narrow-minded old man, who is led by Klinglin, a man of very mediocre capacity; on the other side, by a valiant but inexperienced young prince, and by a general, who has never commanded ten thousand men. In Italy, Beaulieu has excellent points; but I fear that war in the mountains, which is strange to him, will make him commit great faults. He has just opened with a misfortune. On the 10th, he forced the French at Voltri; he believed that by attacking them on the whole line, he could drive them before him, as in the plains of Flanders. On the 14th, the French attacked the post of Sotto and another with a vigour which is peculiar to them. At the very commencement, M. d'Argenteau, who occupied the centre, lost his cannons and baggage; a part of them was retaken; but the corps of M. de Colli was turned, the posts were lost; fifteen hundred men, taken in an ambuscade, were forced to lay down their arms. More than three thousand prisoners are in the hands of the enemy, who, on the 14th, marched upon Acqui. There is reason to tremble. M. d'Argenteau lost the army in the same manner last autumn. The French would have hanged a general who had conducted himself as he has done; the Emperor has retained him in his command.* Europe is in a critical position : this long duration of the war makes me shudder.

* When General d'Argenteau presented himself to Beaulieu after his defeats, Mr. Drake, the English minister, was present. " Where is your army, Sir ?" said Beaulieu to d'Argenteau. "General, I do not know," answered d'Argenteau.—"In that case, Sir, a General, who cannot give an account of his army, deserves to be cashiered, and put under arrest. Officer, the gentleman must be

" You will have found in the English papers the official documents of the overtures of peace, made on the 8th of March by the minister of England, in Switzerland, and the answer of the Directory, dated the 28th. They confirm you in two things, of which I wrote to you at the time : that there has been a good deal of by-play in order to negotiate, but that the Directory would be inflexible.

LETTER FROM MALOUET TO MALLET DU PAN.

"London, May 8, 1796.

" There is, my dear friend, always an interval of two months in our correspondence ; those who suppose it to be so active, so combined, are much mistaken. Here and elsewhere they do not doubt that we are in very frequent communication. They call you the committee of Berne corresponding with the committee of London, as they called me the Austrian committee whilst I was at Paris ; and one of the reasons which have always been the cause that our individual good sense has never produced anything, is the want of concert and communication, which, in times of trouble, has some little similarity to a conspiracy. But must not all honest people conspire for the

conducted to Pavia." D'Argenteau was transferred from Pavia to Vienna, and instead of being judged by a council of war, some months afterwards he was at court, ornamented with military orders and loaded with favours. When Beaulieu went to attack the French, he communicated his resolutions to Mr. Drake, who represented to him the danger of attacking thirty-five thousand Frenchmen with a force beneath twenty thousand men. " There is the positive order of the Baron Thugut," answered Beaulieu ; " my head is at stake." (Details communicated by Mr. Drake.)

re-establishment of order? It seems, my friend, that you alone occupy yourself with it, because we are here quite dispersed, quite destitute of credit and means. Idle conversations, which lead to nothing, are all our labours. However, Montlosier has been extremely anxious to throw a bomb into the camp of the enemy. He has just published letters which he has addressed to me on the effects of violence and moderation in French affairs. They are very clever, contain accurate views, fine reflections, and some blunders. D'Entraignes and Ferrand are ill-spoken of in them; I should have wished that what refers to them was less bitter, without being less strong.

"I do not receive your work, so long ago announced, and I hear much talk about it: it is even said, that you are bitter against England, which I should be sorry for, because, besides the succour of all kinds which the emigration receives here, it is not enough known how England, in all her enterprises on France, has been deceived by the French. Do not think that it is the ministry which has projected and combined any of those fatal operations in the interior; it has always been provoked, tormented, teased by our schemers, and I have reason to believe that the cabinet has yielded reluctantly on more than one occasion. No less difficult is it for you to know well what are the real views of England in this war. I have taken great pains to ascertain the opinions of influential men, and those who pass for the most enlightened, and I have come to the conviction, that they are more occupied at home and abroad with their own safety than with ambitious calculations."

CHAPTER XI.

1796.

" Correspondance pour servir à l'histoire du républicanisme français"—Letters to M. de Sainte-Aldegonde, and to the Chevalier
de Gallatin, on the events of Italy—Letters of Count de Montgaillard—Pichegru—Letters on Paris by the correspondents of
Mallet—Letters of Mallet—Victories of the Archduke Charles, &c.

SINCE the " Considérations sur la Révolution Française," Mallet du Pan had published nothing ; that which
he announced to his friends, printed at Hamburg, at
Fauche's, and corrected by the Abbé de Pradt, appeared at
last under the title of " Correspondance politique pour
servir à l'Histoire du Républicanisme Français."* "I have
written," he says to the Abbé de Pradt, " rather for
France than for foreign countries.   The Directory may do

---

* Mallet inserted the following declaration :

" The author disavows all writings and letters which impostors
have circulated under his name ; he has published nothing since the
year 1793, the date of his ' Considérations sur la nature et la durée
de la révolution,' printed at Brussels." This declaration does not
permit us to ascribe to Mallet several works which are attributed to
him from an air of resemblance which they have with his own. The
fact is, that Mallet had founded a school without desiring it, and
that numerous pamphleteers, not without talent, wrote in his style.

what it pleases, I shall penetrate into it. My plan has been to say here what numbers of sensible people can and dare not say, at Paris. It is a seed which falls on a field ready prepared. It is not to you nor to our party, I speak —it is to those who must be brought back to us."

The 'Correspondence' is composed of the first eight letters which Mallet proposed to publish successively. Its subject is the finances of the Republic ; but it is preceded by an introduction, which is, to speak the truth, the chief piece of the work, and by an *avant-propos*, which is itself a piece full of interest. The author commences by explaining himself on the object of his writing.

" It is not sought to favour any system or any claim ; any more than to flatter the passions of any party, to copy their mutual recriminations, or to lose ourselves in repetitions, which have no more weight on contemporary opinions than the pamphlets, for or against the bull ' Unigenitus.' There will be no imitation of the simplicity of those who hope to assuage fury by reasonings, to convert the wrongheaded by the picture of experience, and to bring back to principles of morality and justice souls whom the spirit of the age induces first to ask : How much is it worth ?

" It would be besides a disgraceful thing to consecrate one's pen to the entertainment of that crowd of idlers and indifferentists for whom, from one end of Europe to the other, as at Paris, the Revolution is scarcely an event of curiosity ; egotists besotted by the love of pleasure or by interest, and who, according to a very just definition, would willingly burn their friend's house to get a couple of eggs cooked.

" The author speaks for those numerous healthy and independent minds who have preserved their reason intact in this deluge of public errors. He deems it an honour to be their organ. Although the world is almost divided between the ignorant and the mad, experience, morality, and knowledge will not always be refused. Opinion, justified by time, is also a power. When wickedness and incapacity have filled up the measure of their works, they appear in court, and the day of wisdom comes with that of repentance. There are among the expatriated French, there are in France, and, I am happy to think so, in the rest of Europe, numbers of those men, who unite rectitude of heart with that of ideas; the conformity of their views and sentiments forms a less fragile coalition than that of political interests. Every hour of the reign of folly tightens the bonds of this union and augments its adherents. The publication of this work aims at lending it new arms.

" We must certainly admire the courage which characterized the declarations of many sections of Paris, the writings of M. Morellet, Marnésia, Lacretelle, Suard, Guiraudet, and some others; but they could only show the scene in profile: crime on the throne would soon have crushed the painter and the palette, if they had dared to represent this fundamental demonstration, this truth in fact and theory, of which M. de Lally-Tollendal supplies us with the happy expression: ' *Liberty in the monarchy, servitude in the republic.*' Such is the epigraph of the work of which the first pages are presented to-day, and which will make up for the silence to which all well-informed or undeceived citizens are condemned in France."

Mallet fully expected to stir up all sorts of hatred and fear; in particular, he braves beforehand the indignation of the most contemptible and odious of all the species that a revolution engenders.

" The author expects to incur another kind of hatred, that of those cautious amateurs of the revolution, who, while feigning to be affected by its excesses, extol the causes which have produced them ; of those Philintes who sweep over the victims of republicanism in order to have the right to weep for its reverses ; of those Jacobins of good society who express regrets for Robespierre, at every turn which seems to favour royalty ; of the mob of unfeeling persons from whom six years of carnage and nameless atrocities have not drawn a sigh ; and, finally, of the numberless votaries of fortune who call their calculations or their pusillanimity moderation, and who, when a true description is given of the sanguinary innovators whose genius they admire, exclaim that they are outraged."

In another passage, which it is but just to Mallet to reproduce, this strong thinker grapples with those who, from hatred of the sanguinary aberrations of the revolution, wish to proscribe intelligence itself.

" There has been formed in Europe a league of fools and fanatics, who, if they could, would deny to man the faculty of seeing and thinking : the sight of a book makes them shudder ; because the light of knowledge has been abused, they would exterminate all those whom they suppose enlightened ; because the criminal and the blind have rendered liberty horrible, they would govern the world by the sword and the cudgel. Persuaded that without intellectual men, the revolution could never have been seen, they hope to put it down with imbeciles. They approve of all motive power except talents. Poor men! who do not perceive that passions, far more than knowledge, overthrow the universe; and that if intelligence has been injurious, still more intelligence is required than is possessed by the wicked, to restrain and vanquish them. The advantage is known which the Jacobins of all countries draw from these allies; they also wish to have only ignorant people and swordsmen. It is not altogether useless to oppose this double Vandalism, and to show that French republicanism has been the work of perversity, it is not less that of silliness and ignorance."

This introduction is, perhaps without excepting even the "Considérations," the most clever and vigorous that Mallet wrote; it is still the same character of the French revolution so often drawn by him; but he is never reduced to repeating himself, and each time he makes the light play upon some new feature of his subject; his arguments seem inexhaustible. After having demonstrated that the republican institution was treason against the public sovereignty, he shows that it has perpetuated itself by this treason: founded on conspiracy, a continued conspiracy has prolonged its existence.

"Such has been," he continues, "such has been, since the 10th of August, 1792, and without interruption up to the present moment, the rotation of this republicanism, every minister of which could say of the French what Narcissus said to the Romans:

"' J'ai cent fois, dans le cours de ma gloire passée,
Tenté leur patience, et ne l'ai point lassée.'

R 2

" The Republican Convention erected its power and that
of its present successors on the revolutionary government,
namely, on the absence of all laws, and consequently of all
liberty.   Towards the end of his days, J. J. Rousseau,
when his hallucinations had worn off, wrote to the Marquis
of Mirabeau, that the problem of liberty consisted in
finding a government which would place the authority
of institutions above the authority of men.   The French
legislators have discovered the government which an-
nihilates the power of the laws, in order to deliver the
citizens, and private, public and natural rights to the
discretion of a few men.   Thus, what no known despot
dared to invent, our century owes to representatives of
the people.

" This unparallelled introduction of the revolutionary
government is the only novelty which till now has resisted the vicissitudes of time.   Each faction, on obtaining
the supremacy, finding this instrument at work, has taken
care not to put it out of order ; it has passed from hand
to hand with undiminished power.   It was marked one
time by a veil of moderation, at another by a constitutional
idol.   It is this change of costume which has caused simple
minds, with which Europe abounds still more than France,
to believe that this desolate land would at last have a legal
regulator, and that liberty would flourish under a positive
and inviolable legislation.

" The French nation is no longer the dupe of these
political masquerades ; but the existing terror of the revolutionary government perpetuates their effects and enhances
all their rigours.   The usurpers of this arbitrary and
boundless sovereignty have only to point with the finger

to the tomb in which they have interred liberty; people recoil from fear, and slavery appears clemency.

" French republicanism has, therefore, been, is still, and will eternally be, nothing but unlimited submission to an unbridled tyranny. In observing the prodigies of the revolutionary power, there is as much embarrassment in comprehending how it has been able to establish itself, as to conceive how it can possibly end. Men of no standing have said to a polite nation, and one renowned for its honour, and characterized by its vanity: be coarse to be republican; become savage again to show the superiority of thy genius; leave off the habits of a civilized people to adopt those of galley-slaves; disfigure thy language to elevate it; speak like the vulgar under punishment of death. The Spanish beggars treat each other with dignity; they show this respect to mankind even in rags; we, on the contrary, enjoin thee to take our rags, our slang, our *tutoiement*; dress thyself *en carmagnole* and tremble, become rustic and silly, and prove thy rank as a citizen by the absence of all education. To day the red cap or the *lanterne*; the pantaloons or the guillotine. A year hence thou shalt be shot if thou hast a green collar. . . . Whoever swerves from our creed shall be delivered up to the executioners, and we shall be his heirs. We will make of carnage a public solemnity, and call it revolutionary justice: we have subjugated thee with words and punishments, we will lull thee asleep with statutes: the children shall go and perish on the frontier to secure our safety; we will rob the fathers in order to provide for our profusions and relieve us from dangers.

" This is the liberty that France still enjoys. And what would be the height of disgrace if it was not that of mis-

fortune, is, that so monstrous a power is formed and supported without the lustre of talents, the weight of personal
credit, the claims of genius to explain and justify the public
submission.   One must go to the frontier to find in the
armies great services and some names worthy to be cited ;
while these armies themselves, without influencing the
internal revolutions, remain neutral witnesses of them, and
abandon the destinies of the state to some obscure conspirators, whom Cataline would scarcely have wished for
his public criers.

" A distinctive characteristic of this populace of demagogues has compensated for their capacity : by dint of
audacity they have rendered genius useless ; to audacity
they owe a statue.   He amongst them who said to them
from the tribune, *dare !* understood his epoch, and deserved a triumph : he has perished on the scaffold (Saint-
Just).   It becomes easy to be clever when one has got rid
of scruples and laws, of all honour and justice, of the
rights of one's fellows and the duties of authority.   At
this point of independence, most of the obstacles which
modify human activity disappear ; one seems to have
talent when one has only impudence, and the abuse of
power passes for energy ; but on discarding these vulgar
mistakes, the question arises whether, after the fault of
commencing an incalculable revolution, there is greater
ignorance than that of never knowing how to terminate it."

The whole work is rich in moral and political thoughts,
which the idleness of our time will not take the trouble to
look for, and which, nevertheless, our present generation
needs to meditate on.   We will venture to cite some more
pages of this remarkable work.

"It would be erroneous to suppose that the spirit of republicanism has sprung up in France only since the revolution. The independence of manners, the relaxation of duties, the inconsistency of authority; the impetuous heat of opinions in a country, where the want of reflection transforms them immediately into prejudices; finally, the American inoculation had infused this spirit into all the reasoning classes. Most of the malcontents in France proclaimed themselves democrats, as most of them do at present in the rest of Europe. The people alone remained strangers to this effervescence. A Frenchman hates all superiority so much, that by effacing that of the King, he became incapable of supporting any. The system of equality drove away that of liberty; the balance of powers seemed an aristocracy: each busy-body said to himself: 'I shall participate in the command, and will not recognize that of any one.' There was, therefore, no medium in ideas, nor discretion in enterprises: they steered towards the republic, under the monarchical flag, and when in 1791, the breakers frightened the pilots, they wished to resuscitate royalty:—that was only a carcase pierced with a thousand poniards.

"Nothing better describes this spirit, the forerunner of the republican revolution, than a profound observation of Mr. Morris, Minister of the United States. This envoy, a man full of intelligence, penetration and experience, prophecied from the commencement of the revolution the circle which this torrent of enthusiastic prejudice, hurled into the midst of the most active passions, was about to traverse. Barnave, on coming up to the States-General, was eager to make enquiry after one of the legislators of the United States, and met him in a club. After the first compliments, the French deputy harangued a whole hour about liberty. The phlegmatic American did not interrupt him for one minute, but towards the end, he showed some inattention ; Barnave, perceiving that it was time to finish, asked him what he thought of his principles : ' I think, Sir,' Mr. Morris answered coolly, ' that you are far more republican than I.'*

" Miltiades imprisoned, Aristides banished, Socrates condemned to drink hemlock, had disgraced Athens in the eyes of French republicans ; the existence of the order of patricians forbade their turning towards Rome ; they therefore signalised their wisdom by fixing on the youngest of republics, the United States of America. And, with equal good sense, instead of modifying the principles of the new world, to suit the maturity, the population, the character of the old world, they exaggerated the democracy of the United States, and rejected its correctives.

" This epidemic of political constitutions, which succeeded in France and Europe to that of puppets and balloons, is the offspring of conceit even more than of fanaticism. There is not a small shop-keeper enlightened by the study

* We do not seek, by this quotation, to revive accusations against a man, whose death has honoured the scaffolds of the Republic. History will be able to form a judgment on the misdeeds of M. Barnave ; it would be atrocious and absurd at the present time to arraign anything but his errors. Whatever blame may be attached to his conduct, during the first two years of the revolution, we must not forget his devotion to the King and the Queen after the journey to Montmedi, nor his repentance, nor his efforts to defend the monarchy which he helped to shake, nor his sufferings, nor his long captivity, nor the courage of his last moments.

of the 'Heloïse', not a schoolmaster who has translated ten pages of Livy, not an artist who has skimmed Rollin, not a witling turned politician through conning over the logogryphs of the 'Contrat social', who does not in these days draw up a constitution.

" Meantime, while theorists are searching for the philosopher's stone of speculative politics, society gradually crumbles away, and its ashes settle at the bottom of the crucible. As nothing presents fewer difficulties than the perfecting of what is imaginary, all restless spirits expand, and move freely in this ideal world. This is one of the principal causes of the success which has attended the Gallican innovations. They leave far behind them all known systems of free government, and intoxicate the brains of fools, while they inflame the passions of the mob. People begin with curiosity, and end with enthusiasm.

" No man who feels the dignity of his nature will ever fail to recognize the claims of the human race, or the respect which social liberty has a right to demand from governments. Nature certainly never intended that nations should, like flocks, be the property of those whom necessity has charged with the duty of protecting them. The government of Morocco is, no doubt, a blessing when compared with the rule of five-hundred revolutionary atheists; but reason will ever invoke the absolutism of justice; and there can be no justice without inviolable laws; no inviolable laws without a positive constitution to act as their safeguard.

" This need, however, varies infinitely, according to centuries, nations, physical and moral conditions. To attempt to satisfy it on an unvarying system, is to remould the bed of iron in which a tyrant stretched the limbs of his victims.

To begin the legislation of a state by isolated political laws, is to lay the keystone of the arch before building the edifice.

" Above and beyond all else, the people are deeply interested in the civil and judicial laws ; these embrace the citizen in his cradle, they touch him at every point of his existence ; by them he is enfranchised, authorised and regulated in the exercise of his daily functions ; from them he learns the limits of his rights and the circle of his duties ; there he recognizes himself as husband, father, son, inheritor, giver, receiver, seller, buyer, master, servant ; in these meet all relations and all needs are reconciled ; from them that vast reciprocity of transactions which composes the social economy, derives its development and security ; in them, finally, justice takes its place by the side of legitimate independence, and general order with the exercise of individual faculties.

" The civil and judicial laws alone form the citizen ; for they embrace him in all respects, and defend him in all his legal actions. Political laws enclose him merely in an eccentric circumference ; they regulate public power far more than liberty itself, of which they form the complement, by the security they ensure to the people for the maintenance of civil institutions.

" But the present generation is sacrificed to the caprices of ecumenic legislators : the next generation will have still to deplore that deluge of the human reason which has realized in France the picture Montesquieu draws of Syracuse :— ' Syracuse, always abandoned to license or oppression, the victim of its liberty and its servitude, always receiving each as a storm, contained an immense population, which never

had a less cruel alternative presented to it than that of
surrendering to a tyrant, or of becoming such.' Let us
consider too, that unanswerable reply to the everlasting
argument which assumes even to-day, in the mouths of
the sincerest men, to absolve the revolution for its transitory crimes in favour of its durable benefits : ' Is it not a
condemnation of revolutions to adjourn their benefits to the
time when their principles and the actors in them shall
have lost their influence? Was it worth the trouble of
beginning them in order to attain such a result? Can a
more stupid, and at the same time more abominable, calculation be conceived, than that of reaching abundance by
universal impoverishment; liberty by the most degraded
and bloody slavery, virtue by infamy, morality by atheism,
national prosperity by the misery of the citizens ?

" You will perhaps allege, that revolution and republic
are not identical, and that, government once formed, men
of property and character assuming the reins of administration, a system subversive of all order, all property, all
freedom, will acquire the character of a popular and yet
stable organization.

" To this prejudice, Sir, I can but return one word
of reply, viz :——that the Republic having hitherto been
founded and maintained solely by revolutionary force, it is
bad logic to infer that this incentive is not necessary to
it. I will add that, on the day when men of property and
character shall have weight in the government, their first
need will be to overturn it, in order to revert to the only
protection possible in a state like France, that of a monarch
who defends the laws against a million usurpers, without
having the power of becoming one himself."

This pamphlet, written in characters of fire, made a great sensation, and excited strong animosity. Mallet had foreseen as much : but the prospect had not availed to stay his pen,—" I shall raise," he wrote, " a whole crop of malcontents. I wrote as I should write twenty years hence. Nothing remains to me but independence : I must exercise it to console myself."

All his friends, while congratulating him, added that they were not free from uneasiness as to the consequences of a daring, which would exasperate the terrorists and the Directory. But for Mallet the essential point was that his work should penetrate into France. His wish was satisfied. At Paris, the pamphlet was at once reprinted by various houses, and three editions were sold in two months.

Notwithstanding its success, the " Correspondence pour servir à l'Histoire du républicanisme français " stopped at this first section. The movement which dragged onwards the destinies of the Republic had received a sudden impulse: the point of view as well as the interest of the political observer was already displaced. Bonaparte's victories in Italy gave a new aspect to the affairs of the revolution, which threatened now to become wholly military. The following letters attest the clear-sightedness of Mallet, who, at the first rumour of this daring conquest, sees and predicts with precision the triumphal progress of the French arms across revolutionized Europe ; for, in this signal progress across Italy, Bonaparte was essentially the man of the revolution, and personified all its spirit, boundless daring, revolutionary enthusiasm, and utter absence of principle, in the means and application of victory.

LETTER FROM MALLET DU PAN TO COUNT DE SAINTE-ALDEGONDE.

"May 4, 1796.

" My last letter, my dear Count, will have prepared you for fresh catastrophes. After their defeat on the 16th, at Dégo, the Austrians entirely abandoned the Piedmontese, and have all fallen back on Alessandria, Bosco, Acqui, thinking only of the Milanese territory. The Piedmontese corps of M. de Colli, sixteen thousand strong, had, up to the 17th, repulsed all the attacks of the French; but these, once freed from the Austrians, united against their ally. They attacked him in great strength in his new position, covering Mondovi. On the 19th, 20th, and 21st, the fight was carried on with unexampled fierceness. At length, on pain of being surrounded, M. de Colli was, on the 22nd, compelled to retire upon Cherasco, Fossano, and Savigliano. Not an Austrian moved to come to his aid. Entering Mondovi, the French gave a ball there, and next day did the town the favour to levy an enormous contribution, to lay hands on whatever was necessary for them, and to press five hundred young men into their army. The Court of Turin summoned M. de Beaulieu immediately to join his Majesty's troops for the defence of Piedmont, as otherwise peace would be treated for. On his refusal, an envoy was dispatched to the Spanish minister at Genoa, to open a negotiation with the French minister.

" Pushing their point without the loss of a day, and although weakened by the loss of fifteen thousand dead or wounded, in the actions from the 10th to the 22nd,

the French forced M. de Colli on the 26th to quit
Cherasco and retire ; he threw a portion of his troops into
Coni and took his road to Turin with the other. That
same evening the French arrived at Carmagnola, at five
leagues' distance from the capital. The dread of a siege
took possession of the inhabitants ; a serious movement
arose among the people ; the hatred and indignation
against the Austrians were its principal motives. There
was no alternative in this crisis. On the evening of the
29th, a truce was signed between Bonaparte and the King.
The former demanded the right of garrisoning Coni, Alessandria, and Tortona ; at the same time the Count de
Costa, nephew of the Archhishop of Turin, and the Count
de Revel, went to Paris to sue for peace.

" You may consider the French army replenished for
six months in men and provisions. So much success and
glory, and the revolutionary spirit, will raise them up
battalions—armies—at every step. The allies have lost,
since the 10th, at least fourteen to fifteen thousand men,
seven thousand of whom are prisoners, and among these
two lieutenant-generals, colonels, and officers in great
numbers. Seven French generals were killed.

" The places surrendered will ensure the French a retreat
on Piedmont ; but I am not aware yet whether this article
is ratified. Beaulieu holds the garrisons of Alessandria
and Tortona : he will not yield them of his own accord.
The respectable and unfortunate King of Sardinia is left,
amid his enemies in triumph at the gates of Turin, and
his allies as dangerous for him as his enemies. What a
lesson for secondary states ! Such has been their fate
everlastingly in coalitions with the great powers !

" If Beaulieu quits his present position, Genoa will be at the mercy of the French. A column will descend the Levant strand, penetrate to Modena, Bologna, and even Rome, without having to fear a battalion. They will revolutionize all on their route. I predicted to you last year, that at their approach Italy would explode like a powder-cask. The conquest is nothing ; the revolutionary subversion is a disaster unexampled since the invasion of the barbarians. They will give a quietus to the Catholic Church and the Pope, make immense booty, *Sans-culottise* all, and retire gorged with rapine, after having overturned all the Italian governments.

" The King of Sardinia's compulsory peace will entail that of the King of Naples, and, in my opinion, that of the Emperor. There is no connexion between the safety of Lombardy, of Tuscany, of all Italy (if possible), and the sacrifice of the Low Countries. The Austrians expect to be attacked on the Rhine ; you will see them recross that river. The play is over, my dear Count—let the curtain fall. England will remain with its enlightened *Chouanneries*, its ministerial pamphleteers, its damaged colonies.

" No member of the royal family has chosen to quit Turin. The French exact as conditions of a truce the restoration of Coni, Alessandria, and Tortona. The army of the Alps, consisting of twenty-five thousand men, is about to support that of Italy in the conquest of the Milanese territory. At least fifty or sixty thousand Austrians would be required to defend it, and there are not half so many."

LETTER TO THE CHEVALIER DE GALLATIN.*

" June 12, 1795.

The commencement of this letter is a mere repetition of the preceding one.   Mallet continues :——

"As to the Swiss whom you mention, they reserve themselves for the afterpiece.   They have received news calculated to create anxiety ; the proceedings, notes, and insolence must surely inspire some alarm.   Undeceive yourself : their security is really what it seems.   They are annoyed when tiresome people point out their danger : they prove by $a + b$ that it is impossible that the French should quarrel with the Swiss ; that reason, policy, interest . . . . this humbug, my dear friend, is literally the answer sent me by the worthy avoyer Steiguer on my communicating to him a valuable letter from Paris, which informed me : ' Our brigades will be in Berne and Zurich, and the tri-coloured cockade mounted in Swiss caps, while your

* The Chevalier de Gallatin, of an ancient Genevese family, was a man of considerable talent and information.   After having served with the Swiss guards in Holland, he retired to Geneva, where he married a Mademoiselle Mallet, a lady of merit.   The Revolution of 1794 drove him from his country.   He joined a number of his compatriots who had taken refuge at Berne ; and formed a connexion with Mallet du Pan, who recommended him to the Duke of Brunswick : this Prince attached him to his person and appointed him one of his intimate counsellors.   The Chevalier, having become Count of Gallatin, passed after the death of the Duke of Brunswick into the service of Bavaria ; he was appointed Minister Plenipotentiary from that Court to Paris at the epoch of the allies' entry in 1814 ; and occupied this post till his death.

senates still deliberate whether and how peace or war is to be declared.' As for me, I shall not wait for the result. My expulsion is already canvassed in a whisper ; at the first raised voice, I shall depart, without asking one day's respite.

" My work has been in circulation here these two days, and produces considerable excitement. I now hang upon a thread."

This correspondence shows us how little Mallet du Pan approved of royalist conspiracies ; and because he was not a plotter, d'Entraigues disliked him. Not so Count de Montgaillard, who persisted in openly calling him his master, and in making him the confidant of a great intrigue in which he was actively engaged. These confidences were for a long time confined to hints and mysterious predictions, and Mallet, out of courtesy to a nobleman who displayed a warm friendship for him, let him run on. It appears that at the moment selected for setting fire to the train—that is to say in the spring of 1796—Montgaillard became more explicit ; at any rate his letters are sufficiently intelligible in our days. The *friend* of whom he speaks is no other than Pichegru : as to Mallet, he thought he had guessed, or he had learned the secret, without putting any the more faith in it. At the beginning of May matters were in an admirable train.

Montgaillard writes : " My friend's behaviour is perfect ; rest assured that he will prove himself what I maintained him to be ; he has charmed the Archduke and Mr. Wickham, and will, I hope, get on. On Wednesday he communicated to me his final resolution, which has been tried and approved. My friend enjoys the confidence of the house whose service he has quitted ; he has an understanding with it, and it assists him with its credit. The work will be commenced on this understanding. I will answer for nothing, because it seems to me that a number of blunders are committed, though this is most positively denied. The truce will be broken very nearly at the time I indicated to you in my preceding letters. The patriotic army is recruiting on the lower Rhine, but continues utterly disorganized. The man about whom I have said so much to you, and who plays so important a part in the letters I left in your custody, will, immediately after the first reverse, be what Camillus was : this is a settled point. Then he will begin to act. Rest assured that he sees clearly, and as he ought."

These illusions were soon at their height in the Prince of Condé's camp. The King, dismissed from Verona by the Venetian States, appeared in person at Condé's army, despite the opposition of Austria, and his reign commenced. Montgaillard gives the following narrative : " The King, my dear Sir, on Thursday reviewed the rear-guard ; yesterday the centre ; on Tuesday he will review the van-guard. As to the many-coloured cavalry (two thousand three hundred and thirty-eight men), posted in the Black Forest, whence they do not appear destined to return yet a while, they will not be inspected. Altogether these amount to eleven thousand eight hundred and sixty-seven available men, well equipped and mounted, and perfectly prepared for active service ; in a word, Mr. Wickham and Mr. Crawford, who go to and fro between Fribourg and Reigel, were quite surprised at the aspect of this army.

They never omit saying: ' Sire,' and ' Your Majesty;' and the King has said to them the most flattering things with the utmost dignity. The King has displayed, under all circumstances, ever since his arrival, a self-possession and modesty which have astonished even those who knew him best: he now occupies his true position. He is neither too much a king, nor too much an emigrant ; but an imposing personage to satisfy men by the minutest details of his conduct, and to inspire hope in the greatest sticklers on such points ; he says nothing but what wisdom (even the wisdom of a revolutionary period), reason and policy may approve. Oh, that flattery may not mar this fair promise ! M.M. Jaucourt, d'Avaray, and La Vauguyon are arrived. M.M. Flaschlanden and Saint-Priest, who left Vienna on the 2nd of this month, are expected every moment—in one word, a Council is formed. Mr. Wickham attends there ; M. de la Tour is expected this morning. Every thing is on the stir and is excited ; the King has no house except that of the Prince of Condé. His Majesty has written to Vienna and London, whither Lord Macartney has proceeded from Venice (though he was charged by his court to follow the King, whithersoever he might think fit to go), after assuring the King that he should forward his interests, much more by this voyage, than by accompanying him to Reigel. The King has laid before his army the insult offered by the Venetian Senate. I know not whether the Doge will pay his second visit to Versailles : this may still be questioned. Last Thursday the King saw what are styled the Republicans : they requested that he might be made known to them ; he remained on horseback alone, and was saluted by the patriots, whom he begged not to cry, ' Long live the King,' as he did not wish, he said, to compromise them ; but assured them that they were his children, and not less dear to him than.those by whom he was surrounded.   The Archduke has sent the King a very plausible letter ; Marshal de Wurmser has written him an admirable one : such is a tolerably exact bulletin of his first week of royalty."

To this rhapsody, Mallet responds from Berne, on the 19th of May :

" Along with your details concerning the King and the Prince of Condé's army, news reached me of the Republicans' arrival at Milan.   I confess to you that the contrast chilled my very heart,   What ! such minutiæ, such hopes, such plans, occupy men's minds, while the French Revolution mounts the capitol !

" Europe is ruined, and by her own choice.   In former days, two hundred thousand barbarians invaded the Roman empire, then possessed of all the advantages of unity, science, discipline, entrenchments, innumerable fortresses. To-day six hundred thousand barbarians pour down upon a hundred states, corrupted, divided, besotted, governed by puppets of straw.   Our modern Goths far surpass in facilities and means those who once changed the destiny of Europe.   The rights of man, equality, the people's sovereignty, will share the triumph of the Rhenish laws.   Long ago wise men foresaw this catastrophe : fools laughed at it, and accused as Jacobinical a foresight which yet required no great exertion of intellect.

" Beaulieu, flying post haste to the Tyrol, leaves the field clear to the French.   There is no Fabius for them to fear, neither have they to win a battle of Cannæ.

Italy is theirs. Trees of liberty, tricolors, requisitions, enormous contributions, follow their steps. They will transport Italy into France : this magnificent country will be stripped, spoiled, sacked. The conquest of Lombardy alone is worth more than all their acquisitions these three years.

"Whether the King of France abide in the north or south, on the Rhine, or the Neva, appears to me absolutely indifferent. The monarchy will infallibly be re-established ; but most probably neither you nor I will witness the event. All hope has abandoned me. Do not build in any way on the good will of your friend. I believe him honest and loyal, but he is powerless."

Nevertheless, Montgaillard resumed his epistolary labours, to inform Mallet of a further development of the great affair, the rupture of the truce, brought about by the *friend*—that is to say, by Pichegru :

" A letter from my friend, which the Archduke received on the 20th, at half-past eleven o'clock at night, has determined him, without one moment's hesitation, to break the truce. You may then feel certain, that on the morning of the 31st, cannon will be fired. God grant that the repeated promise may be fulfilled, that they may be duly aimed, and not directed against opinion or terri-tory : as to the rest, entire confidence is reposed in my friend ; his advice and plans are followed, or at least entirely approved of. This friend guarantees success ; but he daily insists on the emigrants only doing as he wishes, that is to say, nothing : I even suspect he means to leave them in the lurch. I hope and trust that this will encounter no difficulty. The first ten or twelve days will decide the success or failure of my friend. To enable him to fulfil his engagements, the Austrians must obtain the first success, and so I expect they will."

Mallet on his part writes to Montgaillard on the 29th of May.

" What then do you build upon ? On the present moment, or on the predictions of Nostradamus ? You talk of a hundred and sixty-five thousand men, of plans, of wisdom, of fine speaking, of attacks, of head quarters. These are phantoms within the darkness of death. Let the curtain fall—the play is over. It is useless to change one's mind : when five years of irremediable faults have precipitated ruin, then it is too late to own it.

" Italy passes in the lump into the crucible of the revolution. Three electors and a stadtholder have been expelled : the Kings of Sardinia and Spain wear their crowns by favour of the Directory. The Pope sends embassy after embassy to Paris to obtain mercy, which he will not obtain, any more than the King of Naples. Talk to me about the eleven thousand four hundred and fifty-two men of Condé's army, and of the pamphlets of Tinseau, and of all the miserable busy-bodies about you ! At this moment your letter of the 24th reached me. Your infatuation is inconceivable."

A few days later it was Montgaillard's turn to despair.

" Mülheim, June 9, 1796.

" I have just quitted the head-quarters of the Archduke and Wurmser. All is over. The best opportunity and the most efficacious means which have offered themselves these six years, have been wasted. The whole line from Basle to

Dusseldorf was attacked at once ; the lines were to be abandoned by the French. The generals sent word to the Archduke and to Wurmser ; the latter had received the most pressing invitations from several towns of Alsace, where my friend was posted, ready to shake everything, only awaiting the moment appointed by the Austrians, and possessed of the most valuable correspondence at Paris. Yesterday, they were in Alsace, which, on the 15th, I will answer for it with my head, no longer sided with the Republic. I cannot express to you the degree of certainty inspired by circumstances prepared for a year past, with a combination of means, regarding which my sole merit was activity and fidelity to my King. It is for the sake of my friend alone, that the truce was broken ; and if I could see you, and explain to you the state of things, of which the greater part were only known, and still continue so, to my friend and myself, you would not accuse me either of infatuation or prejudice, and you would not tax me with mistaking our hopes for realities.

" I repeat, my dear Sir, my head is as cool as my heart is warm : I did hope everything, and to-day, I tell you with the same conviction and, unhappily, with the same reason, I now hope absolutely nothing." *

* According to Fauche-Borel, another agent in the negotiation, Pichegru's original plan was to join the Prince of Condé with twelve or fourteen thousand of his picked men, and thus to march arm-in-arm with him, heading his grenadiers, to Paris. The Prince durst not take upon himself the whole responsibility of so bold a step ; besides, he scrupled thus to quit the Austrian army. He consulted Wurmser, who, following the instructions of his Court, firmly opposed Condé's soldiers passing the Rhine, unless the towns of Alsace were ceded to him, to be occupied by the Austrians. The dismayed

In default of the confidential correspondence with M. de Sainte-Aldegonde, in which a break here occurs of several weeks' duration, we will give some extracts from the letters sent from Paris to Mallet by his two usual correspondents. They relate to Babeuf's conspiracy.

LETTER FROM A CORRESPONDENT TO MALLET DU PAN.

" All our newspapers will occupy you for a month to come with the great conspiracy of the terrorists ; and you would not understand much about it.   The fact is, that this is the work of concurrent circumstances, at least as much as of people ; that, in a nation inured to changes these seven years, Babeufs are always to be found, as surely as Marats and so many others, who give the signal for murder and disorder ; that a republic founded on the principle of equality will always be disturbed, so soon as any form of government tends to restore social order.   It is not probable that the *sovereign people* should at once reject the new government also ; but it is certain——it is a positive fact ——that this people regard the Luxembourg with almost the same sentiments with which they regarded the Tuileries before the 10th August.

" The comparison is strikingly correct.   Both parties

Prince rejected Pichegru's plan, and other means were sought for ; but from this moment Montgaillard appears to have played an equivocal part.   Fauche-Borel brings a heavy charge against him, and the Count's subsequent conduct gives but too much colour to the accusation.   Compare Fauche-Borel's " Mémoires," vol. 1 and 2, with the " Relation " of Count de Montgaillard, who lays all the blame of this failure on the Prince of Condé.

lean on I know not what ill-omened reason, which has never led them to commit anything but follies.

"The Directory would have rejoiced to keep well with both parties, in this conflict between the revolutionists and the advocates of Government; but I was compelled to adopt some decisive course. I do not expect it will remain long in office.

"The discovery of the conspiracy has failed to affect the external aspect of Paris. Here a group of *Sans-culottes* threatens the Pope and the Luxembourg Directory: further on, some *muscadins* wait in file for opera tickets: every where are seen women dressed with such luxurious elegance as has not been beheld at Versailles since 1788. Bricklayers and tatterdemalions mount guard at the posts of the sections: picquets of cavalry riding in the faubourgs and along the quays: the Sundays are kept with masses, and dancing: the decades equally celebrated by idleness; everything abundant and everything dear for paper, and certain articles even for money.

"The Catholic religion is observed with remarkable exactness. The first communions were numerous in the churches of Paris and in those of the country. I counted two hundred young communicants at Saint-Germain l'Auxerrois."

"23 Messidor, Year iv.

"The royalists are now convinced that dependence on foreign aid is vain; that open insurrection is a murderous folly; that amelioration can only be expected from time, from a moderate system of internal government, from the elections, and from a wise choice of the depositaries of power. Tell those who grieve to see French blood flow—tell those who nourish this sentiment as a duty—that the highest objects of their esteem and gratitude should be the men who assume every aspect and every mask to allay the revolutionary carnage; who, still too weak to stem the calamities of war, at least prevent the blood of families from staining the scaffold; who, at the hazard of their lives, and often amid distressing duties, save the miserable remnant of those illustrious houses, mown down by the scythe of Couthon, while Germany, England, Spain, and Italy, look on terrified or subdued. What a lesson for the *Sans-culottism* of Berlin, London, and Vienna! May its reign be over with us. Tell also those who madly cavil about the shades of crime to be punished in the counter-revolution, that there are certain princes, certain Swiss cantons, who think themselves delightfully secure, and who only owe their exemption from spoliation to the neutralism (pardon the expression, it conveys the idea), to the neutralism of Pastoret, Dumolard, Boissy, Thibaudeau, Pelet, &c., all gallows birds in right of not having prevented what all Europe could not restrain. It is also their useful influence and courageous perseverance which save us from the vengeance of *Vendémiaire* and from the murderous projects of Tallien, Merlin, and Babeuf."

"16 Thermidor.

"The soul of France is on the frontiers: whatever party men may belong to, whatever opinion they may entertain, they speak of nothing but the success of the army, and are unable to understand so many victories.

Armies always conquering and never conquered,—what then are the troops and the generals, what is the policy of the Emperor? A man, thirty-six years of age, named Moreau, who was studying law at Rennes ten years back, and who had never served before the commencement of the revolution, crosses the Rhine, and fights day after day : Jourdan does as much on his part. The Austrians continue constantly to retreat, acting on the defensive ; but they will not give battle, or cannot succeed in gaining a single one, —or rather they do nothing but defend and abandon their positions.

" All these victories are not barren victories. The countries occupied do really serve for the supply, clothing, and payment of the troops; and, in spite of the exaggerated resources and the four thousand millions which Calonne attributes to France, it is evident that our armies could not have continued to subsist on their own soil, if the Austrians had had fifty or sixty thousand more men to impede the conquest of Italy and of the right bank of the Rhine. Now, it seems to me that there was no occasion to be either a great statesman or a great general to manage this, and that the cabinet of the King of the Cannibal Islands would have set about taking his measures somewhat better than that of Vienna. One of the sutlers told me, as to this point, that their business was confined to the provisioning of the fortresses, and that the armies lived at the expense of foreign countries.

" Amid these incomprehensible events, a philippic by Mallet du Pan has just appeared. One Maret, a *ci-devant* scullion, and who prints and sells all the books of this kind, has produced an edition of it, and has had the impu-

dence to sell it at three livres.   As three livres are worth
at least twenty-four to the old amateurs, few would have
been able to purchase it; but, another man having similarly counterfeited it, and selling it at thirty sous, the first
has been obliged to lower his price, so that it has circulated to a certain extent among the public, and the poor
aristocrats lend it to each other.   All agree that not only
is this little work the best which the author has produced
on the revolution, but that none of the others is compar-
able to it, and that many passages are worthy of Tacitus
or Montesquieu.   One thing is desired and not found in it.
It were to be wished that, after showing the evil, he had
indicated the remedy; for it is natural for the unfortunate
to believe that he who developes the cause of their calamities so well, knows also the means of mitigating them. But,
on the contrary, his work withdraws hope: he assigns no
term to the revolution, and his readers are more unhappy
after perusing it than before.

"I am of opinion, and you must perceive the same
yourself, that our rulers, whether the Directory or the
two councils, work well enough together.   The repulse
of the enemy, the tranquillity of Paris, the handsome
emoluments they share, and which make them so many
cannons, plunge them, without their seeing it, into a
kind of carelessness or lethargy as to their political
divisions.   They all think of nothing but enjoying themselves, eating and drinking; and certainly it is vastly
pleasant for a class of men who, but for this, would
almost die of hunger.   Three fourths of them buy national property, being persuaded that it is only proprietors
who can take any interest in the common weal. The others,

whose nothingness forbids them to aspire to such exalted destinies, consider themselves no less happy in having an income of from ten to twelve thousand livres in hard cash—a sum exorbitant and out of all proportion to the actual state of fortunes and the extreme scarcity of money. All this does not prevent the hot-headed of both parties, in private intercourse, from treating each other harshly enough, and with energetic epithets.

" The Directory gets on sufficiently well with the ministers, and the legislative body leaves them to themselves. One hears of no citations to the bar. They give entertainments and dinners ; and to dine just now with Citizen Bénezech is much what it used to be to dine with M. de Breteuil. There is nothing frugal in all this, nothing republican ; the whole difference consists in the quality of the guests. Among them you will find sergeants, or of a yet lower grade, become generals ; some constitutional bishops, having wives and families, become members for the department and at the head of offices, and some Septembrists playing the penitent. Add to these, some marquises, some counts, some priests, fundholders and heads of families, virtuous and ruined, napkin in hand, behind the chairs of an assembly brought together by crime and folly, and you will have a tolerably faithful idea of the agrarian law put in practice by the most sensitive, generous and enlightened nation of the world.

" The people of Paris, in general, are not to be pitied. The little money extant circulates only to pay for commodities of primary necessity : the artizans gain as much as they did in 1790, and more ; the public-houses begin to fill. The landlords, fundholders, clerks, a portion of the shopkeepers consume their savings or starve ; but these people will not change the government. Nowhere is the cry of ' Long live the Republic !' heard, not even in public festivals. The people are for ever cutting their jokes upon the Directory, which lets them alone. Talk is free enough in the *cafés*, and Mallet himself would not have thought his words would be retailed in public."

LETTER FROM MALLET DU PAN TO MARSHAL DE CASTRIES.

" July 13, 1796.

" M. le Maréchal,

" I return an immediate answer to the letter you did me the honour of addressing me on the 25th of June, and which reached me only last Sunday.

" Bonaparte is very probably at Rome. A column of his troops is at Leghorn. He overruns, ransoms, subjects Italy with greater ease than if he were subjugating a department of France. All the sovereigns of the country, to the defence of which they have not chosen to sacrifice a sequin or a soldier, are now raised to the dignity of sutlers to the Directory. Bonaparte, passing the Appennines, feels no uneasiness about the Austrians : he knows very well that he would have twice enough time to go to the extreme point of Calabria and come back, before they would get rid of their dawdling and irresolution. This war would eternally offer the same results, were it to last ten years ; so that my only wish, all the winter, was for peace. It would have been better to lose one province by treaty than four by defeats.

" We await with the extremest anxiety a battle in the

Brisgau : it will decide the fate of Suabia, and probably that of Switzerland. Europe has come to the conclusion so vainly foretold these four years. They must either pass under the yoke, don the *bonnet rouge*—or fight : fight they will not, except retreating, and soon this frightful crisis will end in treaties like that of the King of Sardinia.

"This is the first moment, since the origin of the revolution, in which all hope and all courage have abandoned me. I no longer perceive any indication or near cause of alteration. The course of time and events will bring it finally ; but such a revolution is indefinitely adjourned.

"Receive, &c."

LETTER FROM MALLET DU PAN TO THE CHEVALIER DE GALLATIN.

"July.13, 1796.

"I have received, my dear Chevalier, your letter of the 15th of June, the note of the same date, and your answer from Hackemburg of the 27th. Since you are aware, on the 15th of June, of the fact you mention, do you suppose my correspondent (the Emperor) can be ignorant of it ? Above all, do you imagine he would place the least confidence in the news, if it came from me ? What has been the use of all those I gave him ? The reply has been given ; it is a protocol calling out for information on all points : ' Don't talk to us about that ; we have no occasion for the future ; don't let its image trouble the present ; leave us to eat, drink, trifle, and die, without being incommoded.' One must be an idiot to meddle with these people's affairs : once for all, experience has cured me of the profession of intelligencer general. Besides, it will happen just the same either way. They will equally capitulate after being well beaten. Their only difficulty is as to the how, and with a kind of decorum ; but at the rate they are going, they will soon be delivered from these minor scruples.

"The conquest of Italy is a mere tour to Bonaparte. He raises all the sovereigns of the country in succession to the dignity of sutlers to the Convention ; he treats them like vassals, and is quite right. Master of Leghorn and Tuscany, he will hold the Grand Duke to ransom. He himself went to Rome, after having taken, in four days, the duchy of Urbino, the Ferrarese territory, and Romagna.

"Genoa participates similarly in the benefits of neutrality. Faypoult has demanded the expulsion of the Austrian minister, the dismissal of the Governor of Novi, the closing of Spezzia to the English, the surrender of the two ports to the troops of the Republic, twenty-four millions, the recall of the exiles and other rascals condemned for revolutionary offences. The senator Augustin Spinola, distinguished for his firmness in the various past commotions, has been condemned by the French military agency to be shot, and to the confiscation of all his property. The pretext is a rising of the peasants in his fief of Arquetta. This magistrate escaped to Corsica : not a single voice, not a single effort, against the condemnation. All the moderately respectable magistrates the Republic contained, are keeping within doors, or have left the territory.

"Bonaparte chastises and despoils Italy with less than seventy thousand men. The Austrians do not interfere with him. Proud of having held the gorges of the Tyrol, waiting for their eternal reinforcements, changing generals every week, cowed like hares, they will not attempt even to relieve Mantua, and the season will have elapsed before they pass the Adige.

" The French will have full time to consummate their military executions, to carry off their immense booty, and to retire, leaving Italy in a state of anarchy, and cankered with the spirit of revolution. They have compelled the King of Sardinia to sanction a French theatre in Turin : they neglect nothing to pervert Piedmont, whose fortresses they labour at dismantling.

" I informed you of the Swiss decree against the emigrants. I know that the Directory is about to require immediately the expulsion of Mr. Wickham. It had demanded the recall to their country of the exiles from the pays de Vaud, and the mounting of the tricolor cockade by all the French : this was unanimously refused. This country, however, is not the less wounded to death by the ambition, the mania, and the miscalculations of the young men, who absolutely have the upper hand of the old. Yet the story of Genoa petrified them all.

" I have not experienced anything the least disagreeable through my work. It would have been awkward to persecute me, while my pamphlet is reprinted, and sells in the very midst of the Palais Royal."

THE SAME TO COUNT DE SAINTE-ALDEGONDE.

" August 11, 1796.

" What has become of you, my dear Count ? I am uneasy at your long silence ; but I presume it must have had the same cause as mine, namely, the fear of interception of the

couriers.   I now learn that they pass freely, and hasten
to renew our correspondence.   Notwithstanding the noise
made by the decree expelling the emigrants from Switzerland, three-fourths of them remain.   Several have returned
voluntarily to France, where they are not in anywise
molested.   This is beyond contradiction the least bad
course for all who have not made themselves too conspicuous.

"Here is a fine series of events.   During the breach in
our correspondence Suabia has been lost, almost without
a blow.   The Austrians find out now that it is not all
to play a game with hypothetical armies on paper.   The
Archduke seems fixed at Donauwerth, between the Danube and the Lech, whence his line extends as far as
Bregentz.   The campaign will end in that quarter, in the
circle of Bavaria.   General Moreau and his troops behave
discreetly in Suabia.   No violence and very little disorder.
Franconia, like Suabia, is in the hands of the French.
The army of Sambre-et-Meuse is approaching Egra : we
shall see it in Bohemia.   I know not what means of
resistance the Emperor possesses on that side ; but I conceive them to be very inadequate.   Maria-Theresa was in
a worse position—but then she was Maria-Theresa.

" You know that the French army, after the springing
of the mine at Mantua, was attacked, on the 29th July,
by Marshal Wurmser, and lost all its entrenched positions
on the Adige, Lago, Peschiera, Salo, Breschia, more than four
thousand prisoners, and as many slain.   On the 2nd, this
army, reduced to forty thousand at the utmost, comprising
all its scattered detachments, was retiring on Lodi: we shall
see them in Piedmont before a fortnight is over, unless the

cabinet should come, according to its wont, to snatch the victory from the hands of its general by enfeebling and baffling him. The feeling of the people, from Naples to Nice, is a fanaticism of rage and horror against the French. I was much mistaken in thinking them disposed to insurrection. The revolution has met with no partisans in Italy, except among the nobility and the ministers. The court of Rome surpassed all the others—even that of Florence—in baseness, in prostitution, in meanness of all kinds. I hope sincerely that the King of Naples, the Emperor and the Venetians, who are arming to an extraordinary extent, will deprive the Pope, once for all, of the power of putting his states at the mercy of the first comer, after scandalous refusals to contribute in the slightest degree to the salvation of Italy. The people is very right-minded at Rome, in the Ferrarese territory, and in Romagna ; but all is rotten in the upper classes.

" I have not much to tell you about Paris. They trouble themselves very little about the government ; and the government, which knows the fact, only seeks to live as long as it can. It feels no more anxiety as to the royalists—and it is right. The spirit of movement, insurrection, conspiracy, is stopped for a long time to come. All the malcontents, the middle classes, the men of letters, the Vendémiairists, even the royalists, who are nick-named ' men of Verona,' are completely disabused by the events of the war. There are none now but some old women of the Marais to resemble that knight of St. Louis, who, on hearing of the exploits of Bonaparte, said, ' Don't you perceive that these are old gazettes of Louis XIV. reprinted ?'

" You may look for the approaching disgrace of Bona-

parte.   He had the audacity to say to the Directory, ‘ I
have received your treaty with Sardinia; the army has
approved it.’ ”

Austria, it seems, is never to be in a state utterly
desperate: there is no putting an end to her.   She may be
pushed to the edge of the abyss, but she does not fall
down: this has been proved over and over again by her
history for the past age.   When Mallet wrote to his friend
—“ this Viennese Cabinet holds so strange a course of
conduct that the preservation of the monarchy will be a
miracle,”—the Archduke Charles was saving the Empire
by chasing Jourdan and the French from the Danube, preparing the retreat of Moreau, and thus ruining the daring
plan of Bonaparte, who proposed to join the two generals
with his army in the heart of Germany.   Mallet announced this news to M. de Sainte Aldegonde:

“ September 17. 1796.

“ The Archduke has enrolled his name among the greatest.   This memorable fortnight will stand out in the
strange history of this war, which seems to be directed by
opposing genii, destroying each other’s work, as in fairy-
tales, as soon as it seems accomplished.   This resembles
the campaign of 1704 : the Court of Vienna was on the
eve of destruction, when the battle of Hochstedt brought
it back from the further end of Baravia to the left bank
of the Rhine.

“ After losses so immense, the army of Sambre-et-Meuse
will scarcely be able to recover itself this campaign.   But
Beurnonville will replace and succour it ; your armed neu-

trals will let it have its own way, and thus spoil the certain opportunity of driving the French once for all from the right bank. The Emperor will have saved Europe for the third time. They have shown, and continue to show, energy at Vienna, and all their faults have arisen from a false security. Yet this is the moment the King of France chooses to publish a declaration, in which he announces that he has quitted Condé's army, because he would not fight against his subjects in defence of the Austrian possessions. This pretty sally will amuse France, and raise indignation at Vienna."

TO THE SAME.

"October 12, 1796.

"Moreau and his army, by dint of waiting, have found themselves shut up between Engen, which you passed at five leagues' distance from Schaffhausen, and the lake of Constance—that is to say, in a diabolical barren country, on a space of fifteen leagues at the utmost. His columns of the east, beaten at Bregentz and Lindau, pursued with boundless hatred by the peasants, have thrown themselves into Switzerland since the 22nd September. Upwards of ten thousand of these unfortunate men, mostly wounded or maimed, deserters or fugitives, traversed Northern Switzerland to reach Basle. The adjoining cantons allow this transit without any precautionary measures, order, or regulation whatever. They made them disarm, it is true, but a quantity of baggage defiled.

"They are roused here in good earnest; and their vigilance is reinforced by a note from the Imperial Minister, which was accompanied by a letter from Count de la Tour, wherein that general intimated to the Swiss that he would pursue the French on their territory, if they gave them asylum or free passage. The whole people, especially in the rural districts, murmured loudly at this inundation of freebooters and incendiaries. The anti-French party, which had for six months fallen into a wretched minority, regained all its advantages. By a majority of eighteen votes to twenty, it was resolved to arm at once ten thousand men, besides the reserve of the same strength, to march them to the frontier, and to prohibit all passage under any circumstances. All this was executed in less than eight days. M. d'Erlach, deputy at Zurich, induced that canton to adopt the same measures. Six thousand men were assembled : all the other cantons, with the exception of Basle, adhered to the plan of Berne, and furnished their contingent of twenty thousand men. This rising of Switzerland, and its object, will incense the Directory."

LETTER FROM COUNT DE SAINTE-ALDEGONDE TO MALLET DU PAN.

" Bremen, November 3, 1796.

" . . . . Louis XVIII is still at Blankenburg, where he is much beloved by the inhabitants. His suite is far from numerous. I am not aware of what goes on in it ; because, not wishing to put myself forward in the least, I hold aloof, and above all carefully avoid any correspondence which would put me in relation with it. I want none, except with Scotland, where I meet more than ever with proofs of friendship, interest, and confidence. They are

pained there—this is between you and me—to see that
the King is so remote from the times, and allows himself
to be thus misled as to his true position. Efforts are made
unceasingly, and I am certain of it—efforts are made, I
say—to place it clearly before him. They would desire to
act the part of mediators between him and the interior; but
does not this part seem to you too difficult of accomplish-
ment? Do you think it feasible, even with the best intentions? They desire at Edinburgh to be as much as
possible in correspondence with the interior, and to augment,
or rather doubtless create, partisans there. They wish to
work on sure ground—in short, the strongest desire prevails
of coming to an understanding." . . . .

LETTER FROM MALLET DU PAN TO COUNT DE SAINTE-
ALDEGONDE.

"November 2, 1796.

"We have then an English embassy, *in fiocchi*, at Paris.
No one, except the asses of journalists, believe in a peace.
The English can obtain it only by sacrificing their allies,
Belgium, Holland, &c. Paris does not change its colour:
it is the same spirit from one end of France to the other—
discontent and nothingness, a longing for quiet under any
government. Save at Lyons, royalty is but a vague
reminiscence.

"The emigrants return in shoals, and get their names
erased from the list. A fund is opened for the purpose at
Cochon's office. They pay, and are reinstated better or
worse; but this dangerous passport can be depended on
only for the moment."

TO THE SAME.

" November 6, 1796.

" My dear friend,

" I ought to have answered your two excellent letters
of the 8th and 9th of October ; but a recent absence, the
uncertainty of the issue on our frontiers, and the departure of my son for England, and then the robbery I
experienced eight days afterwards, of a box in which I
had sixty-five louis in crowns, by a thief, evidently well-
informed, and whom I have not been able to trace—all
this has prevented me from writing.*

" The imperialists have, indeed, committed mistakes ;
but these mistakes must be balanced against the difficulties.
If we had been told on the 30th of July, that on the
30th of October not a Frenchman would remain on the
right bank as far as Sieg ; that, of two hundred thousand,
not fifty thousand would return to their place of departure ; that in six weeks they would be driven from the
Danube to Dusseldorf, and from the gates of Munich to
those of Strasburg ; that the Austrian hussars would be
ranging Lower Alsace for these three weeks, after having
overthrown the lines of Quesch ; acknowledge how incre-
dulous we should have been. The Archduke has displayed
great talents—and what is far rarer, character—sustained
activity and celerity, and an emulation of patriotism and
greatness, which has elated his discouraged troops—in

* This money was stolen from Mallet by a servant, who had been
several years in his service, and who soon afterwards retired with his
booty to a small property in the pays de Vaud. Twenty years later
this man died, leaving to Madame Mallet by his will, the interest of
the money he had stolen.

fine, what no prince of his blood has displayed before him, an union of gentleness with severity, of frank affability with the maintenance of his dignity. To these qualities he has joined a personal bravery, which has excited something of the same quality in the most timid. At the attack of Kinzig, on the 19th, his troops were wavering : he placed himself at the head of a battalion of Hungarian grenadiers, superseded the officer who commanded the attack, charged in front, and carried the town. There is stuff in this young man, and I congratulate myself on having thought so in 1793.

" The Directory had really favoured the project of a visit to Vienna ; they professed to have not the slightest doubt on the subject ; Paris re-echoed their intention, while the rest of Europe has despatched imperial negotiators. Notwithstanding, it is a proved fact that this power, accused of desiring peace, and treating for it, ever avoided making or entertaining a single proposal ; that, betrayed by their allies, a prey to all the perfidy of the circles, aware that two hundred thousand French were on the frontiers, they braved the danger. This they did because they really saw it, whereas hitherto they had only read about it. The reign of illusion is over, and now steps are taken which might have prevented three campaigns, if half so much energy had been displayed three years ago."

LETTER FROM COUNT DE SAINTE-ALDEGONDE TO MALLET DU PAN.

" November 24, 1796.

" Before long the King will quit Blankenburg, and go, they say, to Zerbst, a small principality belonging since the death of her brother, the Prince of Anhalt, to the Empress of Russia. I cannot say what his political projects are, though I am aware that several are in agitation : when I have anything certain to communicate, I will do so. I know for a certainty—but this is between ourselves —that attempts have been made to prejudice the King against you. In these attempts, I can assure you, Monsieur takes no share whatever. The knowledge of our connexion has led to a like attempt in regard to myself. However, we are both of us perfectly indifferent to any attack of low intriguers, and our conduct is too blameless to afford any ground for a serious reproach. I make myself quite easy in regard to disfavour wholly unmerited, and am determined never to be a time-server nor a courtier. I offered my own and the services of my family to Louis XVIII, soon after his accession to the throne ; I received an evasive answer ; I took the hint, my dear Mallet, and, what is more, I requested my friends never to utter my name in his presence, nor in that of any of his court. I disdain to be their flatterer or their hanger-on. I was not born to play such a part. My conduct has been in keeping with my birth and principles. Very different is the conduct of his unhappy brother, who pays me the greatest attention, and who would deem himself the most fortunate of Princes, if he could act as mediator between France and the King, and fix the crown at any cost on the head of the latter. Should it ever happen, my dear friend, that proposals are made you, on the part of his Majesty—no improbable surmise— in spite of prejudices, be sure to have the agreement in writing, and signed by the Prince's own hand. There is but one man who really enjoys his confidence, and even with him he is not perfectly unreserved, and that is Count d'Avaray, his favourite ; all others he deceives. With this exception, he is the most polite, the most amiable, and the best informed of all the Princes. He has turned everybody's head at Blankenburg ; even at Brunswick he is an object of interest and admiration."

LETTER FROM MALLET DU PAN TO THE CHEVALIER DE GALLATIN.

"November 30, 1796.

I congratulate you on becoming a Brunswicker, my dear Chevalier, and congratulate myself on having received your letter of the 14th, more punctually than you did mine. You say you regret my absence, because where you are I should have been more decidedly useful. I am not quite convinced of my usefulness, nor certain whether that would be the best stage for its display ; but what I do discern very clearly is, that I cannot waste the little means and money I have, on which my family have the first claim ; that I am not in a situation to be the generous counsellor of any body, nor disposed to further any one's views, by asking charity. I have been too long fool enough to lose my time in anti-revolutionary knight errantry, in scrawling memoranda to be torn up as waste paper, by the parties concerned, and to play the part of secretary and laughing-stock to a set of prying inquirers. I will not stir till I have fixed upon some settled mode of life, and I will not again be so foolish as to neglect my own affairs while looking after those of other people. The future looks darker than ever in my eyes. Every wise father of a family must give up public life, and be persuaded that every day's necessities cannot be put off like counter-revolutions. . . . . .

"Then you do not think that Mr. Pitt wishes for peace? I have good reason for not being of your opinion. The Spanish war, so agreeable to the privateers, embarrasses the government. We see the ports of the ocean and of the Mediterranean closed against the English, who are compelled to build warehouses in London for heaps of goods unsold ; credit and commerce suffer together ; money disappears. But, however anxious the ministry may be for peace, it is not likely they will propose a treaty to five scoundrels and a Goth of La Croix ; they demand an effectual, useful, and honourable treaty ; were this granted, the war would soon be at an end. At Vienna they are immovable on three points : a cumulative peace with England, no separate treaty, the integrity of the Empire, and the restitution of Belgium, or an equivalent for it. I doubt whether Mr. Clarke will procure any modification of these conditions.

"The progress of revolution in Italy is rapid. If Bonaparte is not driven into Piedmont before the winter, that country will become a theatre of crime."

LETTER FROM MALLET DU PAN TO COUNT DE SAINTE-ALDEGONDE.

"November 26, 1796.

"My dear Count,

"I have received your delightful letters of the 4th and 13th. I confess to idleness, but you will forgive me in consideration of my having been much troubled and occupied.

"The history of the Infant of Spain, like that of the Orleanist faction, is one of those thousand and one delusions which have amused the emigrants and the King's counsellors for the last five years, like the scalded dog which fears cold water. I wrote to you at the time an account of the private intrigue of Tallien; but that very Tallien at the present day has not credit enough to appoint a clerk, much less to set up a King of France. Spain may be induced by her desires to form expectations; but not a word, not a treaty, not a partisan, not the shadow of assistance will she get from any of the governing powers.

"The government is detested and despised; no confidence is placed in the present state of things : in general monarchy would be preferred, if one fine day, people on awakening could but find it already established without violence or danger; but the dread of this violence or danger is a thousand times stronger than the desire for monarchy, which becomes more and more transient and imaginary. The universal passion is to pillage and spend—no one is actuated by any other. There is no such thing as opinion; all institutions, past or future, are matter of derision, but many in all classes find it their interest to favour the Republic. The fatal line of conduct to which the King has pledged himself, and in which he persists, has caused a rooted preference for what is considered by every individual as most accordant with his own advantage. I repeat, that, as it is nobody's interest to vindicate the rights of the nobility, clergy, and parliament, and as the people have endured all the calamities of a victorious revolution, in prosecution of its privileges, it is the height of folly to suppose that this same people will risk another revolution to restore what they have won. The absurdity of such an idea is unexampled and inappreciable. Never in my estimation were affairs in a more hopeless condition: I have long ceased to discern light, means, or final result."

TO THE SAME.

" December 18, 1796.

" I have commissioned our Abbé, the financier (the Abbé de Pradt, a great financier and a great strategist), to give you a supplement to my Italian gazette. You are overrun with lies about that ultramontane country, as well as ourselves : the truth is, there have been lost, on both sides, about ten or eleven thousand men, between the 1st and 20th of November (the loss has been most heavy on the part of the French, both in killed and prisoners). After this great slaughter, Bonaparte found himself master of the Adige, and is so at this moment. Mantua continues in a state of blockade and destitute of provisions. General Alvinzi is established on the right of the Brenta, from Padua to Bassano and Fontaviva in a semicircular line, reaching to the corps of Davidowitch, posted at Ala, and in the Italian Tyrol. Reinforcements are arriving ; preparations to resume the offensive were making on the 5th. If not, Mantua will be taken ; and with that fortress, Italy will be lost. But will the advanced season, the course of tardy and indecisive operations bring back Alvinzi to the passage of the Adige ? I doubt it. Consequently, a hundred thousand men will be wanted next year, and will find it difficult to effect that which fifty thousand, with better officers at their head, could easily have executed this year. Italy is fatal to the Austrian arms. Here are four generals and four successive armies destroyed or repelled ; hence I conclude that there is some radical defect in the management of this war. The imperialists have to do with the most daring, the most active, the swiftest mortal that ever existed : his head is brimstone and he has hind's feet. You may think what chance their deliberate movements, their heavy columns, their distant corps, can have against a hawk that darts upon the enemy at the most unexpected moment : he still has from twenty eight to thirty thousand effective troops, which will amount to forty thousand as soon as the reinforcements, which for some time have been passing the Alps and the Col de Tende, arrive. He enlists all the brigands and the fanatics, disciplines them, and next year they will be soldiers. This magnificent country is become a volcano : it will be consumed in a year, if the French stand their ground. Depend on this truth, whatever you may hear to the contrary ; they are all unaccountably blind at Vienna on this head.

" I feel no surprise at what you tell me about the prejudices of a certain august personage in your regard and mine; I was well aware of the feeling—at least towards myself; but what has one to do with the other ? Why punish you for thinking as all men of sense think at the present day ? Luckily, your superior intellect and noble mind render you indifferent alike to contemptible proofs of favour, and unmerited disgrace. Following your example, I shall not take the trouble to exculpate myself: it is truly a happiness to be altogether independent in such desperate circumstances, in the midst of men who by their proceedings would ruin the most promising combinations. I am as much in the dark as yourself as to any other plans; but I can assure you that these agents in France act most injudiciously, and would do much better if they did nothing at all. Adieu."

CHAPTER XII.

1799.

Delicate questions addressed to Mallet du Pan concerning the dynastic interests of Monsieur and his son—Conspiracy of the Marmousets—Letter from M. Necker—"Lettre à un homme d'État"—Letter from Mallet to M. Michaud, of "La Quotidienne," concerning the conduct of the Directory in regard to the Republics of Venice and Genoa—Sensation at Paris—Rage of Bonaparte—The government of Berne, intimidated, decrees the expulsion of Mallet.

A LITTLE more than fifty years ago, when the Republic of France was in the plenitude of its power, four personages openly laid claim, or secretly aspired to hold the sceptre of France on the day it should resume the monarchical form of government. All four during the interval between the republic of that day and of this, have had their turn as King, all four have enjoyed that dangerous supremacy—Napoleon, Louis XVIII., Charles X., Louis Philippe ; one alone, Louis XVIII., preserved it till his death ; the others ended their days in exile. During the period now in review, from 1796 to 1797, Bonaparte has already attained the summit of a command in the name of the republic ; at the head of his little army of emigrants ; Louis XVIII. flatters himself each passing moment will place him on that throne, which is his by rightful claim ; that popular favour which is to instal the Duke of Orleans in the place of Charles X. begins to display itself, and as yet troubles no one so much as Charles X., for the Count d'Artois himself, less concerned than might have been conjectured about the pretensions of the lawful King his brother, is too impatient to substi-his own or those of his son. The Count d'Artois, canvas-sing in favour of his son, in case his own claims should be set aside, is no gratuitous assumption : the following questions unreservedly put to Mallet du Pan by a devoted friend of Monsieur, may fairly be adduced in support of the assertion. We admit that M. de Sainte-Aldegonde proposes the queries in his own name alone ; but his words clearly indicate that he was incited to do so in com-pliance with desires well known to himself.

LETTER FROM COUNT DE SAINTE-ALDEGONDE TO MALLET DU PAN.

" Bremen, December 18, 1796.

" I feel more deeply than any, how much harm the King has done himself by persisting in following the false track he has traced out for himself. I am quite willing to leave off talking of this Prince : it is impossible to serve him against his will, and, since he will ruin himself, and we cannot prevent it, we can only confine ourselves to barren wishes. It is his fault, and that of the men who surround and blind him ; but I am too much attached to Monsieur, and love him too well, not to ask you, in my name, and for the sake of our friendship, to give me an answer as soon as possible to the following questions.   It is myself alone who puts them, so that you are at liberty to reply to them on a fly-sheet, and solely for my own use ; or else to reply, if you prefer, in such a manner that I may be able to communicate your good advice, if they choose to follow and profit by it.

" 1st. What should Monsieur do to make himself and his son, the Duke d'Angoulême, well known in France ?

" 2nd. Supposing mediation possible, what should the Prince do to put it into execution ?   Between ourselves, he lays much stress on this project, and nothing would give him more pleasure than to see it succeed.

" 3rd. What should he do, to turn to profit the favourable disposition shown towards the Duke d'Angoulême last year ?   For you will agree, my dear Mallet, that, since the King does not know how to resume the crown, and, on the contrary, loses it beyond retrieving, it is essential in that case that it should devolve on his nephew and his heir.   This implies no change of dynasty. Louis XVIII. would resign his right to his nephew, and there an end of it.   Monsieur is the best of brothers and of subjects ; but he ruins himself as well as his son by adhering too closely to the course the King has prescribed —a course which he does not by any means approve, I am certain, and which he follows only out of respect and attachment to his brother.   I am well aware too that he does all in his power to undeceive him and open his eyes ; but he has laboured at this vainly a long while."

LETTER FROM MALLET DU PAN TO COUNT DE SAINTE-
ALDEGONDE.

"January 8, 1797.

" What can I add to my previous replies to the question you repeat as to the desires of Monsieur ?   The
subject is dreadfully delicate.   The Prince cannot release
himself from obedience to his brother, and from their
common interest : he is obliged to follow the course
adopted by the latter.   If he abandoned it, without formal
authority from the King, consider to what that first step
might lead.   That is the capital point of the difficulty.

" Monsieur cannot take a distinct and active part
without the consent of the King ; giving him to understand the necessity that exists for an apparent diversity in
their line of conduct.   But will not the very proposal
offend ?   Can he hope to obtain his consent ; if not, how
can he act without incurring the most serious consequences ?   The more I reflect on it, the more impracticable do I consider the project.

" The only step to be taken is to pave the way for
acquiescence in the Prince's views, by informing people of
his sentiments : for this purpose he must express them in
conversation ; his attendants must lead to the subject and
dilate on it : the gazetters will next take it up, and from
them it will be transmitted to the French papers.   A still
better way is to show a readiness to wink at past offences,
in respect to those emigrants whom the Puritan party
regard as not sufficiently strict, and to treat them with
esteem and respect. To indulge personal considerations can

produce nothing but mischief in the prosecution of political designs; all prejudice against individuals, however just apparently, must be sacrificed: things, aims, and means, must be contemplated in their true light.

"A mediator must be accepted by both parties. But men's minds in France are still far removed from negotiations about royalty.

"These precautions might benefit the Duke d'Angoulême, in case France ever offered him the crown; but I dare not advise any act whereby to provide for such a moment and foster these dispositions: this would be to contest the crown with the legitimate king, to divide even the royalists, to open a fresh abyss beside the one we would fain close. All efforts should then be confined to such demonstrations of benevolence, moderation, and greatness of soul, as may tend to strengthen popular prepossession and direct it towards the Duke d'Angoulême. Landmarks should be erected, but the proposed route kept secret: events may be profited by, if they occur, but should not be brought about —an odious position, I admit, but enforced on pain of destroying union and overthrowing every principle."

M. de Sainte-Aldegonde acknowledged that he detected no flaw in Mallet's reasoning; and the two friends, abandoning the Princes to their fruitless projects, thenceforward only dilated in their correspondence on those various events which occupied the end of 1797, and the commencement of the following year. The victorious aggressions of the French Republic, its projected descent upon England, the critical position of the British empire, which emerged suddenly and with heroism from the dishonour cast upon it by

the Directory's rejection of its pacificatory overtures ;
Paul I. at St. Petersburg, Bonaparte in Italy, the Archduke with the troops, Venice taken, Switzerland invaded,
internal conspiracies rendered impotent, the Directory victorious both within and without, yet more than ever
threatened with speedy overthrow ; finally, France, with its
emigrants, weary of exile or else flocking back to their
country, France surfeited with revolutions, yet not cured of
them, waiting impatiently for the arrival of a master who
should liberate it from the republic and its five despised
tyrants ! what a conflict ! what a moment ! All is to be
hoped or feared, when logic, even that of passion, is
silenced, as if leaving events to be decided by the fortune
of a few men. It was indeed with breathless interest that
Mallet du Pan watched the confused scenes of that drama
of which all Europe was the stage.

We, to whom history shows in one view the valuable
results of this unprecedented turmoil, and the unequalled
glory achieved by a great captain of thirty years of age,
do not endeavour to realize the feelings of the lookers on.
Yet we should not count for nothing, when estimating these
glorious epochs, however glorious they may be, the sufferings of contemporary generations ; it promotes the philosophy of history to place beside the undetailed accounts of
historians, the testimony of men who lived through the
events they speak of. Memoirs are history, the history of
the parties concerned : but letters are sincere and tell us
much more. Let us return to those of our hero and his
friends.

LETTER TO MARSHAL DE CASTRIES.

"January 4, 1797.

" Monsieur le Maréchal,

"I am deeply and most gratefully affected by the fresh proof of interest conveyed in your last letter : I recognized in it the high honour which characterizes all your proceedings, and those especially by which you have honoured me. It is quite true that last autumn I was robbed of what, under present circumstances, I could but ill afford to lose : I have been unable to discover whether the thief aimed at my papers or my purse. By resolutely reducing myself to necessaries, I can maintain for a time myself and family : if I had to seek a model of resignation and philosophy, you would furnish me with one, Monsieur le Maréchal ; you, who show yourself so superior to adversity, and who benevolently embrace those even who, like myself, have no claim on you but that of a respectful attachment. You bestow your benefits too nobly for me ever to accept them without necessity : this necessity does not as yet exist : should it arise, you invite my confidence—I should apply to you.

"Again and again we have seen the port, Monsieur le Maréchal, and still the storm drives our vessel back upon the open sea. The horizon seems to me blacker than ever. This absurd English embassy at Paris has ended, as all sensible people foresaw it would end. I do not agree with those who view it as a mere farce of the English government; Mr. Pitt especially would not, I think, have been sorry to adjourn the quarrel, obtain a respite, and settle matters for the moment by a *mezzo-termine*. The

Directory has commenced and will carry on a fearful war with the English, by shutting against them the European ports : it will let them cover the ocean with their squadrons, while its armies prevent their trading on the continent.

" The ambiguous conduct, vacillating principles, and timidity, which have characterized this war, have offered the republicans advantages which they fully appreciate : they will never be made more moderate, because their disposition, circumstances, crimes, and perpetual aim, combine to carry them to excess in everything. They have vested their safety and glory in the dissolution of all states : inconsistent on all other subjects, this plan is ever kept in view."

LETTER FROM MALLET DU PAN TO THE ABBÉ DE PRADT.

" January 25, 1797.

" It is not for nothing, my dear friend, that I have turned Alpine marmot : the winter numbs and torpifies me. This is why I have still to answer your amusing letter of the 31st December : our worthy Europe has had its day, and is turned into so many open madhouses. I fancy the new Emperor of Russia is an answer to the question you ask me : he sets off very much as his father did ; I hope his end will not be similar. I see him bitten with the rage for innovations, philanthropy, and popularity ; he is smitten with Frederick the Great, and thinks to imitate him by wearing a large hat, a scanty, buttoned-up coat, boots, and a black cockade. Such ape's tricks show the calibre of a man. I wish with all my heart that he may emerge safe and sound from these facetiæ.

" On the subject of its fleet (the Irish expedition), the Directory answers with Philip II., that it was not sent forth to do battle with the winds : in fact, it encountered no other foe ; and the five hundred men of war figuring in the English ports and almanacks, have barely captured two or three sloops which the storm gave into their hands. What has become of *la Fraternité*, Hoche and Admiral Morand (they arrived at Rochefort), is not yet known. Be their fate what it may, two-thirds of the fleet have returned, to the consolation of their party. Paris thinks no more about it : a new commencement must be made ; and doubt not that it will be made : these men are not so easily rebuffed. The capital has forgotten both Malmesbury and the fleet. These events afford a theme for the babblings of scribblers and *frondeurs ;* the remainder of the public do not bestow on them three days' attention. By this time Europe has received a fair specimen of the pacific inclinations of the Republic—and knows the vanity of that treaty mania which possesses it and to which it ever returns. Its envoys are received like the dregs of men, disgraced, spit upon, loaded with insults from the Luxembourg, from good and bad society, from water-carriers, and from those potentates who, at Paris, administer the dictatorship of the world.

" You call Madrid the Berlin of the south ! It is the evil genius of the south and of Europe : the Directory has no more faithful servant than my Lord Prince of the Peace, first-class Spanish grandee, Captain-General, superior to the Cid in right of the royal remunerations bestowed on him. The royal family has yielded to the solicitations of its friends the regicides, and made up a little kingdom for the Duke of Parma, comprising the territories of Modena,

Ferrara and Bologna and the legation of Faenza. The
Chevalier Azzara, Minister from Alcudia to Rome, has
threatened and insulted the Pope, to compel him to own
himself a vassal and administrator of the French Republic,
to revoke his bulls, and to make a friendly gift of more
than half his states.   He has declared to his Holiness, on
behalf of his King, that, as a temporal prince, the occu-
pant of the Holy See deserved but little consideration ;
that as head of the Church, he might, taking into account
the spirit of the age, think himself happy at being the last
Pope who would die in the chair of St. Peter.   I have read
the declaration."

LETTER FROM THE SAME TO THE COUNT OF SAINTE-ALDEGONDE.

" February 9, 1797.

" It is long, my dear Count, since I have sent you any
but sad tidings.   This time I have to announce two events
yet more lamentable, which fill me with dismay.   The
first is the surrender of Mantua, which capitulated on the
23rd instant, in consequence of the defeats of the 14th
and 16th ultimo, defeats which, it is now clear constitute the greatest disaster of the war.   What will be
the effect of this dreadful reverse in Vienna ?   Will it
create consternation, or call forth a noble desperation ?
They are lost, if they do not now exert all their energy,
and without an instant's delay.

" I think I informed you in my last letter that the
Directory kept an eye upon the royal agents and commissaries manœuvring at Paris, Lyons, in the Jura, &c., and

let them go on their own way, ready all the while to pounce on them at a moment's notice. You will have seen by the papers of the 1st that they did not wait long. This conspiracy (of the 12th Pluviôse, year v.) is true in all its details—that is the point of the drama. I had written to a man whom I suspected of being the accomplice, or the confidant, of this ridiculous attempt, entreating him, for his own safety and that of his family, not to let himself be carried away by such follies and such fools. On the 22nd of January, he replied in a tone of raillery, adding : ' Addle-headed fellows alone see the slightest difficulty in re-establishing the monarchy without any modification ; we need only—' Here followed an outline of the plot, just as you see it in the public prints; the whole sent by the ordinary post. Were these unhappy creatures paid by the Jacobins or by the King ? The government was looking out for a conspiracy—would have paid two millions for it—and gets it for nothing. What do you say of plotters who go and carry full powers from the King to the very barracks of the guard of the Directory ? Which are the most to blame, these stupid instruments, or those who select them ; who invent such projects ; who put them in execution on the eve of the elections, just when the government was falling into disrepute, when it was reduced to maintain its ground by itself conspiring against the constitution, when public opinion was rising like a hurricane against its agents and its tools ? I am personally acquainted with three of the arrested chiefs ; I would not have trusted them to carry a letter from one street to another.

M. Necker has just published a work in four volumes,

entitled ' De la Révolution française.' As soon as I have read it, I will let you know what I think of it."

TO THE SAME.

" March 8, 1797.

" My dear Count, when I delay writing, pray conclude either that I am occupied in some pressing business, or have nothing of consequence to say, and you will never be mistaken. The fact is, that for a whole fortnight I was deeply engaged, in compliance with a request from one of the ministers of a great neutral power, in drawing up a report on the subject of the Directory's external policy. I set before him visible and tangible proofs that Europe is actually at the foot of the gallows, and did not pretend to conceal that I see no possibility of a remedy, to judge from the conduct pursued by all the cabinets during the last three years. I placed before his eyes a terrible and faithful picture. As he will probably cut it up into curl-papers, I have sent a copy to my son in London, directing him to print it, with a notification which shelters me from reproaches for its publication.

" The ridicule cast upon the Marmouset conspiracy reflects on the cause and on the King. Pray do not fancy the plotters are discouraged by this adventure; they will repeat it as often as occasion may offer. M. de la Vauguyon's letters and instructions, which appeared at the trial, prove that d'Antraigues * is in good earnest the constructor-in-

---

* We here restore this personage the name he had assumed ; we have hitherto, through an oversight, called him d'Entraigues. If

chief of these machines, and possesses the King's letters-
patent for the manufacture.   Did I ever tell you that three
months ago he said to an acquaintance of mine, 'Montlosier thinks me implacable, and he is right : I shall be the
Marat of the counter-revolution ; I shall strike off a
hundred thousand heads, and his shall be the first ?'

"Have you read M. Necker's last work ?   It is beyond
comparison the best thing he ever published ; no book
could be more truly useful to France at this moment.
His analysis of the Constitution of 1795, is a master-piece
of political sagacity.   His critique on that of 1791; his
severe animadversions on its authors, the passage on
equality and several others, are quite the order of the day,
and show a very superior mind.   It is a pity he should be
too verbose.   His style is, however, less bombastic in
this than in his preceding works."*

we may belive the Abbé de Montgaillard, "Hist. de France," vol. 1,
p. 46, this upstart first changed his own name of Avenel for that of
de Launay, and finally designated himself Count d'Antraigues.

* Mallet warmly expressed his satisfaction in his letter of thanks
to the ex-minister, who had sent him a copy of his work.   M.
Necker was not insensible to the compliment, and addressed the
following reply to Mallet ;

"Coppet, March 12, 1797.

"I did indeed venture, Sir, to direct a copy of my work on the
French Revolution to a person whose talents and views I have long
admired.   I was amply rewarded by reading the letter you did me the
honour to write me, conveying so frank and so flattering an expression of approval.   Pray accept my grateful acknowledgments.   The
public mind at Paris must be favourable to the opinions I have
offered and the sentiments I have sought to embody, as I have
reason to believe my book has met with a tolerably extensive success,

TO THE SAME.

"March 19, 1797.

"The new follies at Blankenburg, of which you have given me an account, pass my conception. One would think the King had laid a wager that he would ruin himself in spite of circumstances. I confess I am surprised, not only at so impolitic an instance of injustice, but also at the insult offered to the sacred memory of the late King. And where is the use of granting a brevet of promotion? It is in imitation of the King of Cockayne, who shakes his bauble, and says: ' I reign.'

"What has happened to the Duke de la Vauguyon? I have just seen a letter of his, announcing that he is leaving Blankenburg. Has he been disgraced, or has he resigned, or is he travelling on business? He was one of the props of the Marmouset* conspiracy. A little before it was discovered, he said to an acquaintance of mine, ' The kings of Europe will be deeply humbled when they see the King of France, whom they have so neglected, issue forth from this village, to mount the throne.' They were all expecting to see a deputation arrive from Paris, with the crown and a carriage.

The conspiracy, as I wrote to you, is happily buried

and been distinguished by the approbation of various classes of society.

"The details you so kindly give me are extremely interesting, and your age and talents render you our debtor for a complete history of this memorable period.

"I have the honour to be, Sir, with sincere regard,

"Your most humble and obedient servant.

"NECKER."

in contempt and oblivion. Many more persons have been arrested, among the rest Madame de Soucy; these pretended accomplices are all as innocent as myself. The public take an interest in the accused parties from a hatred of the Directory, of Merlin, and of the Jacobins. I do not think that this affair will make any difference, except to the heads of the three chiefs. No one thinks about it now; the public mind is too much pre-occupied with the elections and their possible consequences. People are beginning to rouse themselves; the assemblies will be tolerably numerous. What is thought, said and preached is exactly the reverse of what was thought, said and preached in 1789; the government and the republicans are treated now as the King was then: public opinion is making great strides.

"M. Necker's book has produced a prodigious effect at Paris; it has contributed much to mature and strengthen right views. Lally's work has also proved useful and valuable."

About this time, the end of March, 1797, the pamphlet which Mallet du Pan was having printed in England, appeared in London under the title: "Lettre à un homme d'Etat sur les rapports entre le système politique de la République Française et celui de la Révolution.*

---

* This pamphlet of forty-eight pages has the following lines for a motto :

> Ce sont là les héros qui gouvernent la terre :
> Ils font, en se jouant, et la paix et la guerre ;
> Du sein des voluptés ils nous donnent des fers.
> A quels maîtres, grands dieux ! livrez-vous l'univers ?
>
> VOLTAIRE, *Triumvirat.*

The author's object was, to demonstrate to the second-rate powers who have thought to defend themselves against the Directory, under the shelter of neutrality, that it was no longer a question of their susceptibilities, or jealous, or prudent fears, as to the equilibrium which might be broken by the partition of France ; that France was all powerful, and that the question now concerned the independence and integrity of Europe. That Europe, opposed face to face to a victorious revolutionary government, with a military force strong both through its principles and its conquests, must no longer depend either on the internal manœuvres condemned beforehand, or on negociations of peace, of which the probable futility is shown by Lord Malmesbury's dismissal from Paris within twenty-four hours, nor yet on continuing the present war. Mallet maintained, that at such a crisis nothing less than the intervention of all the neutral powers would suffice.

" Whether or not it has been their interest hitherto to take no part in the war, now it is indisputably their interest to propose conditions of peace ; so by their influence, and if necessary, by their armed interposition, while making such sacrifices to the French Republic as circumstances dictate, they will be able to overawe it into abandoning its projects of ruin and universal devastation. There is then no safety so long as Europe remains in its present state of division, conflict, and selfishness ; no safety, unless all the great powers unite in effecting a moderate peace, such as may save Europe from the shame of becoming tributary to the revolution, and the heritage of its enactors."

M. de Hardenberg, in writing to Mallet, admitted the

striking justice of these observations, especially where they
attack the blind selfishness which more or less swayed all
the governments; but added, at the same time: " I am
a cipher in the plans of the Berlin cabinet, and for several
reasons am well pleased that so it is. Circumscribed in
my sphere, I become contemplative like yourself, Sir. Still
I am persuaded, that not even our most spirited proceedings could produce and carry out that unity of principles
and measures which is essential to the attainment of our
object. Good can only be effected by an amendment in
persons and principles in France itself, whether it remains
a republic or becomes a monarchy,"

Mallet's pamphlet, published in London, took his friends
by surprise at a moment when most of them were in repose,
yielding to allusions for very listlessness. They agreed in
saying that Mallet must have been out of temper when he
wrote it; and expressed their opinion almost with vehemence to his son, who, being at that time in London, had
been commissioned by him to direct the publication of
the " Lettre à un Ministre d'Etat." With the forgetfulness of self which characterized Mallet in his home
and among his friends, he had, though overhelmed
with business, advised his son, who since 1794 had acted
as his secretary, to try his fortune in a country where he
had received a part of his education, and with whose
language he was conversant. Mallet hoped that the friends
he possessed in London, and the estimable qualities of his
son, might be the means of obtaining for the latter some
situation under the English government. But the esteem
and respect, expressed in all quarters, for the father, availed
only to secure a warm and friendly reception for the

son, who, disappointed in his hopes, in October 1797 rejoined his family at Berne, after making a short stay in Paris, whence he announced to Mallet the approaching catastrophe of the 18th Fructidor.   The journey did not, however, prove wholly useless to the young man, as during his sojourn in London he lived in the society of his father's friends, Mallouet, Lally, Montlosier, and Macpherson.   All these conceived a true friendship for him, and retained it during the rest of their lives (as late as 1843, Montlosier wrote him a very affectionate letter from Randanne) ; but he was exposed to a few squalls in the drawing-room of the Princess d'Hénin, the rendezvous of such royalists as were distinguished for rank or talents.   Not only the tone of the " Lettre d'un Homme d'Etat" appeared too violent and discouraging to exiles who, in the progress of events in France, thought they discerned a near prospect of return to their country : they also found fault with some expressions, perhaps rather too unguarded, respecting M. de La Fayette ; expressions, peculiarly ill-timed, when General Fitzpatrick was on the point of making a motion in Parliament to obtain the intervention of the English ministry on behalf of the illustrious captive.   This motion neither produced, nor could produce, any further result than an expression of interest for M. de La Fayette ; but Mallet's son thought it right somewhat to modify the language of the pamphlet, in compliance with the wishes of his father's friends.

Events, nevertheless, soon justified the predictions of our journalist, and proved that he had not exaggerated the danger.

The Emperor deliberated on making peace with France, leaving England to struggle alone.   And while Mallet's little work was exciting attention, and serving as a text for the discussions of foreign politicians, who had, for some time, widely differed from each other, Venice, Genoa, and soon after Piedmont, revolutionized and conquered ; Portugal and Switzerland humbled ; England herself threatened in her insular position, beheld to their cost their neutral policy followed by the very consequences foretold by the author of the " Lettre à un Homme d'Etat." But between the moment which gave utterance to the prediction and that which witnessed its full realization, France found itself on the verge of a royalist revolution (18th Fructidor), skilfully prepared by the election of the new third estate, seconded by the divisions of the Directory, strong in the intrigues and ascendancy of General Pichegru, yet destined to fail at the critical moment. Mallet was in the secret of these hopes, and for an instant shared them ; but soon laid them aside when he saw the effect produced on the public mind by the Emperor's suit for peace to the conquerors of Italy.

LETTER FROM MALLET DU PAN TO COUNT DE
SAINTE-ALDEGONDE.

"April 16 and 19, 1797.

" The Paris elections augur well. The choice of deputies for the rural cantons will most probably fall upon the Abbé Morellet, Quatremère de Quincy, Fleurieu, La Harpe, Dufresne, d'André and Viennot. These are the very men I should have selected. Do not be surprised at seeing the name of d'André ; he is wholly devoted to the King, has tendered his submission, is employed, is a skilful coadjutor ; he has worked with

x 2

energy on the plan he laid before me here a year ago. Desmeuniers would not have been amiss; I class him among sincerely reformed constitutionalists, and he was also entirely in the King's interest in 1791 and 1792. As for the schemers and old intriguers, their efforts and their boastings have signally failed.

" All this is inevitably bringing on a crisis. The alarm is sounded in the camp of the Directory and the Jacobins ; they will have recourse to violence. Should this not succeed, they will be ruined, and the Republic with them, before six months are out; but I dare not yet flatter myself with hopes of their failure. I also dread the irritation and anger of the thrown-out constitutional trumps and the unconciliatory spirit of the ultra-royalists. If all the partisans of monarchy do not pull together, if there is any attempt to hasten the catastrophe, if any idiotic conspirators meddle in the matter, if any fresh blunders come in from Blankenburg to make havoc in our plans, we shall again sink to the bottom.

" The happy issue of the elections is the result of a measure long since recommended by me, and at length determined on six months ago ; the formation of political associations bearing the name of philanthropic institutions, and having for their ostensible object the defence of the constitution against the anarchists. These associations have spread rapidly and extensively."

" April 19, 1797.

" Before you receive this, my dear Count, you will have learned the result of the Paris elections. The Jacobins and the Directory are floored by the returns—

especially by those of Fleurieu and Emmery. The latter, a member of your Constituent Assembly, was brought in by the party of the King, to whom I believe he has tendered his submission, persuaded to do so by d'André. It was he who induced the Court of Cassation to claim jurisdiction over the proceedings of the Council of War. I am well acquainted with Quatremère de Quincy, a man full of courage, imagination, talent and inflexible principle. In the Legislative Assembly he showed himself the most vigorous opponent of the Gironde and the Republic, and was wholly and gratuitously devoted to the King. The old constitutionalists have been no better treated than the republicans (I am speaking of the principal schemers, the well-known intriguers). Not a single word of Rœderer, Montesquiou, the Bishop of Autun, &c.; they are unanimously thrown out. Desmeuniers has come off no better—he has not even been named for the department. The Parisians never decided better. They have chosen as deputies men of property, upright and moderate men, strangers to the various revolutionary crises. They desire no commotions, no violent counter-revolutions, no precipitate measures; the deputies are to slide France into a monarchy, not to throw her into the risk of breaking all to pieces for the second time.

"Lyons has made two extraordinary returns; amongst others it has chosen Imbert-Colomès, avowedly an agent of the King, three times an emigrant, conditionally erased from the list, and having actually spent the whole winter with us. He has an excellent heart, is well-principled and zealous; but his talents are middling, and his mind over-excited. At Grenoble, and in the south generally, similar elections. Pichegru is returned in the Jura : this nomination is perhaps the most important of all. Pichegru has long been altogether ours."

TO THE SAME.

" April 29, 1797.

" You will see the consequences which the peace with Austria will produce in the interior. Hoche and his Franks, Bonaparte and his Vandals, will be let loose on France : they will make quick work, I assure you, of the journalists, orators, law-mongers, and mutinous citizens. The new legislature might prevent this catastrophe, by disbanding the troops, refusing the subsidies, and taking upon themselves the regulation of military affairs ; but that is the last thing the poor devils will think of doing. Enraptured with their victories and their peace, they will let themselves be muzzled ; the martial sabre will silence the artillery of tongues and pens, and a new revolution will open upon us, while all the ninnies in and out of France are speechifying about the admirable disposition of the public mind.

" The Directory are about to exert their utmost strength against England ; at any cost they are bent on destroying her, subverting her constitution, sacking her, and levelling with the dust this superb monument of human industry. If they succeed, all Europe will be buried under the ruins."

TO THE SAME.

" May 7, 1797.

" You must be impatient, my dear Count, to know what are these famous preliminaries. The French papers of the

2nd will tell you their substance : here is the commentary
—at least such as was sent to me from Genoa and Turin,
on the 29th April. Belgium, the country beyond the
Meuse, Liège and Lombardy irrevocably lost ; compensation made to the Emperor by the spoliation of Venice,
which is to be robbed of all its *terra firma* from the
Adige to Trieste ; the territories of Brescia and Bergamo
incorporated in the Republic of Lombardy. There is some
talk of giving Ferrara to Venice, but nothing is settled
regarding this wretched equivalent. The King of Sardinia
is to receive the imperial fiefs, and a part of the Ponente
strand belonging to Genoa. According to the Italian
papers, twenty thousand French will remain in Lombardy
to protect and fortify the new republic, on which, it is said,
an annual tribute of thirty millions will be imposed. What
do you say to this wholesale move ? Can you find a prece-
dent for such robbery in the whole history of Europe ?
Depend upon it, before a month is out, the Italian Republic
will have consumed Piedmont, Genoa, Venice, Tuscany and
Naples : it is a fire-ship placed there for the very purpose,
and the Directory holds the match. Bonaparte is hastening
back to Paris, and his army is about to re-enter France,
with the exception of twenty thousand men left in Lombardy. The Directory and the republicans count on his
aid to strengthen them ; the Emperor revives the revolution. The haven we had almost reached now seems
farther off than ever. I have known few such bitter griefs
during the last seven years. We are cast back into a
bottomless abyss : there is no kind of calamity that I do
not see impending over France and Europe."

Clearly as it had been foreseen, the fate of Venice and
Genoa, occupied and ultimately revolutionized by French
troops, and subdued to the republic under the name of
democracy, painfully affected our politician.   On this
occasion he endeavoured to influence public opinion
among the French, by pointing out to them that the
revolutionary and conquering policy of their government
menaced their own country with imminent slavery under
new masters.   Towards the end of May, just as the
Directory were accomplishing this fresh act of spoliation,
the " Quotidienne, or Feuille du Jour," then under the
direction of M. Michaud, published in an express supplement a " Letter from Mallet du Pan to a Member of the
Legislative Corps" (Dumolard), on the declaration of war
against the Venetian Republic.   This letter was succeeded
by a second on Genoa, and a third on Portugal.*   " I
have addressed a series of epistles," writes Mallet, " to one
of the Five Hundred ; they are ignorant of everything
connected with politics, and idiotically allow the Directory
to arrange such matters just as it pleases ; they do not
perceive that they are forging for themselves chains whose
weight will crush them sooner or later."†

The letter on Venice, published in the " Quotidienne,"
began thus :

" That the revolutionary spirit, which has now taken
refuge among the Jacobins and a few of the rulers, should
have planned the ruin of a republic thirteen centuries old ;
that it should persist in using war as an instrument for

* " Quotidienne," Nos. 410, 413, 414, 421.
† Letter to M. de Sainte-Aldegonde, June 4, 1797.

subverting society; that its indiscriminating fury should embrace monarchies and republics, friends and enemies of France, powers neutral, peaceful and belligerent—all this, Sir, creates no surprise in my mind. I never doubted either the existence of such a project, or its progressive realization, as soon as circumstances should allow of its development—all this falls within the order of the day. But, Sir, there is one thing that does not fall within it; one thing which calls forth wonder no less than grief: that one thing is the precipitancy of your council, of some among your colleagues—men estimable alike for talents and conduct—in affording their concurrence and sanction to a work of darkness so disgraceful to the French name, so utterly at variance with the maxims and the aims of the wise members of your legislature.

"What! after the cursory perusal of a manifesto; whose every line should awaken mistrust; without raising a doubt; without making a single inquiry; in the midst of a hue and cry you sign a declaration of war! sign it against a neutral and powerless state, for the last two hundred years attached to France by the inalienable bonds of nature, interest and reasonable policy! sign it without even deigning to consider whether so cruel a sentence may not bury this venerable monument of courage, constancy, and wisdom, under the fragments of its fundamental institution!

"Yes, Sir, this manifesto should have put on his guard any man at all acquainted with the history of the times, and who had bestowed the least attention on passing events. Is it for a general in a rising republic to declare

war as a sovereign by his own private authority? Does
the Directory authorize this general, without having any
other legal title to this usurpation than an article of the
constitution wholly irrelevant to the circumstances, and
which could never apply but in cases of imminent danger
to France and the army? This is the question that should
have suggested itself to you all, and which you have lost
sight of in epithets and imprecations. How could any one
of you fail instinctively to perceive, that all promoters of
this unexpected declaration would seek to deceive you as to
their motives, to conceal their illegality and injustice?

"A terrible and novel instance, this, of the peril of such
deliberations in a numerous and public assembly, where
enthusiasm ever precedes reflection, where the destiny of
states is dependent on a war of words, and where the
great majority are so unacquainted with the positive, historical and material facts, on which depends the solution of
political questions. You have here, Sir, a true statement
of facts. I submit the picture to your candour, and to
that of your colleagues. I have no fear that any one can
disprove my statements; authentic and plenary proofs of
their veracity are lying on my desk, and what I here offer
is a mere summary."

Here follows a powerful narration, where the dazzling
glory of the conquest is not allowed to cast a shade over
the injustice of the usurpation, and the perfidy of the
means. The letter terminates with these words:

"Sir, I bring to a close this too lengthy letter, which
already can be of no avail, except as history: Venice is at
an end. That government which six months since was

pictured to us in the attitude of menace and heroism, has afforded an unparalleled instance of pusillanimity. It has dissolved itself.

"This aristocracy, fruitful in great statesmen and warriors, this institution of centuries which our Visigoths call an oligarchy has made room for a revolutionary democracy. Your troops are within its walls, and I only speak of a corpse. But I cannot suppress one important observation. No sooner was this act of abdication consummated, and a municipality, chosen by the vote of your generals, had replaced the successors of a Morosini, Cornaro, Mocenigo, than the people arose in fury, hoisted once more the banners of St. Mark, attacked and forced the houses of the new magistrates, and threatened to bury Venice beneath the wreck of its honour and its government. But none the less for this will your rhetoricians allege the desire, the sovereignity and the insurrection of nations as the justification of these exploits! They will assert as boldly as ever, that this was a popular revolution which scarce one inhabitant among ten thousand promoted.

"One truth, however, remains incontestable : it is, that on *terra firma* as in Lombardy, in Lombardy as in Piedmont, in Piedmont as in Belgium and in Germany, it is the people, and the people only, who have resisted the revolution, who repulsed it with their wills, and would have repulsed if with their untrained arms, if governments without talent, if certain classes abased by selfishness and enervated by opulence, had not hailed with open arms their scourge and their ruin."

In another letter to the "Quotidienne" on the fate of

Genoa, Mallet dilates yet more forcibly on the strange position of the councils.

" Danton called the last Convention the great committee of insurrection for all mankind.   Have you inherited his morals and his maxims ?   Are you aware that from one extremity of Europe to the other, every man, endued with a shadow of sense, probity, love of order, justice, true liberty, asks himself with surprise and indignation the motives of the silence maintained by your councils ?

" Is this, they repeat on all hands, that legislative body which ushered itself in with such an encouraging display, which was to restore to earth peace, justice and mercy ? Will it prefer an obscure complicity in plans which prepare for Europe and for France an era of blodshed and darkness, to the great glory which awaits it, and to the approbation of all who possess a conscience ? "

These letters produced a great sensation, and contributed to bring forward that agitation of opinion on which Mallet and such members of the legislative body as shared his views, had counted ; for the articles of the " Quotidienne" were based on a plan of conduct agreed upon between several members of the Ancients and of the Five Hundred.   Mallet wrote on the 22nd June to his friend, the Count of Sainte-Aldegonde :

" I have been, and still am, in a crisis of urgent occupations, of which you may have seen two specimens in the ' Quotidienne :' some more will appear, and there is no time to lose ; we must strain every nerve to arm the legislative body against the Directory, and to put an end to this mad system of universal revolutionizing.   My part is taken with several leading members of the majority; I shall serve as their precursor and trumpet. These two letters have aroused all Paris, the cataract has been removed and the blind are enlightened. I am told that the bomb will burst in the tribune without delay, and that the Directory will be called to account for its exploits against Venice and Genoa, and for those which it prepares elsewhere."

In fact, not one Directorial paper durst dispute the truth of these letters, of which every word was correct. They had been read at Clichy before being circulated; and on the strength of the impression they had made, it was decided that Pastoret and Dumolard should ascend the tribune to question the Directory. Dumolard's speech was a paraphrase of the "Quotidienne's" philippics—a commission was appointed accordingly.

Meanwhile, these letters had roused the ire of Bonaparte, then in the heyday of victory and triumph; and the bold author who had dared to raise his voice was soon sensible of its effects. The General sent immediately for Haller, a Bernese patrician, who acted as his chief Commissary at War, and informed him that if Mallet du Pan was not immediately expelled from Berne, his country would sooner or later feel the effects of his resentment. This notice was not thrown away: communicated without delay by Haller to his friends in Berne, it brought down on Mallet du Pan a storm which the vindictive general failed not to increase, the Directory falling into his views as a means of revenging their own wrongs, and threatening to require the authorities of Berne to institute proceedings against Mallet du Pan, on the ground of

communications sent by him to the royalist journals.
At Berne, the French party, and those men who dreaded
above all the displeasure of the conqueror of Italy, began
sounding an alarm in the councils of the Republic.   One
of the most violent against Mallet was M. de Haller, a
young patrician, related to the Commissary, and who,
endowed with great talent, at that time professed ultra-
liberal opinions, with the same warmth and even fanaticism, which he afterwards displayed in defending absolute
governments, and writing in favour of the Roman Church.
On the other hand, Mallet numbered warm friends in the
councils, such as his friends, d'Erlach, and the virtuous
Avoyer Steiguer; but the prominence of the latter had
gained him enemies among his colleagues; and they, siding
with the intimidated members of the council, carried the day.
In virtue of the ancient treaties concluded between Berne
and Geneva, Mallet was a co-citizen of Berne, and as such
had a right to residence and protection within the canton;
but though up to this time these treaties had been invio-
lably observed, they were now about to be set at nought to
disarm the anger of the Directory; as if pretexts were
ever wanting to the displeasure of those who mean to be
provoked.   The motion for Mallet's ejection from the
states of the Bernese Republic, was twice canvassed in
the secret council, and twice thrown out; on the third
occasion, the decree of dismissal was carried.   Mallet
learned his sentence from his friend Baron d'Erlach.

"Friday morning.

"My dear Mallet,

"I am deputed to inform you of something which
drives me to despair.   The Avoyer Mulinen has just

informed me that he has orders from the secret council to bid you depart, and he has begged me to warn you of this, as he cannot avoid executing his orders with all possible expedition. The pretext alleged is, that a contributor to a French paper cannot be tolerated. In my indignation I refrain from all comment. The public and the French papers will offer it in my stead. If I can serve you in any manner, be it what it may, command me. Adieu."*

Thus was Mallet sacrificed to the terror inspired by the Directory and their general. It was but too evident that the legislative body was a mere cipher in their eyes and in those of other governments, and that to appeal to it from Directorial despotism, after the example of the " Quotidienne's" correspondent, was an unusual waste of courage. The " Quotidienne" fearful of such generous rashness, had affixed to the articles their author's signature, without giving him previous notice. While thanking

* Baron d'Erlach, writing some time afterwards to Count de Maistre, expressed himself even more indignantly : " I have communicated your letter, Monsieur le Comte, through my wife to M. Mallet ; I have not yet seen him since my return : I believe him to be on the point of departure ; for you know the mean, cowardly, and truly republican injustice used towards him. He has always employed his own pen in the defence of governments ; he upheld our's in particular at a critical period, and his reward is expulsion. Gratitude appears a virtue unknown to republics ; or rather it is incompatible with them, and the more a man deserves, the less he must look for it ; fools alone excite no man's suspicions, and are made much of." Count Joseph de Maistre's " Lettres et Opuscules inédits ;" Paris. Auguste Vaton. 1851, vol. 1, p. 54.

M. Michaud for his personal conduct, Mallet would not deny that he considered himself ruined by his underlings.

The manner in which the decree of banishment was communicated to the victim of this mistaken policy, the universal disapprobation with which it was received by the public, testify that during his four years' residence at Berne, Mallet had secured the esteem and respect of its inhabitants. He had additional claims on the good will of the government, and, forgetful at it may have seemed of more than one service rendered by its guest to the Republic, it was not really so. From every quarter, expressions of esteem and regret reached the exiled man; and so great was the public outcry against this measure, dictated by weakness, that the council began to repent of it, and informed Mallet first, that he was allowed two months for the arrangement of his affairs, and afterwards, that he might prolong his stay at his own pleasure without any cause for uneasiness. But he was no longer safe; besides, cut to the heart, he was not a man to stay one day longer than was necessary, accepting favours from those who had outraged his rights. When he had departed, leaving his family behind him until he should find them a retreat, a noble Bernese, who in his youth had contracted a friendship with the poet Gray, and who afterwards became known as an entertaining writer and agreeable companion, M. Victor Bonstetten, wrote to Madame Mallet, to offer her the use of his country-house. " I should consider myself," he said, " the happiest of my fellow-citizens, could I soften the inpression left in your mind by our criminal weakness in M. Mallet's regard." While expressing a hope that her husband would forget the treatment he had undergone, he added: "I wish I could hope myself to forget it."

The worthy Avoyer Steiguer was not behindhand in the anxiety displayed by the Bernese to testify their sympathy with their courageous co-citizen. He wrote as follows :

"September 7, 1797.

"Sir,

"I cannot express my sorrow at your leaving us. My unbounded affection and esteem for you, my gratitude for the services you have rendered to my thankless country, and for the many proofs of interest and good-will you have shown to me in particular, make this departure, Sir, very bitter and very painful to me. Continue to feel for me that precious friendship with which you have hitherto honoured me. I shall always deserve it by the sincerity of those sentiments of devoted esteem, with which I have the honour to be, Sir, your very humble and very obedient servant,

"STEIGUER, Avoyer."

The expulsion of Mallet du Pan, was the initiatory step in the canton's unfortunate course of concessions to the Directory. This act of weakness, and the ill-dissembled joy with which its instigators received Bonaparte's consequent congratulations,* made known to the Directory

---

* M. d'Erlach, at that time deputy from Berne to the Helvetic diet, wrote to Mallet on the 27th July : "The Avoyer Mulinen has just received a letter, dated Lugano, from M. Wurstenberguer. He has been to Bonaparte on the subject of the Helvetic council, and was well received by him ; and Bonaparte having inquired whether there were any emigrants at Lugano, went on, without waiting for his

that Switzerland also might be worked upon by intimida-
tion; and thenceforward their agents ceased not to employ
this weapon with that consummate skill which · had en-

answer, to express warm thanks for your expulsion, and great complaints of you.   This proves Bonaparte to be your personal enemy;
and you may imagine whether, after this demonstration on his part,
which M. Wurstenberguer has doubtless made known at Berne,
there remains any hope of success, should you demand, or cause to
be demanded, the revocation of your sentence.   Bonaparte also
inquired whether he was within three day's journey of Berne.   The
dread of him at Berne must be excessive.   I have been blamed on
account of the Diet not having written direct to the General, an
omission which might greatly affront him: I answered that, in all
matters, whether public or private, I always first consulted the
dictates of honour, and invariably followed them; that I had never
been guilty of a cowardly action, and was incapable of advising
one.

"Wurstenberguer's narration is curious: nothing can exceed the
insolence of this conqueror.   The first day he kept him waiting an
hour in his ante-chamber, thronged with ministers, envoys, &c.
Afterwards M. Haller presented him; and all he got was, 'Ha! ha,
come to dinner to-morrow;' then Bonaparte went off without saying
a word to a creature, though all the world was prostrated; hastened
down stairs, jumped into his carriage, and took a drive surrounded
by his guards.   Next day he asked: 'To what canton do you
belong?' 'To Berne.' 'And this gentleman?' 'To Uri.'   This he had
repeated, and then he said: 'Ha! Uri, democratical, that is well.'
At table he seated himself on his left hand, having on his right the
Commissary of the Executive power for the collection of statues,
pictures, &c.   He talked constantly in an under tone with the latter,
not once speaking to Wurstenberguer.   After dinner he told him
about his excursion to Capo di Lago; then W—— thanked him for
having had his escort disarmed, and Bonaparte answered: 'Yes,
certainly, it is quite right in a neutral and friendly country:' next
followed the gratifying remarks on yourself and the emigrants.   M.
W—— appeared delighted with this reception, and my colleague also."

abled revolutionary policy to effect so many wonders with such rapidity. Some months later, French cannon was destroying old Switzerland.

Though this termination of a fatal policy had been but too surely foreseen by Mallet, the advantage of his correspondence required him to remain within reach of news from France; moreover, the struggle which had commenced between the Directory and the royalist party supported by Pichegru, might produce such important results, that he thought of remaining provisionally, if not at Berne, at least in Switzerland. But events followed each other in quick succession, and the subjoined letters reveal the nature of Mallet's hopes, founded on the hoped for dissolution of the Directory, and demonstrations on the part of the Ancients.

LETTER FROM MALLET DU PAN TO COUNT DE SAINTE-ALDEGONDE.

" July 1, 1797.

" Those letters on Venice and Genoa, my dear Count, were really an answer to the questions of certain deputies who tormented me to write, to supply them with arms, and to tutor them. They have produced a prodigious effect: not one Directorial paper has dared dispute a line of them: they contain only truth from beginning to end. They were read at Clichy before being circulated; it was determined to throw the bomb; thence the motions of Pastoret and Dumolard—you will have perceived that the latter has only paraphrased my letters. The Directorial party will use

Y 2

every effort to stifle this appeal, to retard and to weaken the report of the commission nominated *ad hoc*.

" This party consists, not only of Jacobins, but also of intriguers and standers-still, mostly constitutionalists of 1791. Dumas and Fronçon du Coudray are its chiefs among the Ancients ; Thibaudeau among the " Youths." Vaublanc, Pastoret, &c., pass from one party to the other: these gentlemen will support the Directory so long as it allows them to share in posts and profits : they scowl on it when it shows too much favour to the Jacobins. You will have seen these parties clearly defined in the debates on the colonies, on the treasury, on the motion of Henri de Longuève, sometime your worthy colleague.

" Do not suppose the peace with England concluded : descents will have their course . . . . I certify you that the Directory settled and commanded the invasion of Hanover and the sack of Hamburg. The threats of the Emperor and of Russia effected the adjournment of this project towards the middle of last month. Allow the unhappy men to re-enter, who return as they set out. The decree for the recal of the emigrants since the 10th August, will be prepared immediately."

TO THE SAME.

" July 29, 1797.

" My dear Count,
" I received your letters, dating from the 1st to the 13th, amidst a flood of occupations, to which was added a necessary journey to Zurich, which took up eight days. I am still much pressed, overwhelmed with work and corres-

pondence with France; circumstances render this more
active than ever, and I alone sustain the burden. The
strange behaviour I encounter here adds to the weight. I
cannot tell you where I shall pitch my tent; but you may
count on my removal towards the middle of September.
I meet with demonstrations of repentance here for this
cowardly degree of expulsion; but I know how to appreciate these regrets: they wish me to regard this act as not
having taken place, and to solicit its annulling. I would
have died rather than descend to so shameful and misplaced
a proceeding; for I was fully persuaded that the slightest
accession of fear, and one word from Bonaparte would
renew the panic, and the sentence of my expulsion.

"Paris is at a crisis which will ripen, or blight our
cause for ever. The conspiracy of the triumvirate, of the
club of Salm, is a positive fact. The councils were about
to be subjugated, purged, proscribed, by the troops which
were being brought forward. Pichegru headed all the
lists of proscription: he is pre-eminently odious to all the
Jacobins. Recollect what I wrote to you about this general
two years ago: be persuaded that he is going to play a
conspicuous part, and that all our hopes rest on him. The
people place full confidence in him, and will joyfully march
under his command. Twenty-five thousand resolute men
can be reckoned on in Paris alone. . . . It is quite certain
that Pichegru said to the Directory, on the 20th: ' Since
they are determined we shall mount on horseback, we *will*
mount! your Luxembourg is not a Bastille; it will be
reduced in a quarter of an hour.' . . . These words so
frightened the triumvirs that they served out cartouches to
the guards, gave them drink, and awaited an attack in

the night. The *Réveillère* beat like mad. This division in the Directory will infallibly lead to an outburst : at the first cannon-shot, the three members will be outlawed. They have missed their aim ; the Five Hundred hold the ball ; they have resolved to throw it : should success attend them, our troubles will not be ended, but they will be greatly mitigated, and in a fair way of termination. Should they lose courage or fall, the future is dreadful to look at. Adieu, etc."

TO THE SAME.

"August 17, 1797.

" The councils and the Directory have been vying with each other in incapacity. They have deferred the contest through mutual fear ; they have embraced after the fashion of Cleopatra embracing Rodogune, and as Nero embraced Britannicus, the better to stifle each other. The council can do nothing but issue decrees ; they afford a new proof that a great deliberative assembly in France would never be anything but a mass of confusion, or a set of firebrands. Pichegru is an eagle amongst them, but he is ill seconde d he will execute wonders, but is more remarkable as a general than as a senator.

" Paris has displayed, as usual, a degree of stupid and disgraceful indifference. On the day when it was resolved that the troops should march on the capital, Ruggieri* made twenty-five thousand francs. The people have been much put out by the re-establishment of the National Guard, which obliges them to resume their muskets. My

---

* A famous keeper of an eating-house.

son, a witness of all these particulars, cannot recover from his horror and astonishment. Paris offers so hideous an aspect in every light, that it has been too much for the honourable feelings of this young man : he has let me know that he cannot bear to live there, and intends to join me. I expect to see him in a fortnight. My dear Count, the affair is not at an end——far from it : nothing will terminate without a violent crisis ; I should be rash were I to predict the issue of events."

TO THE SAME.

"September 2, 1797.

" Here I am then, a constitutionalist at Blanckenburg; What a droll title ! The Baron de Breteuil on my first visit conferred on me this fine appellation, and when I observed that I had periodically and day by day attacked the constitution in its rise, progress and fall, he confessed that he had never read, and was not in the habit of reading, any periodical work. After such an admission I have reason to be proud of a letter four pages long, addressed to me by the favourite, in which, amid high-flown compliments, he reproaches me, in the name of his master, for having stated in my letter on Venice, ' that he asked for delay as regarded the Venetians.' This demand——about which, by-the-bye, I never wrote a word——forms the ground-work of a long series of deductions. I replied to all his politeness as civility required ; and as to the charge in question, that I had referred to protestations, and not to delays ; that Charles XII. protested at Bender, Charles II. at the Hague ; that such a formula can imply nothing that is not honourable, &c. Think of anybody's attaching

importance to such miserable trifles, and writing four pages
to me about it.

"Do not hope for an abdication. Doubtless it would
wonderfully facilitate and tend to bring about more
speedily a distant result. My son, who has just arrived
from Paris, where he has lived with many of the principal
actors, and attentively marked their conduct, assures me
that all hopes are fixed on the Duke d'Angoulême and the
Princess Royal. The King has strengthened all the prejudices that existed against him. The stiff partisans of
hereditary right alone demand that no change may be
made in the order of succession; these are merely a handful, and the looking for men of principle in France is like
seaking pearls in the sands of the ocean.

"The Lameths and the Duke d'Aiguillon would have
been arrested (the warrant was signed by the minister),
but for the interference of the Bishop of Autun.

"The Five Hundred are no more unanimous in their
aim than in their operations. Some of them wanted
violently to attack the Directory, and still intend to do
so. Willot has never ceased holding forth on the subject;
he is a resolute, ardent, and courageous man. Pichegru
advised the same line of conduct; but the lawyers, the
drones who have to decide, set themselves against it and
will not deviate from the constitutional line."

LETTER FROM MALLET DU PAN TO THE CHEVALIER DE
GALLATIN.

"September 5, 1797.

"You, less than any one, will have felt surprise on
hearing of the glorious sentence of proscription of which

I am the object. More than once have you predicted this event : I give you credit for your prophecy—you had good reason for what you said. Since your departure, the government has sunk lower and lower in moral power and judgment. Old maxims, prudence, honour, reflection, decency—all has been thrown overboard. The leaders, encouraged by the promotion of all the students of Göttingen, have chosen them as the arbiters of the state, securing their vote by flattery. This new batch has metamorphosed the spirit of the government : mortifications and insults have been heaped on our respectable Avoyer Steiguer. Counsellor Sinner is at the head of the party ; he denounced me to the Two Hundred in a discourse *ad hoc,* in which he apostrophized the Avoyer Steiguer and d'Erlach. Would you believe it, one of these young philosophers, an acquaintance of yours, made a speech to exhort the Two Hundred to turn their mind to the dogma of the sovereignty of the people, and to acknowledge it ? You may judge how these people would afterwards be able to resist the slightest impulse.

" It would require volumes to make you understand the position of affairs at Paris ; it cannot be condensed into a few lines. Conjectures are vanity, and predictions, folly. I shall attempt no more than to put you on your guard against the exaggerated accounts of the journals. The quarrel between the councils and the Directory cannot be settled save by the overthrow of one or other of the two powers. Place no confidence in rumours of conciliation ; a deadly combat is waging which may be prolonged to an indefinite term, as, through want of means on either side, cunning and stratagem have full play. Each party in

attacking the other, endeavours to seem as if it were con-
stitutionally defending itself.   The Jacobins, unaided, are
too few in number, too universally hateful to be formidable ; without support from the government and the
armies, they are done for.   The only real strength of the
government lies in the troops abroad.   Had it not felt its
inferiority at Paris, it would doubtless have cashiered the
Five Hundred two months ago.   Pichegru is its most
formidable enemy ; he alone in France enjoys esteem,
personal credit, and public confidence.   A decree, and
Pichegru will carry with him the majority of the nation
and decide the engagement if one takes place ; but the
Directory is backed by divisions and want of skill in the
councils, weakness among the Ancients, and by the policy
of the drones.

" The Directory has also in its favour the power of
plotting, and projects the nocturnal carrying off of eighty
deputies.   Perhaps by this time the plan has been essayed.
Since the 29th, the threatened deputies have passed the
night from home ; and assembled in one house, they kept
in readiness to mount and rally their adherents.   Undoubtedly, the advantage of physical force is on their
side."

On the eve of the day on which Mallet wrote these
lines, the 18th Fructidor, the Directory, despite Carnot's
opposition, forestalled Pichegru by a stroke of policy, by
having the legislative body invested by Augereau, who
had been sent them by Bonaparte, and Pichegru, Carnot,
Barthélemy and fifty-three deputies of both councils
arrested.   Mallet's testimony concerning the projects at-

tributed to these deputies deserves to be remembered ; he expresses it repeatedly in letters to his friend Sainte-Aldegonde.

LETTER FROM MALLET DU PAN TO COUNT DE SAINTE-ALDEGONDE.

"September 17, 1797.

" . . . . You can conceive the weight added to my troubles by the recent events at Paris. Was I wrong in warning you against delusions ? Once more we are upon the fathomless sea. The future no longer admits of conjecture. What will not usurpers dare who have with impunity, without a shock or trembling, carried out such an attempt ? Some day it will be returned on their own heads—but when ? You see how true was what I wrote to you of the meanness of this legislative body. Exclusive of the majority of the proscribed, and some dozen others, the remainder have no more head than a string of onions. Their imbecility, the constitutional chicanery of Thibaudeau, Emery, Vaublanc, have ruined those honourable men who had resolved to carry the Luxembourg by main force, in the middle of August, and who for prudence sake were induced to defer this project.

" Montgaillard has twenty times related to me in the same terms his conversation with d'Antraigues. I have had in my keeping for two months the papers concerning this negotiation, which places in so striking a light the wisdom of the Prince de Condé. Do not try to cast a doubt on a single word of this narration, any more

than on the declaration of Duverne de Presle ; the whole
is strictly true.   What say you to a dethroned king
who selects such grooms as these for his confidential
agents ?   What say you to this d'Antraigues, who, having
to escape by passing through a French army, leaves this
pretty conversation in his portfolio ?   Either he is fit
for a madhouse, if he could be guilty of such imprudence,
or he deserves the halter, if he betrayed his secret to
get out of difficulty.   Finally, what say you to Montgaillard,* who babbles about such a negotiation to everybody he meets, who from Italy corresponded familiarly
with the Directory, who has re-entered France, who lives
in or near Paris, who was neither sought out nor disturbed ?   As for Duverne, take notice, that he lived four
years at the expense of the English, accompanied by a
girl whom he called his wife, lodging at Berne, and
keeping open house there for a year ; and now he goes
and declares that the English were paying him to ruin
France and the monarchy.   Such revolting impudence
and baseness are enough to disgust one with any cause."

TO THE SAME.

"Zurich, October 11, 1797.

"My dear Count, there has been no conspiracy of the
legislative body against the Directory, though eighty depu-

* A common friend, to whom Montgaillard had entrusted his
papers, withdrew all the letters of Mallet du Pan and sent them to
him at Berne.   This saved him from the annoyance of witnessing
the publication of a correspondence expressive of more confidence than
was merited by so dishonest a man.

ties had conceived a plan of resisting it even by force. The affair of Pichegru is an old story of 1795, not in the least applicable to present circumstances. This general still kept in mind his own views and object, but had formed no project other than that of his colleagues. I repeat, that Montgaillard gave me at the time the very same account which the wise d'Antraigues preserved to enrich the Directorial portfolio. I then doubted the truth of Pichegru's reply; but there can be no doubt of the plan he at that time adopted, nor of the deplorable follies of the Prince de Condé and his satellites.

" The declaration of Duverne de Presle contains only certain facts with which I was previously acquainted; it was the turning-point of the drama, like everything else that is concocted in that shop. The Directory was as well aware of it as the King, and lay in wait for our schemers at the defile; but these counter-revolutionary stratagems have no connexion with the Five Hundred, the great majority of whom are wholly guiltless of direct co-operation in these designs.

" The catastrophe of the 18th Fructidor was the means employed, not the end aimed at, by the faction. Seeing that the elections brought in none but anti-revolutionists, and aware that any constitution in France must annul the revolution, they resolved to be quit of them. To overthrow the Councils was an easy task: devoid alike of resources, concert, or fixed aim, knowing each other only by the exercise of speech, they were vulnerable on every side, and could readily be got rid of at pleasure. Several of the proscribed, Camille Jordan, Imbert, Dumolard, Lemérer, Pastoret, Doulcet, Duplantier, Polissard, &c., are in Switzerland, and engaged in preparing a protest. They have been ruined by the 'Ventre,' by Thibaudeau in the Five Hundred, and Tronçon du Coudray in the Ancients. Alexandre Lameth and d'Aiguillon have sallied forth and crossed Switzerland, whose inns and roads were for three weeks crowded with fugitives. There have been some commotions at Marseilles and Aix; on the 22nd September, there still existed at Toulon a body of six thousand Terrorists; some troops were preparing to chastise the mutineers."

Abroad, this catastrophe at Paris entirely disconcerted the plans of the moderate royalists, whose hopes rested on the progress of their own opinions, and on the Council of Ancients. The Princess d'Hénin's clique at London began to discover that Mallet's predictions were not those of a visionary, and each endeavoured to secure for the future such resources as might fall within his reach. In this state of affairs Malouet, anxious and disheartened, begged Mallet's good offices with the court of Vienna, to aid him in obtaining the naval supervision of the Adriatic, now dependent on this power through its recent acquisition of Venice by the treaty of Campo-Formio. Mallet, then destitute of a place of refuge, and unable even to obtain from Vienna a reply to his request for permission to sojourn at Fribourg, had it not in his power to render his friend this service. Still, the letter Malouet wrote on this occasion to his friend's son well deserves perusal, as also a few pages from Mounier, then reduced to the necessity of setting up a school at Weimar. The minor traces of the effect of revolutions on the lives of individuals possess the advantage of recalling us from the stern generalities of history, and, from the solicitude professed in our day for the destinies of mankind in the abstract, to the general feelings of humanity : they re-awake our sympathies. History but too commonly leaves to poets a motto she also should adopt :

Nil humani a me alienum esse puto.

The portraiture of such distinguished men reduced to a precarious existence, in exile, suffering and anxiety, may not strictly belong either to history or politics, but claims a place in a picture of the revolution. Did we possess the letters of some illustrious Roman exile, driven during the civil wars to keep school in the land of Mithridates, they would assuredly not be devoid of interest.

LETTER FROM MALOUET TO M. L. MALLET.

"London, November 24.

" I know not, my dear young friend, what can have become of my letters to your father. I delayed my reply to you for three weeks, because you announced a change of abode without giving me any address ; I then wrote to you at Constance, next to your father at Fribourg in Brisga, and at Constance ; finally, I write to you at Berne. If this reaches you, enquire for the three others : there is one from Lally at Fribourg. These letters are interesting to me, and may perhaps be so to you, as they communicate to your father an idea which is working in my mind, and which is far from chimerical. I have a notion I might undertake the management of the Emperor's marine in his new possessions on the Adriatic. In fact, there is but one step from superintendence at Toulon to superintendence at Venice; and as the hereditary dominions of the House of Austria have not as yet produced any overseer of marine, I do not see why I should not come forward as a candidate. On the other hand, there are two reasons why I should: the first is, that the Emperor, whether he means to make little or much of the new arsenals, ports and sailors he has just acquired, must at any rate want some one who understands such arrangements as relate to police and interior administration. The second reason, which I might call the first, saving the respect due to sovereigns, is that I know not what to do or to be. The colony of St. Domingo is dead or dying, and my deputation too. Here, nothing seems open to me. You know what England is to a foreigner: charity is bestowed on him, but nothing more. I have no debts, but I have no money; I therefore naturally wish to live by my labour where it may be of some use; and you may be sure, my dear friend, that if I were to be employed in the way I speak of, I would find a situation for you too. My wish then is, to know whether your father, by means of his friends and connexions at Vienna, could be of any use to me; or whether he could point out to the Princess de Bouillon, who is at Frankfort, and whom I have addressed on the subject, what steps she must take in order to succeed. I suppose your father has kept up a correspondence with the Archduke. I have informed him that I could collect here, and take away with me, the wrecks of the administration of Toulon, engineers, port-officers, masters of vessels, &c. And I think this little colony need not be despised by the Court of Vienna; for, in a new territory so acquired, the natives of the country cannot be employed with much confidence by the new Sovereign, while exiles like ourselves are necessarily attached to the power which affords them subsistence. It is for you and for your father to enlarge on my text: I leave it to the friendship of you both ; and, if there is a plank for me in the wreck, the port I reach shall be also that of my friends.

" I have followed your policy, your plan of observation, since our separation. You were brought up in too good a school not to have already a share in your patrimony, which consists in sagacity united to correct views. Your father fails in his conjectures and combinations only when none but disingenuous minds can guess. This peace of the Emperor seems to me big with a new war : the pacification of that great French sink becomes more and more distant. In the present state of Europe, my friend, you will agree that I could not do better than go to Venice for the carnival, taking care to make off at Lent. However, if I were once overseer of the Adriatic, I would defend the ground foot by foot, and should thus be the better able to offer my services, in case of need, to the Grand Signor. Don't treat my suggestion as a joke. I am quite willing you should laugh at it on reading my letter ; but, after you have finished, be serious again, and work in good earnest for the success of this great enterprise. Here, my friend, I can do nothing to serve you. I will only tell you by way of supplement to Montlosier, or as a repetition of what he said, that we flatter ourselves with hopes of early peace with Spain, and a new coalition of the powers of the north and south. Tell your father to endeavour to turn it to better account than the first. I send my most affectionate wishes to both of you."

Mounier, also, had written to Mallet du Pan, from Weimar :

"In the details you are so kind as to send me, I am sorry to find none personal to yourself. You do not inform me whether you are to remain in Switzerland, whether you have received an answer from your friend at Vienna. I went to know all about you—even to the description of your house, your vexations, and amusements ; I was too intimate with you in Switzerland not to have become attached to you irrespectively of politics.

" I hope your relation with V . . . . is not interrupted. Pray, my dear friend, overcome your repugnance, and make provision for the future. I know that your independence of character must render any kind of solicitation very painful to you, but it is a great sacrifice which you owe to your children. As for me, I should be quite as anxious as yourself to despise fortune, if once assured of the requisite, yet I neglect nothing to ensure future resources. My present occupation has been very unpleasant to me, except for a few days. Want of continuous employment and lethargy, and the ill-humour and *ennui* which result from these, are almost as bad as in Switzerland. I have several projects for the maintenance of my children. If those do not succeed, I shall be forced to take to literary employment, in which I should be most happy to have you for a colleague : if fortune were to condemn you to the same resource, perhaps our names in conjunction would find some favour."

In another letter Mounier announces to Mallet, that the kindness of the Duke of Saxe-Weimar has settled his plans.

" Yesterday I came to Weimar. I passed several days at Gotha, and the rest of the time at Erfurt. I was very well received at the Court of Gotha by the Duke and Duchess, although one is generally accused of excessive aristocracy, and the other of democracy. This Prince treats the French with the most touching humanity : he has welcomed those whom the Elector of Mayence had dismissed from Erfurt, and overwhelms them with courtesies and kindness. If he ever entertained, as is asserted, democratic principles, it can only have been through a mistaken idea of doing public good. He now holds the soundest opinions ; and all the emigrants he has received have followed his good example, and treat me very well.

" The possibility of our return to France appears to me very remote indeed. You have still some means of waiting before taking a decisive step ; but as for me, my dear friend, I had to accept the first endurable opening which offered in such sad circumstances. The young man I am with could not procure me a pension, unless I consented to follow him several years more. I therefore gladly accepted the proposal of the Duke of Weimar, to place me in an educational institute in one of his countryhouses. This will enable me to remain with my children.

" I do not think I can get young men from Berne. But show the prospectus to your friends, and tell me what you think of it.

" Write to me as soon as possible, and believe in my sincere attachment.

" MOUNIER."

CHAPTER XIII.

1797—1798.

Mallet du Pan is forced to quit Switzerland—Fribourg, in Brisgau—
The Abbé Delille, Messieurs Portalis—The Directory orders the invasion of Switzerland—Mallet's letters about these events—Union
of Geneva with the French Republic.

THE triumph of the Directory, and the Peace of Campo-
Formio, by which Italy and the neutral states were shortly
after left at the mercy of Bonaparte, changed the aspect of
affairs, and the position of Mallet in Switzerland.   Mallet
had been recalled to Berne by his private affairs ; he was
again obliged to quit that city towards the autumn,
shortly after the return of his son, to whom he had
entrusted the task of continuing his correspondence with
M. de Hardenberg and M. de Souza.   He applied himself
to seek a place of safety, and he wandered about for the
purpose during several weeks, from Zurich to Schaffhausen, to Basle, to Constance ; from which last town he
wrote thus to his family.

" My mind is occupied night and day with our difficulties, your anxiety, with the inconveniences, loss of time,
and the expenses of this unsettled life, which resistance

renders so irksome, and which would be tolerably pleasant, if I could have directed my course immediately towards Fribourg.

" This wandering life, this idleness, new faces, the kind of unsettled existence, so ill-accordant with my taste, weigh sometimes upon my spirits. My health, however, is happily very good—thanks to temperance and plenty of exercise. I was delighted with the appearance of the lake, and of the Rhine, which surpassed my expectation. In many points, I conceive it superior to the Lake of Geneva, though the shores are less wooded. But the banks of the Rhine are very different from those of the Rhône, which is narrow, gloomy, and rapid, when it leaves Geneva.

" My society is limited to two or three acquaintances, among others, M. Cayeux, formerly treasurer of the Prince de Condé, and a friend of Duchemin. From him I have received unbounded attentions. With the rest of the _émigrés_, with one or two exceptions, I have but little intercourse. Their excitement is unbounded ; their tone and manner truly ridiculous. In the Emperor's dominions they speak of him and of his minister, and of England, as people speak of them in the clubs of Paris.

" I saw Portalis at Zurich ; but I only knew his name, after having conversed ten times with him, by mere accident. He called on me twice ; but unfortunately we had not an opportunity of being alone, which annoyed us both. Doulcet arrived the day before I left."

At first, Mallet had thoughts of settling in Zurich, where he had met with a hearty welcome, and which testified a lively indignation at the conduct of the government of Berne ; but fear soon displaced this generous disposition. " The Jacobins and the moderate party are uneasy at my remaining here; the matter was discussed the day before yesterday in the council, but no molestation has ensued as yet. I saw the head of the Commission, explained my case to him, and assured him that, as it was not my intention to remain here, I wished for only eight or ten days. This term has even been extended, and all passed with much courtesy and consideration. Here the emigrants are allowed only forty-eight hours. The general list of strangers at the inns is printed, and that every day : this list goes to Bacher and to Paris : they took the precaution of removing my name from the list."

Mallet was obliged similarly to give up hopes of Neufchâtel. The Prussian government had been sounded, and preserved silence. This amounted to a refusal ; they feared to grant authority. The historian, Müller, then Imperial Counsellor, had strongly urged the exiled journalist to imitate Pellenc, and direct his views towards Vienna. Mallet had frankly replied that, wearied, worn out, with eternally fighting for others at his own expense, and being exposed to persecutions, derangements, vexations of all kinds, he had resolved to put an end to them ; and, if the war recommenced without his being sure of a livelihood, to retire to Anspach or Brunswick, where he had been offered an asylum and provisional means of establishment ; and that he would see about gaining thence England or Holland, and fix in one of those countries in peace, once for all. Müller entered into his reasoning, but conjured him to give the preference to the Emperor's service, and await an answer from Vienna.

Events thickened, and no news came from Vienna. Mallet then reverted to the idea of establishing himself in London. But, as it was too late to start for England that same year, he took the route of Germany, and stopped at Fribourg-in-Brisgau. Hence, he wrote to M. de Thugut, requesting him to obtain permission for him to pass the winter in the states of the Emperor, and at Fribourg in preference to Lower Suabia, of which that minister had spoken. He thus concluded his application : " Your Excellency will pardon my urgency, in considera- tion of the pressing nature of my position : I venture to hope from you, and from His Majesty's government, the compassion accorded to the innocent in distress, and which I claim on grounds that will transmit my name to my descendants unstained, whatever may be the degree of misfortune in store for us." We recognise here, as in all Mallet's letters, that tone of natural elevation, that self-respect, which he never permitted any of his corres- pondents to forget. But this letter of a man, who for three years had had relations with the cabinet of Vienna, remained unanswered. Fortunately, Baron de Sumeraw, Governor of Brisgau, took it upon himself to give Mallet an asylum, which he offered him in the most flattering and generous terms.

Mallet's family, bidding adieu to Switzerland, rejoined him at Fribourg—the first step, as they foresaw, of the wandering life to which they found themselves con- demned ; for, since their country withdrew its protec- tion and security, there remained to them no assured residence or tranquil retreat. However, their exile was softened by the companionship of the distinguished men

who partook in it.   In fact, scarcely had Mallet reached
Fribourg, when he received letters from several emigrants,
and from victims of the 18th Fructidor, from Messrs.
Portalis, the Abbé Delille, and the Abbé Georgel among
others, all of whom begged him to obtain from Baron de
Sumeraw permission for them to come to Fribourg.
This permission was granted; but Portalis and his son
were obliged nevertheless to retire to a sorry village in
the Black Forest, whence they often issued to see their
friends, for emigrants of recent date even this was a
great favour.   In the society of these companions in
misfortune, Mallet du Pan and his family passed this
sad winter.   The liveliness and inexpressible charm of
Delille's society, the pregnant and highly interesting
conversation of Portalis and his son, contributed to
mitigate the cruel impression of the events which passed
almost under the eyes of the exiles.   Nothing, indeed,
had availed to restrain the Directory, long determined to
swallow up Switzerland in its system of revolutionary
invasion : its intrigues and threats had commenced active
operation from the latter months of 1797, and its armies
completed it by the taking of Berne in the opening days
of 1798.

It may be conceived with what interest Mallet watched
the progress of the invasion, the efforts of a too tardy
resistance, powerless or surrounded with dangers, but
finally glorious, and more worthy of Switzerland.   Many
portions of his familiar correspondence turn upon these
events.   He was informed at first hand, and often by
express ; so that these narratives, condensed, but full o
stirring matter, possess an accuracy perfectly historic.

LETTER FROM MALLET DU PAN TO COUNT DE SAINTE-
ALDEGONDE.

" Fribourg, in Brisgau, November 13, 1797.

" My dear Count,

" Here I am boxed up in this town, where I have received your two last letters. No period, since the emigration, has been more bitter to me than the two months just
past. Compelled to quit Berne, roaming through Switzerland, freezing with fear all the cowardly Swiss among
whom I appeared, bandied about every day according to
the chances of peace or war, unable to adopt any course of
action before the necessity for action itself, wasting my
time and money on the high roads, far from my family,
which had remained at Berne till I should select an asylum,
and heart-broken by the last events in France, I have had
every possible opportunity of taking my degree in stoicism.
This advantage at least I have gained, that of becoming
convinced that I must give over——leave off ruining myself
to defend men who cut your throat and their own——and
settle down somewhere definitely. I am irremoveably
fixed on leaving for England in the spring : the dangers
of that island are no objection. We are, upon the continent of Europe, what the victims devoted to the infernal
gods were among the ancients : it was thought sacrilege to
give them refuge. I hope to remain where I am for the
whole of this winter. You will scarcely believe that they
were nearly refusing me hospitality here ; that at Vienna they
were uneasy at my being near the Rhine, and that, but for

the generous interest of the chief of the local government,
I might perhaps still be houseless.

"Switzerland is on the brink of ruin.   The Directory
dislodges it from all its intrenchments one after the other.
After Mr. Wickham's departure,* the immediate suppression in Switzerland of all the crosses of St. Louis, and of the

* Mr. Wickham, by departing of his own accord, had forestalled
the Directory, which was deliberating on demanding from the
Bernese government the dismissal of the English envoy.   We have
here an opportunity to insert a note, equally authentic and interesting, which has been communicated to us by that diplomatist, whose
name has already occurred more than once, and will again appear
in these Memoirs.

"It would be an extraordinary delusion, as to the mission of Mr.
Wickham in Switzerland, and a very vulgar error, to consider that
mission as having had no other object or result than subaltern plots,
and anti-revolutionary conspiracies.   Beyond doubt, Mr. Wickham
organized, found funds for, and held the thread of a number of
enterprises and movements, well or ill-combined, having for their
object the overthrow of the Directory and the revolutionary faction,
then mistress of the destinies of France, and the re-establishment of
order and monarchy.   But, if his official correspondence should ever
be published, it will prove the extent and certainty of the intelligence he had with Paris, and other parts of France; and the
eminent services which these means of information enabled him to
render his country.   To give some sample of this, we cite the
following facts :

"Mr. Wickham had such early information of the conclusion of
the treaty of Basle, in 1795, between France and Spain, that he
despatched a courier to Lord St. Vincent, who commanded the
allied English and Spanish fleet, in the Mediteranean, to give him
notice of the fact.   A great number of English were then in the
Spanish ports in assurance of perfect safety ; and this communication enabled the English Admiral to take the measures necessary
for warning them of their danger, and giving them time to provide

Order of Merit, was demanded, together with an amnesty to all conspirators banished from Switzerland, right of fixed domicile to all French republicans, without special sanction ; in fine, Basle has delivered Richer-Serisy, bound hand and foot, to the Directory. This unfortunate Serisy provoked

against it. Lord St. Vincent expressed his warm gratitude to Mr. Wickham.

" On another occasion, he despatched a courier to the British Ambassador at Constantinople, desiring him to send a messenger to India forthwith, in order to inform the government of Bombay that a fleet was about to set sail from Texel, with the ostensible object of steering for the coast of Ireland ; but in reality destined to re-capture the Cape of Good Hope. In consequence of this intimation, equally prompt and opportune, the Dutch fleet, which had set sail for the north, to avoid the English Channel-fleet, found a strong English squadron awaiting it at the Cape, and had no choice but to yield.

" At another time, Mr. Wickham, having learned the intention of the Directory to send diplomatic agents, ostensibly on scientific missions, to the Imaum of Muscat, and several Indian princes, caused them to be all intercepted by the British Consul at Bussora, who obtained a prohibition of their further progress, and gave them safe-conducts to return to France.

" Lastly, in 1797, Mr. Wickham communicated to Lord Grenville, in a confidential letter, a fact of the highest importance, viz. : that the two principal chiefs of the rebellion then brewing in Ireland, Lord Edward Fitzgerald and Arthur O'Connor, were in conference with General Hoche, at Basle ; a fact unknown even to Wolfe Tone, the avowed agent of the Irish Directory at Paris. In consequence of this communication, Mr. Pitt, in 1798, at the moment when the rebellion was about to burst forth in Ireland, had O'Connor again arrested—he having been previously acquitted on an indictment for alleged high treason ; and the result of this second arrest was a confession from O'Connor, which contributed essentially to the discovery of the plan of rebellion, and the persons implicated in it."

his fate. I supped with him at Basle two nights before his arrest; I conjured him to depart and follow me; but he, fool-hardy and self-confident, despised my advice.—Adieu."

TO THE SAME.

"Fribourg, in Brisgau, December 14, 1797.

"I think, my dear Count, you are mistaken in looking for a new war, or serious difficulties, from the Congress of Rastadt. Two causes will remove all obstacles; the threatening and all-powerful rod of the Directory, and the understanding they are generally believed to maintain with Vienna. Do you think that any of the injured parties are either in a position, or in a humour to do anything but complain?

"The solemnities of Rastadt are, then, a mere farce. The individuals concerned will set forth a whole library of statements; the pamphleteers will babble; this nonsense will raise a laugh, and the negotiation which is to open on the 25th will, I expect, be nipped in the bud. A new war could only arise from the Courts of St. Petersburg and Berlin forming an alliance with England; but it will be infinitely better to leave the latter to its evil destiny, and await the revolution with crossed arms, affecting to assert again and again that there is nothing whatever to fear, and that, in fact, the Directory is composed of the best fellows in the world.

"Bonaparte went from Rastadt to Paris on the 1st, in the wake of three consecutive couriers despatched by the Directory. He treated the imperial deputies like dogs, receiving them with his hat on, and having their names announced without looking at them as they were introduced. This hero will return for the opening of Congress.

" Nothing less than the horrors heaped upon the Venetians, and those in store for them, can make us conceive the boundless joy with which they pass beneath the imperial dominion, once so odious to them. The heads of the state, the patricians, the large proprietors, themselves invoked the loss of their independence.

" The papers will have informed you of the atrocious note by which the Directory has just demanded of the Swiss the expulsion of all the emigrants, the arrest and extradition of all those sentenced to exile. Switzerland being on the eve of an utter crash, it will be a service to the emigrants to remove them. Whither will they go? what will become of them?

" I have quite made up my mind to leave here in April. Perhaps I shall pass some weeks in Brunswick before embarking for England. There is no more drawing back. I must make myself some resources, and fix somewhere. The continent offers me nothing but persecution, disgust, the universal prohibition against writing, and the certainty of starving. Adieu."

TO THE SAME.

"January 13, 1798.

" The true object of the association, or rather of the conferences at Rastadt, has not yet been entered upon. There has been nothing but jeremiads, complaints, memorials, against invasion, inactions, brigandage, and the contempt of the armistice displayed by the French. All this jabber was so much time wasted. The French legation refused to listen to anything, and the proceedings finished with the invasion of Mayence. The Congress has the look of a funeral, and indeed is an interment of the Holy Roman empire.

" You will hardly believe it—but the fact is indisputable : the Bernese deputies to the Congress are the only ones who dare speak and show some energy. They put to shame the whole herd of formalists, cancellers, Excellencies, and Monseigneurs. They have not crossed the threshold of the French legation, and keep glued on to that of Prussia, which weeps and wails like the others.

"This shows you the spirit which reigns in Berne. The gauntlet is thrown ; the Swiss crisis has matured with a rapidity proportioned to the violence of the Directory and its choleric pride. You will have read its decree of the 8th Nivôse—a patent of insurrection addressed to the subjects of Berne and Fribourg. This decree was made known in Berne eight days ago. In twenty-four hours the government made a reply, which one would be tempted to date from the eve of the battle of Morat : ' We are accountable for our actions to none but God, ourselves, and our faithful subjects." Next day they proceeded with the trials of the arrested rebels, four of whom must have been beheaded the day before yesterday. Thus, war is almost as good as declared. The Directory sent a new summons on Monday for them to declare whether Berne would take arms against the French Republic, and whether the government had arrested deputies from the remonstrant communes. Night and day work goes on in the arsenals ; the essential and decisive point is the fidelity of the people.

That of the German canton has stood firm ; it displays zeal and devotion. In the Pays de Vaud, this sentiment is less universal. Lausanne, long the hot-bed of intrigue and revolt, has just resolved upon a petition to claim its rights. Zurich, Soleure, Fribourg, and Lucerne, remain linked to Berne, and determined to aid it. The diet, sitting permanently, adopts strong resolutions : vigour offers some chance of salvation, cowardice would destroy all. Of this they are now convinced at Berne. But what can they do, abandoned by all, betrayed by the very one of their neighbours who would have the strongest interest in maintaining the independence of Switzerland ? They will perish, but honourably, and with some hopes for the future. This small spot of earth rivets attention : I shall soon have to give you news full of interest. I am not less affected and agitated at its fate. Indeed, I cannot witness without sorrow the annihilation of the noblest monument of wise and paternal administration existing in the world."

TO THE SAME.[*]

" January 25, 1798.

" As the occupations of my father prevent him from writing to you, he desires me to-day, M. le Comte, to put you in possession of the last stupidities of our country. To be occupied with politics is a sad task just now ; but, as it is not as dry as it is sad, one puts up with it. We are here in a kind of desert, destitute of resources, far from our friends, and having no advantage but that of

* This letter is by M. Louis Mallet, who sometimes assisted his father in his correspondence.

being situate between two theatres of action. You will
have learned from the papers, the defection of Basle at the
Diet of Arau, and in its sequel, that abandonment of the
Helvetic union which was an insurrection in due form :
castles burned, pillage, a rising of peasants *en masse*,
the feebleness and fall of the government —nothing was
wanting to it. Most of the honourable magistrates have
resigned ; and the rest have formed themselves into a permanent club, with some peasants and friends of the *grande
nation*, to make a constitution founded on equality and
the rights of the people.

" Here, then, is one side of Switzerland seized by the
revolution ; and you know, M. le Comte, that, when the
canker has affected one part of the body, the disease very
soon becomes incurable. However, the canton of Berne,
without cutting off communication with Basle, has taken
some precautions, and troops have marched to the frontiers.
The diet preserves its unanimity and energy ; but it seems,
nevertheless, that they seek to renew negotiations with
Paris. The senate of Berne, desirous of knowing the
people's wishes, has demanded from all the communes a
renewal of their oath of fidelity. The whole German portion of the canton has taken it with enthusiasm, the greater
part of the Pays de Vaud with some restrictions, and the
rest has refused——that is, four of five small towns who
called for the restitution of their ancient rights, and the
estates which they had a right to convoke under the Dukes
of Savoy to accept new imposts. As the Bernese have
not imposed imposts, they did not assemble these estates ;
but, since these towns have protested that they would take
the oath on being satisfied, a commission has been nomi-

nated to hear and redress their grievances. This little experiment has given them courage, and clubs and corres ponding committees have been established in all the towns The rural districts, faithful hitherto, have been inundated with emissaries who demonstrate the folly of paying tithes ; and it seems these fine reasons are beginning to make all the more effect for being seconded by all the decrees of the Directory and by fifteen thousand men of the army of Italy, who must have traversed Geneva within the last few days, and formed a camp in the Pays de Gex, to support their friends and brothers. Meanwhile, the Government, which has not yet lost its senses, has formed a camp at Payerne, and has brought forty pieces of cannon over the gorges of the Jura, in order to uphold its *clemency* with reasons somewhat demonstrative, should the *respectful* applications degenerate into revolt. All the German portion is full of courage and energy, and resolved on supporting government.

" The French allege that they propose to hold possession of the Pays de Vaud and the Valais, because the Emperor intends to take the Grisons. An army of fifteen thousand Austrians, which is at this moment marching on Bregentz, would seem to give some colour to this apparent absurdity. These divisions of territory will only end when France dispenses with allies. Meanwhile, she always takes care of herself, and appropriates, like the lion, on many grounds of claim. Here it is for the Cisalpine country—there for Holland—elsewhere for the rights of nature. Pretexts are quite as abundant for taking as for ceding."

TO THE SAME.

"February 1, 1798.

"My dear Count,

"Switzerland is gone. We shall soon have to say the same of the rest of Europe. There were no other means of preservation than those I had mentioned to you, and which I had recommended with my utmost strength to the parties concerned. Berne would have adopted it; but the other cantons, the diet, the trickeries of Zurich, have ruined Berne and Switzerland.

"In lieu of seconding the masculine vigour of Berne, its firm replies to the Directory, and its opening measures, Zurich and the diet declared they would no longer lend their aid to acts of force and severity. They offered to send deputies to negociate with the factious of the Pays de Vaud, to receive their petitions, and employ conciliatory methods. Berne, not to break the union, yielded, stayed the march of its troops and its provosts: the deputies spoiled all. Their presence and their pathos emboldened the rascals, discouraged the well-affected—pulled the machine to pieces. Meanwhile, twelve thousand French troops of the army of Italy, led by Ménard and Rampon, traversed Geneva and took up their position at Versoix and the frontier. These scoundrels, mere boys for the most part, beardless, in rags, unshod, led by officers who look like beggars, and more similar to highwaymen than soldiers, very soon made the fermentation overflow. Ménard published a declaration to the country, inciting it to rise against its tyrants, and promising to support it. Then— and although the great majority of the country was sound-hearted—the revolt broke out in all directions. The magistrates were arrested or compelled to fly, their chateaux broken into, the public chests and receipts seized, Bernese property sequestrated, and many of the land-owning gentry who were government officials, forced to escape. Corps of volunteers were armed. In fine, revolution was rampant.

" Berne, whether resolved on abandoning the Pays de Vaud—which it is impossible to defend without the command of the fort of l'Ecluse and Geneva—Berne, which committed the unpardonable mistake of not commencing the offensive six weeks ago, concentrated its forces—that is, all those of the German canton—on the position of Morat. They have fifty-two battalions, a score of squadrons, a powerful artillery. Such was the state of matters on the 28th. Count d'Erlach, formerly a colonel of Schomberg, and field-marshal, is the commander of the troops : he is an excellent officer, a man of sense and courage ; but, subordinated as he is to republican counsellors who are constantly deliberating when action is demanded, what can he do ? Both officers and soldiers display determination : the latter demanded to be led against the enemy, bayonet in hand, without wasting time in sharp-shooting. For all this, I look upon the game as lost. In case the first position should be forced, there is no alternative between this last chance and abandoning the ground. The French take them in flank by the Pays de Vaud, and by the canton of Basle, into which Augereau must have marched yesterday with fifteen thousand men before him, and the corps of Saint-Cyr to the west, on the frontiers of Erguel. Lucerne and the small cantons support Berne, and behave admirably : the democratic cantons are the

best, the most deeply enraged against the French.   Basle
has made its first revolution ; Zurich totters ; Soleure wavers.
The whole district will relapse into barbarism : the consequences of the revolution will be frightful.   I foretold them
fully, and altogether in vain.   Berne repents bitterly having
ill-treated me. I was besought, a month ago, to return and
give them my co-operation. I answered I would do so, if the
plan of which I have spoken to you were adopted : but
that to make myself the auxiliary of any other measure
would be a fruitless sacrifice.

"I shall hasten my departure by the end of March,
and perhaps sooner.   My dear Count, the Abbé did not
say a syllable too much—not even enough.   What times !
what men ! what masters ! Adieu, &c."

FROM THE SAME TO THE ABBÉ DE PRADT.

"February 17, 1798.

"I received your letter of the 26th, my dear friend,
and that of the Count eight days ago.   In my last I
informed you both of the fortunes of our south ; it is the
same spirit from one end of Europe to the other.   The
cause must be sought for in the character of the age.
By dint of urbanity, epicurism, luxury, all the rich, the
high-born, the landowners, the men of society, are absolutely, as it were, boiled to rags.   No blood, sentiment,
dignity, reason, or ability.   The love of ease is the only
instinct remaining to them.   They are like the Indians
whom the Moguls found lying on palm-leaves, at the
moment when they came to assassinate and rob them.
No one thinks of what he will lose, only of what he may

preserve. Essentially, it all reduces itself to the following calculation : " How much will you leave me if I betray to you my country, my laws, my altars, the dust of my fathers, my honour, my posterity ?" When nations have reached this point, they must perish. For thirty years government in Europe had been a masquerade : the old momentum kept things going. But, at the first shock, these crazy machines crumbled to power, and we find out how rotten they were.

" Switzerland has not yet settled its accounts ; they will struggle between battle and poison. I have traced you the genealogy of these follies *;* the Diet has ruined Berne, and the Diet has ruined itself because it *was* a Diet. The dread of furnishing the allies with a pretext for departure, if the offensive should be adopted, kept Berne immovable, whereas it would, with a single motion, have swept beyond the Jura the first French columns which came to favour the revolt. A hundred thousand peasants, dwellers in town and country, only begged to fight : in reply they were presented spontaneously, and solely in order to disarm the Directory, with a political revolution, a new mode of government : they conjured their Majesties to preserve their authority, and lead them to battle. The more the people showed energy and patriotism, the more did the governing bodies entangle themselves in rigmarole. At Arau, a municipal, commercial, and wealthy town, of the Canton of Berne, where Mengaud had thrown his firebrands and produced an insurrection, the peasants interfered, broke the gates open, sawed down the tree of liberty, arrested the chiefs, and restored go-gernment. A similar scene was witnessed at Olten. At

Soleure, the peasants demanded the detention of all the partisans of France and of revolution ; the trembling magistrate thought he did a great deal in allowing the rascals to escape to Basle, the refuge of all such worthies. In the Pays de Vaud itself, the intrepid men of the Jura valleys never would submit, either to the insurgents or to their allies ; and they sent three thousand volunteers to Berne, to aid the government. Troops, generals, people, women, children, demanded war : all the efforts of the government, or rather of the party which has prevailed for the last four years, were confined to the attempt of cooling down enthusiasm, temporizing, giving time for the arrival on the frontier of ten thousand Frenchmen under the command of Brune and Schauenbourg.

"This temper in the people having, however, alarmed the Directory, it made proposals for a negotiation ; and the snare was fallen into at once. Four deputies from Berne are at Basle, to treat with Mengaud. I was informed the day before yesterday, that the latter's ultimatum had been despatched on the preceding day to Berne, and that the return of the courier would decide on peace or war. Such is the state of things. The Directory aims at adding Switzerland to the Cisalpine territory, and imposing on it the same measures—a total subversion. The cantons would be glad to remain under their semi-revolution. The population are absolutely against any that would derange their civil and political economy, and denaturalize them. But in this point, as in all others, they are betrayed, and the shepherds, I fear will open the fold to the ogres.

"Excuse me from speaking of Rastadt. The Emperor

drowns himself in the jargon of his expounders. The French got him into a corner with curt and trenchant replies: what on earth do all these empty pedants mean with their *distinguo*, their morality, their good-humour? " Bring them a map of the Rhine, since they don't know it," said Trielhard, " they will there discover what the left bank means." But do not imagine that the cession, the dishonour, the insults to be swallowed, all the humiliations they endure, are the serious matter. The petty secular princes have made their bargain with the Directory, and sell the empire for a mess of pottage. The imperial deputation would retract ; but, as soon as it attempts to display any vigour, all the mongrels who are waiting for their pickings set to barking. There has been a quarrel between the ministers of Bavaria and of the Emperor. The former was forced to resign."

TO THE SAME.

"February 21. 1798.

" I have just received my letter from Switzerland. The promulgation of the new Jacobin constitution which the Directory thinks of imposing on the cantons, has excited indignation and a general revolt in all classes and in all the cantons (except Basle, which is no longer Swiss). Any government which should dare to propose the adoption of this farrago, or any attack upon the independence of the country, would be massacred. All the contingents of the cantons are assembled in the Bernese. They marched off with transport ; the small cantons offered to triple their's. Sixty thousand men have been collected, without counting the masses of the population and the landsturm. On the 20th, a definitive conference must have taken place between the deputies from Berne and General Brune ; in this peace or war will have been decided. They were much out of their reckoning ; for the Swiss demand the recall of Mengaud, and the complete evacuation of the Helvetic territory, including Erguel. The Directory insists on the independence of the Pays de Vaud, the constitution, and a sum of money."

LETTER FROM MALLET DU PAN TO THE CHEVALIER DE GALLATIN.

"February 28.

" The Swiss had it in their power to change the face of France and Europe ; they prefer to dishonor themselves by the most ignominious and stupid abasement. When I speak of the Swiss, it is not of the nation : peasants, troops, a great majority even of the middle-classes, women, children, have but one longing, one cry, one sentiment. Full of rage against the French and the innovators, they have implored a score of times to be led bayonet in hand against the enemy. Such was the feeling of Soleure, of Berne, of Lucerne, of the small cantons, of three-fourths in Zurich and Fribourg. In four days, they would have driven the French beyond the Jura, chastised the Pays de Vaud, and occupied the Pays de Gex. But the canker is in the ruling bodies : it is the guilty party of the fawners on the revolution and the republic, those puissant imbeciles who had so well calculated the effect of the brotherhood with France and that of peace, who have rendered nugatory the patriotism and intrepidity of the population. Without their asking for it, these have thrust upon them pernicious innovations, to serve as a bridge of communication with the Directory. The latter, which contemplates a total subversion, a new and not a repaired edifice, takes no account of their advances ; of this, the slightest good sense should have forewarned them. The insolence of demands increases. They have sent from Paris the ready-made code of a republic one and indivisible, according to which Switzerland is divided into departments, with a Prime-Directory and two councils. This extravagance still further inflamed the people : the magistrates thought it enough to be frightened at it. However, the general outcry has compelled them to make declarations for maintaining the integrity and independence of the country ; but they have persisted in the line of conduct most likely to destroy both. The justice of the Directory, the virtues of its chiefs, have been appealed to ; they dabble in treaties and conferences, &c. Thirty-five thousand Bernese, twenty thousand in the contingents, remain stationary for three weeks in sight of thirty thousand French, at the utmost, unprovided with magazines, munitions, or artillery. The pretext is, that the country is not at war ; they wait to be attacked : the invasion of territory does not count as a hostility. Fellenberg has proved it. A terrorist, named Brune, ex-general of the revolutionary army, annoys and trifles with Berne in parleys, the upshot of which is, that he is not invested with the necessary powers. Whilst these are asked from the Directory, fresh forces advance, and in a fortnight, perhaps, Switzerland will have eighty thousand men to do with. The avoyer Steiguer and four or five others alone have stood firm. Their adversaries run, nevertheless, an enormous danger ; for the peasants, who regard them almost as traitors, threathen to take vengeance on them for the loss of their glory and their freedom.

" As for the Pays de Vaud, Lausanne is on the threshold ; the church of St. Lawrence is a Jacobin club ; the most atrocious motions are the order of the day ; the property of absentees has been confiscated ; the peasants, all the young men, flee to Berne. Geneva is unanimous in rejecting the incorporation ; it will be compelled to it, and the play played out. The Pays de Vaud and the Valais will be swallowed up in like manner ; that is decreed in the council of the gods.

" Does Europe think the Directory does enough ? Are men sufficiently satisfied with its promptitude and honesty ? Will they always look on at this inundation, as at a Pinetti's theatre, or Jonas's tricks, so much a head ? Are they glad enough to be still on their feet while all crumbles round the last remaining governments ?

" P.S.—— My letters from Berne, of the 25th, apprise me that an armistice for a fortnight has been concluded at Payerne between Brune and the Bernese, pending the answer of the Directory : it will expire on the 2nd March. The Bernese deputies at Basle, at whose head are Tillier and Rengger, the doctor, have urged over and over again that the preliminaries demanded by the Directory should be agreed to——viz. abolition of the secret council, and of the council of war, total abdication of the men now in power, provisional government chosen by the friends of the people, and compensation to the Arau scoundrels arrested and sold to France. On the 24th, the Two Hundred and the deputies of the communes in conjunction rejected *in pleno* all these abominations."

TO THE SAME.

"March 14, 1798.

" In contempt of an armistice, the French attacked unexpectedly the rear of the canton of Soleure, whilst their General, Schauenburg, advanced from his quarters at Berne on the town itself. Two days previously, Berne had given full unlimited powers to d'Erlach d'Hindelbranck. On the first hostility, and on the expiration of the truce, he was to attack, and had prepared to do so. The deliberation concerning him had not finished, when an aide-de-camp of General Brune arrived very opportunely with an application for a new conference at Payerne. The traitors and the fools seized occasion by the forelock, and the deputies were despatched to Payerne on the 28th February. That same day, the powers of d'Erlach were diminished, and he, as well as Colonel Gross who commanded at Arberg, was forbidden to attack. The French profited by these acts of madness or perfidy to attack and march forward. The detachments from Soleure of Dornach and Thierstein, surprised and overwhelmed by numbers, were compelled to retire. A colonel, in understanding with the French, afterwards yielded them the last passage, sent off to sow dismay in Soleure, and retired, leaving six hundred peasants of the valley of Balstall shut in. They fought like lions ; two-thirds of them were slain, and a number of women were butchered with their husbands and children. Soleure opened its gates to Schauenburg on the morning of the 2nd.

" Brune, on his side, seized on Fribourg during the night between the 1st and 2nd. An officer with a detachment on the road stopped him, sent in vain to demand succour from Fribourg, fought bravely, and, after losing two-thirds of his troops, reached the town with his cannon, burst the gates, found all the inhabitants asleep, and was followed by Brune an hour later.

"At the news of the fate of Fribourg and Soleure, the Lucernese should have fallen back on Saint-Urbain, and the contingents of the small cantons should have followed their example, leaving the Bernese alone to settle the matter with the Zurich contingent. They fought on the 3rd and 4th, and with advantage.

"The position of the army being strengthened by a part of the fugitive contingents, the French were attacked at Fraubrunnen on the 5th. The action was very sanguinary; but the battle was at last decided in favour of the enemy, by the French cavalry and by the defection of a portion of the confederate troops. The Bernese retreated with great loss to the neighbourhood of Berne, where Schauenburg and Brune arrived on the evening of the 5th, and received the capitulation of the town, a capitulation of very little importance. The flower of the patrician youth, all of whom above the age of fourteen had joined the army, has perished. These several actions have been very destructive on both sides, and the road from Fraubrunnen to Berne was covered with dead.

"I cannot tell you exactly what has become of the Bernese army since the 5th. There are no more couriers. What I know for certain, up to the 8th, has reached me by a letter of that date from Monsieur d'Erlach, despatched to me last Saturday by his wife, who has taken refuge at Sekingen with Madame de Watteville, her sister.

"After the action of the 5th, it seems that the army

and the peasants followed the example of anarchy set by the government, and fell back on Emmenthal and Oberland, and on their villages; but, in the fury of desperation, believing themselves betrayed and misled by the treachery of the emissaries, they turned their rage against their most intrepid defenders, accusing the most strenuous enemies of France and her revolution of having delivered them up to France. They massacred their General, Erlach, and many others; the Councillor Herport shot himself. The peasants overrun the fields like tigers, and kill all they meet with. M. de Watteville, of of Lentzburg, and Colonel Berseth, going to Baden on business, have been attacked and wounded, the latter almost mortally: both were saved by the Lentzburg people, who ran to their assistance. The Soleurese have also killed one of their chiefs.

" In the midst of these scenes of slaughter and crime, numerous villages were burned by the French. I conversed yesterday with a young countryman of Argau, who had escaped the destruction inflicted on all his family besides. He told me, crying bitterly, that his village was a mere ruin, and that his father, mother, two sisters and brother had been massacred by the French. These last carry off everything, cattle, horses, furniture, and all the moveables. Such is the condition of this country, which was previously and justly the envy of Europe, and which would doubtless have triumphed, if that infamous party, engaged as we have seen for five successive years in preparing their country's misfortunes, had not disorganized and complicated everything, and brought matters to such a point that resistance could be nothing else but a butchery. M. d'Erlach and the avoyer Steiguer were, on the 8th, still at Berne, where Brune has established a garrison and maintains some discipline. Geneva, our native place, is drawing towards its last day, and will be annexed by fair means or foul.

"On the 10th, the French marched on Zurich, already besieged by the peasants of the lake, and we shall see there the same scenes of horror repeated."

From this moment the communications were interrupted, and as Mallet, although but a very short distance from the frontier, received no more expresses, his letters contain the reports only which reach him about the misfortunes of the great cantons, stripped and completely subjugated by the French republicans, under pretence of deliverance, and about the resistance of the forest cantons, which were preparing, with a heroism worthy of their ancestors, to drive back the terrible revolutionary bands.

Soon afterwards, as Mallet had long anticipated, the ancient independence of Geneva fell into the common gulf into which the French revolution promiscuously hurled principalities and republics.

Bonaparte, on his return from Italy, had said that the independence of Geneva was of consequence to the Republic; that, if it did not exist, it ought to be created. The French government on several occasions, and even recently, had declared through its envoys at Geneva, that it would respect the independence of the Republic, and would keep its promise, leaving to tyrants the prerogative of perjury.* Suddenly, on the 16th of April, a corps of

---

* The envoy Adet, when he delivered his credentials in a public audience, said : "I assure you that the French people will never do

eighteen hundred men enters the town by its three gates, and the Republic is annexed to France, notwithstanding the unequivocal vote of the citizens. The French learned this new exploit of the Directory by reading the " Moniteur," the insolent bulletin of the resident Desportes : " Geneva is full of joy !" The treaty of annexation excepted three Genevese, with Mallet du Pan at their head, from the honour of belonging to the French nation.*
The Directory did not know, when thus revenging themselves, that they were conferring on this courageous man a glorious distinction, worthy of a true republican, and the bravest defender of liberty.†

anything contrary to your independance. This word given by me, the French Republic will keep : tyrants alone have the prerogative of being perjurers." M. Resnier, on presenting the council of Geneva with the colours given us by the French Republic as a token of alliance, said also : " May the tricolour flag be a seal of the glorious proof that the French people is the most decided partisan of your independence." Finally, M. Desportes himself has told us several times that " if his government chanced to forget its principles of justice, he would never afford it his services."—*Letter from M. Bellamy Wyss to Mallet du Pan.*

   * It forms the third paragraph of Article I, of the treaty of annexation of the Republic of Geneva to the French Republic :
   " The French Government, considering that the so-named Jacques Mallet du Pan senior, François d'Yvernois and Jacq. Ant. Duroveray, have written and acted openly against the French Republic, declares that they can never at any time be admitted to the honour of becoming French citizens."
   † Professor Paul Henry Mallet was arrested at M. Tronchin's, at La Boissière. He was mistaken—or it was so represented—for Mallet du Pan ; but he was released some hours after his arrest.

CHAPTER XIV.

1798—1799.

Mallet du Pan repairs to England with his family—His first letters from London—The " Mercure Britannique "—" Essay on the destruction of the Helvetic League "—Entrance of Russia into the Coalition.

WHEN Mallet heard that his country had ceased to exist, he was no longer on that continent whence he was everywhere rejected. The society of Fribourg had dispersed towards the end of March ; MM. Portalis went to Holstein, whither they were invited by Count Reventlow ; and the other members of the little circle, seeing the close of winter, and the end of the permission which had been granted them, approach together, prepared for departure. The moment had come also for Mallet to take some step. Communications with France were closed to him, and his private correspondence with Vienna being thus deprived of supply, was a source no longer to be relied on. England, who since her abandonment by Europe, showed herself haughty and decided, had a peculiar attraction for him ; and indignation and discouragement had made him more than once meditate quitting the continent for this island, protected against revolutionary invasion by the ocean, by her constitution, and by the public spirit of her inhabitants. " As for the public, my dear friend," he writes to the Abbé de Pradt, " you must leave the continent if you wish to address it ; for there is no longer a place where a line can be printed against the Directory and its manœuverings. I have only been tolerated here under promise of keeping silence. What then would you have me do in Germany ? I have but one regret, and that is, that I did not leave five months since. Your continent horrifies me with its slaves and executioners, its degradations and cowardice. It is only in England that one may write, speak, think and act. That is my place ; there is no other for any one that wishes to continue the war."

But the certainty of a situation which would enable him to be useful, and to maintain his family at the same time, was necessary to a man of his character, too proud to ask a share of emigrant subscriptions, too conscientious to let his pen droop while his strength permitted him to hold it— while it could serve the cause of justice and society. Now, as he had been told, he could not calculate in London on the support given to political writers by some continental states. Still, his friends induced him to hope that a political journal, analagous to the old " Mercure de France," would have some chance of success there. This idea had been already suggested to him at Berne, by a Scotch gentleman, Mr. Mackintosh, and it was encouraged by Mr. Wickham, who promised to promote its execution.*

* It was at this period that the government of Berne, wishing to disarm the Directory by means of prudent concessions, asked the

Old Lord Liverpool, President of the Board of Trade and Secretary for the Colonies, and Mr. Windham, then English agent to withdraw. The following letters, written at that time by Mr. Wickham to Mallet du Pan, possess some interest:

"Berne, October 10, 1797.

"I hasten, my dear Sir, to thank you for your very obliging letter of the 7th. I shall write immediately to my friends on the subject, about which Mr. Mackintosh has been conversing with your son.

"You are perfectly right in thinking that an undertaking of such a nature as that which you contemplate, could not possibly succeed without having at least the secret protection and the favour of the government; and I will make it my duty to obtain, as soon as possible, its opinion on this subject. Meanwhile, I advise you to write to Mr. Reeves, and ascertain from him confidentially, if there would be any means of entering on this undertaking with his concurrence alone. I will write him about it on my side, after having had an interview with your son. You will be kind enough to sketch me out the general features of such a journal as you conceive most practicable and useful in the present crisis; we will discuss your ideas, propose our own, and I will send the result of the whole to London.

"It is not impossible that I may follow you soon, judging by the turn things seem to be taking. You have doubtless heard that a certain M. Mengaud has come here with a firm determination to drive me away. For myself, personally, I wish him every success in his mission, for I shall not be sorry to spend my winter near a coal fire. But, in spite of the strange things we see, I cannot persuade myself that he will succeed. All I can say is, that I shall raise no kind of opposition: to appear even to know anything about it, would be forgetting on my part what I owe to my position, and to the dignity of the Helvetic confederation."

"October 19, 1797.

"My dear Sir,

"I write you these few words to inform you, that, yielding to the

Secretary at War, had been both sounded on this project by a friend, Mr. Reeves,* and gave it their cordial assent. England is the natural country of those generous men who

repeated and earnest demands of persons whose friendship has great claims on me, I have promised, against my own conviction, to remove from Berne for some time. I have not yet communicated to any one the resolution I have taken ; but I shall have a conversation on this subject to-morrow with the avoyer, M. Steiguer.

" I have the strongest reason to believe, that, after this first blow, the Directory will not long withhold their second. I am firmly persuaded that those who desire my removal, do not know what they ask. However, I owe them all possible marks of attention and respect, and I should be the most unhappy of men if, by a misplaced resistance, I was the means of bringing misfortunes on their heads.

" It is the opinion, possibly well founded, of one of the best and wisest magistrates here, that the Directory will begin the attack with him and others of his colleagues, by accusing them of corruption ; and I think I perceive that those even who are most above such a suspicion, dread it particularly ; they feel that such a charge would suffice to deprive them of their people's confidence, and would justify the timid conduct of some cantonal governments.

" I shall not stay more than a day at Zurich, and as I shall neither receive nor pay any official visit there, I shall enjoy your society; without inconvenience, we can talk over the matter about which I wrote you recently. I anticipate great pleasure also in seeing M de Salis and M. de Saint-Gratien.

" If peace or a long truce is agreed on, I fear this country will be suddenly attacked, and in that case God only knows what the consequences will be.

" I am, with the most sincere consideration, my dear Sir, yours, &c.,

" WICKHAM."

*John Reeves, counsellor, author of a " History of the British Laws," from the time of the Saxons, to the reign of Philip and Mary, and of a much esteemed treatise on the laws relating to English navigation. He had taken a very active part in an associa-

place at the service of their friends something beyond feelings and good advice. Reeves, while informing Mallet of his efforts, offered him his house until he had made suitable arrangements for himself; he sent him also a remittance of a hundred louis, to defray his travelling expenses. Mallet, therefore, prepared to start for London with his family; but his resolution was scarcely known, before proposals of co-operation reached him from all parts, on the subject of his undertaking. He very prudently declined them.

A more delicate request was sent him by M. de Sainte-Aldegonde. Monsieur invited him, in the most flattering terms, to set out for Hamburg, whence a vessel, which was coming to take up the Count d'Escars, would convey him to his residence at Edinburgh, where he desired to converse with him on various topics. "The proofs of attachment," said the Prince, "which M. Mallet has afforded me on several occasions, induce me to think that he would experience some pleasure in receiving new marks of my esteem and confidence."

This letter came too late, and only reached Mallet in England, which was a fortunate circumstance for him; for his health was very much shaken, and this visit to Scotland would have greatly added to the fatigue and difficulties of his removal, without conducing in all probability to any useful result.

Mallet left Fribourg with his family and passed through

tion called that of the "Crown and Anchor" (the name of the tavern in which its meetings were held). The object of this association was to enlighten the people on the revolutionary intrigues of the partisans of France and French ideas.

Brunswick, where the Duke, who had more than once offered him an asylum in his states, loaded him with politeness and kindnesses. He reached the port of Cuxhaven, where he embarked in the latter part of April. On the 1st of May, after three days' voyage, they touched the soil of England. On their arrival in London, our Genevese emigrants met with the most hospitable and cordial reception from all their English and French friends, from their compatriots, and from a crowd of emigrants of all shades of opinion, from the Bishop of Arras to the Chevalier de Grave, a Girondist. At the head of the former were Malouet, Lally-Tollendal, Montlosier, Lord Fincastle, Macpherson, Mr. Oliphant, Mr. Reeves, and his two anti-Jacobite coadjutors, Mr. Bowles and Mr. J. Gifford. Among his fellow-citizens, he had especial cause to be gratified at meeting the Chevalier d'Yvernois, his former political adversary at Geneva, where he had been conspicuous amongst the most fiery representatives, but who had now returned to moderation and truth, and was devoted to Mr. Pitt's government; Du Roveray, who shared with d'Yvernois and Mallet the honour of being excluded from the treaty of annexation of Geneva to France; Etienne Dumont, once the valued assistant of Mirabeau, now occupied in publishing the works of Jeremy Bentham, an amiable man, and a rare and enlightened spirit; the Achard family, and Rigaud, member of the Royal Academy of Painting, to whom we owe the original of the excellent portrait of Mallet, engraved by Heath.

The delight of these first moments was keenly felt by Mallet, who was deeply touched by his friends' affection, and the satisfaction of having obtained an asylum in a country where he found, what he had vainly sought on the whole continent, a government full of resources and supported by opinion, a people animated by a powerful public spirit, and ready to sacrifice everything for the maintenance of its honour and liberty. He wrote to his friend, the Chevalier Gallatin, then at Berlin :

" London, May 18, 1798.

" We landed on the 1st, and arrived here on the 3rd, after stopping twenty-four hours at Yarmouth. From that moment I have been in a complete whirl and confusion, overwhelmed with receiving and returning visits, with the cares of settling myself, and with the hubbub of this colossal city, which I find increased again by a full third. Mr. Reeves, my friend, pounced upon us just as we were, carried us off from the mail-coach, and lodged us at his house. I am there still. This hospitality has given me leisure to choose my neighbourhood and residence at my ease.

" I have met here with a friendly and very favourable reception. My plans are under examination ; I do not hurry, and have had little time yet to occupy myself much with my personal affairs. I will discuss that chapter with you another time. I must place Mr. Wickham at the head of those who serve me with the most intelligence and goodwill. He is Under-Secretary of State for the Home Department : that is his province, and he fills his position with applause. It embraces the police, to which he has given an activity, a direction, and an extent hitherto unknown.

" I fancy myself in another world and another age. This is the period when it may be well said, *Et penitus toto divisos orbe Britannos.* On the other side of the sea I have left the continent struggling in the convulsions of a ridiculous peace, which it tries to obtain or preserve. I have left it in the midst of the benefits of this peace, that is, not knowing what to resolve on; suffering from anguish, division, and terror; daring neither defence, nor union, nor complaint; devoid of all patriotism, and unable to combine two means of safety.

"Here they are in open war, crushed with taxes, exposed to the rage of a most exasperated enemy; and security, abundance, energy, reign everywhere : in cottage and in palace I have not perceived one symptom of timid disquietude. This spectacle of public spirit has surpassed my expectations, and that greatly. The nation had not previously acquired a knowledge of its power and immense resources. The government has taught it the secret, and diffused boundless confidence. These dispositions attain an extravagant height; I find much fanaticism here, but exclusively amongst the sound part of the nation. It abhors France, the revolution, the Jacobins, the Directory, as France hated the aristocrats in 1784. Woe to the partisans of the doctrines of the day! This class, which has prodigiously diminished, is in dejection and obscurity. There is no more safety for any one who does not show himself a true Briton.

"We have had a recent and remarkable proof of this popular sentiment, in the enthusiasm which the escape of Sir Sydney Smith has produced among the people; even the children talked about it in the streets. Three days afterwards, the King struck Mr. Fox's name from the list of the Privy-Council, and no one hardly speaks of it.   I will say nothing of the opposition ; it only exists in the Whig Club, and the ' Morning Chronicle'.

" It is difficult to imagine more skill, energy, conduct, and activity, than the Ministry employs in everything relating to the safety of the state.   Its foresight embraces all possible contingencies ; measures are taken and means all ready, from the embarkation of the French in their harbours, to the invasion of London itself, where they would find everything prepared for their reception.   To the regular troops, to the old and supplementary militia, to twenty-thousand volunteer and select cavalry, armed associations are added in all the parishes.   Their office is to enforce the law, to watch the seditious, to guard the waters, to check fires, to repress the least movement.   A million men are under arms at the present time.

" You may conceive that I am in my element : I no longer need periphrases to give currency to my opinions ; I have no further fear of being driven away for failing in respect to Merlin.

" Commercial matters being highly prosperous, the fate of the continent is a cause of too little anxiety.   (I am speaking of the public, not the government.)   There are national prejudices with regard to it, in which I have already made a breach.   I have made use of the note you sent me ; I have considered its justness and consequences ; I have been very well understood, and I think that the continentals will perceive a great improvement in this particular.   But with all this, contempt for the submission of the continent, and impatience to see it change this attitude, are universal sentiments. The national impetuosity acknowledges neither obstacles, considerations, nor circumstances."

Meanwhile, thanks to the active zeal of Reeves, the affairs of the new "Mercure" made rapid progress, the chances of success augmenting daily. Encouragements were received from different classes of English society, and even from the continent, which justified calculating with full certainty on the success of the journal. Mallet, sick and enfeebled, entered on the task with much more calm good sense than enthusiasm or pleasure. The late Lord Liverpool, who came to dine in Cecil Street sometimes, was interested in the work. "I remember," says Mallet, "the cold and diplomatic manner of the taciturn Lord Liverpool; he appeared to me of all men the least adapted to attract confidence and encourage independent talent. Still, he took a real interest in my father's enterprise, and even busied himself with the means of securing its success. Some of his ideas on this point were whimsical enough: thus, he recommended Mallet to associate with him, as coadjutors, Peltier and the Abbé Barruel; the only difficulty he saw in this strange combination was the union of a Catholic ecclesiastic with a Genevese Protestant. The Abbé would succeed, no doubt, but the Calvinist bigot caused him great apprehension. Mr. Windham, whom we sometimes met at dinner at Mr. Wickham's, formed a perfect contrast with Jenkinson (Lord Liverpool). Nothing could surpass the charm of his courteous demeanour and his frank and benevolent manners. For the rest, Mr. Wickham, the amiable Macpherson, Mr. Trevor, Mr. Romilly,

Mr. Batt, and a number of other friends and persons of note, either from their official position, or in society, or literature, took a great interest in establishing the 'Mercure,' and zealously exerted themselves to procure subscribers."

These gentlemen ultimately approved the plan proposed by Mallet himself. It was resolved not to make the "Mercure Britannique" an ordinary gazette, but a work especially directed against the French Republic and its government, against everything done and promulgated by the Directory—a consecutive and uniform system of opposition to it, founded on facts, and the most candid discussion.

"It is by broad sketches," said Mallet, "by incessant instructions on the past and the future, by retrospection and the pictures of the past, that I propose to conduct this publication, giving it a methodical and connected form. There is no other work of the kind in Europe, and it is without doubt the most necessary. Experience is lost, if we do not perpetuate it at the very moment by writings which fix its impress. Innumerable prejudices have been established both on the continent and in England, on the force, the success, the duration, the nature of the French Republic; on the skill of its governors, on the irresistible impulse of the revolution, on the means of retarding its approach. These prejudices, which hold the first rank amongst the obstacles to the formation of a new continental league, shall be daily attacked."

A prospectus drawn up with these views was distributed by the journalist's friends, and we may easily imagine how subscribers would respond to this appeal.

It had been calculated that five hundred subscribers would afford a sufficient revenue for Mallet and his family. But the concurrence of the government was not to be reckoned on. The English minister had indeed assisted the " Courrier de Londres," an ultra-royalist journal, written without talent, by means of subscriptions for the emigrants, amounting to fifteen hundred livres.* But all that could be obtained for the " Mercure Britannique" was confined to the communication of some official papers, and a subscription for twenty-five copies intended for the conquered French colonies. The Court of St. James was then perhaps the only one in Europe, where a writer of this class did not become the object of especial distinction on the part of persons placed at the head of government. Now, with the exception of personal subscriptions and some insignificant testimonials of interest, Mallet received no marks of official attention from any man in place : he was never summoned to any minister. But his reputation, and soon his work itself, did him better service with the *élite* of the English public. The five hundred subscriptions were rapidly exceeded, and quickly rose to nearly eight hundred. This was of course little enough in comparison with the fifteen thousand subscribers Mallet had left on the French " Mercure," but considering the circumstances, this modest number was reckoned brilliant. Although Mallet's son, whose familiarity with the language of the country rendered the task comparatively easy to him, was entrusted with all the business and financial department of the undertaking ; the periodical labour was a heavy burden to Mallet, who engaged to furnish a

* See " Mémoires de Fauche-Borel," vol. III.

political essay of sixty pages every fortnight. An elaborate and complete article was always expected from him, and probably he would not have been suffered to give those pages of feeble composition and filling-up matter, which are the ordinary resource of periodicals. The co-operation of many editors would not have been satisfactory, and besides, his independence would not have permitted the assiduous co-operation of regular coadjutors. Moreover, his old friends, the monarchists, so long in agreement with him in their appreciation of the French Revolution and the means of opposing it, weary of awaiting the re-establishment of a government according to their wishes and principles, had insensibly reduced their hopes to such an organization of modern France as should secure to so many French exiles a return to their native land, by offering them some shadow of repose and some remains of their property. These dispositions had inclined them towards the Whig party, who always showed themselves favourable to peace, and desired negotiation with France at any price, rather than the continuance of a struggle the necessity and wisdom of which they disavowed. By following this course they had gradually deviated from Mallet's views, who did not admit that circumstances justified such a policy. These divergences occasioned, from the very first, a coolness between these veteran soldiers of a common cause, which, however, did not last long, and did not for a single instant disturb the warm attachment of Malouet, ever candid, but ever devoted, and a most affectionate friend. As for the ultra-royalists, they were not long in perceiving that the editor of the "Mercure Britannique" was not favourable to their chimeras, or disposed to espouse their extravagant impetuosity and pretensions. He had hardly landed before they sought to win him over to their side.

"I have had an interview with Baron de Rolle," wrote Mallet to his friend Sainte-Aldegonde ; " he appeared quite under a misapprehension, which I often meet with among many other Frenchmen, with regard to my supposed influence with ministers. From this conclusion they proceed to dictate to me the counsels I should inspire, especially in inducing the government to decide upon fresh attempts on the interior. I have undeceived M. de Rolle as to this illusion, and told him plainly that my unalterable decision was, not to play the part of councillor of state here ; and that if any man in office asked me my opinion, it would invariably be, not to retard the inevitable division which will sooner or later break out in the dominant faction, by giving them a ground of union in rash enterprises, which could not meet with any success.

" This system does not find favour with the Chouans, petitioners and others, who appear quite exasperated because millions are not thrown to them, on the very first requisition. Of course, they conclude from my reserve that I am devoted to the British government. These poor men are as happy in their inferences as in their projects and information. I take no notice of all this nonsense ; I must, the same as every one else, pay my share of tribute to the indomitable spirit of discord, malignity, and despotism which consumes the refugees."

Mallet du Pan, therefore, set himself alone to the task, and unfurled his flag. Seeing already, as he thought, that France, transformed as she was by the revolution, was fatally condemned to extend her invasions over Europe, and that no concession or offer of alliance, no manifestation of sympathy, could have any other effect than to suspend this irresistible impulsion, so dangerous to the peace and to the liberty of the world, all these threatened interests must be united in order to form a formidable barrier, capable of arresting the conquering impetuosity of France. But the moment had not yet arrived : that combination of force and of public spirit, which was at a later period to check the billows of the empire, and which Mallet implored with a deep sense of their necessity, could only be the result of circumstances difficult to foresee at that time. To obtain it, in the epoch in which Mallet was writing, would have been to open eyes that would not see ; it would have been necessary, by the picture of a recent past, and of a present sufficiently terrible, to overcome the universal sloth and listlessness, at least, to force conviction on those who were interested, and reflection on the governments. This is what Mallet du Pan wished at least to attempt in his publication ; and as his hopes entirely reposed on the people, who, in his opinion, had shown themselves so superior to the governments, he purposed addressing nations much rather than cabinets.

Having formed this resolution, he could not open the campaign better than by retracing, with a most energetic pencil, the last crime of the Directory——the destruction of the Helvetic league, overthrown much more by the cowardice of Swiss governments and councils than by the French armies. This recital, he hoped, would show undisguisedly the morality of the French Republic, the odious hypocrisy of its protestations and pretended love of liberty, the darkness of its intrigues, and the uncontrollable avidity of its agents. The first numbers of the " Mercure Britannique" were, in fact entirely filled with a description of this event, and yet the misplaced patriotism of too many French writers persists in promulgating on this subject false colourings drawn from the official lies of the Directory.

"All powers," observed Mallet in the preface, "may read therein their destinies and their duties. If any still flatter themselves with the hope of reconciling their existence with that of the French Republic, let them study this terrible monument of its friendship.

"And yet, what people had more claims than the Swiss to the favour of the French Directory? What people could concede a greater number of sacrifices? Consider the catastrophe which closed five years of patience, deference, and hope. Consider the point attained now-a-days by efforts to avoid war!

"Let governments and nations, therefore, cease to expect their safety from counsels dictated by a servile policy; let them be assured that the revolutionary association of Paris will conquer them on the morrow of the day in which they have so dishonoured themselves. Providence has not connected peace with the forgetfulness of all courage, nor security with terror. Nations and sovereigns are condemned at the tribunal of the revolution; the fall of one is inseparable from the misery of the other. Switzerland is now lamenting her misapprehension of this truth; she renews the picture which a writer of the middle ages has left us of Athens, after the invasion of Alaric, the empty and bleeding skin of a victim offered in

sacrifice.   She has nothing left but rocks, rubbish, and
rhetoricians."

We must not expect to find in this work the calmness of
the historian, or the *sang-froid* of the political philosopher,
whose only passion is to discover the logical relations
between cause and effect.   The author terminates his
preface thus :

" I forewarn a class of men, very sensitive to their own
misfortunes, very indifferent to those of others—who would
forgive the French Republic the desolation of the globe,
provided it was kind enough to spare *them*, that they will
not find in this work what they are pleased to call moderation.   I invite such persons to preach it to the oppressors,
and not to the victims.   And besides, all the impartiality
permitted by historical exactitude will be found preserved.

" With Switzerland I have lost country, relatives,
friends ; all of it that remains to me now are heart-rending
reminiscences.   I should, perhaps, be without an asylum
if heaven had not reserved me a harbour in which I can
accuse, without fearing them, infatuated tyrants whose
haughty impotence vainly threatens this last bulwark of
old Europe.   It is under the protection of an immovable
nation that I here deposit my recital and my grief.   Without
her magnanimity I should still be experiencing the torment
of silence."

There is no exaggeration in these expressions ; Mallet
had really an intense interest in this work ; it was his only
refuge for all that he had lost, for all that his country had
lost.   " How many times," his son tells us, " have I seen
my father, when employed at this task, disturbed, agitated

rise suddenly and stride up and down the room, until
he had succeeded in mastering the powerful emotions
which were swelling in his soul." There is, indeed, too
much emotion in the "Essay:" indignation bursts forth
with too much vehemence; and the accent of accusing
eloquence prevails too naturally in it, for the work to be
considered as a history, properly so called. But its historical exactitude and veracity are not the less unimpeachable,
the essential portion of the recital being both solid and
deeply interesting. The whole of the first part, devoted to the
analysis of the causes which led to the fall of the Confederation is, to use the expression of Dumont, a masterly
sketch of the lofty efforts made by a republic threatened
by foreign invasion and distracted by intestine discords.
The first chapter, in particular, the subject of which is the
moral and civil state of the canton of Berne before the revolution, is a picture of the manners and government of that
happy people, the interest of which will never be
lessened either by the lapse of time, or the change of
ideas.

These first numbers of the "Mercure Brittannique"
produced a lively sensation wherever they reached, but
especially in England, where the fate of the cantons had
excited much sympathy, and among the Swiss exiles; for
the avenging book penetrated with difficulty into the
country of which it related the destiny. On all sides
Mallet received acknowledgments of lively, sometimes im-
passioned, approbation. Nothing affected him more than
the letters of some Bernese gentlemen, especially that
which was addressed to him by the very secretary who had
shown himself so ardent in procuring his dismissal in the

previous year——that Charles de Haller who nobly expiated
his error by his energetic efforts to re-establish his
country's independence.*

"Rastadt, January 22, 1799.

". . . Although you have written with a pen of fire,
you have given a very incomplete account of the horrors of
Unterwalden.   I perceive that circumstances, and distance
from the places, have thrown difficulties in the way of procuring sufficient information.   If I was not pressed for time
to-day, I would send you some details which would make
your hair stand on end, and which I noted down hastily on
paper.   No Swiss newspaper has dared, and no German
newspaper has wished, to insert them.

" I have been here for two months in the midst of this
wretched and servile Congress, whose eyes, however, open a
little every day, and in which fear alone restrains and com-
presses the feeling of horror and revenge with which all
souls are penetrated.   We read the numbers of your ' Mercure,' with the admiration which genius and virtue inspire,
and with painful sentiments of the disgrace and humiliation
of the continent, the merited punishment of cowards who
have lost every principle of honour and duty.

". . . Every Bernese will eternally preserve at heart
his admiration of your magnanimity, and his gratitude for
your Essay on the destruction of the Helvetic confederation.
Alas ! we had great need of your pen to preserve the little
honour we have preserved, and to withdraw attention from

* This is the same Charles Louis de Haller, grand-son of the great
Haller, who afterwards acquired celebrity by his conversion to
Catholicism, and by his work on the " Restauration de la politique."

the victims' blame, to scorn and horror of the assassins. No, good will was not wanting to combat this scourge, but immoveable firmness, and, above all, capacity. Twenty times, when reading this work, worthy of Sallust and Tacitus, sobs have hindered me from continuing. Alas! it is not yet known in my unhappy country; I have sent it here, where it is read and purchased with avidity, in spite of the inquisition of a Bonnier or a Jean de Bry, and the servile condescension of an Edelsheim, the Margrave's minister. If Berne requires justification, she is justified now. Already, on the 25th of March, her elected representatives had the honour of being excluded by the brigand Brune. There is no longer a single patriot to be found in that city. Our tribunals, communes, &c., are deposed by the Directory, and they send us proselytes, treacherous spies to tyrannize over us. Tillier himself has just been displaced. Virtuous Mallet, enjoy universal consideration in that fortunate isle. Receive, in particular, the tribute of my respect. Yes, in the pride of my heart, I think I have some resemblance, if not with your talent, at least with the principles of your character, with the sentiments of your soul."

The success of these early numbers of the " Mercure Britannique," was complete and popular; the succeeding copies, devoted to an examination of the relative position of France and the other states of Europe, corresponded to this first effort. The expedition to Egypt, the defeat of the French fleet at Aboukir, and the triumphant daring of Nelson, which followed, filled the whole English nation with enthusiasm, at the very moment when the Irish revolution had just been crushed, and the descent of General

Humbert had failed ; and furnished our journalist with important materials.

Towards the close of the year, the efforts of England to form a new coalition began to shake Mallet's incredulity. He had no doubts of England when he saw her government and the entire nation earnestly at work.   But what success would attend her endeavours to give a movement to the empire and the Emperor, and to withdraw them from Directorial negotiations in which they sacrificed even their honour ?   Or could the Emperor possibly remain indifferent to the last acts of the Directory, which, not content with having put to flight the King of Naples, drove him from his dominions, which were transformed into a revolutionary republic, and by stratagem consummated the ruin of the King of Sardinia, thus overthrowing the two kingdoms which had escaped in Italy ?   At the end of November he wrote again to one of his friends :

" King, ministers, commerce, and the nation—all are characterized by a manly tone : confidence is at its height ; the opposition, disunited, without chiefs or plans, is reduced to a score of discordant units ; but, as prejudices exist with regard to the Emperor, it is still thought that he will await hostilities, and as I doubt the Directory's commencing so soon, the matter stands postponed.   It has perhaps been thought desirable to get the Russians into Bohemia before making a demonstration.   These temporisings will be likely to spread far and near, if dictated by any other motive.

" As yet I catch a glimpse of clouds only, and always the same perspective in the distance, the triumph of the revolutionists in the midst of total disunion.

" . . . . Barthélemy and Willot are about to arrive. Pichegru is re-established; his destination is ready at the first sound of the tocsin. He is the only individual who has inspired me with any confidence for the last ten years When to his talents are joined forgetfulness of self, *sang-froid*, reserve, phlegm, and much good sense —*that* is being very strong in France, and indeed everywhere. Always the same wranglings amongst the royalist agents, who are cutting one another's throats. As long as the King reposes confidence in this sort of intrigue he will retrograde."

But to return to Great Britain: " The budget next week," he says, " will be brilliant, and crowned with success; John Bull's purse is open." This budget, memorable in the annals of the British empire, was in effect presented by Mr. Pitt. The " Mercure Britannique," in giving the *résumé*, expresses itself in these terms :

" Since the existence of deliberative assemblies, I doubt if any has ever comprehended a development of this nature, equally astonishing in its extent, its precision, and the talents of its author. It is not merely a discourse that the minister has pronounced—it is a complete course of public economy, a work; and one of the finest works on real and speculative finance that ever distinguished the pen of a philosopher and a statesman.

" His deductions might be added to the learned disquisitions of the Adam Smiths, Arthur Youngs and Stuarts whom the minister has honoured by his citations from them—famous reply to the modern Vandals, who, because a sect of enraged sophists has meddled, in France, with the government of the universe, would cast into the fire libraries, science and the learned, and bring Europe back to the condition of the Huns and Franks. There is no adulation in this judgment; such adulation would be gratuitous. I have not, thank God, the reputation of being a flatterer; but I have no hesitation in saying that, whether English or foreigner, adversary or friend of Mr. Pitt, all will agree in their opinion of this grand achievement."

In deciding on immense sacrifices in order to bring over Russia to its system of defence against the Directory, the English government had reckoned on the effect of this great measure in inducing Austria, and even Prussia, to resolve on breaking with the Directory and forming a new coalition. But the old spirit of Austrian diplomacy was perhaps still more alarmed than persuaded by the prospect of a Russian auxiliary army setting foot within its states. Mallet, who for five years had seen this sort of consideration carry habitual sway in the councils of the powers, exerted himself in the "Mercure" to dissipate its unhappy influence, and to scatter the chimerical fears which closed the eyes of the parties interested to the sole and actual evil——the obstinate and boundless ambition of the French Republic. "She has put Europe under an interdict," says he, energetically: "she devours her, leaf by leaf, like an artichoke." The Directory, on the first news of the Russian alliance, had lost no time in representing to the Congress of Rastadt, in a threatening note, that this active intervention of Russia was equally dangerous to Turkey and the Germanic Empire; and it soon inundated the public with writings designed to spread alarm about the approach of these auxiliaries. The " Mercure" refuted these alarms vigorously, and laughed from the first at the plodding brains and antiquated reasoners who gave credit to the commonplace arguments of the Directory. " Some baron or other of the Empire," said he, " whom the French will leave without a bed within six weeks, is investigating the question, whether the Russians are not coming to dismember Germany."[*]

" Far from being a source of alarm to the independence of the Germanic body," the writer asserts, " Russia is, from her position, her necessary and natural support. Does any sensible head harbour the idea that she can have ambitious views on the smallest territory in Germany, or can favour the ambition of any other power desirous of aggrandisement there ? Will it ever be her interest to tolerate the deliberation or the usurpations of Austria and Prussia ? She seems, on the contrary, to serve them as a mutual safeguard, and to form between them an intermediate bond, calculated to prevent a shock, or the danger even of their collision."[*]

Reminding the powers a second time of the disastrous history of their distrustful policy, Mallet offers them a safe thread to extricate them from the labyrinth of their procrastinations and uncertainties, the best guides in this emergency, the tactics of the Directory. " Every hour the Directory is reiterating an appeal to Europe to abridge her differences and adjourn her dissensions. With arms outstretched, from the Texel to the extremity of Cala-

* " Mercure Britannique," t. ii.
† Ibid., t. ii, p. 17.

bria, it traces her destiny more vividly than supernatural visions could represent it.   If it is obeyed, he who enjoins the Emperor not to permit the advances of the Russians, may soon bid him descend from the throne."

Whether these reflections had been anticipated at Vienna, or Paul I. had by threats forced the Austrian cabinet to this decision, as Mallet thought; or whether finally the summons of the Directory, commanding the empire to arrest the march of the Russians, had at last aroused their depressed courage, the Emperor determined to break with the Republic.   But the Directory was before-hand with him, and ere Europe was informed by it of the recommencement of the war, the French army had passed the Rhine, and, overrunning the neutral states, had penetrated into the empire.   The Congress of Rastadt was dissolved, and the plenipotentiaries dispersed.   Then occurred the deplorable event to which the name of Jean de Bry is attached, although he was the most unfortu-nate victim.   The three French plenipotentiaries, returning under a safe-conduct from the Austrian generals, were stopped by some Imperialist horsemen, and sabred ; Jean de Bry escaped.   At this news a cry of horror arose in Paris, and the Luxembourg had no difficulty in exciting public indignation.   Since then, no French historian has failed to pause, with patriotic and generous emotion, over this episode in the wars of the revolution.   This mas-sacre of the plenipotentiaries was a crime against the right of nations ; but what authority is there for imputing to the generals of the imperial armies, the fury of a picket of hussars (they belonged to a frontier corps) ; with what object could they have given orders for the commission

of the most useless of all crimes ? And were the men of
the French revolution entitled to the privilege of declaim-
ing so loudly on the right of nations ? Mallet du Pan
was not to be intimidated by these clamours, or by the
funeral solemnity in honour of the victims of Rastadt, at
which Merlin, President of the Directory, pronounced this
anathema against the Emperor : "Woe, everlasting disgrace,
implacable hostility to the atrocious house whose outrages
have dishonoured the age of reason and enlightenment !
May such a government be excluded from all communication with human society !" Mallet related the event, and
found no difficulty in demonstrating that the crime of so
heinous an action could not be charged upon a government which had released Drouet, the postmaster of
Varennes.*

* "Mercure Britannnique." No. 19. "The Directory," he says
further on, "knows for a certainty that the tragedy of Rastadt,
absolutely unconnected with all the Austrian commandants, was the
result of a casual project of highway robbery, which would have been
prevented if Bonnier had not, in an arrogant humour, made up his
mind to brave the obstacles attending millitary orders and a dark and
stormy night." Mallet then passes in review the political character
and the antecedents of the plenipotentiaries themselves, and he
honourably distinguishes Roberjot, the Secretary of Legation, from
his two revolutionary colleagues. "He is accused," he says,
"of having also voted for the assassination of the King ; this is a
mistake ; for at the time when Louis XVI was tried, this envoy was
a member of the Convention, which he did not enter till some time
afterwards : he did not participate, at least openly, in any of the great
revolutionary crimes. During his mission to Hamburg he conducted
himself with discretion and moderation, and carried away the regrets
of more than one unfortunate to whom he had shown kindnesses.

"The chief Secretary of Legation, M. Rosensthiel, deserves much

less than Roberjot himself to be confounded with his superiors.
Since his name has unfortunately been connected with theirs, I owe
him the justice of wiping away the stain which this association
might cast on him.   I knew M. Rosensthiel, an Alsacian, for eight
successive years.   He was the pupil and friend of the celebrated
Pfeffel, and employed in the department of foreign affairs, in which
he had acquired the esteem and confidence of the last ministers of the monarchy.   His probity, his attachment to the
King, and his principles were such, that he was dismissed by
Dumouriez when this general entered on the foreign department.
No one detested the revolution more heartily, and he was well
punished for it : cashiered, afterwards imprisoned, forgotten, ruined,
and the father of a numerous family, he accepted, in 1796, the consulate at Elsineur, as a means of subsistence.   As he is perhaps the
only individual now in France well acquainted with the history
and public law of the Empire, the Directory employed him at
Rastadt, where his urbanity, modesty, and prudence, contrasted
much with the shameless conduct of the supreme agents of the
Republic."

CHAPTER XV.

1799.

Battle of Zurich—Letters from the Count d'Artois (Charles X)—
to Mallet du Pan—Two letters of Portalis communicated to Louis
XVIII—The "Mercure"—Violence of the ultra-royalists in
London against Mallet—Peltier—Reparation—Letters of MM.
Portalis and Quatremère de Quincy.

SIGNAL successes at the commencement, and reverses at
the end, distinguished this first campaign of the Confederation of the north. Its generals, by the rapidity and
harmony of their operations, retaking from the French
almost the whole of Italy, carried the limits of the revolution back to the frontiers of Dauphiny; but Switzerland
and Holland, evacuated at first, beheld the armies of the
Coalition, hitherto triumphant, succumb, after five months'
victories, in consequence of irreparable and but too
palpable faults. They had neglected to take advantage
of the public spirit and the indignation of the Swiss,
and ended by destroying the resources offered in this
important element of war, by devastating the country, and
delivering it up to its intestine dissensions. Mallet's letters,
far more than his " Mercure," in which he was obliged

more or less to restrain himself, put us in possession of all
that he thought of this disastrous mismanagement.

LETTER FROM MALLET DU PAN TO THE CHEVALIER DE GALLATIN.

"London, July 16, 1799.

" My dear Chevalier, we are embarking a great expedition which our emigrants destine for the Chouans, but
which I destine for the mouths of the Scheldt. Probably,
these twenty-five thousand English hope to find an army
in the neighbourhood to second them; otherwise the expedition may easily degenerate into a silly undertaking.
Holland is, I believe, quite ready to throw off the yoke,
and will not require enormous levers to set her in motion.

" Suwarrow is more nimble than the Archduke. He
has, however, played a hazardous game. An intelligent
witness of the battle of Trebia assures me that it was long
undecided, and that to have lost it would have been utter
destruction.   Switzerland offers many more difficulties,
and greater forces to contend with.   Massena has received
reinforcements: it was really too stupid to imagine that he
would voluntarily evacuate Switzerland; and yet he was
supposed to be at the Archduke's quarters.   Switzerland
is the finest intrenchment for Franche-Comté; and so
France will be defended in the cantons.   The position of
the Reuss would be abandoned, if the Austrians marched
in full force on Lucerne; but everything is prepared to
take the position of the Aar and Jura.   Hard blows will
be required to dislodge the enemy thence.

" Meanwhile, Switzerland is full of division, discontent

and uncertainty. All the letters I receive thence make me sigh. I have submitted to the government here all that I have been requested to submit on the subject; but to what avail? They pay no regular attention to these remonstrances; they proceed by jerks, and think that everything can be done by means of money and a few levies.

" You know that the Austrians have not re-established a single government! The indignation is general, both here and at St. Petersburg. What is their object? What can be the meaning of their unintelligible policy? They slight Suwarrow, they cannot agree about anything: they wished to exile the forty-five thousand Russians at their arrival on the Lower Rhine. These, however, stood firm, and will march to Switzerland. Suwarrow intends to lead his army over Mount Cenis, to join the new-comers and fifteen thousand Swiss who will be levied, and to march upon France with his eighty thousand men. The Austrians will do what they please. It is expected that they will profit by the opportunity, to take off a few shavings from the King of Sardinia, regarding whom they carefully avoid saying a single word in their proclamations."

TO THE SAME.

" West Horsely, September 6, 1799.

" My dear friend, I have just received here, at a distance of thirty miles from the great abyss, your packet dated 4th August. The south-west wind, which has prevailed for the last three months delays all the packets. Convey my thanks to your friend Colonel Constant for his instructive letters. What he says is but too true, and accords with all my other tidings from Switzerland : every one pourtrays it under the like colours.   But M. C——— has not told you that the conduct of the Swiss springs naturally from that originally pursued towards them.   One false measure was heaped upon another ; the emigrants, and those in France, both strove to rule from afar a distrustful and touchy people who would not be ruled by them ; I know not what faults were not committed.   They suddenly stopped short after the taking of Zurich, as if to keep the inhabitants in suspense as to their fate : they acted on no fixed plan of restoration ; they knew neither the arts of command nor of persuasion ; they disgusted men of credit whose influence would have done much with the people ; they gave way to ridiculous predilections ; they neither sought to excite, nor to sustain a national movement.

   " The work is too palpably beyond the strength of those who strive to accomplish it.   Besides, eighteen months of revolution have sensibly deteriorated the national character, already sunk greatly below its reputation.   The event has proved that Switzerland now possesses no men of distinguished talent ; their skill to reconstruct will not exceed their power to preserve.

   " It had been lightly determined to despatch Monsieur into Switzerland—he was sent for from Edinburgh.   Enthusiasm was at its height ; this plan was after all given up, and the Prince has immured himself four miles from my dwelling-place, and intends to await the ripening of events.

   " You are quite right in saying that England ought to assume a high tone in Switzerland.   She would rejoice to do so ; but she possesses only one, and that a secondary vote in such matters. Russia will support her; but I repeat that the reorganization of Switzerland, its well-being as such, is hardly thought of. One end alone is aimed at; the raising of a few regiments to be sent into France, and the expulsion of the French from Switzerland, not for the advantage of the Swiss, but for the sake of facilitating access to the mouth of the lion's den.

" After making proper representations, and adducing facts to give them weight, I sank back into my obscurity, and shall come forth from it no more. A foreigner is too unfavourably situated to play the censor: he excites displeasure, he gives occasion to slander, he provokes the enmity of the irascible and haughty. We must let the world go its own way. When I am asked for advice I shall frankly give it; but shall take good care not to meet applications half-way.

" I am living here in a charming place, where I lay aside the thought of politics, and where for a fortnight past I have hardly looked at a newspaper. I enjoy a true *otium cum dignitate*, and dread the day of my return to my detestable scribbling; no man was ever more weary, more sick of it than I am.

" Adieu. Accept my warmest salutations; let me hear what goes on, and particularly what takes place between St. Petersburg and Berlin. M. Fagel has not yet appeared, and will, I expect, remain on the continent."

TO THE SAME.

" London, October 28, 1799.

" Two months ago the future history of Switzerland was written in legible and unalterable characters. It was worth while, indeed, to complete the calamities of this country by making it the theatre of war, and then after all to march out in this way. The official reports will have given you a very inexact notion of the occurrences from the 25th of September to the 8th of October. I can assure you, on most certain and most respectable authority, that Massena did not lose eight hundred men on the 25th and 26th. There never was a stranger battle. The Russians did not execute a single manœuvre ; all their dispositions attested their ignorance and the haughty incapacity of their general. Refusing to follow, or even hear any advice, he allowed his rear to be surrounded : never could he be induced even to post a corps of observation on the Zurichberg, where the French entrenched themselves without firing a gun. By a sort of verbal capitulation, Korzakoff had been left at liberty to retreat by the way of Winterthur ; but as he had never made a reconnaissance at a league's distance from Zurich, and had arrived there by way of Eglisau, he disdained the former road, which was safe, set off on the latter, and fell in with the French columns and batteries posted at the back of the Hange Berg. His lines broke, seized with a panic. Here they suffered their heaviest loss of prisoners, artillery, baggage, &c. In my number of the 27th you will read an entirely new account of this action, drawn up from authentic information. The ignorance of the Russian officers was everywhere the same. They pillaged Zurich before abandoning it. The peasants killed as many as they met, in revenge for their habitual depredations.

" Suwarrow would have been irrecoverably lost, if Colonel

Clinton, Tinseau and Varicourt, who were conducting him
into the recesses of the lesser cantons, had not induced him
to abandon his mad resolution of proceeding further.   The
following saying is attributed to a great captain, who
inhabits the same town as yourself: " Suwarrow is just the
man to obtain great advantages at the opening of a campaign, and to let himself be taken or killed before its
close."   This horoscope has nearly proved a true one.

" Many cry treason against the Austrians, and lay the
blame of the reverses on the Archduke's retreat.   Without
undertaking to justify it, it is but fair to remark that that
member of a league whose forces and proximity render him
the most important, and who incurs the greatest danger in
case of ill success, ought to have the preponderating vote.
The Court of Vienna had required that the Russians should
be placed at its disposal.   They refused, for the sake of
executing, without its aid, a chivalrous design, which was
to conduct these same Russians to Paris.   Then the ill-
feeling broke out, and each followed his own private plan.
In my opinion, it would have been better to conform to
the views of Austria than to run the risk of its displeasure.
We have no spirit of conciliation."

In London, the defeat of Suwarrow before Zurich, and
that of the Anglo-Russians in Holland, caused consternation
to take the place of the joyful excitement of early hopes ;
for the success of the coalition in Italy had intoxicated all
minds, especially in the emigrant world.   " If," writes
Mallet du Pan, " any one had denied that in Holland,
Switzerland and France, the great body of inhabitants
would come forward to meet their deliverers, he would
have been proclaimed a Jacobin.   Our emigrants set me

down as such for doubting whether they would be at Paris in October."

This last clause alludes to a storm, which the impracticable editor of the "Mercure Britannique" drew down upon his head, and of which we must here say something.

Since his arrival in England, Mallet, as we have already said, had made it his study to keep out of the jealousies with which the emigrants harrassed each other, to the great damage of their position. He had dispersed their illusions, as to the influence they attributed over the English government to his personal advice. Monsieur, however, had not given in, and had developed, in a letter addressed to Mallet, the length of which compels us to reserve it for the conclusion of these memoirs, his views on the situation of France, the King, and what circumstances demanded of the English government, which, if it desired to overturn the Directory, should begin by recognizing the rights of Louis XVIII, and giving him public marks of respect and interest. He returned to the eternal idea, so long opposed by the man he affected to consult. " It is only," he declared, " by resuming his rights by force of arms, that the King will be able to preserve the authority needed to govern a great nation, and at the same time ensure to it the inestimable blessing of a good and wise constitution, calculated to produce the happiness of a long series of generations. A sovereign restored to his throne by means of a compromise of whatever kind, receiving the law instead of laying it down, would never have, and never gain, power enough to impose it on ill-subdued factions. It is necessary," he continued, " that the British government, nobly calculating its broadest interests, should restore to

the King of France an army which the enemies of mankind have wrested from him to plague the world. To
this great end must tend all the general and special views
of those who possess elementary means sufficient for
carrying them out. To demonstrate its importance and
prove its necessity, is the fitting task for men on whom, as
on you, Sir, nature has bestowed that nervous eloquence
which confers an incalculable power on just ideas. Speak—
thunder—do not fear : you cannot say too much on the
subject to a cabinet capable of appreciating your opinions.
It feels the danger by which it is threatened, and has its
eyes open to the truth ; but it needs rousing to come forth
from its habitual circle and rise to the height of the cir-
stances in which it is placed."

The most remarkable fact about this letter is, that it was
in answer to a note in which Mallet counselled a passive
expectation. "They are on fire to act, and I recommended
inaction ; I shall not have met with success," thought he.
However, Mallet confined himself to his previous advice ;
and, as events had again taken a turn favourable to the
fortunes of the Princes, he was left to himself. But the
ultra-royalists, the intriguers who carefully fostered their
exaggerated hopes, watched with a jealous and scrutinizing
eye every opinion, every expression, in Mallet's writings,
which might be interpreted as opposed to the old *régime*,
or to constitutional modifications. Some of these " white-
cockaded Marats," as he had once called them, made a
comfortable livelihood out of the plots and intrigues whose
management was confided to them. As sounder political
views would soon have put an end to this profitable trade,

they cried louder than any others, and persuaded the zealous royalists that nothing could possibly induce the Bourbons to bend the knee before Baal : they detested all who were courageous enough to question their exclusive right to political influence.   For his own comfort, Mallet would have done better never to notice their repeated attacks ; but he lost patience, and addressed to these monomaniacs lessons for which they never forgave him.   The occasion was as follows :

In the summer of 1799, at the height of the hopes excited by the defeat of the French army in Italy, the question of a constitution was debated more hotly than ever among the emigrants, who fancied themselves on the eve of returning to France with the King.   Had the King anything to do beyond restoring the old *régime* precisely as it had been ?   On the other hand, a Parisian gazette had spoken of a constitutional King, whom people were disposed to find in the Duke of Orleans, ready to accept conditions.   About the same time, Mallet had received from his friend Portalis two letters, full of the strongest and justest reflections on the real chances of a monarchical government in France, and on the spirit and conduct to be displayed by the King.   One of these two letters, more especially, is an admirable theory of the system, altogether new to France, which Louis XVIII., at length enlightened by such repeated advice and the reflections of exile, adopted in part, and sincerely applied himself, after 1815, to establish for the good of the kingdom.   Mallet du Pan, foreseeing that the sagacious author could not allow him to give to these letters a publicity, which indeed he himself considered unreasonable,* hastened to communicate extracts to the King, without naming the author. We conceive there can be no indiscretion in quoting here a letter so honourable to the mind and character of Portalis :

LETTER FROM PORTALIS TO MALLET DU PAN.

"Emckendorff, August 11, 1799.

" . . . . My dear Mallet, you are quite right in complaining of follies and exaggerations. The military plan of the Cabinet will be of no use either to France or to Europe, unless it be directed by a political plan. It will be easy to enter France after beating all the French armies ; but to enter France without aim or plan, or merely to take a stroll there after the Prussian fashion, would be an error worse than the first.

" It seems, from what you tell me, that the Russians would propose to penetrate into the French territory, even without the Austrians, should the latter decline to follow them ; that the King and his adherents would be presented to the people, and the national temper be thus sounded by way of experiment. It is forgotten then, that success never crowns steps which betray more hesitation than confidence, and that minds should not be left to roam when they can be recalled only by fixing them on a definite point. In merely showing the King and his adherents, too much is done, or too little. There is a medium between the policy of the conqueror, and the hesitation of the victor, who has the appearance of coming to receive the law, when he can impose it.

* He requested permission to publish them, but Portalis declined.

" A republic has never been seen or known in France There are no republicans. The whole nation is tired of the revolutionary system. The lassitude which succeeds to all such revolutions, has brought back all minds and all hearts to monarchy. I do not speak of the Jacobins, who are but a handful of men whom the mere show of justice will dispel.

" There is no occasion for proceeding by imperative proclamations in order to make the French nation royalist. Were such proclamations necessary, they would be useless. It does not seem to me that the choice of a King can be a subject for deliberation, unless it is to be made a motive for civil war. Some courtiers may hesitate between such and such a person. But the nation sees the King without ever seeing the man. I think I may say that the mass is weary of choosing and deliberating.

" But, if minds should not be left in uncertainty, neither should they be thrown into fear. The King should present himself, not as the head of a party, but as the head of the nation. He should respect whatever is the result simply of events and circumstances. It is the fate of every empire to experience gradually or violently inevitable modifications. Any blind or intemperate return to worn-out institutions, which have not been able to maintain themselves, would compromise the security of the new monarchy. A rising nation has need of a guardian—an old and oppressed nation of a liberator.

" The equity of ancient Rome confirmed the decisions of a slave. The policy of the new King ought to destroy that only which was produced by error or violence. Even those things which must be re-established should not be so by express laws ; that would be imprudent. Thus, it is necessary to revert to the memory, the recollections of men, and to their habits, which are even less effaced than is imagined. Nobility, restored by a law, would lose all its dignity and ancient glory. It is wiser to assume that it never was and never could be destroyed, because it belongs to the feelings, to respect for hereditary virtues and ancient services, and to whatever, in the language of Cicero, authorized, even in republics, what the orator calls *jus imaginis*.

" But a liberator must bestow reasonable laws, not laws of passion or resentment. National institutions to replace those which exist no longer are indispensable. It is not enough for a king to have a court, for it is courts which ruin kings. A guarantee is required for the security of the throne and the liberty of the people. This guarantee must not be a constitution, a volume long. The permanence of the judges, so necessary to individual liberty, and the concurrence of a deliberative assembly in the enactment of taxes and laws—this is all the constitution necessary in the legislature. The organization of this assembly is the most difficult and delicate point. But models are at hand, which require only to be modified according to local circumstances. One thing is certain :—that a plan must be settled beforehand : it would be adopted in the first moment, which will be one of lassitude, and would not be adopted in the second. At the first moment, the ambitious are silent, the mass alone is active and of consequence : at the second, the mass disappears, and the ambitious or the theorizers resume their sway.

" To sum up. If an entrance be made, let it be with the confidence of strength, with the dignity of reason. No

capitulation must be made, as if with a vanquished people.
The language of protection, rather than of command, should
be adopted ; but this language should be neither timid nor
dubious.   Nothing is to be feared from the nation, at the
moment when you come to defend it against its oppressors;
but time must not be lost.   You must instruct and reassure, and effect the great result of destroying all parties
for the general good of the nation, instead of appearing to
subject the nation to a party.

" But, my dear Mallet, I perceive that I prose too much
on politics.   I speak to you with confidence, and under the
seal of friendship.   I risk my observations, and submit
them to your judgment.   Generally speaking, it is a great
mistake to print much on these subjects ; if a thing is to
succeed, it must be secret.   A revolution should not be
published like a pamphlet.   The emigrants talk and write
much more than they ought."

FROM THE SAME.

" September 23, 1799.

" I know, my dear Mallet, that I may speak to you
with confidence and under the seal of friendship, without
fear of any indiscretion.   Since you desire it, I continue
my last conversation with you.

" If the revolution were to be accomplished, I am convinced no one would be willing to have it.   They have been
too well taught, that it is almost more dangerous to change
than it is unpleasant to endure.   But we must start from
facts as they are.   Given such and such circumstances, what
is the best plan to adopt ?   That is the problem of politics.

" The old government rather crumbled to pieces than was destroyed. If its forms appeared still sound, its spirit had departed. There remained nothing but a huge body, soulless. The proof of this is visible in all that has occurred. When the institutions of a state are still living, civil wars arise without revolutions. But here we have had the sad sight of a revolution without civil war. That gives us the measure of the corruption which infected all classes. That happened which was inevitable ; those who had something to preserve, became cowards after having been fools. Those who had nothing to lose, and all to gain, possessed the energy and power of endurance of which the habit of the enjoyments and comforts of life deprived the upper classes of society.

" All was dissolved ; and, what is worse, the dissolution was like that which succeeds to death, not that which a violent crisis may produce, and which takes place sometimes in a body full of life.

" In this state of things it is not enough to re-establish ; it is necessary to regenerate, to deal with men even more than with things, and create, so to speak, a new nation.

" I can understand that it is easy to say : ' Let us resume our places ;' but what is easy to say, is exactly what it is least wise and most difficult to do. I speak of the independence of the King, who alone can guarantee the rational liberty of the nation. I do not wish the King to compound with the factious or ambitious ; he would find as many systems as heads ; but I wish him to become the supreme arbiter of events, interests, and rights. He owes much to the fidelity and sufferings of those who have not disjoined their fate from his. But he cannot repay them better, than by giving them that only which they can preserve in safety.

"It would be a mistake to suppose that it is inconsistent with the dignity of the King not to re-establish all the old institutions. The pride of kings may revolt at being dependent on certain men. But their wisdom calls upon them not to ignore the dependence of things, a dependence from which no human power can escape. The art of governing is not a metaphysical and absolute theory. It is subordinated to the changes which occur in a nation, and to the situation in which they may be placed. There is a saying of St. Augustin, which seems merely religious, but which appears to me of deep meaning in politics : 'He,' says that father, 'who created you without your concurrence, cannot save you without it.' '*Qui creavit te sine te, non potest salvare te sine te.*' I prescribe to royal omnipotence no other limits than such as divine omnipotence prescribed to itself.

"All the malcontents in France are not royalists ; and the majority of the royalists may be made malcontents, if there is a show of distributing them into classes more or less favourable. I speak to you on all these matters with the more frankness, in that I owe it to circumstances to be utterly disinterested. I will not say my wisdom—but chance, at least, has so ordered it that I belong to no party, and have, in consequence, been always in a better position for seeing and judging correctly. I did not emigrate, and never approved the emigration, having always considered it absurd to leave France in the hope of saving her, and to place oneself under foreigners to avert or terminate a national broil. On the other hand, I did not choose to interfere in the changes and reforms projected by the first revolutionists ; perceiving that they wanted to make a new heaven and a new earth, and aspired to form a nation of philosophers, when they should have aimed at forming a nation happy and contented. I have lived in solitude and dungeons ; I said then, and still say : ' *Obliviscor eos, obliviscendus et illis.*' But I have not become unjust. The subjects who showed themselves more loyal, should not scorn those who did not follow the same path. I do not speak of those among them who, living by the abuses, had no interest in reforming them, but of those who remained faithful for duty's sake, and on principle. To them I say : Could you be useful ? Be indulgent : the mass of men, before experience, never is what it can become only through it. All men have passions ; they have no right to complain of those of others ; but if they have any influence, they must endeavour to guide them well. What man in this revolution must not reproach himself in some respect ? When, in 1789, the movement began in France, the mistake was committed of showing the same indulgence to a handful of spouters and rioters, as would have been displayed to the most formidable faction. But now it would be wrong to treat the revolutionary factions which have arisen, as lightly as a handful of rioters might be treated. If threats are held out, if humiliating distinctions are declared, incalculable evil is produced. It is not courage I dread in the factious, but fear ; for that may endow them with the courage of desperation. One would rather be oppressed than degraded.

" I may add, that the mass of the people will not move ; and that there will be no useful auxiliaries but the men

who have rushed into the armies and into the parties,
which the revolution has disaffected and crushed.   I unhesitatingly believe that men's minds are well disposed for
the re-establishment of monarchy, provided the King
adopts the precaution of announcing that he comes not to
enslave but to abolish all tyranny, and provided he surround himself with men having no interest in vengeance,
and who, forgetting their particular grievances, will devote
themselves solely to the public good.   No time must be
given for cavillings or ambitious speculations.   Let there
be no ambiguity of speech; and let the plan proposed be
national and impartial, suited to existing circumstances—
a plan which will testify to all France, that the King has
framed it without personal bias and with entire independence."

Marshal de Castries, on receiving these extracts, replied
to Mallet: "Seldom have I seen letters better written or
better conceived, Sir, than those from which you send me
extracts.   I should suppose them your's, did you not inform me to the contrary.   I consider it my duty to transmit them to his Majesty, since you allow me to use my discretion in the matter."

These letters did, in fact, strike Louis XVIII.: and, by
his desire, or at least with his sanction, Malouet addressed
to the "Mercure" a letter, in which, after recommending a
legal government, a limited monarchy, as the best means
of decomposing the revolutionary power, he pledged himself that such were Louis XVIII.'s views, an assurance
which, for the moment, removed any necessity for requiring explicit engagements.   "You know as well as I do,

Sir, and as certainly," said Malouet, " that, independent of the wise and gentle character of Louis XVIII.; his experience, his extensive acquirements acknowledged by all, his distaste for arbitrary authority, enable him to perceive the danger and inadequacy of this in the present state of men's minds."*

It was at the express desire of Louis XVIII., that Mallet inserted this letter, regarded as so important by the King and the Marshal de Castries. But the storm burst on poor Malouet; he was furiously attacked, and branded as a traitor and an apostate. In particular, Peltier, a clever and unprincipled writer, signalized himself by the violence of his invectives in the " Ambigu," a periodical he conducted in London. Then Mallet du Pan, who wished to answer his friend's letter, in order to demonstrate the unsuitableness of this species of public declaration, which ought, he considered, to be reserved to the King of France himself, opened his article in the following striking manner :

" No sooner does a man undertake to proclaim the King's indulgence, clemency, and justice, his aversion from arbitrary power, his discrimination between the errors to be repressed and the truths to be respected in the opinions of the age, than a cry is raised to contradict this eulogium, stigmatize the object of it, and notify to France that the King's virtues are chimerical.

" All parties, even the most respectable, have their nervous victims ; let their most imperceptible fibre be touched, and straightway they will cry out murder. Legal government is proposed to them ! They choose neither legality nor

* " Mercure Britannique," v. iii. p. 485, No. 23.

government. Their science of social administration consists in hanging, putting to the sword, subduing men's wills with reference to no other rule but that of their own caprices, in tolerating no laws but such as reduce the people beneath their dominion, but leave themselves wholly free, and in despising every restoration which would terminate the misfortunes of France and the perils of Europe, unless it also secured to a privileged few the exclusive right of disposing at their own pleasure of the monarch and the monarchy.

" These disguised *bonnets rouges* have, like the Jacobins, their formularies, their system of terror, and even their *Père Duchesne*. Yet, however impressive may be the *crescendo* of their clamours when they behold common sense approach the Capitol, it is proper to undeceive the French of the interior and strangers, who might judge of the intentions of the King of France, of the true royalists, and of the immense majority of the emigrants, by the outpourings of certain isolated individuals to whom the revolution is and ever will be a revolt of the *faubourgs*.

" Whatever may be the resolutions of Louis XVIII., every loyal Frenchman must bow to them : till they be made known, it is doing the Prince but little honour and but poor service, to deny him such qualities and principles as are calculated to win the hearts of his subjects. King of twenty millions of Frenchmen, fully as much so as of those among them who shared his exile and the glory of his adversity, he will doubtless sacrifice none but guilty and encroaching interests, and will respect every legitimate right."

This lesson, and above all the appellation of *Père*

Duchesne, stirred up a storm among the pure royalists, and thenceforward Peltier was Mallet's fierce and irreconcileable enemy, and levelled at him and Malouet a pamphlet which had all the characteristics of a manifesto. Mallet relates the incident to M. de Sainte-Aldegonde:

" You will have read in my first two numbers a letter by Malouet, which the King approved, and which M. de Castries urged me to publish. This letter raised a storm among the emigrants: you have probably seen my remarks on the subject. Though the generality of the French approved of it, the Jacobins of the party were resolved to have the last word: no sort of atrocity has been spared us: the King himself, and the Marshal, whom they called a patriot, met with no more consideration. Finally, they caused to be prepared by Peltier a coarse and insipid libel, which was read in full committee, at M. de Barentin's and afterwards at the royal agent Dutheil's house, to brothers and friends. Two other writings of like calibre and tone succeeded. The English papers of every shade expressed the general indignation; this rose to such a height that the Bishop of Arras made Monsieur promise to testify his displeasure and impose silence on these maniacs. In the midst of this turmoil, which failed to disturb me, a message reached me from Monsieur, with an invitation to visit him at a given day and hour. Malouet had received the same intimation. This interview took place in the presence of the Bishop of Arras, Count d'Escars, and the agent Dutheil, who underwent the mortification of witnessing my reception. You may believe nothing was wanting. Monsieur very gratefully put me in mind of our connexion, conversed with me alone for twenty minutes in the cabinet, and vied with his chancellor in applauding me, and blaming the intemperance of the clique headed by Count de Vaudreuil. I answered them that, for my part, I was become by use callous and indifferent on the head of attentions of this sort ; but that I begged them to consider what effect such hare-brained publications would produce in France, and what opinion of their safety under the King would be formed by those who have some faults to reproach themselves with, when they find that not even Malouet and myself find favour. All these truths and many others were well received : everything was admitted ; and at the end I found myself a consummate aristocrat. I know not how far sincerity pervaded this interview ; I neither seek to ascertain, nor care ; but certainly this proceeding does honour to the Prince's judgment, and it has produced a good effect : he spoke to me reasonably and amiably.

" Such, my dear Count, is a faithful relation of this grand adventure, which occupied for a fortnight the gossip of our French societies. The libellers have been snubbed but will resume their functions on the earliest occasion— that is, at the first crown-piece offered them. You should have been the first confidant of this story ; but for the last fortnight, strolls, a love of the *far niente* and rural distractions have prevented my resuming my pen."

Though justly satisfied with the Prince's courtesy, Mallet laid no great stress on it. It had cost him an effort to quit the country, where he was taking a few day's rest, in order to wait upon Monsieur. At the first news of this call, conveyed to him by his son, he had answered : " Here I am beyond the turmoil of political passions ; at peace with all around me. I am free from my cough and irritation, and I cannot forego these advantages, having but a few days wherein to enjoy them. You must then make my excuses to Monsieur until my return."

In his answer to Mallet's letter, M. de Sainte-Aldegonde, speaking of his friend's interview with Monsieur, offers a remark worthy of attention: "The striking honour done you by Monsieur is just on his part, and deserved on yours; but I am too sincerely your friend not to tell you frankly that this homage, to which your good sense will not attach undue importance, is a forced homage got up for the occasion, counselled by the opinion of sensible and right-minded men, advised by the Bishop of Arras, and of which you will undoubtedly not be the dupe. They will coax you still more this winter, when they are certified that the allies cannot penetrate into France this year; then you will be consulted, and in high favour. But at the first trifling success that attends them, they will not deign to look at you. The princes will ever be the same; they will never employ men but as individuals of a class; and Monsieur, with all his grace and affability, will prove as unchangeable as the rest."

In relation to the termination of this incident of the letter of Malouet, the editor of the "Mercure" says in his number for August: "After all, what are all these things to me, except as matters of opinion, and in connexion with my desire to see justice and humanity triumph; the only advantage I anticipate from the return of the King is to see monarchy succeed to the republic: I shall be neither the better nor the worse for the change." "In fact," says M. L. Mallet, "my father's mind had become familiarized to the prospect of never returning to France, and had he survived till 1814, he would have gone to end his life at Geneva."

Before leaving this chapter, let us return to other exiles, whose letters afforded compensation to Mallet du Pan for the folly of the bustling royalists of London.   MM. Portalis and Quatremère de Quincy, who remained in Germany, often wrote to their Fribourg friend.   In their retreat these men of judgment kept a watchful eye on Germany.   Then, as well as at present, that country contained its political metaphysicians, systematic and fanatical admirers of the revolutionary idea, and the best fellows imaginable, amongst its illustrious men, who still retained, in respect to the French Revolution, illusory fancies, which reality was slow in dissipating.   Our exiles, escaping from that Liberty with which they had been in such close contact, and which they had seen exercising the most despotic tyranny, were astonished to find in the midst of retired societies of men, still strangers to the misfortunes of France, a sympathy in the abstract, on the principle and application of which they themselves set as much value as it was worth.   On this and other accounts, the following letters are interesting.

LETTER FROM M. DE PORTALIS TO MALLET DU PAN.

" Emckendorff, April 9, 1798.

" My dear Mallet, here we are arrived, not without difficulty, at the place of our destination.   You have heard that we were overturned twice in one day.   A few days after, we were overturned twice in an hour : near Cassel we were overturned for the fifth time, and then we got rid of our coach, which as yet had not succeeded in getting rid of us. The rest of our journey was very comfortable.* We met with a reception answerable to the earnestness of our invitation. We live in a companionship grave, but agreeable. We are among persons of information and integrity.

" The affairs of Switzerland have made the greatest sensation here; but all reduces itself to regret. They can deplore, but not succour. Everywhere one meets this corrosive philosophy, which eats into the very bone; all must absolutely change, for nothing can endure longer. Some one observed to me the other day very smartly, that the 18th Fructidor of France might very probably be the 10th of August of Europe. The country I am in at present is peaceable; but should it cease to be so, I should certainly join you. I shall never forget the sentiments with which you have inspired me; you are one of those rare persons whom one cannot know without entertaining a better idea of men."

FROM THE SAME.

"Emckendorff, June 24, 1798.

" You have arrived then at the true country of liberty. You are right in saying that elsewhere one sees only irre-

---

* Portalis, Junior, describing these accidents to his friend M. Louis Mallet, said: " We have had everything broken and have experienced that accident which the Abbé Delille numbers among the greatest calamities; we broke down when equidistant from the two relays. At the moment we deeply regretted his little pasteboard Paris cabriolet, whose lightness he so energetically lauded to us, and which might be called a pocket cabriolet."

E E 2

solution in those who govern, and a tendency to anarchy in those who are governed. The north, however, is not approaching a revolution. Philosophic ideas are confined to the universities; they do not make way among the people. I notice here a singular phenomenon: several ministers of religion preach infidelity from the pulpit; the faithful then desert the parish, or oblige the minister to return home and fetch the books he had been in the habit of reading to them on high days. The government dares do nothing; but it is sufficiently protected by the sluggishness of mind in the people, and by the ancient customs of society.

" You will have heard of the new revolution in Holland; it is that of the 18th Fructidor turned inside out. When will the end come of all these movements which agitate Europe? I see nothing but shoreless ocean; passion has assumed the empire which prejudice had lost. But prejudice moves in a confined circle, within which its effects can be traced, whereas passion subtilized by reasonings knows no limit or circumference.

" England must be a noble sight. That nation proves that there may be enlightenment without its abuse, and that the public spirit which unites is better than the philosophic spirit which isolates.

" No one will be better able than yourself to portray the causes which led to the Helvetic revolution, the violence which attended its consummation, and the facts which followed it. There, indeed, the government broke up in despite of the people, and the force of the people could not hold out against the corruption of the government. In less than two months, I have seen the institutions of Switzerland in full vigour, and witnessed their sudden disappearance.

"Nothing new in France. They dance, suffer, live from hand to mouth, and reading the papers is their only essential occupation. As for me, my dear Mallet, I live quietly in my retreat with the worthy hosts who afford me hospitality. The country is agreeable. Beside the house we live in, we have a fine lake and forest; art procures all the fruits which nature denies: the character of the people is gentle; there is a good deal of information in the upper classes of society, and more religious principle than might be supposed is still to be found among them. Every lord, with wise moderation, gives his vassals their liberty: he makes them land-owners, does them good without quietly, and seeks to impart to them the love, not of change, but of labour and industry. It is interesting to see human nature actually reviving and issuing from the chaos of feudal serfdom.

"I am very glad that Madame Mallet's health is re-established. I beg you to give her my respects, and don't forget to remember me to your amiable son. Pray send me a copy of your "Révolution Helvétique," as soon as that interesting work appears. My hosts, who are fully aware of your merit, await it impatiently. My young companion shares all my affection for you, &c."

TO THE SAME.

"May 22, 1799.

"My dear friend,

"It would be unreasonable to complain of your silence, knowing, as I do, how fully your time is occupied. The successes of the Austrians seem to restore the Germans to some degree of energy. Your "Mercure" exerts considerable influence over the public mind, and a few such men as yourself would uproot the fallacies which desolate the world. The German professors encounter some checks; one of them who openly inculcates atheism, has just received his dismissal; this is the celebrated Fichte, professor in the University of Jena. This sophist maintained, that if Kant's was the philosophy of modern times, his own was the most modern of all philosophies. You see that the generations of these pretended philosophers succeed each other rapidly. Fichte's affair employs all the writers of Germany. It is amusing to see distinguished authors fighting about abstractions or lologriphs; but very strange to see the public take part in disputes they do not understand. The talk used to be of blind faith—I fear now-a-days we may talk of blind philosophy.

"Fichte said to Kant: 'You may have sparkled for a moment, but you understand nothing: it is I who have solved the riddle. I fancy I can hear these two madmen, of whom one said to the other: 'You set yourself up as God the Son; but if it were so, should not I, who am God the Father, know something about it?' But I detain you too long over this philosophical drivelling. I would not have mentioned it to you, but that at this moment it occupies all the governments and all the writers of Germany.

"The Austrians have ceased their operations on the Rhine; they seem intent on nothing but Italy: nevertheless the evil does not lie there. It is asserted that Prussia demands the independence of Holland: were this the case, I should discern in such conduct symptoms of a political system. I wish the Austrians would turn their minds to Switzerland, without which they cannot even possess Italy securely.

"The newspapers announce that Rewbell has quitted the Directory. I should be amazed if the pentarchs had not made a serious choice this time.

"The horrible assassination of the French ministers at Rastadt remains a mystery, judging from the different circumstances alleged. I am not easily convinced of a crime, above all, of a gratuitous crime, that could only serve to injure the Government, for which it was committed; but I wish the truth may be elicited.

"I have not seen Quatremère; he is fifteen leagues off, and the severe season which continues after the endless winter, offers no temptation to travellers. Judging from what I hear, Quatremère may very well settle in this country. The Government is mild, and appears to consist rather of things than of men. This happiness is attributed to the disposition of the Prince Royal, and to his good choice of ministers.

"On the occasion of the affair at Rastadt, it was resolved to put the army into mourning. News reaches us that this measure gave rise to discontent, and that all the soldiers said openly: 'We are left to perish by thousands, and not a word said about it; and all this fuss is made about two pitiful lawyers.' Adieu, &c."

LETTER FROM QUATRÈMERE DE QUINCY TO MALLET
DU PAN.

Eutin in Holstein, August 18, 1799.

" You wish, Sir, that I should continue writing to
you, though my present position and distance from the
scene of action must render my correspondence very
meagre.   I shall avail myself of your permission ; this
intercourse is too advantageous to me to be neglected.
Unfortunately, the only return I can make is but a
poor one.   I am delighted that you find something
honourable in my present wearisome retirement.   Expelled
from France with the utmost rudeness, I had arranged
nothing with the very few friends I then possessed, as
to the choice of such acquaintances as might offer abroad,
or the means of being, during my stay there, of service
to the good cause, and of use either to myself or to
others.   You know I was bound straight for England,
when the winter frosts blocked the way against me for
the next three or four months.   Dumas, whom I have
mentioned to you, offered his services to me in this
country, and procured me two acquaintances in this little
town, the only persons whom I frequent, or could keep
me here.

" The intimacy with one especially, Count F. de Stolberg, is after my own heart, and accords entirely with
my taste.   The truth is, I have contracted during this
execrable revolutionary contest—that unfortunate party
spirit which measures its hatreds and friendships by
greater or less conformity of political views.   Now, Count

Frederick de Stolberg, possessed of literary reputation, a celebrated poet, a man of genius, virtuous and religious, is also the most anti-revolutionary Frenchman I ever met, and you know that the species is not very common, above all, in Lower Saxony and Denmark.

"A thousand times I have been tempted to write against the stupid infatuation felt in this part of Germany for a revolution which they no more understand now than on the first day; for I do not speak of those who do understand it, or of those who are still its champions. But what has always restrained me is my precarious condition here, and my distance from the resources of a great town, resources essential to the utility of such a project. It excites my indignation to see that, out of ten journals, there are at least eight in these parts which write at the dictation of the French Directory. You have already, Sir, in some of your numbers, attacked these apes of revolution. Pray do not forget them, when occasion serves. Germany——at least such parts of it as I know, or can make out from the very small loophole I command——is cankered far deeper than might be supposed ; and scholastic philosophy is more certainly noxious than even the worldly and frivolous philosophy of France.*

* See in No. 17 of the " Mercure britannique," the opinions and translation of a work by M. de Gentz, then Councillor of War at Berlin, who, having translated the works of Burke and Mallet du Pan on the French Revolution, was engaged in publishing in the " Journal historique," some historical and political essays, "in which," says Mallet, " great depth of thought and a forcible style are to be admired. The following reflection of the German author, and that subjoined by the editor of the " Mercure," deserve notice.

" The enthusiastic admirers of the revolution endeavour, on the

" But, Sir, in treating of these subjects, I recommend you, even for the sake of your remedy proving effectual, never to omit making exceptions in favour of the sound German philosophy. I have noticed that the genus of philosophers is even more irritable than the *genus irritabile vatum.*

" Among true philosophers, you may rank Jacobi, whose opinions and character I value and love more and more highly. I do not deny that he was slightly infected with the mania of the constitutionalists of 1791. I fancy, it was under cover of such a profession that Dumas made his acquaintance and won his friendship ; I even suspect this was my title to share in the acquaintance. My very decided disapprobation of this foolish hypocrisy, seemed at first to jar with the habits of the house ; but nothing in the world would now induce me to resume the mask ; so I maintained my somewhat provoking demeanour. Dumas who, when he visits this town, lodges with Jacobi, has more than once given me an opportunity of ridiculing or depreciating this sect, which only lacks members ; and I have always seen that these discussions invariably redounded to my

contrary, to keep in the background those blemishes which have defaced it from the cradle, and represent it as the immaculate production of human reason in its state of gradual development. This last solution possesses the advantage of being vague, and offering an imposing idea.

" Such Germans as admire the revolution willingly adopt this mode of explaining it, but refuse at the same time to admit that the progress of knowledge may produce revolutions. The contradiction is palpable. If the progress of knowledge sufficed in France to overturn everything, one does not see why it should not boast the like virtue in other countries."

advantage, and that Jacobi was more friendly with me than ever afterwards. In the main, his opinions are excellent ; and to become more decided, he only requires to be a little less good. But what a good fault is this !

" You give me news, Sir, of Barthélemy and Villot. Should you have an opportunity of seeing them, put them in mind of a colleague who sympathized deeply in their sufferings, and sincerely rejoices at seeing them in safety. You are better acquainted than myself with Barthélemy ; his short appearance on the public stage of revolution precluded my visiting him often. Dumas flatters himself that in him he has an additional constitutionalist. He lays wait for him at Hamburgh, and tries to settle this point. I know not what to believe of these hopes. You must have seen that in the drama of Ramel care was taken to class and associate Barthélemy with those ingenious ancients, that is, members of the Council of Ancients, who ask justice at the hands of injustice itself, and expect their executioners to be judges. Barthélemy does not seem to me, however, to have remained firm in this sublime part to the end, and the unconstitutional flight of Synamari must, I think, diminish somewhat of his credit with the sect. As to Villot, I know him much better ; he is brave, frank, active, clever, and his views appear to me indisputable.

" I occupy my time with works by which I should hope to effect some good, were the crisis prolonged, and its result postponed indefinitely. Then I should wish to turn them to account in England, and then I should count on your kindness to facilitate my entrance there."

In retracing the picture of these disastrous times, which

witnessed the sacrifice of so many feelings and interests, it is refreshing to pause for a moment in contemplation of these noble friendships, and the sentiments of attachment and esteem entertained for each other by distinguished men and philosophical minds, who, without previous connexion, when cast by the tide of revolution on foreign strands, recognized that they were worthy of each other.

CHAPTER XVI.

1799—1800.

Return of Bonaparte—The 18th Brumaire—The " Mercure Britannique " and Mallet's correspondence on these events—The Duke
of Orleans (Louis-Philippe) in London—Mallet's opinion of him—
Mallet's health declines—His disquietude—Letter to Mr. Wickham
—He is obliged to suspend the " Mercure "—His death at Richmond—General retrospect—Private character of Mallet du Pan.

ALL the excitement aroused in the emigrants by the
victories of the Archduke and of Suwarrow, cooled down
when the disastrous issue of the campaign in Switzerland
and Northern Holland became known. But hope revived
stronger than ever on the news of the events in Egypt,
where the French expedition, as it was said, had just been
ignominiously deserted by its leader, and at Paris, where
the Directory, torn by intestine conflict, and an object of
public odium, was evidently on the eve of downfall.
Barras was already engaged in making terms with
Louis XVIII, when the aspect of affairs changed on a
sudden, and the Revolution, instead of succumbing, found
an asylum by sacrificing the republic. On the 9th of
October Bonaparte disembarked at Fréjus. The once so

brilliant hero was held by all Europe to have vanished from the scene. The correspondence of officers, intercepted by the English cruisers, had revealed in the army of Africa a deep resentment against the leader of the enterprise ; his star was eclipsed, and his glory seemed to have disappeared together with himself.

The conduct of Bonaparte, judged from the only point of view then possible, was unjustifiable ; his departure for France was nothing but the flight of a defeated general of no genius, the desertion of his army an act of cowardice, which ruined him for ever. Mallet was deceived, like the rest ; and the hopes which the dissensions and blunders of the Directory reasonably gave him, served to obscure his habitual clear-sightedness. He supposed the beaten General had gone to some retreat to hide his ill fortune, and withdraw his person from the hatred of that Directory, of which he had been the terror. His sudden appearance opened Mallet's eyes. One evening several emigrants were together at his house, when the news arrived of Bonaparte's return to France. The company treated the fact as totally insignificant, and talked lightly of it ; Mallet alone became serious, and declared that, in his eyes, the event was of immense importance to France and to all Europe.

The 18th of Brumaire and its sequel soon followed, and proved that he was in the right ; and the " Mercure Britannique," in relating and expressing an opinion on this revolution within a revolution, attested for the last time the profound sagacity of the philosophic historian, whom circumstances had made a journalist. All then written by Mallet on Bonaparte and his prospects, deserves to be recalled. We reproduce here only the most remarkable passages.

The author of the " Considérations" had a full right, and exercised it, to call special attention to the summit attained by the revolution and liberty, after ten years of crimes and calamities suffered by the French nation.

" *Gladiorum impunitate, jus vi obrutum, potentiorque habitus prior, discordiaque civium antea conditionibus sanari solitæ, ferro dijudicatæ.* These words of a Roman historian comprise the history of France, ever since it undertook to proclaim the authority of knowledge and laws. Whether it be that national impetuosity will not wait for the slow effect of moral and political resources, or that the spirit and violence of factions are incompatible with every means of gaining the ascendant, except that of assault; or finally, that the genius of revolution and of its actors resorts invariably to plots and surprises for settling disputes—force has constantly been the sole legislator in this arena of republican gladiators. Whoever wished to do harm, whoever attempted to do good, has found himself reduced to sum up the number of muskets on which he could count; for the people, weary of the combatants and the combat, has long regarded itself as the stake of the game, and not as one of the players.

" Thus, republic and liberty have been merely lies and profanations. If the authors and coadjutors of the days of the 9th and 10th, who demonstrated it in fine speeches, and proclaimed it in their manifestoes, had had the humanity to hasten that demonstration, two generations would have been spared, millions of citizens preserved to their country and their families, and Europe and France saved from a war equally dreadful in its cause and its effects : the disturbers, the factious, the fanatical, the reprobate of all countries would not have risen *en masse* to serve and imitate that generation, to-day publicly condemned by its admirers, those sublime institutions which to-day are termed works of darkness, folly, and ignorance ; that succession of iniquities, brigandage, executions, and crimes, to which a revolution so ill-conducted, according to its new masters, owed its existence, its so-called laws, and its duration.

" The cannon-shot of Barras, directed by Bonaparte, solemnized, on the 6th of October, 1795, year III., the free and unanimous consecration of the constitution.   On the 10th of November, 1799, that constitution, whose sentence of death was delayed by contempt for four years, falls under the sabre of the same general, and perhaps of the same soldiers who had enforced it by cannon-shot on the impressible heads of the citizens of Paris.   It is the priesthood itself which breaks the sacred ark : its defenders, so intrepid, so stern at any, the slightest irreverence with which the malcontents seem to threaten it, avow to-day that they were fools, and most unjust proscribers.

" This repentance and this contrast are, in our opinion, the most memorable lesson and the most useful consequence of the political metamorphosis which has just changed the apparel of republican France.   We know not whether to adopt the pompous expression of one of the orators of the day—she has donned the virile toga. Let her efface, if she can, the stains of blood and filth which soiled her robe of glory and of youth.   Let her appear at length, were it but for six months, under a human aspect; the producers of her new arraying will not be undeserving of gratitude. Public esteem may then applaud the consequences of an operation whose nature and means, and many of whose actors might terrify, far rather than reassure, the friends of true freedom, justice, and permanent tranquillity."[*]

Next follows a sketch of the Republic dragging on from the 18th of June (30th Prairial), between a tottering government and an anarchical legislature; Sieyès stands in the foreground, preparing the revolution.[†] Then comes the fall of the many constitutions solemnly proclaimed, and then overturned with enthusiastic joy. Mallet notes the universal satisfaction with which the revolution of the 18th Brumaire was received in France, and unhesitatingly declared his approval of it, for the following reasons:

"The delirium of enthusiasm exaggerates these advantages, but it were unjust to contest them. Is it then

---

[*] " Mercure Britannique," vol. 4, No. 29.

[†] Mallet did not believe that this had been concerted between Bonaparte and Sieyès. " It is positively false," says he, " that there was a concerted plan, that Sieyès had sent for the Solon of Egypt, or that the latter had obeyed any order. No sooner had he arrived from abroad than he proved that he wanted no orders, and that it was his place to command. He displayed such daring and haughtiness as fully attested the exalted opinion he entertained of his own consequence, good fortune, and ascendency in crises. Disdainful, cold, interrogative, and taciturn towards his civil superiors, but insinuating with the soldiery, dissimulating his objects and his passions, he was sought after by both parties; the Jacobins loaded him with adulation and proofs of confidence and deference, while they flattered themselves he was led by them."

nothing to be preserved, though but for one year, from the
ravages of a faction under whose rule no man could sleep
in peace, and to find it expelled from office at the moment
of general fear, lest it should burst out again with fire,
assassins, taxers, and agrarian laws all over France ?   Is it
nothing to have seen disappear with its downfal those
execrable and execrated assemblies, where, under the name
of representatives of the people, mercenary speakers,
ignorant maniacs, and cowardly accomplices from the most
guilty factions have regulated, for eight years past, the
fate of Europe and of France, while perpetuating their own
power and the nation's servitude ?   At length we are
freed from these councils of folly and iniquity ; at length
that shifting oligarchy, composed of seven hundred and
fifty fabricators of contradictory and oppressive decrees, is
dissolved, after a reign which ranks with the deluge and
the black plague.

" By calling to military account this fundamental and
indissoluble Senate, by adjourning it in an arbitrary manner,
by reducing it to two secret committees empowered to
prepare its final suppression, and a new system of representation, all the dogmas of 1789 are thrown into derision,
all previous constitutions are destroyed, and the detestation
with which they were regarded by every enlightened man
is ratified : the tribunal of the 10th November has annulled
the decrees, and overturned those principles which founded
the republic and its institutions.

" It is very doubtful whether three Consuls and two
legislative commissions will remedy these deep-seated
disorders, these calamities of which the root remains
untouched.   It is neither impossible nor improbable that

fresh convulsions will result from the collisions of authorities of institutions, of ambitions, of untried systems ; but not the less will France have revived for a time under a more tolerable government, and emerged from the state of terror and subjugation to which the Directory and the Jacobins have reduced it, since 1797.

" By concentration, government acquires more strength to curb factions, more means of obedience and protection, more resources for the maintenance of order, security and obedience : its most secret deliberations afford less field for variance ; and if it obtains a wider power for evil, it also becomes more independent for effecting good. Such talents as it may possess will no longer be counteracted by incapacity and ignorance, or by the innovating and factious turbulence of cohorts of successive legislators, and a continual succession of assistants.

" Whether the new rulers be honest or perverse ; whether or not they hide pernicious views under a semblance of justice, interest, experience and necessity, they are alike precluded from resorting to revolutionary tyranny.

" Hence proceeds the ostentatious promise of a peace, the chief object of the national desire ; hence the immediate abolition of the law of hostages and forced loans ; hence those declarations in favour of property and civil freedom ; hence the suppression of the oath of hatred against royalty —not, indeed, as some dreamers have conceived through any love of monarchy, but in order to annihilate one invention and ensign of Jacobinism, one formula of conspiracy, one insult to all kings, many of whom it will be attempted to conciliate.

" Hence proceed those overtures of peace to the Chouans,

and that mission of delegates into the departments to dethrone the Jacobins and reassure the rest; lastly, hence those appointments, of which the majority obtained the public vote, and of which many deserved them. By comparing the list of the late officials with that of their successors, we learn to understand the effect produced by this revolution.

"The expulsion from public offices of a crowd of intriguers, sharpers, odious and inefficient intruders, has been hailed with joy. Assuredly, I would not trust myself to the mildness, or justice, or moderation of the heads of the actual government, were their passions put into opposition with their promises and their duties; but they cannot choose their own line of conduct.

"'On ne voit pas deux fois le rivage des morts.'

"The vindictive Jacobins will never forgive the authors of their ruin. Were one tempted to imitate them by reviving their measures, one must also reclaim their protection, and return under their supremacy.

"It follows then, that the new arbiters of France, encountering only two classes essentially opposed to them —namely, the anarchical republicans and absolute royalists, will associate, not in their authority, but in its functions and securities, the party called Moderates, which consists of all who shrink from public shocks, dread spoliations, and showed no more courage in resisting the oppressors, than a disposition to tyrannize. Numbers of ancient constitutionalists, abstract royalists, mitigated republicans, theoretical people, ambitious and intriguing, but not ferocious men, against whom the Jacobins closed the doors of distinction ; lastly, the throng of peaceable citizens, to whom all forms of government are alike indifferent, so long as themselves are secured from troubles, assassins, thieves and pitiless innovators, will be summoned to this alliance. This will result in obtaining more consideration for those classes of society who have hitherto borne the brunt of tyrannical power."

Proceeding to analyse the event itself, Mallet at once recognized it as belonging to an entirely new order of facts :

" This revolution appears to us as fundamental as that of 1789. Here are entirely new materials, means, results, architects, and times, which will probably impress the future with a character far different from that produced by previous commotions, which, notwithstanding their variety, replaced the republic in its former position."

After showing that this is the first revolution in which military power has absolutely lorded over civil power, in which the process, the language, the actors, were all martial, Mallet dilates on the prominent persons, and sums up all the suggestions then canvassed by universal curiosity on the subject of Bonaparte and his intentions :

" What Frenchman is there so simple as to doubt that as chief of the army, and political chief of the Republic, Bonaparte does not possess in fact, and for the moment absolute power ? The more we fathom this extraordinary man's conduct on the recent occasion, the more we recognize the elements of his genius and character, as they appeared in Italy and Egypt, in every time and place. In a wisely regulated republic, such a citizen is hurled from the Tarpeian rock ; in a republic like that of France, this citizen ascends the Capitol with power to reduce it to ashes, should he be forced to descend once more, or if the Consular sceptre is insufficient to his safety and dominion . . . .

"There exists no conformity between the systems, wishes, and opinions of the crowd, who applaud this change, who expect and receive advantages from it. Some believe themselves in the way to a more perfect republic, which will put an end to disturbances, and maintain an invariable balance between public powers. Others think they are on the eve of such a concentration of authority, that they place a constitutional monarch at the head of the government; but while thus uniting royalty with the republic, each individual prepares the contract union according to his own notions, and names, as his interests or theories may suggest, the candidate to whom the crown will be awarded. Lastly, a third class, more careless as to the fate of public laws, surfeited with constitutions and popular troubles, not desirous of a royal counter-revolution, but ambitious of fortune, posts, and renown—ever ready to devote themselves to any one who takes the lead in right of genuine superiority, no longer recognize the State, except in the person of Bonaparte, or tranquillity and stability, except under a military dominion, headed by a chief capable of governing all factions.

"The persons least able to satisfy public curiosity as to the aim and consequences of the 18th Brumaire, would be, I fancy, the directors and abettors of the event. The position of the chiefs, and their desire of safety, were its prime motives. An accusation and a decree from the majority of the councils, in collusion with two or three directors, would have sufficed to depose Sieyès, and to hurl him from the Luxembourg to Guiana. The utmost obscurity would scarcely have shielded Bonaparte from a similar fate; his exaltation, his hopes, his fortune, his life— even his glory—were at the mercy of the first officer who, warrant in hand, might terminate by his arrest the uneasiness of a government which his overbearing tone offended, and which could not tolerate so formidable a rival. It was a deadly war : the choice lay between becoming head of the Jacobins, or head of the French Republic—Bonaparte could not hesitate.

" We shall not waste our time in refuting that shallow opinion which, confounding a change of the republic and its rulers with a return towards monarchical principles, has so gratuitously ascribed to the authors of this master-stroke, a leaning towards the re-establishment of royalty. They approach it neither in fact nor in desire, and if they tend towards a reasonable constitution, it is but thereby to prolong the burial of true monarchy, and to stifle the germ of its resurrection.

" Heroes capable of defeating Austrians, Cossacks, and Mamelukes, are common enough, but we rarely meet with a Timoleon or a Thrasybulus. The vulgar ambition which deposes and overturns established authorities, either to succeed them itself, or to obtain a sanction for its own whims, is far removed from the generous and elevated spirit of a chief, strong in power, talents, and credit, who profits by the crowning moment of his fortune to renounce himself, and restore to his country its legitimate superior, and the laws which secure its liberty.

" Bonaparte was master, dictator, and sovereign of

France in the hall of Saint-Cloud.   Perhaps he was not
so in the same degree on the morrow ; but, in preserving
the elements of his greatness, he destines the crown for
his own head, were the recasting a crown in question.
Like Cæsar he has rejected it——but with the understanding
that he might have taken it, but preferred restoring it to
the people.   He seems only to have desired the honour of
this refusal, and a legal authority sufficient to conduct
him, by means of laws dictated by himself, to an illustrious
repose.

" This, at least, is the opinion of acute observers ; but
while they thus interpret his present views, they eschew all
conjectures as to what may follow.   Doubtless, while
repeating to himself that he rejected the dignity of
dictator, of protector, or of prince, he has repeated far
more frequently, and been far oftener reminded by his
flatterers, that it was in his power to become so.

" May he not have prescribed, as the condition of his
splendid renunciation, that his plans be followed in con-
structing that new order of things which he allows to take
the place of his personal domination ?

" Were this conjecture just, we might predict, especially
taking Bonaparte's character into consideration, that any
one who forms a different conception of liberty will be
viewed as an enemy ; and that any opposition to such
acts of legislation and acts of government as he may
please to enjoin, will restore to his ambition the utmost
force it is capable of.

" In such a situation, a definite aim and boundary are
seldom assigned ; but the course of events decides all.
Bonaparte's head is in the clouds ; his career is a poem,

his imagination a store-house of heroic romances, his stage an arena accessible to every outburst of intellect or ambition. Who shall fix the limit where he will arrest his course ? Is he sufficiently master of his feelings, of things, of times, and of his own fortune, himself to fix it ?"

These last views, so steadfast, so penetrating, and which the event proved so just, as to the probable conduct of Bonaparte, were diametrically opposed to the wild fancies to which the exaggerated royalists, and the King himself, had reverted since the 18th Brumaire. They were bent on discerning in the conqueror of the Directory a second General Monk, who only sought to concentrate the power within his own hands in order to restore it to the legitimate monarch. Meanwhile, numerous emigrants profited by these party delusions, and by the recall which seemed evidently addressed to them by the moderation, and all the acts of the First Consul, to return to France ; many others, while preparing to follow them, paved the way for their proceeding and justified it, by lauding the conduct of Bonaparte. Mallet, as we have seen, did not subscribe to this new faith : he mistrusted Bonaparte ; he believed him destitute of moral principles, and ranked him among those statesmen who regard their fellows as slaves and dupes, incapable of being actuated by any motive but that of interest. His anterior policy, and the portion of his character drawn out by his conquest of Italy, gave colour to this opinion :

" It may be," says Mallet, on occasion of the First Consul's letter to the King of England, " and in fact is, very indifferent to the French—even to most of those who are called *just thinkers*—whether or not Bonaparte violated

public faith, infringed the laws of war, outraged public
rights to the uttermost in the persons of the Lombards,
Venetians and Genoese.   So long as he governs the nation,
freed from the Jacobins, with clemency and justice, his
conduct in foreign relations will affect no one: but I think
strangers are justified in instituting a somewhat more care-
ful scrutiny, and in not so soon forgetting the past.

" It is to be remarked, that men in whom is found a
combination of force and astuteness, of violence and dissimulation, and whose actions are prompted by love of fame
or ambitious energy, are usually guided, not by morality or
enthusiasm for certain principles, but by their own position.

" In a previous number of this work we remarked, even
before the proceedings attempted relative to his Britannic
Majesty, that the policy, requirements and necessity of
circumstances would decide the question of peace or war in
the mind of Bonaparte, a sovereign of a sovereign people ;
and would decide it far more imperiously than private affection or opinions.

" The honesty of his proceedings results then from these
calculations, and not from virtue.   If cogent reasons enjoin
the termination of the war, he will finish it, without his
character being affected for the better or the worse.   In
like manner, he will re-commence war the moment his
interest dictates a change of measures."*

At the same time, however, Mallet du Pan did ample
justice to the First Consul's superiority over the men he
had displaced, to his system of firm and conciliatory government, and to the hopes he awakened.   No contemporary
gave a more faithful picture of all Bonaparte did during

* " Mercure Britannique." v. 5, No. 34.

the first three months of the Consulate, to renovate France, and to make the nation feel itself the object of an equitable, fostering, concentrated and anti-Jacobinical government. So much impartiality exposed the author of the "Mercure" to the charge of fickleness, and he did not escape : he was even accused by persons who, a few years later, figured amongst the most assiduous courtiers at the Tuileries.

His peace was disturbed by these annoyances, but his judgment remained imperturbable.

LETTER FROM MALLET DU PAN TO THE CHEVALIER DE GALLATIN.

"London, January 14, 1800.

"My dear Chevalier,

"I refer you to the 'Mercure' for my opinion on the late revolution at Paris, and its consequences. These poor simple emigrants, who happily enjoy blindness as a support under their misfortunes, had conceived that Bonaparte laboured for them and for Louis XVIII. Would you believe, that here certain men in office shared this inconceivable infatuation ? Yet this is the tenth year of the revolution ; but the longer I live, the more convinced I become that the habit of interpreting it by contraries is incurable.

"In the same way they are persuaded, I know not why, that the reign of Bonaparte and of his political system will terminate within twenty-four hours. They build on the *Chouans*, the public poverty, the finances, the Jacobins and other common places in great repute since the commencement of the war. As to me, I recognize an enormous power vested in the hands of a man who knows how to use it, and who has on his side the army and the public. This is a totally new order in the revolution : we must acknowledge that eighteen-twentieths of the French are perfectly indifferent to the republic and the monarchy ; but that they naturally must be, and are, at the feet of the first superior who protects them against the slaughterers, who guarantees their existence from the genius of revolution, who will afford them without convulsions the advantages of a firm and tutelary government, exercised by a man in whose talents they repose confidence. Bonaparte is king : how long will he continue so ? Who can solve a problem which depends on external events and so many incalculable chances ?

" You have heard that this potentate has written a letter to the King of England, as from one equal to another, in which he catechises his Majesty, and gives him lessons on the love of peace. This overture has been answered in a negative note ; but, as the latter must beyond doubt, have been sent to your worthy sovereign, I do not speak of it. Opinion is more than divided on the subject of this note, which is far from meeting with universal approbation. What it proves, is the great confidence placed in the perseverance of Austria ; otherwise, it would be impossible to account for so peremptory a refusal to negotiate. On the other hand, numberless reports are spread abroad about Prussia, her intimacy with France, and the preparations she is making. Until you undeceive me, I shall look upon these rumours as so many idle stories."

LETTER FROM THE SAME TO THE COMTE DE SAINTE-ALDEGONDE.

" London, January 14, 1800.

" You have no doubt both heard and read in the papers that Bonaparte has sent a letter to the King of England, written in an unusual tone, in which he reads him a lesson on the love of peace, and asks him if there is no means of coming to an understanding. This letter is written as from one equal to another. The answer returned was a note couched in a most negative sense, in which, after much recrimination, it is declared that the re-establishment of the Bourbons would be the only true and sure means of pacifying France and Europe, and in which it is also stated that, although it is not intended to dictate any form of government to the French, yet theirs is too new to inspire any confidence. Such is the general sense of this answer, which is far from being generally liked. A government must have great confidence in its allies to risk so proud and peremptory an answer ; it will create a fine uproar at Paris.

" The Chouans are relied on here beyond all measure, and a descent is being prepared to suppport them ; but, as this expedition will be but slowly proceeded with, and hardly ready by the spring, I greatly fear that, when it does land, there will be no more Chouans left. As for me, I place not the slightest reliance either on *chouannerie* or descents, and I have excellent reasons for doing so.

" How innocent were all those simpletons who were *naïve* enough to think that Bonaparte was working in the cause of Louis XVIII.! There was not one *émigré* here out of a hundred and fifty, however, who doubted it, including even the most reflective. Were the revolution to last a century, these innocent creatures would still remain at their A, B, C.

"Monsieur is passing the winter here: he hopes to return to France through the projected expedition. I have not seen him again; but yesterday he sent to me, begging that I would have my last number reprinted in the epistolary form, for circulation in France; he also requested me to take it to him when finished. Such rubbishing attention is, doubtless, thought a fine sop for those who are neglected.

"Great reliance is placed here on the Court of Vienna: they must indeed be terribly afraid there of falling out with Russia, who forces them to do whatever she likes. The next campaign will be a warm one—but will it be the last?"

TO THE SAME.

"February 27, 1800.

"I was right in my opinion of that impertinent freak of the Chouans, which was disapproved of at Mittau, and encouraged here, and on which I hear raised the most extravagant expectations, that still continue to dazzle people, in spite of their constant repetition. One must have lost his senses, to think that a parcel of peasants and highwaymen, divided under twenty leaders, without either a commander-in-chief, connexion with one another or subordination, would be able to resist the most experienced troops of Europe. Bonaparte, moreover, attacked and vanquished them as much by persuasion as by arms. He granted them everything, churches, priests, bishops; struck off the lists of the proscribed names of the *émigrés* who happened to be among them, and abandoned them to the election of local magistrates, &c. The great stupidity of the leaders was that of not capitulating in time. Frotté is taken, and I tremble lest he should be executed. All these projects cause shame and horror; but it is useless to expect anything else.

"I have not seen Monsieur again: he hardly receives any one but his courtiers, and is more bespattered with adulation than he ever was at Versailles. The object for which he wished to see me was not worth a moment's attention; my objections had not been able to make them change their opinion; but the course of events has exercised more influence than I could. I ardently wish to be entirely forgotten in that quarter, because there is nothing at all to be done with people who are not sincere, and who, while feigning to consult you, have already resolved to disregard every sensible thing you may say.

"You have doubtless been informed of the Princes d'Orléans, and of their reconciliation with Monsieur. The Duke said nothing about repentance and pardon, as his royal Majesty's valets took care to spread about;* he

* "The "Mercure Britannique" relates the proceeding of the Duc d'Orléans (Louis-Philippe) in the following manner: "The Princes of the house of Orléans, that is, the Duke of that name, and his brothers, the Duke of Montpensier and the Count of Beaujolais, who had taken refuge in the United States, and afterwards at Havannah, have arrived in London. It is at the very moment that a

spoke of his faults and his devotedness, but with a proper nobleness and reserve. I shall not dilate upon the very favourable impression made here by the Prince, on both the English and the French. It would be difficult to have a better-formed, more enlightened and more culti-vated mind, or to have greater power over language, to show more good sense, to possess more knowledge, or more simple and winning manners. He, at least, has learned to profit by adversity. . . .

"You appear to put great hopes on the approaching campaign. My dear Comte, this has been our disease every winter, but I am now radically cured. We shall pay Bavarians and Suabians, and give Austria a subsidy to enable her the more conveniently to procure herself peace. I do not doubt that all these forces will fight most wonderfully; but it is not to be contested that the French are in a state to oppose them in a very different manner to what they were a year ago. With respect to the counter-revolution to be brought about by foreign arms, I would as soon hear talk of conquering the moon.

parcel of mad fabulists still affected to believe and to spread about that the republican Sieyès, whose love for thrones is so well known, was preparing one for the Duc d'Orléans, that this young Prince has united himself with the heads of the House of Bourbon. He presented himself before Monsieur, and, in a conversation as honour-able for the one as the other, expressed with nobleness and loyalty the sentiments his honour and duties dictated. Monsieur received his protestations with sensibility and cordiality, and with such expres-sions as they were fitted to inspire.

"The Duc d'Orléans has written to Louis XVIII. a letter, equally worthy of his birth and his fidelity."

" Bonaparte has succeeded more and more in rendering his government popular : to accomplish this, he adopted the only true means, that of inspiring all parties with confidence.   The blunt and positive refusal given here to enter into negotiations with him has been of great use to him in every quarter.   The *émigrés* are leaving this place, as they are every other, in crowds.   What determination shall you take ?   Shall you not also be tempted to return ?   I will not venture to give you any advice with respect to your so doing ; but I ought not to hide from you how remote I consider the period when will be witnessed the re-establishment of Louis XVIII, and of the former monarchy.

" Adieu, and receive my best wishes."

LETTER FROM MALLET DU PAN TO THE CHEVALIER DE GALLATIN.

" London, February 28, 1800.

" I do not think, my dear Chevalier, that I have been honoured with any letters from you since the 13th of December, which letters reached me, according to the amiable custom of the country, two months after date.

" Mr. Pitt has opened his budget, and raised a loan of twenty millions, at four and three quarters per cent., the interest of which will be paid by an additional tax on tea and spirits.   This loan, obtained at so low a price, is a strange circumstance, and ought to make the French Government reflect.   The rise, however, which at first took place, did not maintain itself, and it is easy to foresee that the slightest circumstance would cause a deterioration which would, perhaps, be considerable.

" You would greatly err, if you supposed that the immense support obtained by the minister on the question of war and peace, proves any great adhesion to the former of these two things. More than a hundred members of the House of Commons always vote with the ministry, and nearly twenty in the Upper House abstained from voting altogether. Again, many members, though they totally disapprove of Lord Grenville's answer, support the ministry from principle, even in its faults, against an opposition which has lost all respect. The latter has recommended its usual litany, its eulogiums on the revolutions, its apologies for the Republic, its panegyrics on Bonaparte—nothing more was necessary to give the finishing stroke to its unpopularity. Its orators have not, on questions of this nature, the slightest skill, judgment or knowledge. Generally speaking, it appears to me that, during these famous debates, all spoke of everything except of the question itself.

" This question will be brought before the House again to-morrow. Tierney, who is, without doubt, the leading man of the opposition, will make a special motion against the continuance of war for the re-establishment of French monarchy. He will, it is said, enter into detail at great length, and ask for an account of the sums of money that have been lavished on Monsieur, the King, the Chouans, and the Royalists in active service. If Monsieur were not so entirely surrounded by flatterers, who turn his head more than it was turned at Versailles, he would, I think, do well to return to his retreat at Edinburgh.

" I suppose Baron de Castelnau has informed you of the particulars relating to the Duke d'Orléans. It is easy to see that the latter has not been spoilt by his courtiers, and that he has turned his misfortunes to good account. There are very few Frenchmen who are equal to him in learning, judgment and intelligence.

" According to the reports made to the government by the Royalists, the Chouans amounted to a hundred thousand men, who were all intrepid and invincible, provided they were well supplied with money. Whatever Bonaparte might do, it was asserted, they would at least hold out all the winter. Plans were drawn up, enumerations made, and expeditions projected for this long campaign, which lasted three weeks, and ended in the most disgraceful manner, scarcely without burning a pinch of powder. Another project of a similar nature is in course of preparation : one would be inclined to laugh if he were not forced to weep.

" In good truth, my dear friend, when one sees how affairs are managed, and how, after eight years' experience, they are still directed in the same circle of visions, of stubborn disregard for evidence, of wrong-headedness, of divisions and selfishness, one ceases to take any further interest in the future.

" Bonaparte is the only one who seems to me to understand the question. He guides his bark like a pilot who is well acquainted with the seas on which he navigates. We are inundated with French merchants who come to purchase our colonial produce ; their testimony agrees, in every point, with that of my letters. This Government is possessed of a strength and confidence that very few legitimate governments ever enjoy. The *émigrés* are returning from here, as well as from elsewhere, in crowds, and amongst them are found the most celebrated names. Six months hence, we shall see many of them at the Sultan's court, who accords his protection to all parties, without fearing any. Adieu, my dear Chevalier, my heart is with you."

The "Mercure Britannique" succeeded beyond all expectation, and the increase of consideration which ensued for the editor, rendered his position very honourable and apparently most agreeable. His house became a sort of rendezvous, where the time and occupations of the master were, it is true, but little considered. Those *émigrés* who were friends of the family, and who came and left, as if the house belonged to them, at any hour of the day, were the principal visitors. Besides the intimate friends already mentioned, there were Monsieur de Circé, the old Archbishop of Bordeaux, who had been keeper of the Seals in 1790 ; his nephew, the Chevalier de La Bentinaye, whose gay disposition rendered his company most agreeable ; the Archbishop of Aix, an eloquent speaker, of the most courteous manners, and possessing a heart as noble as his birth ; the Prince of Poix and the Baron de Gilliers. There were also Lajare, the Abbé Delille, and the Chevalier de Panat : Bourmont too was there, clever, graceful and insinuating, who, after having been a Vendean leader, became a general of division under Napoleon : then came Pozzo di Borgo, the future negotiator of the Emperor Alexander, with Mallet's compatriots, Messieurs Saladin, d'Ivernois, Dumont, Doctors de La Rive and Marcet. Mallet was also much sought after by the English, who vied with each other in showing him the most delicate and continued attention. Mallet, however, faithful to his custom, went out into society as little as possible. Yet, as long as his health permitted, he never missed the meetings of a little modest club which had been formed in London in 1798, an imitation of the English ones, under the name of " The Foreigners' Club." It met every month in a dirty street near Leicester Square, at a little French eating-house, where the fare was none of the best, but whence they had banished the eternal beef-steak and the mutton-chop, which, forty years later, gave Monsieur Cottu such a shock, and which had been replaced by *fricandeau* and *vol-au-vent*. Malouet, Pannat, Mallet du Pan, d'Ivernois Dumont, Balan, the Prussian chargé d'affaires, a man of great information and of most gentlemanly manners, gene-rally met there ; Pozzo di Borgo, a man of great imagina-tion and wit, was also an *habitué*. Vansittart, since Chan-cellor of the Exchequer, and his friend, Doctor Beale, author of several pamphlets on finance, came there now and then.

One would imagine that a paper established under such happy auspices, which brought affluence to Mallet and his family, which surrounded him with a crowd of friends, and made him the centre of the most distinguished society, would have imposed but a very easy task on a writer who wielded his pen with so experienced a hand, and who was so well acquainted with political affairs. Unfortunately, such was not the case. What Mallet stood most in need of, but which he could not obtain, was repose with tran-quillity of mind, both which blessings were incompatible with his task. With his mind continually intent on public events, which he was obliged not only to judge but to foresee, feeling himself morally responsible for the influence exercised by the " Mercure," and desirous of seconding, and not obstructing, the government which afforded him hospitality, but, at the same time, incapable of shackling the indomitable independence of his reason, and forced by his conscientious character to use frankness which often offended, he advanced with difficulty in the midst of the dangers that the passions of parties raised around him, which he met constantly in his own circles, and among his most intimate acquaintance.   We have just given a sample of his disputes with the *émigrés;* more than one French Royalist passed from affection to malevolence towards him. Mallet had rendered the Abbé Delille great services, both by asking and obtaining permission for him to sojourn at Fribourg, and by usefully interfering in an affair concerning the pecuniary resources of the exiled poet.   But Delille, with respect to politics, was the most unreasonable of men, and more than once he broke forth in the most unpardonable invectives, even at his host's table, against Malouet and his friends.

The editing even of the " Mercure" was both morally and physically an immense burden, at certain oppressive times.   To find twice a month, for a stated day, matter for sixty pages, with the necessity of rendering that matter interesting and instructive, and then to be obliged to take such pains in polishing his style, under pain of endangering the existence of his journal; to obtain authentic news when communication with the continent was almost entirely cut off; to weigh everything, risk nothing, and to let no occurrence pass unnoticed, was certainly a task of disheartening difficulty.   The government, which had promised him the use of its papers and official documents, sent the former very irregularly, and the latter hardly ever, and what it did send was generally of no importance. Sometimes London and the editor of the " Mercure Britannique" were entirely without news from the continent.* Had Mallet's health been less undermined, he might oftener have been able to fill up these gaps with some of his articles on philosophical or historical literature, in which he excelled. It was in one of those times of dearth, that he wrote one of the best articles ever written on the influence of Voltaire and Rousseau, considered as one of the causes of the revolution ; a remarkable article on the difficulty of writing the history of this revolution ; an important criticism of the " Memoirs of Bertand de Moleville ;" and, lastly, a triple notice of three persons who had just disappeared from the stage of life, on which they had each occupied very different places—Washington, the Avoyer Steiguer, and Marmontel.

Mallet's health became at last a continual source of anxiety to his family. Both at Berne and Fribourg, he had had recourse to long walks about the country, in order to recover his strength and his tranquillity of mind, both which continued application, confinement and meditation, often mixed with great anxiety, rendered imperatively necessary to him. Consequently, his joy at being able to escape into the country to visit his friends the Westons, at West Horseley, and Baron Masères, at Reigate, is vividly depicted in his letters ; but these amusements were of rare occurrence, and his forced residence in London too often deprived him of this precious resource for recruiting his health. He had

* In March, 1799, there were fifteen mails behindhand.

also been accustomed to a mild, leguminous diet, suited to the delicate state of his lungs; but a French exiled physician, who had been recommended to him, and who was endowed with a remarkably vigorous temperament, possessed the medical theory that, in the damp atmosphere of London, it was necessary, according to his own expression, "to box with the climate," and he therefore placed Mallet upon a diet of solid meat and port wine, which could not have been more opposed to the diet suited to him, and which augmented his malady. But yet no sign of declining vigour in his journal betrayed the rapid loss of his strength, undermined by constant fever, or even the profound disgust which had seized on him for the work to which he had bound himself: it was only, however, to his most intimate friends that he testified his increasing repugnance and fatigue. "That horrid 'Mercure' of mine," he writes to the Chevalier de Gallatin, "absorbs the few gleams of intellect which shoot around me in the midst of the darkness visible in which I live. I count the minutes which still remain to complete my second year, and I assure you that no power on earth shall induce me to begin a third one."

The interest offered till now by the life of this courageous writer, is that which attached itself to strong and upright characters, who have remained unshakeable in the public tempests through which they have passed; but when we meet, which we do but too rarely, with men who unite superiority and expanse of mind with firmness of opinion, we must follow them to the end of their career: the evening of their boisterous day has also its flashes of light, and nothing that concerns them is insignificant, not even their silence in the night of their peaceable and unaffected end.

From the beginning of the year 1800, the Countess of Holderness, widow of the Secretary of State of that name, who, from Mallet du Pan's first arrival in London, had given him forcible proofs of the interest she took in his welfare, advised him to consult her own physician, Sir Gilbert Blane, well known by several works of great merit. As soon as that excellent man, who attended Mallet with the most affectionate and disinterested care, had ascertained the nature and seriousness of his illness, he ordered an entire suspension of work.

The patient himself felt only too well the necessity of this ; but he also saw in what a dreadful position the suspension of his labours would place him, as it would deprive him of his sole income—the profits accruing from the " Mercure." How would he be able to provide for the wants of his family ! He had, doubtless, as much right to rely on the bounty of the Government as a crowd of *émigrés* who besieged the ministers, and received subsidies for the support of unsuccessful projects and political intrigues ; but he had never solicited such assistance, and shrank back from so desperate and uncertain a resource. At last, on the advice of his friends, he determined to open his heart to Mr. Wickham, at that moment Ambassador to the Allied Powers in Germany ; he therefore announced to him that he could not, without committing suicide, undertake to support for a third year the responsibility of the ' Mercure.' He complained with great frankness of the little encouragement he had received from the English Government. By this, it will be seen how very

far from the truth were all those who had discovered in
Mallet du Pan a writer in the pay of Mr. Pitt.

"Several circumstances have concurred with loss of
health to render this burden still more heavy : at one time,
it is the ill-humour and complaints of some foreign minister,*
at another, the over-hastiness and calumnies of the *émigrés*,
at whose head the agents of the King distinguish themselves, and then it is the false and mad-brained interpre-
tations put upon both my writings and intentions.   Being
used to such hostilities, I should not take the least notice
of them, were I certain that they exercised no influence on
the government. I own to you, that I am extremely grieved
at not having the slightest pretext for believing that I
possess the approbation of the ministry. I am entirely at a
loss to conjecture what opinion the ministry can have
formed, both of my labours and myself, who, at each fresh
number, am fearful lest I should perchance offend its views.

"I have taken no determination, nor shall I be able to
do so just yet, with respect to the means by which I shall
try to replace an income on which my own existence, as
well as that of my family, depends.   A great many persons
advise me to have recourse to the bounty of the Government, and it is even at their instigation that I importune
you now with all these private details.   It is impossible for

---

* "I have had here a sharp quarrel with the Imperial Minister
concerning my fifteenth number. He will not, I think, be readily
induced to advert again to this subject ; but he has given ten louis to
Peltier to abuse me, and to scrawl, after his dictation, a fine apology
for the surrender of Mentz, the occupation of Venice, the conferences
of Seltz, &c.—*Letter from Mallet du Pan to the Comte de Sainte-
Aldegonde, April* 23, 1799.

me to participate in their confidence; I have no claims to show; I know none of the ministers, and am the most awkward of men in forwarding my own private interest, even when it is supported by justice. How could I, a stranger, hope to obtain a favour that an Englishman does not always succeed in obtaining, even after years of long service? I take the liberty of submitting these difficulties to your judgment. I, for my part, am far from misunderstanding their character. In soliciting what might be called my retiring-pension, I should at least wish, by not remaining idle, to acquire some right to receive it : if, therefore, among the number of places which the present conjunctures have doubtless created, there was one which the Government could give me, and which was not entirely useless, such a *mezzo-termine* would crown my utmost wishes. As my health is too delicate to permit me, at fifty years of age, still to run on, like a stage-coach, which is forced to start in all weathers, and at a stated time, I shall now take care of myself, so that, if I can sufficiently recover my health, I may be able to follow less slavish occupations, and thus prevent it being further endangered. I beseech you to give the letter a moment or two of your consideration, to enlighten me by your judgment, and to direct me in the course I ought to pursue. If it is a chimerical hope to expect anything from the Government, I will lose no time in looking out for some literary employment, in order to ward off starvation.

" I beg you will pardon the liberty I have taken; but you are the only man to whom I would have made this confession ; you will, I think, do me justice enough to believe that necessity alone could have torn it from me ; I trust you will receive it with indulgence, and look upon it as a testimony of the unlimited confidence which your former kindness has inspired me with, as well as of the esteem and unchangeable attachment of your most obedient servant."

This letter met with delay before reaching Mr. Wickham, who was still in Germany with the allied armies; and when his answer, which was couched in the most affectionate terms, arrived, Mallet had already been forced, by the rapid progress of his illness, to give up the "Mercure." He retired to Richmond, where Lally-Tolendal placed a house which he possessed there, at his disposal. It was from that place that he wrote again to Wickham, as follows :

"The rapid progress of my illness has baffled all my calculations, and put a stop to the wishes expressed in my letter of the 20th of January. Since the date of that letter, I have been in a constant state of suffering, which has been increased by the painful efforts I was forced to make, in order to complete the last numbers of the "Mercure." I am obliged to stop it at its thirty-sixth number, as my physician totally forbids me to apply my mind to anything; but the entire loss of my strength rendered such an order superfluous. I thought it incumbent on me, Sir, to inform you of the discontinuance of the "Mercure," before announcing it publicly in my thirty-sixth number, which is almost entirely written by me. I was far from imagining that, when I came to this country under your kind auspices, my labours would have so sad an end. My career of utility is now terminated, and the suggestions contained in my last letter are become useless.

I cannot contemplate, without the greatest anguish, the position of myself and family, left as I am without resources in the dearest country in Europe, where my long illness has exhausted my scanty means, where the climate is unhealthy, and where I am haunted by bitter thoughts on the past, and distressing anxiety about the future. The only resource I have left is resignation and trust in God, and to commend my children to those who, like you, Sir, have never ceased to give me proofs of their esteem."

Though the English Government, whose attention it was difficult to divert from the current and parliamentary business with which they were overwhelmed, and who were probably dissatisfied with the tone of moderation in which the " Mercure" had spoken of the first acts of Bonaparte's administration, continued to remain perfectly indifferent with respect to Mallet du Pan, from everywhere else the most willing assistance and the most obliging offers of services were tendered him. Lally-Tolendal lent him his country-house; Malouet undertook to bring out the last numbers of the " Mercure," and Sir John Macpherson continued to solicit the Ministers, and engaged his friends to bestir themselves also, in behalf of Mallet. As soon as it was known that the editor of the " Mercure," sinking under his task, had let his pen fall from his hand, Mallet received from several of his French and English readers of every station, letters expressive of sympathy and great respect for his character. At last the Government, overtaken by the general interest which surrounded the dying journalist, awoke from its indifference. Mr. Rose, the Secretary of the Treasury, gave Mallet's son, who had translated for him the year before a work on finance, a place as foreign translator and examiner in the Audit-Office, and Sir John Macpherson was informed by Mr. Addington, the Speaker of the House of Commons, that the Ministry was about to adopt some measure with respect to Madame Mallet.   The last days of the dying man were rendered more calm by these circumstances : by being thus reassured about the welfare of his family, he was freed from his most painful anxiety, and from the bitter reflection that his unceasing devotedness to the cause of governments and society had not even procured his family bread.

He was enabled once more to see the fine days of spring, so mild in the neighbourhood of Richmond : he enjoyed them all to the last.   One morning—it was the 10th of May—consumption completed its work, and Mallet du Pan gently breathed forth his energetic soul.

Lally-Tolendal announced his friend's death in the " Courrier de Londres," in the following words :

" M. Mallet du Pan died on Saturday (May 10th), at the age of fifty, at the house of the Comte de Lally, at Richmond, of consumption, the progress of which disease had been accelerated by his labours.   For the last month his friends had lost all hope of preserving his life, and he himself, feeling his strength decline, spoke of his approaching end without weakness or ostentation.

" The affliction of his family and of his friends announced more than anything else his dissolution.   He died without pain, and without a struggle.   The serenity of his conscience was depicted on his face.   The evening before his death, he took a drive out.   He said that he felt himself inspired with fresh life by the pure air and the beauties of Nature ; he spoke with pleasure of the drives he meant to take, and even of his convalescence; but those who observed him closely, had cause for believing that he was less ignorant of his real state than that he was desirous of concealing it from others, and that, up to the very last, he called to his aid all the strength of character he possessed, joined to the goodness of his heart, to spare the sensitive family which surrounded and adored him, as much grief as possible. He once said to his wife and children : " If I could be sure that you will be happy when I am no more, I could die content." During the three days preceding his death, it was remarked that he read over again, with a meditative air, the sermons of Mr. Romilly on resignation and the immortality of the soul."

The next day, when Madame Mallet, whose courage rendered her worthy of the companion of her life, was torn from that house of mourning, taking in each hand one of her daughters, and turning her eyes, filled with tears, towards the chamber where the remains of her husband lay, she addressed him in the following touching prayer : " O ! thou, who art now in Heaven, thou, who wert a good husband, a good father, a good friend, and an honest man, pray for us, and obtain for us that courage of which we stand in need."*

Lally-Tolendal and Malouet, regarding public opinion and their own, more than the humble position of a Swiss family who depended on the kindness of the Government for their existence, decided that the funeral of their friend should be a public one, and worthy of his fame and the universal sympathy felt for him : the affecting style and

* Letter from M. Mallet du Pan, Junior, to the editor of the " Courrier de Londres."

rather pompous warmth of Lally-Tolendal will be recognized in the following extract :

" Yesterday was the day appointed for the funeral of the celebrated and much respected Monsieur Mallet du Pan. It was signalized by an imposing display of grief and respect, of modesty and solemnity.   No greater mark of honour could have been paid, and no greater tribute could have been rendered to justice than was rendered by that assemblage of men of all ranks, belonging to the different countries and religions of Europe, who had hastened to Richmond to offer a last token of veneration and gratitude to the courageous and unshaken defender of European liberty, to the man who, in all the force of the expression, had devoted his life to the extirpation of Jacobinism, to the maintenance of social order, to the cause of legitimate governments, of national rights, of public and private property—in one word, to the grand cause of humanity.   As many of those who came to perform their melancholy duty, only knew him by his salutary writings, they asked for permission to see him before the grave closed over him for ever.   His features were in no way discomposed.   He appeared to be sleeping on the bosom of eternal justice. He had been covered with flowers—lilies and white lilac. The mournful procession set out on foot, at half-past one, from the house of the Comte de Lally-Tolendal, and, passing along the principal street of Richmond, proceeded to the church, and thence to the cemetery.   A group of ecclesiastics walked immediately before the coffin ; among them was observed the minister of the Swiss Church established at London ; he was in deep mourning.   The pall was supported by Lord Sheffield and the Prince de Poix, M. Fagel,

Keeper of the Records of the States-General of the United Provinces, and the Right Honourable Mr. Trevor, member of his Britannic Majesty's Privy Council, and formerly his Envoy Extraordinary and Minister Plenipotentiary at the Court of Turin ; by Sir John Macpherson, Bart., and W. Keene, Esq., both members of the English Parliament ; and by the Comte de Lally-Tolendal and Monsieur Malouet, both deputies at the States-General of France in 1789. The eldest son of Monsieur Mallet du Pan followed the coffin, accompanied by several of his country-men ; then came a great number of English, French, and other gentlemen, among whom were observed Baron Maseres and his brother, Messieurs Granville Penn, Flint, Clarke, Reeves, Bowles, Ryder, Gifford, the Rev. S. Woollaston, the Rev. W. Sparrow, the Vicomte de Souillac, formerly his most Christian Majesty's Commandant of all the French establishments in the East Indies, the Marquis de Thuisy, the Chevalier de Thuisy, &c., &c."

Mr. John Gifford, one of those who were present, wrote the next day to a friend, as follows : " Yesterday I discharged my last duty to my worthy friend Mallet du Pan, at Richmond, and though I was very much indisposed, I would rather have had myself carried there than not shown him this last mark of respect and regret." The son of Mallet placed a very simple inscription over his father's grave. " I think with you," wrote Dumont to him, " that a pompous epitaph says all the less by affecting to say so much. It would be still more out of place to employ an emphatic style, while speaking of a man who loved simplicity, who always introduced it into his habits, and who looked upon it as the safeguard of independence and of virtue."

These details will possess no other interest in the eyes of our readers than that, which is yet great, pointing out honest and courageous talent, thus publicly honoured. It is on this account that we shall also relate what the English government did for Mallet's family.

A few days after his death, Mr. Addington, Speaker of the House of Commons, informed Sir John Macpherson that it was the intention of government to grant Madame Mallet a pension of two hundred pounds out of the Civil List. The various reductions that this pension underwent, reduced it to one hundred and fifty; but that even was a great and unexpected favour, which families of high birth, overtaken by misfortune, often applied for in vain. This pension, and the appointment given to Monsieur Mallet's son, were the contribution of the English government; but the public also wished to offer theirs. Sir William Pulteney, Sir John Macpherson and Mr. W. Keene opened a subscription, of which the maximum for each subscriber was not allowed to exceed ten pounds, so that a greater number of persons might be able to take part in this tribute of respect. The money flowed in rapidly, and soon amounted to the sum of a thousand pounds.

This unanimity, which was honourable and consoling to those Mallet left behind him, was troubled by the malevolence of Peltier, who, as soon as Mallet was dead, did not shrink from slandering the man who had enjoyed the confidence of Louis XVI., and he even represented both Mallet and his friends as more culpable than Collot d'Herbois and Marat. It was Lally who, lending his pen to the son of Mallet du Pan, eloquently resented these outrages, in the name of his friend's family.

But these attacks did not deceive those lofty-minded persons, who, both in England and France—and, in fact, in every place where Mallet's writings were known—confirmed the following judgment pronounced by Lally Tollendal on his friend :

" He was never either the writer of a party or a government; he neither wished to offend or to flatter any one ; he took less umbrage at the accusations of which he was the object, than at the levity of character or fatal passions which engendered them. During the three years of the first Assembly, his analysis of the debates was read throughout Europe as a model of argument, as enlightened as it was impartial; for, while he intrepidly attacked the phalanx of factious members, he concealed neither the faults nor the extravagances of their adversaries. Though he detested the reigning mania for innovations, he neither worshipped abuses nor hated reforms ; and, though he did not hold that the people ought to be without restraint, at the same time he did not admit that they ought to be without rights. It was a touching spectacle for honest people of every country to see a Protestant writer peal forth his thunder in France against the persecution of the priests and the spoliation of the churches, and to behold a republican struggling against the subversion of monarchy, defending the clergy and the oppressed nobility, and incessantly contrasting the true doctrine of liberty and of general welfare with the sophistry and license of faction. How true, indeed, is it, that probity

H H 2

and intelligence suffice to make us consider as sacred
everything which ought to be so, without forcing virtue to
pass beneath the yoke of shame !

" The article he published in 1793, on the causes,
means, and power of the revolution, excited the most
insane clamours ; but all people of judgment viewed it in a
different light, and posterior events confirmed the superiority
and accuracy of his penetration. It may be said that,
since the above-named epoch to the day of his death, all
Monsieur Mallet du Pan's labours were directed to the
carrying on of a social war, in order to arrive speedily at a
liberal peace.   The tranquillity of Europe, the happiness of
France, together with that of all other nations, a return to
the great principles of order, of safety, of property, and of
liberty, occupied all his thoughts ; and had not his health
grown gradually weaker, he would every day have become more and more adequate to the treating of his
subject.

" We do not pretend to say that, surrounded as he was
by so many storms, and moving in so varied a circle of
scenes, and of active and divided occupations, mistakes
never happened to Monsieur Mallet du Pan, while under
the influence of indignation, which was so much the
greater, as the motive of it was the more pure ; but we do
say, that no one deceived himself less than he ; and, above
all, that no one desired less than he to deceive others."

This eloquent portrait is in no way overdrawn : Lally's
friendship has not exaggerated a single feature of it. Such
was indeed the character of the publicist, whom the French
Revolution had brought into notice ; and we are here
entitled to add, such it had ever been, from the very com-

mencement of his career as a political writer, and long
before the course of events had raised before him the stage
of the grand struggle.   Hatred of oppression and arbitrary
power in any form is, we think, the characteristic feature of
his writings and his life; it is visible throughout the
whole of these Memoirs; and, in spite of the severity of his
opinions and style, this virtue has never been denied him
by his political adversaries.   The personal impressions of
Mallet du Pan on the disastrous scenes of the revolution,
may have sometimes given a colour of partiality to his
pen; but they never reconciled him to despotism and the
abuses of monarchy.   In his youth, he was seen to devote
himself, with the ardour of his age, to the cause of an
oppressed minority; but, later in life, impelled by no
motive of personal ambition, he raised his voice against the
acts of resentment and injustice of which his former colleagues were guilty on arriving at power.   Naturally
grave and religious, he defends Voltaire from the calumnious exaggerations which pursue his memory.   When
he was subject at Paris to the strictest supervision of the
official censure, and was constantly thwarted in the expression of his opinions, and had never participated in the
favours granted by the Court to men of letters, he sacrificed his repose and fortune to defend the principles and
remains of monarchy.   On being expelled from his country
by an act directly opposed to the right of nations, which
act had been dictated to the Helvetic Confederation by
Bonaparte's personal resentment, he is the first writer
who, in 1799, in a foreign country, where such opinions
were not popular, renders justice to the good resulting
from the Consulate, and to the conciliatory views the ad-

ministrative talent and genius of the man who had put an
end to the revolutionary form of government.

Mallet du Pan, whom these Memoirs represent as being
attached to such stern maxims, who was so vehement and
nearly passionate in the discussion of those great principles of which he had embraced the causes, was the most
tender and indulgent man to his family, and the most
faithful and devoted friend to those who were intimate
with him : it is no wonder, therefore, that his memory is
so religiously cherished by all who belonged to him.

We have said nothing of Mallet du Pan's personal
appearance. The fine portrait engraved by Heath, after
Rigaud, represents him to us in the last year of his life,
when illness had already sunk his features, and weakened
the expression of his face. Yet, it is the same man as the
one depicted in these Memoirs—or rather in his own
writings—and whom the pious hand of his daughter thus
sketches : " Mallet's person was good, his face noble,
expressive, and full of intellect, and his air grave and imposing. He joined gaiety to observation, and spoke
without preparation, and with great facility. Music and
walking were his usual amusements. He was an enthusiastic admirer of the beauties of Nature, and indulged his
passion so long as his strength allowed him : the garden
of the house where he died was a pleasure to him up to
the last moment of his life."

HISTORICAL, POLITICAL,

AND

LITERARY FRAGMENTS.

(TAKEN FROM THE MANUSCRIPT COLLECTIONS OF MALLET DU PAN.)

IT has been seen that it was Mallet du Pan's custom to note down, under the name of " Miscellaneous," his historical observations, anecdotes, scraps of information, extracts from his readings, and sometimes his own thoughts. The most important of these notes have already appeared in these Memoirs ; but a certain number of them could not find room there : of these latter the most instructive and interesting have been taken to be introduced here. Several of the particularities they serve to illustrate have perhaps already appeared elsewhere ; some are merely fragments of readings and conversations, such as are found in the " Mélanges" of Madame Necker ; but good sense and truth enjoy the privilege of passing for new more than once ; we have not scrupled, therefore, to collect in this sort of *Ana* everything which, without appearing trite, seemed to possess some worth, either as containing thought or representing the history of events, customs,

and literature of the last century.   Though these notes
have been traced rapidly, and with negligence, they are not
without character ; in fact, the " Miscellaneous Papers" of
Mallet du Pan may be considered, for many causes, as
a proper Appendix to the Memoirs which have just been
read.

These notes have been arranged in the same order they
occupy in the papers of Mallet, with the exception that
the observations relating to the revolution have been
placed together, and according to the order of their dates,
as far as it was possible to do so.

1.

At the beginning of the last war between Russia and
Sweden, the Empress composed a burlesque tragedy, in
which the King of Sweden was the hero.   This piece, in
which Gustavus was grossly insulted, was played   at
Catherine's private theatre in the country.   Suddenly, it
was announced that the King of Sweden had landed in the
Gulf of Finland, and that he was about to enter Cronstadt.
The Empress, greatly disconcerted, stopped the play, gave
her orders and arranged the plan of corruption which we
saw tried on the traitors of the Swedish army and fleet.
M. Foscari, the Venetian Ambassador at Petersburg, told this
anecdote to Sir John Macpherson, from whom I heard it.

When the Abbé Delille was at Ferney, he read Voltaire
a few passages of his poem of " Les Jardins," and drew Voltaire's attention to the parallel between the garden of Eden

and modern gardens. Voltaire began crying out against the garden of Eden. "Oh! yes," said the Abbé Delille to him, "your prejudices against the gardener are known." The Abbé maintained that the poetry of the Hebrews was superior to every known lyrical work; and he quoted, among others, the "Super flumina Babylonis." "These rascals," said Voltaire, "complain of the Babylonians, to whom they owe everything. When they came to Babylon, not one of them knew how to read."

Voltaire has introduced sectarianism, and enrolment in letters, and, by so doing, has caused great harm.

During the war of 1778, the English captured a French vessel in which there were several cases addressed to M. Buffon, and others addressed to the King of France. The English Admiralty forwarded M. Buffon his cases, with a polite letter, and confiscated those of the King.

When M. Necker was induced to join the ministry of M. de Maurepas, as President of the Council of Finance, M. Dubucq said to him : "you will perish by the law of Moses, which says : 'Thou shalt not yoke the ox and the ass together.'"

A letter having been read to M. de Sartine about the Bay (*la baie*) of Honduras, an attack on which was meditated, he asked where this abbey (*abbaye*) was, as he did not know it. Hereupon M. de Maurepas said : "Say nothing more about bays to M. de Sartine; he takes them for abbeys, and asks for them for his relations." He did not know what the date of the Hegira was. M. de Choiseul was unacquainted with the situation of Senegal.

The Baron de Breteuil, being put out of all patience by

some person or other, said to him : " If there were three men like you in France, I would quit the ministry." " If your Excellency will wait an instant," replied the person addressed, " I will go and fetch the other two."

D'Alembert pretends the King of Prussia has written to him as follows : " I do not revenge my own insults, but I do those of my friends. If you like, I will undertake to carry off Linguet and confine him at Spandau."

Sédaine was a very honest man. His mother lived at Montbard, in a convent of which Monsieur de Buffon's sister was the Superior : he was a stone-cutter's apprentice at Paris, and earned thirty or forty sous a day, out of which he saved enough to send his mother a few louis every year.

Fréron wrote a play against Voltaire. He presented it to Monsieur de Sartine, who said to him : " Give over ; two foolish things were committed by allowing ' L'Ecossaise ' and ' Les Philosophes ' to appear." " Well then, commit a third one, and we shall all be satisfied."

Helvetius presented his book " De l'Esprit " to the Queen, who was reading it with pleasure, when some one made her remark the danger of such a book. Helvetius was obliged to resign his appointment, and Servier the censor lost his.

A titled lounger was one day at Madame de M * * * 's with the Abbé de Mably. He had just returned from Versailles, and in his enthusiasm he was praising the Court and royal family ; he said that his heart was French, and that he loved his King, &c. The Abbé, who had been greatly annoyed by this idle talk, rose and said : " What the devil have you to do, Sir, with loving the King? He does not love you: Kings love no one. Your ideas, Sir, are suited to the pace of the snail."

After the suppression of the Jesuits, Louis XV. was informed that the Dauphin harboured fathers of that order in his house, and that they held meetings there. Louis XV. had always had some suspicions about them since their dissolution; he gave orders to his attendants to inform him whenever the Dauphin was with any of them in his house.

One day, he was told the fathers were there; but as the Dauphin was informed of the King's visit, the meeting dispersed, and when Louis XV. entered, he only found his son. He acquainted the Dauphin with the object of his visit, and complained of his conduct. The Dauphin tried to justify himself, spoke of his devoted attachment to the society, and said that he placed such confidence in them, that if they were to tell him to descend from the throne, he would do it. "But what," said the King, "if they were to order you to ascend it!" The Dauphin fell back into a chair.

Voltaire was about to purchase a house for the remainder of his life of M. de Villarçeaux; he went to see him at M. Lecouteulx de Molé, where he was supping. While ascending the stairs, he leaned on the Abbé Delille. "Yours is not a heavy weight," said the Abbé, "for a man who is going to buy a house for the remainder of his life." "You are a sly dog," answered Voltaire, "it is not a house, but a tomb, that I am about to buy."

J. J. Rousseau said to M. Romilly: "I cannot drink

wine more than once a day ; my means do not allow me to take any at dinner and supper."

He had written a complete sequel to " Emile," which he burnt in England with his other papers. He was so frightened, that he set out without any money, and paid for post-horses, etc., on the road, with bits of his plate which he had broken up into fragments.

Rousseau was truly persecuted, even by the philosophers. They have injured all those who defended him. They refused to give M. Blin de Saint-Maur the prize for his epistle on Racine. Since M. Roucher praised him, he also has been abandoned by them, and they have brought his poem into discredit.

M. de Bouffon said, talking of Montesquieu's too brief style, that " The President was nearly blind, and so quiet that, for the most part, he forgot what he wished to dictate, so that he was obliged to confine himself to the smallest possible space."

J. J. Rousseau disclosed, one day, to M. Ducis, the precarious and painful state of his affairs, and begged him to use his interest in obtaining some asylum from the government for him, where he could find a shelter, tranquillity, and a little comfort. M. Ducis spoke about him to M. de Roquelaure, Bishop of Senlis. The Bishop, who was moved, offered Rousseau an agreeable home at Senlis, at his country-house, with everything he required. Rousseau at first accepted, but said, the next day, to M. Ducis : " No, my dear Ducis, this will not suit me. M. de Roquelaure is a prelate, and at the head of the clergy ; they would blame him for having offered me an asylum.' Ducis then applied to M. d'Angevilliers, who proposed Meudon, which was uninhabited at that time. Rousseau refused this offer also.

While the whole congregation were on their knees in the church of Saint Mark, an Englishman remained standing in the middle of the benediction. A senator, who perceived him, having in vain sent him word to kneel down, at last went himself to the Englishman, who said he objected to do so, because he did not believe in transubstantiation. "Ed anchè io," replied the senator with animation, "però ginocchione, o fuor di chiesa!"

The Chevalier d'Aumont, Chargé d'Affaires at Dresden, in the absence of Count de Broglie, under Augustus III., had frequent interviews with the ministers, and among others with Count de Waldstorff, a man possessed of wit and information under a rough exterior. One day, conversing with the Chevalier on the subject of his travels, and making remarks on Italy, England, and Spain, he said not a word about France. The Chevalier having noticed this: "Oh, France:" observed the Count, "it is said in our gospel, that when God created the earth, and had united all France in one empire, the remark was made that it would swallow up all the other states. He answered that his immutable will could not be changed, and that France should remain as it was, but that, by way of compensation, all its inhabitants should have their heads turned."

Dr. Johnson most cordially hated Hume and his opinions. "What a man!" said he, "who does his best to persuade his friend, that he has by his side a stone just fit to break his head."

He would never consent to see the Abbé Raynal when the latter was in England.

In his opinion, the happiest life was that of a man of business enjoying intervals of literary recreation, and he considered no one happy or virtuous whose time was not wholly occupied.

Johnson observed of Mrs. Siddons, that she was one of the small number of persons who had withstood the corruption of the two greatest corrupters in the world, money and love of fame.

By Johnson's own avowal, he had often in his youth wandered all night in Grosvenor Square, till four o'clock in the morning, with Richard Savage; reforming the world, dethroning princes, establishing new forms of governments, giving laws to various states. When quite tired out, the legislators went to refresh on four pence halfpenny, the whole contents of their purse.

He had been introduced to Lord Chesterfield, who became his patron. This connexion was not congenial. One day, my lord being engaged, made Johnson wait an hour in the ante-chamber. At last, Johnson saw Cibber, the actor, come out of Lord Chesterfield's study. He instantly left the house indignantly, and never set his foot in it again. Lord Chesterfield used to say that the highest commendation he could bestow on the Doctor, was to consider him in the light of a respectable Hottentot.

The Bishop of Verdun, Nicolaï, chief almoner of the late Dauphiness de Saxe, was proud, ardent and ambitious. "You ring the alarm bell," said the minister one day. "Yes, Sir, when you are setting everything on fire."

Queen Anne had interceded with Louis XIV. in favour of some protestant ministers, who had been sent to the galleys, and claimed them as her brethren. The French Ambassador was commissioned by Louis XIV. to tell her, that he could make no other reply to her request than such as the Queen would return if the King were to ask her for the criminals confined in Newgate. "The criminals of Newgate, Sir," replied the Queen, "oh! I am quite ready to send them to your master, if he claims them as his brethren."

The despatches of ambassadors are generally very carelessly drawn up. They touch lightly on the most important points, omit what is essential, leave out dates, take one family for another, put wrong names, &c.

A councillor of the Parliament of Toulouse observed to the Duke d'Ayen, in reference to the sentence on Calas, that the best horse was liable to shy. "Yes; but what do you say to a whole stud doing so!" retorted the Duke.

At the breaking out of the war, M. de Sartines had made the King a set of marine models. Louis XVI. wanted to know all the odd names, and set about studying them: top gallant masts, brails, rigging, blocks, &c. His valet told him one day that such words quite stunned him: "Sire, Louis XIV. knew nothing about blocks and cables, and his fleets were everywhere triumphant."

Louis XV's valet having forgotten to put on the King's cravat, he put it on himself. The valet returned, looking confused. The King took off his cravat and said to him: "Since you have a mania for putting on a cravat, put it on."

Voltaire being in London with Bolingbroke, Pope, Swift, Dr. Young, &c., poured forth a torrent of impious, but witty jokes.   Young indignantly interrupted him with the couplet :

> "You are so witty, profligate, and thin,
> You look like Milton with his Death and Sin."

Dorat's letters abound in touches of nature.

Latour was taking Louis XV.'s portrait.   He was a gossip, and rudely familiar ; while painting away he talked on politics, and had the impudence to say to the King :— " Well, Sire, so we have no longer a marine ?"   "And Vernet ?" coldly replied his Majesty.

Piron, meeting the procession of the Host one day, took off his hat.   " What, Piron," said some one, " you take off your hat to Him ?"   " Oh," replied he, " we bow, but we are not on speaking terms."

It was Madame de Boufflers who requested Hume to take Rousseau to London : she was his special protectress, and had recommended him to the Princes of Luxembourg and Conti.   After the affair with Hume, he wrote her an insulting letter.   " I think he has lost his senses," said Madame de Boufflers ; " I would rather think him mad than ungrateful."

One of his friends informing him of the death of Louis XV., he exclaimed : " Oh ! heavens, how sorry I am ?" " Why ? you did not know him."   "Ah!" replied Rousseau, " he shared in the hatred the nation has sworn against me; now I am left to bear it alone."

Rousseau enjoyed till 1771 a pension of a hundred louis, assigned him by the King of England.   He having declined it at first, Hume made a second application in his favour, without his knowledge, succeeded, and kept his own counsel. M. Dutens was commissioned to make him the offer, which Rousseau accepted. In 1771, he took it into his head that he would not have had it, if it had been known how ill he had spoken of the English ; accordingly he wrote to the Earl of Rochfort, saying that he thought it right to let him know that he had spoken so and so of the English ; that if this was not thought a sufficient reason for depriving him of the pension, he would continue to accept it, but that he should consider silence as a proof that it was withdrawn, and would beg to decline it. The Minister, occupied with other affairs, set him down as a madman, never sent him any answer, and the pension was refused, and put an end to.

Winter of 1784.—Some wealthy ladies have the insolence to heat their staircases and wardrobes : this is an outrageous waste of wood. M. Beaujon, at the time of the death, had eight hundred *cordes* in his cellars. The Prince de Beauveau, on the contrary, extinguished all his servants' fires, and made them all warm themselves at a great brasier. The Prince de Condé got his wood from Saint-Maur.

Fifty thousand loads is the rate of consumption of a fortnight in a severe winter.

The Chevalier de Boufflers said in a company where the merits of M. de Richelieu were discussed : " He is like a hackney-coach on the stand during a storm : the only one, and therefore engaged."

M. de Valons, ambassador from France to Belgium, was one day at the play with the King of Prussia. The curtain, in the act of being dropped, remained suspended midway, so that nothing was seen but the actors' legs. " I can fancy," said the King to M. de Valons, " that is a picture of the Councils of Versailles." "Possibly," replied the minister, "your Majesty knows by experience that legs have their value."

At one of Louis XV.'s suppers, dangerous political questions were started. The King kept his temper for some time, and said at last, striking with his doubled fists upon the table : " Silence ! the King is here,"—the usher's words when the King enters.

Louis XV. had his own private purse to ensure some resources in case of a general subversion. M. de Bertin was intrusted with the negotiation or investment of this money ; he placed some in one of his loans—" M. Bertin," said the King to him, " is this loan quite safe ?"

Voltaire argued very ill in saying : " It was not Montaigne, or Spinosa, or Hobbes, or Collins, or Woollaston, or Diderot, who threw the brand of discord into their country ; but the theologians, who were ambitious of becoming heads of sects, and soon leader of parties. Let the philosophers only be authorized by the laws of the state to hold their opinions up to adoration, let them have a share in power, and we shall see whether they will not surpass the theologians."

Palissot wrote to Voltaire : " One must not suppose the Capitol in danger whenever the geese cackle."

Montesquieu's son, the Baron de Secondat, possesses two folios written throughout in the hand of the President, with this title on the back : " Esprit Français." It is a collection of songs selected by himself.

Gresset had said that Rousseau was a bear. When the latter passed through Amiens, Gresset called on him, and invited him to visit him. Jean-Jacques answered in mono-syllables, and concluded by saying: " Confess, Sir, that it is easier to make a parrot speak than a bear."

Young Charles Lennox, son of Lord George Lennox, and nephew of the Duke of Richmond, being in a club together with the Prince of Wales and other members of the opposition, was invited by one of his friends to drink a bumper to the health of Fox. He hesitated, but finally consented. When he had done so, he invited his friend, as is usual, to drink the health he should propose, and he gave that of Pitt. The Prince of Wales rose in a rage, told him he was an impertinent fellow to dare propose the health of a rascal like Pitt in his presence, and threatened to strike him. Mr. Lennox rose also : " Don't come near me," he said, " for, if you touch me, I shall kill you." The company interfered to stop the quarrel. The King has just given this brave young man a company in the guards, in the regiment of the Duke of York himself, who was furious.

When the economists assembled, the bust of Quesnay was in the room, and every one bowed in passing it. They starved the provinces in 1771, 1772, and 1773, mystified M. Turgot and France ; never took the least account of political laws in their system ; economic riddle-mongers. Fréville, one of their mouth-pieces, an atheist, and preacher of atheism in the cafés. The Abbé Saury took it into his head to write that people went mad when in a state of starvation. M. Turgot put him into the Bastile. Those two follies of law and " economism" desolated the first, the beginning, the second, the end of Louis XV's reign. It was the economists who gave rise to the trade in grain, carried on by that King. Never were the most fanatical pretenders to inspiration more absurd. They sallied forth like Mahomet, and only lacked his sabre, and his courage. Diderot, who was no friend to them, said that, like doctors, they operated on a dead body. They were near getting into a quarrel with the philosophers, one of them having had the hardihood to say that geometers were deficient in genius.

M. de Buffon prefers Milton to all other epic poets. He has his hair curled with irons every day, and at a less advanced age had it twice a day.

He told us that, being once in company with M. de Trudaine and M. Turgot, the former, the only learned Minister we have had for a long time past, wished to impress M. Turgot with the danger of the free export of grain, the necessity of having magazines, &c., &c. Getting from argument to argument, M. Trudaine said to M. Turgot : " You would run the risk of starving the present generation." " So much the better," replied he, " if we are certain of ensuring the happiness of future generations."

The court will not hear of M. de Condorcet's admission into the Academy, because he is an atheist. One day some expressions of Voltaire in favour of a divinity were mentioned to Diderot. " Pooh !" replied he, " let me hear no more of that bigot."

The Abbé Maury, the first living preacher, has ceased to preach at Versailles, where his boldness was not relished. The King said : " That preacher displeases me."

The Marquis de Chauvelin, whilst playing with the

King, was seized with apoplexy. Some one exclaimed: " M. de Chauvelin is ill !" The King turned round, and said : " He is dead : remove him. Spades," &c.

After the death of Madame de Pompadour, her remains were removed to her mansion. The body being gone, the King, half-an-hour afterwards, pulled out his watch, and said : " If they went fast, they must have arrived."

A duplicate of our Saviour's crown of thorns had been given to M. de Vergennes, at Constantinople. He sold it for fifty thousand crowns to the brothers of a Greek monastery.

Frederick II., King of Prussia, said of the inflexible Beaumont, Archbishop of Paris : " He is the only general who never retreated." This prelate, after the ceremonies and processions on the occasion of the jubilee, which had made a great impression on the people, said to M. de Monthyon : " This gains us fifty years over the philosophers."

When shops were erected about the Palais-Royal, the King inquired why the Duke of Orleans so rarely made his appearance at Versailles. " Sire," replied the Count d'Artois, " ever since my cousin has taken a shop, he only goes out on Sundays."

Buffon had a jacket made of whaleskin. De Lauraguais offered him two hundred louis for it. Buffon declined the offer, and asked him what he wanted to do with it. " Oh," said he, " I should like to make a cover for my chaise of it, it would look so singular, and handsome."

The two following lines in " Astarbé" were suppressed :

La terreur, aujourd'hui, veille aux palais des rois ;
L'amour, le doux amour, les gardait autrefois.

In another play the following line was suppressed; the actor, shewing a dagger, said :

. . . . . Tu vois
La resource du peuple et la leçon des rois.

Mirabeau, disputing with Rivarol on some literary question, went into a passion and exclaimed : " A fine authority you are indeed ! I request you to remember what a difference there is between our reputations." " Very true, Count," replied Rivarol, " though I should have hesitated to remind you of the fact."

The military hospitals in France afford instances of the most disgraceful abuses. Count de Muy, in the course of a tour of inspection in which he was engaged, arrived at Toulon, where the hospital was under the superintendence of M. de H. . ., still at the head of these same military hospitals. M. de Muy found one of the apartments which he proposed visiting, locked : he was informed that M. de H. had the key. His suspicions being excited by what he had seen in the hospital, he had the door broken open by six grenadiers, and found within thirty dead bodies whose burial had been deferred for the purpose of exacting payment for an extra week of the allowance assigned them by the King. Each patient costs the King eight or ten francs daily.——M. de Montbarey was deputed by M. Leclerc to make a tour with the same view : he discovered enormous abuses, furnished a plan by which to save at least five hundred thousand livres, introduced admirable regulations, and ended by being ousted, through the intrigues of the rogues he had unmasked.

Clavière paid a visit to Jean Jacques Rousseau at

Bourgoin, with letters of introduction from Mme. Deles-
sert. Without giving his name he presented the letter
to Rousseau, who, on seeing the name of Clavière,
recoiled and said, turning his back on him, that he wished
him good-night. Clavière begged to express the veneration he felt for him, and his regret that the representatives
had not had the power to be of service to him, &c.
" Sir," replied Rousseau, opening the door, " the only
favour I demand of you is to do me no harm," and turned
him out.

When the Czarina took possession of the Crimea, M. de
Vergennes wrote her word that " the King was determined
not to suffer her arms to pass the Dnieper." The Empress
replied : " The words ' determined not to suffer,' are not
suitable to the politeness of a King of France : as he will
find it impossible to enforce his commands, it is ridiculous
to announce them. My army will march."

Addressing himself to the Abbé Delille, Voltaire said,
pointing to Père Adam : " Look at Père Adam : he was a
Jesuit—you see him laugh at all my jokes about *l'infame*.
Well, I suspect, after all, the wretch is a Christian : what a
hypocrite."

When Pitt the elder (afterwards Lord Chatham) undertook the conquest of Canada, he asked General Wolfe to his
country house, and told him he had selected him. Wolfe
replied he would not undertake the commission unless he
had Lord Townshend as his colleague. " The King, George
II., detests him," said Pitt, " it is quite impossible—think
again." Wolfe persisted ; Pitt mentioned it to the council,
and it was resolved that he should have Townshend.
When the Secretary-at-war presented the commission of

Wolfe and Townshend to George II. that he might sign it, he went into a violent passion, and refused to do so. Pitt approached him, saying : " You must sign, Sire ; it is indispensable that you should : you must sign," and he signed. Townshend had caricatured him.

Adam Smith asked Hume whether he had read Walpole's Lives of the English Painters ? " No," said he, " he has written three volumes in octavo, and we have not had a single painter." Hume had a great deal of conversational talent ; he was gay and light, never profound. Smith was the reverse, and always enjoyed a reputation for strict probity.

The Abbé Galiani hearing of the expulsion of the Jesuits, who had left Spain and gone to Italy, said : " *Gens inimica mihi, Thyrrhænum navigat æquor.*"

He had a favourite and very dexterous monkey which unsealed his letters : Galiana called him " a member of the diplomatic body."

" Mme. du Deffand happened to be at the baths of Plombières with a president's wife, a pretty but very silly woman. One day, they were in the same room together, when the latter, who had been occupied in writing, quitted the apartment. Mme. du Deffand was tempted to look over the paper to see what she had said, and found it was a letter to her husband. That evening, in the family circle, the conversation chanced to fall on absent husbands, when Mme. du Deffand observed : " A certain fairy enables me to guess all the loving epithets that women lavish on their husbands." " I lay you would never guess mine," said the president's wife. " Perhaps I could, Madam ; I know some, very odd and difficult to guess.

I should not wonder if you called him, my dear Tampon."
"Well, I declare, that's it, Madam," said the lady, blushing, "I did call him my dear Tampon."

It is related of Mme. du Deffand, then blind, that, hearing a stupid man prose on for a length of time, she said: "Oh! for heaven's sake, have done reading; shut the book—it is too tiresome."

M. de Vergennes used to say, "that the next most contemptible thing to an author was a book."

Rousseau lodged in the house of Mr. Servan three weeks, and quarrelled with him every morning.

A handsome lady in Gotha, of high respectability, was on the verge of despair for the loss of an only daughter. Helvétius goes to see her, treats her to a string of wise sayings, and begs to suggest one source of consolation. The mourner looks at him weeping, and with an expression of mistrust. "Madam," says he, "have the first child that passes in the street killed, and you will think no more of your daughter."

After the battle of Zorndorf, a Dane, hearing that the King of Prussia had killed thirty thousand Russians in that engagement, observed: "No matter; it is so easy for God to make new Russians."

Danchet having to compliment the King in 1728, on the recovery of his health, had composed eight lines, and began spouting them before the King: "Prince, l'Europe entière à tes jours . . . à tes jours . . . à tes jours . . ." Here he stuck. Count de Charolais, who was present, said to the King: "Sire, M. Danchet is drinking your health." Danchet was dumbfoundered, and fell ill with mortification.

Count Vaudreuil had presented an important request

through the mediation of the Count d'Artois.   The affair dragged on ; he reminded the Prince of his desire in a letter, which he sent by his valet.   The Prince commanded his admission, and despatched him with this message. " Tell your master that he is a fool : was ever a Bourbon known to say, ' I will ?' "

Madame Geoffrin used to say that Madame Necker was not only hungered but famished for wit.

The Abbé Beauregard, in one of his sermons at Notre Dame, before the revolution, exclaimed in a prophetic tone: " These altars will be sullied, these pillars thrown down, these temples destroyed ; and the shameless Venus will in this sanctuary usurp the place of the holy mother of the living God !"   D'Alembert, on hearing him said : " It must be owned that these men die hard."

Piron said, in reference to the " Métromanie :" " It is a monster which devours all my other children."

The harangue of the quakers to James II. was admirable. " We are come to express our grief on the death of our good friend Charles, and our joy on your accession.   We have been told that you belong no more to the Anglican church than we do, which leads us to hope that you will grant us the same liberty that you grant to yourself."

After the return of Cardinal Mazarin, one of the Fron- deurs fell into his power, and sought to excuse himself for having joined that party.   " Yes, Sir," replied the Cardinal, " I understand you.   There is no cause so bad as not to have its apologists.   When Judas betrayed our Saviour, he reasoned thus : ' He is either God or an imposter ; if he is God, he can deliver himself ; if an imposter, I do well to betray him.' "

Philip IV., King of Spain, was present at a play (a burlesque farce) on the death of Gustavus Adolphus, the representation of which lasted twelve days.

M. de Paw wrote to the King of Prussia that the ring of Saturn had been lost. This overturned all the King's notions, his arrangement of the great whole, the work of nature: he was beginning to believe in God. When the ring was found again, he returned to his atheism.

On the 23rd, I dined with good old La Place. He is eighty-two years of age: his memory, his presence of mind, his liveliness, his gaiety, are astonishing. He over-flows with anecdote, and has more in his head than he has printed. He told me that he had an uncle, the captain of a vessel, who, seeing him studying and philosophizing, said: " You are an ass for all your studies. I never read any-thing but a volume of Moréri, which you lent me. Well ! I am happier than you. Take it into your head to reason, and you will never be happy." When he died, he told La Place that he was quite easy, and that God was too good a fellow to damn him.

Favier passed for the first journalist in France. His morals were very loose. He wrote a quantity of reports on foreign affairs. " If not well paid for them," he would say to the minister: " I warn you that I will proclaim in cafés, society, and so on, that such a report is mine, and that the minister stole it from me."

He was tall, stout, strong, sarcastic. M. de Choiseul, after his retirement, having complained to Favier that a memorial was attributed to him against the Archbishop of Cambray, brother to the Duke, and in which the Duke was much abused, Favier replied : " M. le Duc, I don't operate on dead bodies."

1774.—M. de Voltaire told me that Queen Anne of Austria had been delivered of the Iron Mask, while Madame de Beauvais was with her at Saint-Germain. He was, according to this account, an elder brother of Louis XIV. M. de Caumartin told M. de N. . . . . that Mazarin, when on his death-bed, had confessed as much to Louis XIV., and that the imprisonment of the Iron Mask dated from that time.

1791.—All the hypotheses hitherto published about this famous prisoner appear to be mere fables. The Chevalier de Taulés, a *ci-devant employé* in the Ministry of Foreign Affairs, read to me, in 1791, a report in evidence which gives the key to this anecdote. He got the first notion of it from a shabby old book bought on the quay, the " Mémoires du Marquis de Bonnac pendant son Ambassade à la Porte." Subsequently, he sought out further facts and proofs among the records of the foreign office, and found them in the official despatches of the period, as well as in those of Louis XIV. himself.

The following is the statement of the " Mémoire," and of the passage in Bonnac's " Memoirs," (published in 1724.)

" Avedik, patriarch of the Armenians chismatics, was a mortal enemy to the Catholics and the Jesuits, and had inflicted the cruellest persecutions on the Armenian Catholics. By dint of money, the Jesuits obtained from the divan his exile to Chio. Fathers Braconnier and Torillon, Jesuits, who were on the spot, thought of gaining over the officer who had to transport Avedik to Chio. A French boat was taken round to that isle, carried off Avedik, and conveyed him to France, to the islands Saint-Marguerite, when he was transferred to the Bastile in 1698.

" This took place at the commencement of this year 1698 ; the transfer to the Bastile, in the month of September of the same year.

" Avedik having disappeared, the Armenians turned upon the officer ; the grand vizier subjected him to the torture : he confessed everything. The French Consul at Chio, also arrested and interrogated, defended himself better, and denied all. M. de Féréol, French Ambassador to the Porte at this epoch, was threatened and underwent numberless expostulations, annoyances, and demands. The Porte made a formal reclamation for Avedik, with energy, and on several occasions ; the French Government, kept in subjection by the Jesuits, constantly denied any knowledge of the circumstances connected with the disappearance.

" The court, subservient to the society, and embarrassed by a war with half Europe, was afraid to break with the Porte ; and, apprehensive that the latter might commence hostilities, hushed the matter up as much as possible, in order to efface the memory of this detention. The Porte did not forget it till about 1710.

" The name of *Mar-Kialy*, under which the man with the iron mask was buried at Saint-Paul, is composed of two words : *Mar*, which means holy, is applied in the Levant to the patriarch of the Armenians, and *Kialy* is a diminutive of *Michael* in Armenian. In fact, Avedik was called Michael.

"The choice was left him of cutting off his beard, or wearing a mask ; he preferred the latter : this peculiarity and his tawny complexion would have made him be recognized for a Levantine, as well as his accent and language.

"The virtuous Abbé de Nolhac, massacred at Avignon by Jourdan, and formerly rector of the noviciate of the Jesuits at Toulouse, told the Chevalier de Taulès, that Father Layre, ninety years old, had said to him at that time, and with reference to the discussions about the masked prisoner, which occupied the public attention about 1750 : 'That this fact was very far from being worth the trouble which was taken to discover it ; that it was of no interest to any one in France, and that it was only connected with the missions of the Jesuits in the Levant.' "

Another Jesuit had said the same to Duclos.

Father Griffet had been charged by his society and the court, to lead the public astray by false tales and conjectures, in order to defeat inquiry. This he has done.

II.

A popular revolution is frightful and unlimited, when the people are attached to principles and not to men. When they yield submission to Calvin, Luther, Mahomet, and Cromwell, they will never go further than their chiefs, whose doctrine will be theirs ; but if you abandon them to opinions, which they conceive, interpret, extend, apply in a thousand ways, and always loosely, all is lost: the people must be led by sentiments, and not by ideas.

Two revolutions have taken place, the one of a moral character in minds which it has penetrated with truths and semi-truths, the foundation of which will remain; the other, criminal and barbarous, will be the more easy of extirpation, when once the power has fallen from its hands.

Diderot had said: "with a single false idea one may become barbarous." The revolution has furnished a thousand instances of the correctness of this maxim; souls of sensibility, honourable characters have been perverted by errors of the mind, and impelled to the last point of ferocity. They commence by being senseless, they finish by being atrocious.

The revolution is incessantly talked about. The necessity for government is far more urgent: it is government which sways the destiny of the people, and which secures true liberty by the maintenance of the laws.

"Every constitution which requires in its chief more than a moderate portion of intelligence, experience, and virtue, does not deserve to be regarded as established." 'An Essay on the Constitution of England,' by Ramsay.

It is very remarkable to hear the declaimer, Pastoret, make common-place observations, and sympathize with descendants of religionists, whilst an immense number of living Frenchmen are left to suffer, and to be persecuted in the most horrible manner. The religionists were emigrants who fought against the government of their country

in the war of the succession, and who inundated Europe
with libels against the government of their country.   It is
curious to see them at this time protected by the tyrants
of the political emigrants, by those who have proscribed and
pillaged, by those who shoot them.   The comparison of
the religious and political emigrants is just in all points.

Whilst the throne is vacant, all who are influenced by
unrestrained ambition covet and rush at it ; under the
empire of a false sovereignty there are no chimerical projects.   The cowards who reject the King from a fear of
civil war, are preparing the very materials for it.   It is
because they foolishly wish for repose and the constitution, that they will have neither repose nor the constitution.

The national character seems to impel the Frenchman
to recognize as superior only him who was never his
equal.

Some one has justly remarked that leagues in their
plans resemble the "Avare" of Molière, and say as he
did : " I give one and keep three."

Fontenelle said : " In time of war they speak of another
equilibrium of Europe.   There is another equilibrium as
efficacious at least, and as much adapted to preserve
every power—it is the equilibrium of follies."

Great conquests, the establishment of new and extensive sovereignties were constantly preceded and followed
by great religious revolutions, or new political systems ;
but French revolutions are followed by a blank in matters
of religion, and by metaphysical abstractions in politics.

Louis XVI. restored to France her national assemblies.
The first of these assemblies deprived him of his autho-

rity; the second of his liberty, and the third of his life.

The roués of the revolution have sprung from the roués of the boudoir.

Malouet writing to me, in 1791, set down a just and profound thought. "We who reason justly, hardly ever calculate with precision on any event, because the actions of men have very little correspondence with good reasoning. If you notice closely a clever and audacious criminal, you prejudge his conduct according to all the rules of cleverness and audacity—not at all; there is also to be found folly and inconsistency. So it is with the fools and cowards: they have enlightened moments and fits of courage."

Mably, one of the most ardent harbingers of the revolution, could not bear to see the government making reforms and effecting good. "So much the worse," he said, " if they do any good; that will support for some time the old machine, which must be overthrown."

I have spoken previously (see the Memoirs, vol. I, p. 249), of the step which was taken on the 29th of September, 1789, by Messieurs the Bishop of Langres, Malouet and Redon, who were deputed to M. de Montmorin by a great number of their colleagues, in order to make known to the government the projects meditated by Versailles, and to solicit the departure of the King, and the meeting of the majority of the deputies in another place. M. de Montmorin brought the subject before the council, which deliberated on it, and after long debates, the party of weakness prevailed. During the deliberation, the King, who was present, fell asleep and snored for half an hour.

Lord Robert Fitzgerald affirmed to Mounier, (in October, 1794) that during his mission to Paris of 1789 and 1790, he had never received nor delivered a farthing from his government to serve the Revolution.

M. Waker, of Bath, who was consulted in 1790, at Paris, by the Constitutionalists, and had given them a plan with regard to juries, replied to the Committee of Constitution, when his advice was asked about the constitution: "Messieurs, there remains much to do, much to do over again, and much to undo. You have inserted too many republican principles for a monarchy, and also too much monarchy for a republic."

One day he represented to Baumetz, that they should give the King the right of pardoning: "Oh!" replied Beaumetz, "Do not speak to us about the King—he is done for."

It was M. de Staël who said of La Fayette and Bailly, after the sack of the Hotel de Castries: "These gentlemen resemble the rainbow—they always come after the storm."

Mr. Burke made his political profession to Cazalès, by saying to him: "I like kings little enough, and I detest the people."

Old Madame de Mackau said to the Baron de Gilliers, in 1790, that ten years previously, the King, entering the Queen's apartment one morning, when Madame de Mackau was present, said that he had been tormented by a frightful dream, that he had thought he was carried off from Versailles, and put to death on a scaffold. "I fear," added he, "for this monarchy; it will perish by my excess of goodness."

The Abbé Delille said to the Lameths and to Barnave,

who were talking with him, in 1791, about their desire to strengthen royalty : " Ah ! I understand : you resemble the giant of Ariosto, running after his head.   In this head was a hair, which his enemy wished to have ; he resolved to cut off the head in order to obtain it.   Well, messieurs, the abuse was that hair !"

He also said to them : " You put me in mind of the history of a very simple Sicilian, to whom it had just been told that the Viceroy was dead.   Ah ! my God ! said he, the Viceroy is dead.   Ah ! my God ! what a misfortune ! What is to become of us ?   The next day he heard further news, still more distressing.   Eh ! what ! the Arch-bishop is dead !   He sinks into despair, regards himself as lost, and sees no more safety for Sicily.   At last, on the third day, the death of the Pope is announced.   Oh ! once more he grows pale, his arms fall, he loses his speech, goes to bed, draws his curtains, closes his shutters, and awaits the end of the world.   At the end of twenty-four hours, he hears the noise of a vermicelli-mill : he thinks he is mistaken——he listens attentively.   What ! says he, the Viceroy is dead, the Archbishop is dead, the Pope is dead, and they are making vermicelli ! that is impossible.   In order to assure himself, he opens his curtains and shutters a little, looks into the street, sees carriages passing as usual, people coming to purchase as usual also at a shopkeeper's his neighbour.   Then he reflects, and ends by saying : ' After all, it may really be possible that those persons who have just died were not necessary things.' "

D'André has acknowledged to me that the Constitu-tionalists never had any plan——that they lived from day to day, and from motions to motions.   They met in com-

K K 2

mittee, at the Duke de La Rochefoucald's.   La Fayette,
D'André, Chapelier, the Bishop of Autun, Emery, Beaumetz, Crillon, Liancourt, Montmorency, Toulongeon,
formed this committee.   Chapelier, at the end of a quarter of an hour, rose and went to a m . . . . . .   The Bishop
of Autun fell asleep : they never came to any resolution ;
they were jealous of the power of La Fayette, regarding
him almost as an imbecile, who knew nothing but bowing
to the National Guard.

The cabal of Lameth, Duport, Barnave and La Borde
was more compact and systematic.   Its only aim was to
remain in the ascendant.

At the affair of Mons, the French officers and soldiers of artillery fired in the air.   This goodwill saved
Beaulieu.

Dumas, of the Legislative Assembly, told me that,
having resumed his seat for some days in the Assembly,
towards the end of August, and being then president of
the military committee, he found the Girondists in consternation at the progresses of the Prussians.   Brissot,
Kersaint, and others invited him to attend the committee.
There they asked him for maps with full details of the
course of the Aisne, where the enemy was : he sent to
the war-depôt for them.   He told them, with the map
before their eyes, that the affair of Croix-aux-Boix was
decisive ; that Dumouriez, having allowed this most important post to slip from his hands, which he ought to
have defended personally, he found himself cut off from
Paris by the Prussian army, which would force him, by
two manœuvres, to throw himself into the Barrois ; that
the capital could then no longer be defended, and that in

four marches the hostile videttes would be at the gates ; that nothing was to be hoped from the departments of the north, which, if they were well treated, would second the enemy. The intimidated faction fell back on the design of abandoning Paris, passing the Loire, carrying off the King, and making a winter campaign.

The Cardinal de La Rochefoucauld, the Abbé de Pradt, and other emigrant ecclesiastics, have been to Maestricht to see the French prisoners, to console them, and to take them money, linen and succour. Among those unfortunate men, mostly impaired by debauchery, a malignant fever was raging, which carried off the Abbé Fontan, who had escaped from the Carmelites and found safety at Maestricht, and who tended the prisoners with zeal and assiduity. Many of these captives were repentant ; others said they had enlisted without knowing what they were doing, or from misery ; others again were thoroughly perverted. The Abbé de Pradt, having asked a wounded man of the latter party how he could continue serving since the death of the King? " F...., Monsieur," replied he, " why did he fire on us, on the 10th of August ?"

September, 1793.—Drouet of Sainte-Menehould, taken when leaving Maubeuge with eighty dragoons, arrived in chains at Brussels, on Sunday the 6th of October. Several persons have been to see him at the old Hôtel de Finances, in which he is imprisoned. Encountered by a detachment of Austrian cavalry, his escort was dispersed ; he escaped, as best he could across the country ; his horse fell into a ditch and bruised his thigh : he rose again, and being pursued in ploughed land, the horse fell once more into a furrow. Drouet lay flat on the ground ;

a party of Blanckenstein hussars discovered and took him.
He replied to M. de Caraman, who reproached him for
the arrest of the King : "Monsieur, all that depends on
opinion : it was an act of virtue in France—here it is a
crime." To M. Ribes, Receiver-General of Roussillon, he
said the same, adding, that in revolutions it was well
known how they began, but it was not known how they
would finish.

The emigrants of the legion of La Châtre violently
insulted and threatened Dumouriez at Ostend, at the
moment of his return from England. The general,
having, on the order of the commandant, described his
titles, one of those sharpers said to him : "French
officer! that is not true; you are no French officer,"
and a thousand impertinences. Dumouriez restrained
himself, and replied very gravely : "We are not here,
Monsieur, to dispute about titles."

The army of Dumouriez said to him : " F . . . ., father
general, obtain a decree from the Convention to march on
Paris, and you shall see how we will handle those . . . . of
the Assembly."

Dumouriez lives on three spoonfuls of soup, and sleeps
three hours out of the twenty-four, stretched on a truckle-
bed. No one is so laborious as he is. He often gets a
piece of meat, some bread and water placed by his side,
and remains two successive days writing without relaxation. He prides himself on his style, and glories
more in his proclamations than his victory of Jemmapes.
He is a lump of saltpetre.

We find in Dumouriez many traits of the character and
talent of the Count de Broglie, even of his defects. It is

known that he was educated in that school, and employed by the Count.

On the 12th of July, 1793, I was presented to the Archduke Charles, Governor-General of the Lower Countries. This interesting Prince has the judgment of a German, the penetration of an Italian, and the elevation of the soul of a Spaniard. It is known that he partakes of these three nations by his father and mother and his birth and education in Tuscany.

In the month of April, the King of Prussia said to an English friend of mine : " I do not at all understand the Duke of Brunswick ; he is always in want of five hundred men. Whatever directions are given, whatever expedition is confided to him, he always alleges a deficiency of forces. If I gave him two hundred thousand men, he would ask me for a second army, in order to be in a condition to act with the first."

The Duke of Brunswick was strongly inclined on principle to the alliance between Prussia and Austria. I have seen letters of his which give special proof of it : he preserved this sentiment until last autumn (1792). At the present time (July, 1793) he has turned his coat, and secretly labours to break the alliance.

The moment the King was sentenced, the Abbé Lajare was charged by M. Malesherbes to go and see Sieyès, his former colleague in the provincial administration of Orléans. When Sieyès saw him enter, he said to him before he had spoken : " I understand you, he is dead —dead : let us say nothing more about it."

One day, Danton said to one of his comrades, advocate to the councils, in 1793 : " The ancient *régime* made a great mistake. I was educated by it as one of the exhibitors of the College du Plessis : I was there with great seigneurs, who were my comrades, and lived with me in great familiarity. · My studies completed, I had nothing. I was in misery. I sought occupation ; the bar of Paris was inaccessible, and much exertion was necessary in order to be received. I could not enter the army without birth or patronage : the Church offered me no resource : I could not purchase any office, as I had not a farthing : my former college comrades turned the back upon me. I remained without employment, and only after many years succeeded in getting enough to purchase the office of Council-Advocate. The revolution came : I, and all those who resemble me, plunged into it ; the old government has compelled me to do so by educating us well without providing any opening for our talents."

Champcenetz died with his usual gaiety. When his sentence was pronounced, he said : " May one not name a substitute here ?" Executed with Parisot, this latter said : " I die a republican."—" Do not believe a word of it," replied Champcenetz, " he's a charlatan, he's an aristocrat like myself."

M. de Laverdy was guillotined because his farmer, when winnowing corn, threw the husks into a corner ; M. Duruey, for a letter in which a non-emigrant father entreated him to pay at Paris two thousand crowns to his son, who was going to Bordeaux, whence he had afterwards emigrated ; the Duke of Orleans was condemned on the accusation of Brissot, who had ordered him to be imprisoned at Marseilles, and condemned as an accomplice of this Brissot. Madame de Marbeuf was guillotined for having sown two acres with lucerne; a week after, the Committee of Agriculture sent in a report, in which they recommended and encouraged the cultivation of artificial meadows, as a nursery of agriculture, &c. &c.

The Duke de Biron, being prisoner in the Luxembourg, four other prisoners of his acquaintance formed a plan of escape and proposed it to him. He received this proposition with some indifference, made some objections to their plan, and ended by accepting it, when some difficulties had been removed. His comrades corrected the plan, made a calculation of the expense, acquainted him with all some days afterwards, and told him that it would cost each a thousand crowns. Biron, who passed his days in bed, drinking Bordeaux wine, answered carelessly, that he was no longer one of the party, and that this flight did not suit him. They asked him for his reasons. " 'Faith," said he, " I would just as soon remain here. We must get over a cornice, where I shall surely break my neck, and the guillotine is quite as agreeable: besides, that is not all; one must leave Paris, remain hidden in the kingdom, and be in fear of recapture; or go abroad and be insulted by all whom I meet—better to be guillotined." The four captives left him and succeeded in escaping.

When he was before the revolutionary tribunal, he was asked his name. He replied: " Cabbage, turnip, Biron— as you like; it is all much the same !"—" Why," said the judges, " you are insolent."—" And you, empty talkers, come to the business; ' guillotined !' that is all you have to say, and I have nothing to reply." Nevertheless, they commenced interrogating him on his pretended treasons in

La Vendée, &c. " You do not know what you say ; you are ignorant people, who understand nothing of war : finish your questions ; I sent in the account of my conduct to the Committee of Public Safety, which approved of it at the time : it has now changed and ordered you to put me to death : obey, and let us lose no time."

Biron asked pardon of God and the King : he never appeared to more advantage than on the road to execution. The Duke of Orleans read a newspaper, whilst they interrogated him.

In Belhomme's, the private hospital in Charonne, in which numbers of people of quality were confined, they had their etiquette, their ranks, their distinct societies, as at Versailles. M. de Boisgelin, afterwards guillotined, wishing to receive a visit from a former intendant of Brittany, who had had misunderstandings with the province, M. de Noyan, an old Breton, said : " If M. de Boisgelin did that, he was inevitably ruined, and would not have the presidency of the next States of Brittany."

Chaumette had been the author of the first indictment against the suspected, in which he included every body. When Robespierre had him arrested, he was conducted to the Luxembourg, and great was the joy amongst the prisoners there. They proposed to send him a deputation, and Parisot headed it : he passed before Chaumette, humiliated as he was by shouts of laughter from the company, and paid him only the following compliment : " I am suspected, thou art suspected, he is suspected, we are suspected, you are suspected, they are suspected."

It is said that Madame de Lamballe perished through want of presence of mind. When she came out, they cried

to her to say : " Vive la nation !" Two National Guards
held her under the arms. Struck with terror at the sight
of the crowded corpses, still quivering amidst torrents of
blood, she was unnerved, and said : " Ah ! how horrible !"
The people thought that she cursed them. Then it was
that she received the first blows : she fell and was sacrificed
in two minutes.

It was du Vaucel, farmer-general (fermier-général), who
saved Madame de Tarente, after having saved two other
women by means of three hundred louis given to one of
the leading Jacobins. This man objected greatly when
du Vaucel proposed to him the rescue of Madame de
Tarente. He told him, " that is not possible, because she
has the secret of Lacroix, Danton, and of the independents
who had treated with the Court, and they have recommended that she should be put to death." At last, by
means of five hundred louis, the affair succeeded and the
Princess was spared.

Fouquier-Tinville received a pension of a thousand
crowns a month from Mademoiselle de Boufflers, the
pension augmenting a quarter every month from the
atrocious nature of the circumstances. This method saved
these ladies, whilst those who gave sums in full were destroyed.

Others perished for having brought themselves into
recollection, amongst others the Viscount de Saint-Priest,
who was so imprudent as to send a memorial to Robespierre.

The English have restored to the Republic the boxes of
Natural History collected by M. d'Entrecasteaux, taken

in India with a part of this officer's squadron, whilst the Republic confiscates the cabinet of the Princes with whom it is at war.

Boissy-d'Anglas printed on the 12th Messidor, year II. of the Republic, an "Essai sur les fêtes nationales," addressed to the Convention, in which he said : "Robespierre, in speaking of the Supreme Being to the most enlightened people of the world, reminded me of Orpheus teaching to men the first principles of civilization and morality, and I experienced an inconceivable pleasure in hearing him."

On the 8th of June, Chaumette, attorney of the Commune, said, in full council general : "We want a Sunday, but we do not want a Sunday defiled by superstitions. We shall, doubtless, have festivals, but moral festivals. We shall have civil festivals, and the people shall be our God : we do not want any other."

Madame de Saint-Aignan, being brought before the tribunal, Fouquier accused her as well as her husband, who was present, of having shared in the crimes of the Court, of having been an extortioner to the people, and of having promoted corruption. She replied with *sang-froid*, that she and her husband never went to Court, that they had had an income of thirty-thousand livres, which enabled them to dispense with the King's favours, and that it was sufficient to look at her husband to be quite sure that he was a stranger to the gallantries of Versailles. The people applauded loudly, and cried out to her : "Go! thou may'st be gone with thy hunchback." She was acquitted.

The Chevalier de Barry, confined with M. Frisching of

Berne, at Toulouse, was led to the guillotine. On coming out, he said, laughingly, to his comrades in captivity : " The executioner will be much mistaken, when he wishes to take hold of my hair ; for my wig will remain clutched in his hand !"

Madame de Lavergne, the wife of the commandant at Longwy, had gone to hear the trial of her husband, whom she believed saved. She lost her self-possession at the moment he was condemned, and cried, " Vive le Roi !" At her repeated exclamations to die with him, the people, affected, told her to be quiet : she was executed with her husband.

Previous to the Queen's trial, her libellers again gave free course to all their atrocious calumnies on that Princess. They accused her of having lived at Trianon on pasties made of little children, of daily bestowing her favours on six persons whom she had afterwards put to death and made away with, to remove the evidence of her shame, and of having sent two hundred millions of francs a month to her brother. The people were fully persuaded of the truth of all these terrible reports ; and they pursued her with insult on her way to the scaffold.

The Queen made an impression on the people the first day of her appearance at the tribunal, but none at all on the other two days. At the turning of the Rue Royale, it appears that she fell into a deadly swoon. She reached the scaffold without making any movement. The executioner shook her, and told her to get down. She had a return of purely physical palpitation. They were obliged to carry her from the place up to the platform. When her head was cut off, the blood dripped and did not gush out, a proof that all vitality had previously ceased. Three months before, Hébert and his clique had been won over to rescue her.   He made, consequently, a proposition to the Jacobins to remove her from the Conciergerie to the Temple. The matter was referred to the Committee of Public Safety, who suspected Hébert and refused ; and then he, desirous of destroying this suspicion, inveighed furiously against the Queen, and incessantly demanded her death.

Camille Desmoulins entertained a sort of passion for this princess ; he had become attached to her ; he wished to save her.   His exertions and speeches lost him his popularity ; he was sacrificed by Robespierre.   In his letter on Arthur Dillon, one of the most pungent pamphlets of the revolution, Camille Desmoulins called the Duke of Orleans a Robespierre of ayes and nays (par assis et levé.)

None died with more firmness, greatness of mind, or lofty bearing, than the Duke of Orleans : he ranked once more as a prince of the blood. When asked at the revolutionary tribunal if he had anything to say in his defence, he replied : " To die to-day rather than to-morrow : deliberate upon that."   It was granted.

Custine defended himself with talent, and died like a child.   During the sittings the deputies, and amongst others Merlin, came to instigate the tribunal against him.

The representative Dumont, who ravaged Picardy, and arrested and put to death the Duke and Duchess du Châtelet, was at the galleys in 1791 for robbery and burglary : Chabot procured his release.   Fouquier-Tinville, public prosecutor, was clerk to a small attorney.   He was put in the pillory and driven from the profession for having stolen and sold to the opposite party a bundle of papers, in a suit which the lawyer was carrying on. Danton had procured him his post : he procured his death.

It is certain that Danton and his party entertained the project of putting an end to matters, re-establishing the monarch, electing the young King, and reigning independently of him. As for Robespierre, he really aimed at remaining sole master of France. He had hoped to be proclaimed dictator on the day of the fête of the Supreme Being, at the moment he proceeded to burn the effigy of atheism, by the fountains of the Tuileries ; but the multitude gave no acclamations of approval, and cried : "Vive la nation !" This fête, from its ridiculous character, was the commencement of his discredit .... When he saw the Mountain rise against him, on the 9th Thermidor, and threaten him insultingly, he turned to the right, and said to them : "And you too, honourable men, you abandon me ?"

Hérault de Séchelles, convinced that he would not escape, went every day for six successive weeks to see the guillotining, to familiarise himself with this mode of punishment.

Hébert was fair, with blue eyes and a mild countenance. When he was intriguing to save the Queen, he said to Madame de R——: "If I cannot save her, I will have her put to death !" He kept his word. Such was the conduct of Danton towards the King—such was their conduct to all.

This Hébert left more than two millions. The circulation of the "Feuille du Père Duchesne," was so extensive, that upwards of eighty thousand impressions were struck off. The government offices distributed fifty thousand, gratis, to the armies, municipalities, &c. One day, the Mayor of Caen, being solicited about an affair which required the immediate attention of the commune, answered: "I cannot; we have a meeting this morning to read ' Le Père Duchesne.' "

Saint-Just had the boldest and strongest talent of the Committee of Public Safety. His audacity surpassed all imagination. One day, giving orders to Pichegru for the army of the Rhine, the general told him that in a quarter of an hour they should be attended to. " In a quarter of an hour!" replied Saint-Just, " in a quarter of an hour I would regulate Europe." Cambacérès telling him, on his return, of the idolatry of the people and of the enthusiasm for the revolution: " Fool that you are," replied Saint-Just, " you will soon find very different acclamations on their part when we are led to execution."

The Abbé Delille had received permission from Garat, Minister of the Interior, to sell his furniture which he had at Meudon, conjointly with that of M. de Las-Cases. He carries his certificate to a timber-merchant of Sèvres, " procureur syndic" of the department of Versailles, who, without looking at the permission, demands whose it is ? " From M. Garat, Minister of the Interior." " From the Minister of the Interior ? If he was amongst your furniture, he should be sold with it. Go, take back your permission, and apply to the department of the interior."

The Duchess of Orleans has refused pension or payment on account of her property, saying that it was all due to her, and that she wanted her patrimony and the liberty of her children, or nothing. It is not without an object that the revolutionists keep the sons of the Duke of Orleans imprisoned and in France.

February, 1796.—When Tallien was dining one day at Madame Panckoucke's, with Fréron and others, the young King was the subject of conversation. Tallien said that his death would be necessary, and that the death of a child was not to be compared with the happiness of twenty millions of inhabitants. His wife told him he was a monster, passed into another room, and fainted away. Tallien, startled at his wife's condition and his own imprudence, had a very severe attack of illness. He is epileptic.

After the conspiracy of Babeuf, discovered in May, 1796, the Directory had a placard posted, beginning with these words : " A frightful plot is going to take place to-night ; they intend to slaughter the legislative body, the members of the government, all the constituted authorities, and then massacre a portion of the inhabitants, and give the city up to plunder." On reading this, the people said in the market-places : " What a misfortune ! many others have been slaughtered too !"

CONFIRMATORY DOCUMENTS

AND

ADDITIONS.

PAGE 204.

" Il est impossible d'être plus modéré, plus intéressant, plus at-
tachant que ne l'est le Duc de Bourbon."—*Lettre de Lally-Tolendal.*

THIS unfortunate Prince contrived to reside in France
until the restoration, and lived in close retirement after the
melancholy death of his son, the Duke d'Enghien. The
death of his child plunged the Duke and also the Prince de
Condé into profound affliction. It was the Count d'Artois,
then in London, who discharged the principal duty of
going to Wanstead-House, six miles from London, the
residence of the Prince de Condé, to communicate the
tragical end of his brave and noble grandson. An eye-
witness of this affecting scene has related the details which
follow :

" On arriving at Wanstead-House, the Count d'Artois,
as he stepped from the carriage, met the Duke de
Bourbon, who had come to receive him, and who, reading
his child's sentence on the countenance of the Count,
had not the courage to ask a confirmation of the fact.

Retiring with hurried steps, he hastened to his apartments, in which he shut himself up to give full vent to his
grief. His servants hearing his sobs, begged him to permit them to enter and afford their sympathy and consolation; but his grief was too keen, and it was only at the
end of twenty-four hours that he yielded to their prayers.
The Count d'Artois, on separating from the Duke de
Bourbon, proceeded to the Prince de Condé, and accosting
him, said: 'You know, cousin, that I have had to bewail
a brother, a nephew, a sister, a sister-in-law; you have
always shared with me our common misfortunes. . . . .' At
these words, the Prince de Condé fell into the arms of his
friend, the Chevalier de Contye, and hiding his face in his
bosom, he bathed it with tears. This silent scene lasted
nearly a quarter of an hour, at the close of which the
Prince, taking the hand of the Count d'Artois, said to
him: 'Excuse my weakness, cousin, these are the only
tears I have shed since the death of Louis XVI.'" The
Duke d'Enghien was this unfortunate old man's idol; he
thought he saw living in him afresh the heart and the
brilliant qualities of his ancestor, the great Condé.

PAGE 402.

LETTER FROM COUNT D'ARTOIS (CHARLES X.) TO MALLET
DU PAN.

"Edinburgh, July 25, 1798.

"I have received, Monsieur, your letter of the 26th of
June, with your accompanying sketch of the present state

of France ; and the Baron de Roll has not left me in
ignorance, either of the desire which animates you to save
the most just of all causes, or of the constant disposition
you possess to give me proofs of your attachment.

" I have examined your treatise with the most serious
attention ; I have meditated on the grounds and also the
consequences, and acting on the opinion I have both of
your character and principles, 1 wish to communicate to
you my reflections and ideas.

" In the first part of your work you describe, forcibly
and truly, my unhappy country subjected to a despotism
lodged in the hands of an association of factious men,
united by a common crime which confers great strength
on this union, but divided by interests always acting in a
contrary sense; the general discouragement, the servile
apathy of the multitude, the want of men of genius fitted
to reanimate and rally the nation, and lastly, the prodigious variety of systems which destroy all concord
among the chiefs who might aspire to perform this honourable part.

" To all these causes of the cruel slavery of the French,
must be added the scandalous immorality which reigns over
nearly the whole of Europe, and the singular corruption
of all the political principles which direct her cabinets.
This corruption can alone explain the indifference which is
shown for the natural and indispensable chief of a party,
whom it would be necessary to create, if he did not exist,
as an enemy most essentially opposed to that anarchical
oligarchy which holds France under a degraded yoke, and
endangers the whole extent of the civilized world.   I
know that you think as I do—that all sovereignties, all

governments whatever, will be in a state of continual com-
motion until the crater of the volcano, which has exploded
in France, becomes hermetically sealed ; and I do not
imagine I extend my idea unduly, when I connect the
interests of the whole world with the special interest
attached to the re-establishment of the French monarchy.

" You have most clearly indicated, Monsieur, the
principal causes which concur in making the prolongation
of the dictatorial power, a subject of fear ; and in rendering
useless—injurious even—all the half-measures which it
might be sought to employ in contending with it. No one
is more persuaded than I of the inutility and danger of those
trivial and isolated resources of which you speak ; and as
much as in me lies, I will discard all application to them.

" But if, on the one hand, I am convinced of the necessity
of choosing with prudence the moment for action, and of
undertaking nothing unless with a great probability of success ; on the other, my soul is too much affected by the
general danger, and my heart too deeply touched by the
misfortunes which overwhelm my country, not to seize
with avidity all the means which tend to shorten their
duration.

" There exists a very powerful one, the success of which
is far from being improbable. Its trial offers no inconveniences, and its issue would be both prompt and
decisive. The first important step is, to persuade a
government which still preserves a force and energy
capable of saving Europe, that it is not in the actual
authority of the Directory, however imposing it may
appear, that the real power resides. That despotic

oligarchy which weighs upon France, and extends her ramifications over the four quarters of the globe, is herself dependent on the military force, which keeps check within, while spreading affright and making conquests abroad. This force has hitherto belonged to the predominant faction, which is its paymaster.

"They must be deprived of this support : the British government, with a noble calculation of her best and highest interests, should replace in the hands of the King of France an army which the enemies of humanity have snatched from him, that they might disturb the universe.

"Towards this grand end should be directed all the general and specific views of those whose preliminary means enable them to set about the task : it is to demonstrate its importance, to prove its necessity, that those men should devote themselves, to whom, as to you, Monsieur, nature has given that vigorous eloquence which lends incalculable power to accuracy of ideas.

"Speak, and with a voice of thunder ; be in no fear that you may say too much to a cabinet that can well appreciate your opinion. It knows the danger which threatens it—its eyes are open to the truth ; but it requires to be roused before it will come forth from its habitual sphere, and rise to the height of the circumstances in which it is placed. Say to it, Monsieur, that the French Revolution having deranged every kind of moral and political equilibrium, matters are come to such a pass that Europe is inevitably ruined unless the monarchy be promptly re-established in France ; and that it is force, and force alone, that can henceforward effect this re-establishment. Any other species of restoration has become more than improbable; and I do not hesitate to say further, that it would be a misfortune for France and for the whole of Europe. It is only by the resumption of his rights by force of arms that the King will be able to preserve the authority necessary for governing a great people, and at the same time to secure to all Frenchmen the inestimable benefit of a good and wise constitution fitted to form the happiness of a long course of generations. The sovereign who should be re-established on his throne in consequence of any arrangement, receiving instead of giving the law, would never have, nor acquire, sufficient power to hold imperfectly-extinguished factions in check. Fresh intrigues, fresh pretensions, fresh seditions would soon arise to overturn the throne once more, and to bring further troubles on the neighbouring states.

" Truths such as these are well calculated to impress wise and enlightened ministers; but, in order to demonstrate still more clearly the direct interest of the country, tell them, Monsieur, that England is now in the same position as that in which the *éclat* of the reign of Louis XIV. had placed France; that our common enemies have artfully directed, and still incessantly direct, all the ideas of the continental powers to the apprehension lest the empire of the seas leave to Great Britain all the advantage of this tremendous struggle; and that, even on the supposition that the war will be renewed in Germany, the examples of the past ought to prove to British ministers that there is not a cabinet in Europe on which they can safely rely.

" Say to them in addition, that under the circumstances

there is no other faithful and secure ally for England
than the royalist party, in whatever point of view it may
be considered. This party alone makes true common
cause with the British government. But to realize from
this party all the effect it is susceptible of producing,
totally different principles and plans must be adopted from
those which have been followed for the last six years.
So much has hitherto been done to repress and weaken
it, that more exertions must now be used to restore to it
that consistency without which its scattered and isolated
means can avail nothing. Such a party could not acquire
the necessary harmony and act with uniformity, from a
will regulating all others, and directing them to the same
end, without a predominant chief, under the legitimate
chief, to whom he is essentially bound. Everything will
remain in anarchy among the royalists as long as a blind
policy permits the undignified and unsupported position
of a sovereign, stripped of all his property, of all civil
and military power, and left without the slightest means
of making his wishes respected and cherished. This
sovereign, placed in a situation so distressing to himself,
and so fatal to the general cause of all governments, is,
nevertheless, the corner-stone, the fundamental base on
which alone can be established the union, the strength,
and the solidity of this royalist party, this true ally of
England, and all the powers who desire the effectual
re-establishment of tranquillity in Europe.

"This re-establishment cannot be expected to result
from the present state of affairs, and from the confusion
necessarily created in France by the continual collision

of different factions, and the rapid transition from one tyranny to another. The usurpation of the crown by a branch from the natural hereditary line would not lead to a more solid peace, because the seditious and discontented would not fail to make use of this illegality by raising a standard of agitation which would light afresh the whole conflagration.

"The recognition of the rights of Louis XVIII., public evidences of respect and sympathy given to this monarch— these are the real measures which should be taken by every government that wishes to overthrow the Directory, and to destroy that monstrous power which threatens humanity with the worst scourges. This power, as I have previously said, reposes on the army alone, which is still held dependent by the instrumentality of many.

"The military spirit, from its very nature, inclines more to monarchy than republicanism, a kind of government under which the soldier in time of peace becomes suspected and enjoys no consideration. The information I have procured on this important question, furnishes me with strong reasons for believing that the French armies would rejoin the legitimate monarch, if they saw him re-invested with a grand political existence, and sufficiently supplied with pecuniary means to insure their pay during the struggle between the factions and him.

"Such is, Monsieur, the sum of my opinions and ideas on the general situation of affairs. I send it you in confidence, and I shall receive with the same feeling any observations you may wish to offer on it, as well as a further development of your first work, about which the Baron de Roll has informed me.

" With pleasure I take advantage of this opportunity to renew to you, Monsieur, the assurance of my perfect esteem, and of all my sentiments towards you.

" CHARLES-PHILIPPE."

THE END.

LONDON:
Printed by Schulze and Co., 13, Poland Street.

CPSIA information can be obtained
at www.ICGtesting.com
Printed in the USA
BVHW041847290819
R10232900001B/R102329PG556819BVX6B/7/P